DATE

MW00653107

BEHIND THE BADGE

This volume is the logical follow-up to the military treatment handbook *Living and Surviving in Harm's Way*. Sharon M. Freeman Clevenger, Laurence Miller, Bret A. Moore, and Arthur Freeman return with this dynamic handbook ideal for law enforcement agencies interested in the psychological health of their officers. Contributors include law enforcement officers with diverse experiences, making this handbook accessible to readers from law enforcement backgrounds. This authoritative, comprehensive, and critical volume on the psychological aspects of police work is a must for anyone affiliated with law enforcement.

Sharon M. Freeman Clevenger, MSN, MA, PMHCNS-BC, ACT, is the CEO and Founder of the Indiana Center for Cognitive Behavior Therapy and Adjunct Professor of Psychology at Indiana/Purdue Universities. She is certified as a Diplomate, Fellow, and Trainer by the Academy of Cognitive Therapy.

Laurence Miller, PhD, PA, is an Adjunct Professor at Florida Atlantic University and Palm Beach State College. He is a clinical and forensic police psychologist for the West Palm Beach Police Department, the Palm Beach County Sheriff's Office, and Troop L of the Florida Highway Patrol.

Bret A. Moore, PsyD, ABPP, is an Adjunct Associate Professor in Psychiatry at the University of Texas Health Science Center at San Antonio. In 2008, Dr. Moore left active duty service in the U.S. Army, where he served as a captain and clinical psychologist with the 85th Combat Stress Control unit based in Fort Hood, Texas.

Arthur Freeman, EdD, ABPP, ACT, is Professor and Executive Director of Clinical Psychology in Behavioral Medicine at Midwestern University. He is Past-President of the Association for Behavioral and Cognitive Therapies and the International Association for Cognitive Psychotherapy. He is a Distinguished Founding Fellow of the Academy of Cognitive Therapy.

BEHIND THE BADGE

A Psychological Treatment Handbook for Law Enforcement Officers

Edited by
Sharon M. Freeman Clevenger
Laurence Miller
Bret A. Moore
Arthur Freeman

Routledge
Taylor & Francis Group

NEW YORK AND LONDON

First published 2015
by Routledge
711 Third Avenue, New York, NY 10017

and by Routledge
27 Church Road, Hove, East Sussex BN3 2FA

Routledge is an imprint of the Taylor & Francis Group,
an informa business

© 2015 Taylor & Francis

Library of Congress Cataloging-in-Publication Data
Freeman Clevenger, Sharon M.
Behind the badge : a psychological treatment handbook for law enforcement
officers/Sharon M. Freeman Clevenger, Laurence Miller, Bret Moore, Arthur
Freeman.—1 Edition.
pages cm
Includes bibliographical references and index.
1. Police psychology. 2. Police—Mental health. 3. Police—Job stress. I. Title.
HV7936.P75F74 2014
616.85′210651—dc23
2014020351

ISBN: 978-0-415-89229-2 (hbk)
ISBN: 978-1-138-81890-3 (pbk)
ISBN: 978-1-315-74492-6 (ebk)

Typeset in Sabon
by Swales & Willis Ltd, Exeter, Devon, UK

Printed and bound in the United States of America by Publishers Graphics,
LLC on sustainably sourced paper.

The opinions expressed herein are those of the authors, and are not necessarily representative of those of the Department of Defence (DOD); the Department of Justice (DOJ); any government agency including police departments; or, the United States Army, Navy, or Air Force.

CONTENTS

ACKNOWLEDGMENTS

This book is dedicated to all of those police officers and their family members who deploy each day into harm's way in order to keep the rest of us safe. Especially to those officers who responded to the Sandy Hook Elementary School tragedy, the officers and first responders to the Boston Marathon bombing, and the countless other officers who have faced similar horrors and yet continue to protect and serve. We owe a tremendous debt of gratitude to your selfless service.

Sharon M. Freeman Clevenger would also like to thank her husband, Brig Gen (retired) Richard Clevenger who has been exceptionally patient and supportive while this book was in process. Rick, you are my light, my anchor, and my best friend. Special thanks to Nancy, Bryan, and Steve Hough for sharing your stories as police families, and for your personal sacrifices to protect and serve.

Laurence Miller is grateful to his family, Joan and Halle, for their ongoing support of his various projects, as well as admiring their own independent contributions to the field of mental health practice. He would also like to thank his many students over the years for their insightful questions and comments that keep this clinician, researcher, and teacher on his toes.

Bret A. Moore would like to thank his wife, Lori, and daughter, Kaitlyn, for their ongoing support of his work.

Art Freeman is grateful for the opportunity to work at Midwestern University with the finest faculty and staff of any psychology program anywhere, and to the MWU students who challenge and invigorate my work. The professionals with whom I consult ask questions that stretch my thinking in new and exciting directions.

FOREWORD

Outside of the police headquarters building in Philadelphia is a statue that depicts a standing uniformed police officer holding a small child in his arms, symbolizing the protective role of the police officer. This bronze sculpture, by artist Charles Cropper Parks (1922–2012), is iconic in that it portrays the most common role assigned and expected of the police officer in the community and symbolizes the role assumed by law enforcement officers to protect and serve the public. This role may be played out in municipal, state, national, and international settings. It is common across cultures where the rules and roles may, in fact, be different from the roles and expectations of other law enforcement officers (LEOs) of the jurisdictions or even countries adjacent to a particular geographic setting. It is therefore unsettling when law enforcement officers break the law they are sworn to uphold and protect, are used to maintain a corrupt regime, punish those who may disagree with the "powers that be," or operate in self-service rather than in service to the broad public good.

I can recall on many occasions advising my children that the policeman was their friend. If they were in trouble or lost, to seek out the police officer who will help them and get them safely home. We expect the LEO to protect, assist, defend, shelter, safeguard, and shield the weaker and less fortunate. Just as images of police wrongdoing makes the headlines, so do selfless acts of kindness, support, and even the sacrifice of one's life to protect and to serve our communities and society.

What are too often lost are the personal and individual characteristics and behaviors of specific officers when painting the entire group of law enforcement officers with one brush. The corps of LEOs in the United States comprise about 800,000 officers with approximately 12–15 percent being women. There is representation of every religious, ethnic, and racial group among LEOs. In fact, one ongoing mission is to increase the number of underrepresented groups under the broad heading of community policing.

I have had several strokes of good fortune in both my career and my personal life. First and foremost has been my wife, Phyllis. Phyllis was a Justice of the Superior Court in Pennsylvania for over 25 years until her retirement from the bench in 2005. Not one to sit around, Phyllis still keeps a busy schedule. My children have been a source of great pride. My eldest son, Roy, is a Neuro-ophthalmologist and clinical researcher, my daughter Judy is President of the Beck Institute in Philadelphia, and has established herself as one of the major spokespersons for cognitive therapy (CT) through her books, teaching, and lectures around the world. My daughter Alice has literally inherited her mother's judicial gown, and sits as a judge in Philadelphia's Common Pleas Court. My youngest son, Daniel, is a Social Worker and practicing Cognitive Therapist. We are further blessed by our grandchildren and friends. Interestingly, as judges, Phyllis and Alice have worked closely with the police as partners in the broad criminal justice system.

Over the course of the years I have had an insatiable curiosity about how things work, why they work, and how to make them work better. Given that psychoanalysis was one of the main (if not the only) model used to attempt to help people be more adaptive, and ultimately more functional, I trained to be a Psychoanalyst. It was in the course of my curiosity to support the psychoanalytic idea of depression being anger turned inward that my almost six decades of treatment and research began. It was this curiosity that led me to posit a "cognitive" element as the primary source of most emotional disorders. This curiosity first was focused on depression. Later we added the treatment of anxiety, and still later, the treatment of individuals with personality disorders. From rather humble beginnings, just a few professionals at the Center for Cognitive Therapy at the University of Pennsylvania, cognitive therapy has grown to be an international treatment model. True to my need to meet my curiosity, I have developed, encouraged, supported, mentored, and sustained the necessary studies that support the applications of the CT treatment model.

Had you asked me in 1977 what disorders were best treated by cognitive therapy, my answer would have been depression. After myriad treatment studies and literally hundreds of books, CT is seen as a model for the treatment of the broad range of disorders; it has been applied to every treatment application, practiced with every age and developmental group, and in every treatment venue. Just when I think that we have covered it all, the present volume has emerged, focused on those who live and serve "behind the badge": the law enforcement officer. This volume is a worthy follow-up to the excellent volume on the treatment of military who put themselves *Living and Surviving in Harm's Way*, edited by three of the present editors, Sharon M. Freeman Clevenger, Bret Miller, and Art Freeman.

Part of my great fortune over the years has been that our work has generated new thinking and attracted among the brightest and the best therapists, conceptualizers, and researchers. Some were my students over the years such as Art who began working with me almost 40 years ago. Art has trained a number of students who have expanded and extended the CT model. Two of his direct students, Sharon Morgillo Freeman Clevenger and Bret Moore, were directly taught by Art (making them my theoretical grandchildren). Sharon is a Psychiatric Nurse Practitioner who is well trained in cognitive therapy, and is a Fellow, Diplomate, and Certified Trainer for the Academy of Cognitive Therapy. Sharon is also the Founder and Owner of the Indiana Center for Cognitive Behavior Therapy. Laurence Miller is a Clinical and Forensic Psychologist. He serves as a police psychologist, mental health consultant, and examiner for the Palm Beach (FL) County Court, and consulting psychologist with several regional and national law enforcement agencies. Bret is a board certified Clinical Psychologist, a Prescribing Psychologist and Fellow of the American Psychological Association. Bret is a veteran who focuses on the in-service post-deployment problems of members of the military. Art has published widely in cognitive therapy. He is the Executive Program Director of the Clinical Psychology Programs at Midwestern University for their campuses in Downers Grove, IL and Glendale, AZ. He is board certified in clinical psychology, cognitive behavioral psychology, and family psychology.

The editors have brought together a team of contributors who cover the major areas of concern and emphasis in dealing with the emotional and behavioral sequelae of police work. The topics and clear strategies in this book will help therapists and counselors to work with the myriad and complex problems presented by LEOs. These areas include the role of the LEO both from a historical and sociological perspective. They follow this with an essential chapter on assessment and evaluation. This gives the reader a picture of the required tools and purposes of the assessment process. The key for appropriate treatment is the development of a plan for treatment. We recognize that the treatment is guided by the treatment conceptualization, which is in turn guided by the assessment data and goals of treatment. Of particular interest is the chapter on the bidirectional influence of mind and body. There are significant health consequences that are a product of the stress and trauma that are a frequent concomitant of police work. Critical Incident Stress Debriefing (CISD) is a technique for intervention commonly used at times of community or personal trauma. Over the years there has been significant data arguing for and against the demonstrated efficacy of CISD. This chapter brings the issue and questions forward with a discussion of the present state of the science. The next two chapters address both the LEO engaging with members of the military, and the military law enforcement officers that serve in the military, who are responsible for the maintenance of military rules and regulations within the military. Given the multiple venues in which one finds law enforcement officers, the correctional officer is often overlooked. This chapter addresses the special issues involved in treating the LEO officers serving in closed or secure settings.

The editors then shift their focus to special problems and give the reader information and insight into areas that are not often seen by the public. These include the LEO in the legal system, the LEO as an undercover operative patrolling sex crimes (made visible by the TV show *Law and Order: Special Victims Unit*), and hostage negotiation. The LEO may be the first point of contact with mentally ill individuals and therefore have the responsibility to stabilize a situation, protect the public from further assault or damage, and attempt to control the individual. We saw, with horror, LEOs and fire personnel enter the doomed buildings of the World Trade Center. More than 380 first responders died that day, 2,000 were injured and many others have been sickened or have died from attack-related illnesses. The book's final chapter addresses the moment that no family member of a LEO wants to experience, the knock on the door of the LEO chaplain. The chaplain is tasked with maintaining the spiritual health of the LEO, whether the assault is intrapsychic and personally generated, family related, circumstance reactive, or soothing and calming after the loss of a fallen comrade.

With this volume, Sharon and her co-editors have assembled a synergistic group of authors. The content and pace of the book is superb. They have added to the growth and dissemination of the understanding and treatment of this important and significant group of people in our lives. These men and women take on the challenge of keeping our society safer, more secure, and more livable, even at the expense of personal safety and well-being.

Aaron T. Beck, M.D.

CONTRIBUTORS

Monty T. Baker is a licensed clinical psychologist who received his PhD from Nova Southeastern University in Fort Lauderdale, FL. He is a Lt. Col. in the United States Air Force (USAF) stationed at RAF Alconbury, England and currently serves as the Mental Health Clinic Flight Commander. Dr. Baker has presented numerous times at conferences, seminars, and workshops on a variety of mental health-related topics. His publications include articles on crisis/hostage negotiation, law enforcement stress, anger management, suicide assessment, and combat stress/reintegration from war. Dr. Baker's primary areas of interest include law enforcement stress, crisis intervention, and deployment psychology.

Andrea M. Brockman, PsyD, received her doctorate at the Center for Psychological Studies at Nova Southeastern University, FL. Dr. Brockman has published and presented research in the areas of internet crime, corrections, and crisis negotiations. Her clinical and research interests are in the area of police psychology, correctional psychology and crisis negotiations, hostage negotiation, correctional officer stress, and inmate rehabilitation. Her present employment is as a Staff Psychologist with the Federal Bureau of Prisons, at USP Big Sandy.

Brandi Burque, PhD, is currently with the San Antonio Police Department's Psychological Services. She graduated from Nova Southeastern University (NSU) in Fort Lauderdale, FL in 2009 with a PhD in Clinical Psychology. Her practicum training was with the Broward Sheriff's Office (BSO), providing therapy and crisis intervention services to first responders and their families, and NSU's Family Violence Program. She was coordinator of training for the liaison program between NSU and local law enforcement's crisis negotiation units. She completed her internship at the Captain James A. Lovell Federal Health Care Center/ North Chicago Veterans Affairs (VA) Hospital focusing on the treatment of PTSD, substance abuse, and neuropsychological assessment. In San Antonio, Texas she completed a two-year postdoctoral fellowship with

Brooke Army Medical Center's Warrior Resiliency Program where she had the opportunity to work with active duty service members. She was an integral part of the team to develop resiliency and mental toughness training for Army residents and interns. As staff psychologist in the Psychosocial Residential Rehabilitation Treatment Program at the Danville VA Hospital, she provides psychological rehabilitation services for Veterans. Dr. Burque has presented at the FBI National Academy on topics such as PTSD and Critical Incident Stress Management (CISM) and Crisis Intervention Teams (CIT). She has also presented on the risk and protective factors and case studies of school violence to several law enforcement agencies in the Midwest as part of an FBI collaboration.

Sharon M. Freeman Clevenger, MSN, MA, PMHCNS-BC, ACT, is a Psychiatric Clinical Nurse Specialist, and CEO and Founder of the Indiana Center for Cognitive Behavior Therapy, in Fort Wayne, IN. She is Adjunct Professor of Psychology at Indiana/Purdue Universities. She is also certified as a Diplomate, Fellow and Trainer by the Academy of Cognitive Therapy. Sharon was lead editor for *Living and Surviving in Harm's Way: A Psychological Treatment Handbook for Pre- and Post-Deployment of Military Members,* also published by Routledge. She has been a Senior Member of the Women's Police Officer online support group, Policewives. org for seven years. Her other books include *Cognitive Behavior Therapy in Nursing Practice* (Springer, 2005) and *Overcoming Depression: A Cognitive Therapy Approach Workbook and Accompanying Therapist Guide (Treatments That Work)* with Mark Gilson, Arthur Freeman and M. Jane Yates (Oxford University Press, 2009).

R. Trent Codd, III, EdS, is the President and Founder of the Cognitive-Behavioral Therapy Center of WNC, PA located in Asheville, NC. He specializes in delivering and disseminating cognitive and behavioral treatments, including Beckian Cognitive Therapy and Clinical Behavior Analytic approaches such as Acceptance and Commitment Therapy (ACT) and Functional Analytic Psychotherapy (FAP). He holds an EdS in Mental Health Counseling from the University of Florida and a Master of Criminal Justice from the University of South Carolina at Columbia. He also holds a Certificate of Graduate Study in Alcohol and Drug Studies at USC's School of Public Health and he completed graduate training in Applied Behavior Analysis through the University of North Texas. He is a Fellow of the Academy of Cognitive Therapy and a Board Certified Behavior Analyst. His current clinical work is with private psychotherapy patients across a range of disorders, but his early work was with incarcerated juvenile offenders. He produces a popular podcast (www.CBTRadio.org) focused on evidence-based psychotherapy.

Judy Couwels has been employed at the Broward Sheriff's Office since November 1990 as the Manager of the Employee Assistance Program (EAP). She works with the Hostage Negotiation Team as the Mental Health Consultant, provides team training, and partners with the Nova Southeastern University to facilitate learning opportunities for graduate students. Judy has a BS in Psychology from Pennsylvania State University and an MA in Marriage and Family Therapy from Syracuse University. She is a licensed Marriage and Family Therapist, is currently the State Wide Training Director for the Florida Association for Hostage Negotiators (FAHN), and is the President of the South Florida Chapter of the Employee Assistance Professional Association (EAPA). She holds certifications in hypnosis, treating addictions, and as a Criminal Justice Instructor.

Stephen F. Curran, PhD, ABPP, received his doctorate from the University of Maryland in 1977 and is licensed in Maryland and Virginia. Dr. Curran was among the first psychologists awarded the diploma recognizing board certification in Police and Public Safety Psychology by the American Board of Professional Psychology (ABPP). There are fewer than 70 psychologists recognized in the United States for having this board certification. Dr. Curran's expertise is in pre-employment evaluation of public safety applicants, workability assessments and stress management intervention and training. He is active in professional police organizations and a member, as well as Past-Chair, of the International Association of Chiefs of Police (IACP) Police Psychological Services Section. Among presentations are those at the FBI Academy, IACP, and professional psychological organizations.

Robert E. Douglas is the Executive Director and Founder of the National Police Suicide Foundation, Inc., Seaford, DE. The foundation provides educational training seminars for emergency responders on the issue of suicide. He is considered a leading expert in the area of LEO suicide according to Dateline, CNN, *Time Magazine* and *USA Today*. Bob has authored four books: *Death with no Valor*, *Hope Beyond the Badge*, *Healing For a Hero's Heart*, and *The Art of Being You*. Bob served 20 years with the Baltimore City Police Dept., and five years as a Patrol Officer with the Temple Terrace Police Dept. in Temple Terrace, FL. He holds a BS in Criminal Justice (University of South Florida), a Master's in Police Administration (University of Baltimore) and a Master's in Theology (St. Mary's Seminary). He recently retired as the Senior Pastor at Jenkins Memorial Church in Riviera Beach, MD where he served for 24 years. Past service includes Police Chaplain for FOP Lodge #3 (Baltimore, MD), and Chaplain for ATF (Alcohol, Tobacco and Firearms, Washington, DC).

Arthur Freeman, EdD, ScD, ABPP, ACT, is Professor of Behavioral Medicine at Midwestern University, and Executive Director of the

Clinical Psychology Programs at both Downers Grove, IL and Glendale, AZ campuses. He has been the President of the Association for Behavioral and Cognitive Therapies and of the International Association for Cognitive Psychotherapy. He is a Distinguished Founding Fellow of the Academy of Cognitive Therapy and has earned board certification in Clinical Psychology, Behavioral Psychology, and Family Psychology from the American Board of Professional Psychology. He has published 75 books and over 100 chapters and articles. His work has been translated from English into 20 other languages. Dr. Freeman has lectured in 45 countries over the last 35 years. His research and clinical interests include marital and family therapy, and cognitive-behavioral treatment of depression, anxiety, and personality disorders.

Randy Garner is Professor of Behavioral Sciences and former Associate Dean in the College of Criminal Justice at Sam Houston State University TX. He holds a BS, MA, and PhD in Psychology from the University of Houston. His (second) PhD is in Theology and Religious Studies. Dr. Garner had more than 30 years of law enforcement service beginning in 1976 and has worked in all divisions and levels of command. He was Chief of Police for a Houston-area agency in the mid-1980s. Dr. Garner has taught courses in major police command colleges in the country (FBI National Academy, Graduate Management Institute, Leadership and Command College (LEMIT), Institute for Law Enforcement Administration, and Southern Police Institute-University of Louisville). As a Police Officer, Dr. Garner was licensed as a Texas Polygraph Examiner, a Forensic Hypnotist, a Police Firearms Master, a Police Defensive Tactics Instructor, and was an FBI-trained Hostage Negotiator. He has been with Sam Houston State University for more than 18 years and was the founding Director of the Texas Regional Community Policing Institute (TRCPI) and served as the Executive Director of the Law Enforcement Management Institute of Texas (LEMIT). Dr. Garner has authored numerous books and professional publications. His books *Criticism Management* and *Constructing Effective Criticism: How to Give, Receive, and Seek Productive and Constructive Criticism in Our Lives* have been adopted by command colleges, leadership courses, and communication programs across the country. Dr. Garner is the Editor-in-Chief of *Applied Psychology in Criminal Justice*, an interdisciplinary, peer-reviewed, academic journal that examines the social and psychological aspects of human behavior as related to applied societal and criminal justice settings.

Christine M. Heiny is a police veteran of 17 years, having served with both the Dallas Police Department and the Campbell County Sheriff's Department. While in Dallas her specialty was as a full-time SWAT team member acting as both a hostage negotiator and sniper. In Campbell

County her specialities were child abuse cases, homicides, sexual assaults and internal affairs. She has a BS degree in behavioral science and numerous training hours in addiction and currently works as the Assistant Director for the Recovery Center of AADP. Christine spends her free time writing and publishing small books of spiritual inspiration.

Stephen Joseph, PhD, is Professor of Psychology at the University of Nottingham, UK. He received his MSc in social psychology from the London School of Economics and his PhD from the Institute of Psychiatry in London. His research is on positive psychology, psychotherapy and psychological trauma. His latest book, *What Doesn't Kill Us* (Basic Books) was released in paperback in 2013.

Karen C. Kalmbach, PhD, earned a doctorate in Clinical Psychology (Forensic) from Sam Houston State University, TX. Before joining Texas A&M University-San Antonio as a professor in the Psychology Department, Dr. Kalmbach helped to build Harris County's first juvenile mental health court in Houston, Texas. Prior to that she held a faculty position in the School of Criminal Justice at California State University, Los Angeles, where she taught forensic psychology and related courses. While in Los Angeles, she also conducted research in high-risk neighborhoods for the Los Angeles Mayor's Office of Gang Reduction and Youth Development. Dr. Kalmbach has previously served as a director of the Texas Regional Center for Policing Innovation, a federally funded criminal justice training institute. Currently, she also performs clinical evaluations for military and justice system populations.

Laurence Miller, PhD, is in independent practice in clinical and forensic psychology in Boca Raton, FL. He is a court-appointed forensic examiner for the Palm Beach County Court and conducts independent forensic evaluations in civil and criminal cases. Dr. Miller is Police Psychologist for the West Palm Beach Police Department, the Palm Beach County Sheriff's Office, and Troop L of the Florida Highway Patrol, and he provides clinical services and training for law enforcement agencies around the country. Dr. Miller is Adjunct Professor at Florida Atlantic University and Palm Beach State college, offers continuing education training seminars around the country and is the author of over 300 professional and popular print and online publications pertaining to the brain, behavior, health, law enforcement, criminal justice and organizational psychology. His latest books are *Practical Police Psychology: Stress Management and Crisis Intervention for Law Enforcement* (Charles C. Thomas, 2006) and *Mental Toughness Training for Law Enforcement* (Looseleaf Law Publications, 2008). He is a regular commentator on local and national media.

Bret A. Moore, PsyD, is a board-certified clinical psychologist and prescribing psychologist in San Antonio, TX. He is Adjunct Associate

Professor in Psychiatry at the University of Texas Health Science Center in San Antonio and Instructor in Psychopharmacology at Fairleigh Dickinson University. In 2008, Dr. Moore left active duty service in the U.S. Army, where he served as a captain and clinical psychologist with the 85th Combat Stress Control unit based in Fort Hood, TX. Dr. Moore has authored and co-edited numerous books including *Treating PTSD in Military Personnel: A Clinical Handbook* (Guilford, 2011), *Handbook of Counseling Military Couples* (Routledge, 2012), *The Veterans and Active Duty Military Psychotherapy Treatment Planner* (Wiley, 2009), *Living and Surviving in Harm's Way: A Psychological Treatment Handbook for Military Personnel* (Routledge, 2009), and *Wheels Down: Adjusting to Life After Deployment* (APA, 2010). Dr. Moore is a Fellow of the American Psychological Association and is the recipient of early career achievement awards from Divisions 19 (Society for Military Psychology) and 18 (Psychologists in Public Service) of APA.

David Murphy is a Chartered Counselling Psychologist and Associate Fellow of the British Psychology Society. Having first joined the University of Nottingham as a part-time tutor on the BA Humanistic Counselling Practice in 2004, he later joined the Centre for Trauma, Resilience, and Growth (CTRG) in 2008 following a number of years in clinical practice. He moved to the School of Education in 2010 and joined the psychotherapy and counselling staff as a full-time member of the team. He has an honorary contract with Nottinghamshire Healthcare NHS Trust, Centre for Trauma as Psychologist Specializing in Psychotherapy. A significant part of his work has been providing therapeutic and psychological services to police officers and staff following traumatic incidents. Following the South East Asia tsunami, he developed and provided therapeutic support to promote psychological well-being for those from the East Midlands who were involved in disaster victim identification and repatriation processes. He was awarded an Association of Chief Police Officers (ACPO) certificate of recognition for this work.

John Price is currently Director of Psychological Services for the San Antonio Police Department. From 1999 to 2004, he was in private practice. He was a staff Psychologist and Program Director for the Pain Management Program at HealthSouth RIOSA from 1990 to 1998. From 1990 to 2004 he was an outside consultant for the San Antonio Police Department's Hostage Negotiation Team. From 1988 to 1990, he was a psychologist with the San Antonio Police Department. From 1984 to 1988 he was on active duty with the U.S. Army. Dr. Price earned a Doctorate Degree in Counseling Psychology from Texas A&M University in 1986. In 1980 he completed a Master's of Art in Clinical Psychology from Trinity University and a Bachelor's of Art Degree in Psychology from Texas Tech University in 1978.

Stephen Regel is Principal Psychotherapist and Co-director at the Centre for Trauma, Resilience and Growth, Nottinghamshire Healthcare NHS Trust/University of Nottingham, Nottingham, UK. Since 2002, he has been visiting therapist/consultant at the Family Trauma Centre in Belfast, Northern Ireland. He has over 30 years' experience working with trauma and post-traumatic stress disorder (PTSD). He also consults and trains extensively with UK police forces on the provision of post-trauma support. The Centre's Peer Support Training package continues to be delivered to emergency services, social services departments, health trusts, humanitarian aid organizations, and various health/mental health professionals in the UK and abroad.

Vincent B. Van Hasselt, PhD, is Professor of Psychology and Criminal Justice, and Director of the Family Violence Program at Nova Southeastern University, FL. He is also a certified police officer in the State of Florida. Dr. Van Hasselt has published over 200 journal articles, books, and book chapters, including many on crisis negotiations, critical incident stress management, and police stress and mental health. He has served as a consultant to the FBI's Behavioral Science, Crisis Negotiation, and Employee Assistance Units, and is a lecturer at the FBI National Academy on the topics of critical incident stress and the law enforcement family. His clinical and research interests are in the areas of police psychology, crisis (hostage) negotiation, and behavioral criminology. A licensed practicing clinical psychologist, Dr. Van Hasselt specializes in the problems of emergency first responders.

John M. Violanti, PhD, is a Full Research Professor in the Department of Social and Preventive Medicine, School of Public Health and Health Professions, University at Buffalo, NY and a member of the University at Buffalo graduate faculty. He has been involved in the design, implementation, and analysis of police stress and health studies over the past 25 years. Recent projects include a longitudinal study on psychological stress and cardiovascular disease in police officers and the impact of shift work on police health outcomes funded by the National Institute of Occupational Safety and Health. Dr. Violanti's research has focused on a number of topics including assessment of psychological and biological indicators of chronic police stress, subclinical cardiovascular and metabolic disease in police, shift work and health, and the epidemiology of police suicide.

Deloria Wilson, PhD, is an operational psychologist working with Air Force Security Forces personnel. She earned her Bachelor of Arts in Psychology from the University of Notre Dame, IN and her doctorate in Educational and Counseling Psychology from the University of Missouri. She served in the Air Force for seven years as a staff psychologist, director of a learning and development center, Alcohol Drug Abuse Prevention and Treatment program manager, deputy flight commander, and consultant to flying training squadrons and aerospace medicine in matters of airsickness management and performance improvement. She was a Deployment Behavioral Health Psychologist with the Center for Deployment Psychology, which trains civilian personnel to work with military members in providing effective treatments, and led the education and training division at the Warrior Resiliency Program where she helped develop training for psychologists on the issues of resiliency. Her current efforts include helping AF Security Forces with developing resilience training and efforts to support their members during combat and daily operations.

Part I

UNDERSTANDING THE LAW
ENFORCEMENT OFFICER

1

INTRODUCTION

Sharon M. Freeman Clevenger

> Every society gets the kind of criminal it deserves. What is equally true is that every community gets the kind of law enforcement it insists on.
>
> — Robert Kennedy

Law enforcement officers (LEOs) are identified by many other titles ranging from peace officer, trooper, ranger, U.S. marshall, detective, cop, police, deputy and sheriff. Regardless of the title that the LEO assumes, this person takes on the responsibility to place their life in danger, each day, in order to preserve and protect citizens. The role of the LEO has evolved over history. These peace officers are at times reviled, and at other times hailed as heroes. They are feared, respected, degraded, harassed, misunderstood, and courageous.

According to the Law Enforcement Officers' Safety Act (LEOSA) 18 USC 926B, the legal definition of a law enforcement officer is as follows:

A "qualified active law enforcement officer" is defined as an employee of a government agency who:

1 is authorized by law to engage in or supervise the prevention, detection, investigation, prosecution or the incarceration of any person for any violation of law;
2 has statutory powers of arrest or apprehension under Federal Law;
3 is authorized by the agency to carry a firearm;
4 is not the subject of any disciplinary action by the agency which could result in suspension or loss of police powers;

5   meets the standards, if any, established by the agency which require the employee to regularly qualify in the use of a firearm;
6   is not under the influence of alcohol or another intoxicating or hallucinatory drug or substance, and
7   is not prohibited by Federal law from possessing a firearm.

According to the National Law Enforcement memorial page, there are more than 900,000 sworn LEOs now serving in the United States, which is the highest figure ever. About 12 percent of those are female. According to the FBI's Uniform Crime Reports, an estimated 1.3 million violent crimes occurred in the United States nationwide in 2010, a 6 percent decrease from 2009.

What these statistics do not explain are the reasons why a person chooses law enforcement as a career, the hazards of daily life working in law enforcement, and the stress that is experienced by those closest to these officers. The following chapters provide a glimpse into the lives of LEOs, including an explanation of the culture, mindset, and special requirements placed on mental health professionals who work with these officers.

Chapter 2 provides an overview of the life of police officers, their families, and their history. Sharon Freeman Clevenger covers the evolution of the law enforcement officer. These officers carry a major responsibility in both maintaining and overcoming regimes and power centers over the years. The Roman Centurion, the Revolutionary Guard, and the local Sheriff's department, all have carried the burden of establishing, defending, and protecting both those in power and those in need of protection from those same political and powerful elements. This chapter reviews the personality characteristics of the LEO as well as the moral and cognitive requirements. The integration of women into police work, the impact on the families of LEOs, and the dangers faced in law enforcement will be outlined. A case example of a police officer critically injured in the line of duty will be presented as an example of not only dangers of police work, but also the strength it takes to survive a worst case scenario.

Chapter 3 by Stephen Curran describes fitness-for-duty evaluations that set the groundwork for an LEO's ability to function safely in the field. Stephen Curran describes the assessment process relative to the overall collection of data that is important for the mental health provider working with law enforcement. Dr. Curran outlines proficiencies that the psychologist must meet, including pre-employment job analysis and psychological evaluations which include both medical and psychological components for fitness for duty.

In Chapter 4, John Violanti introduces the reader to the psychological and biological stress experienced by law enforcement officers. He provides a masterful review of the biosocial process for understanding the magnitude of both internal and external stress and trauma. The concept of post-traumatic stress is introduced here in an occupation that is routine with episodic moments of intensive danger and incredible stressors. The effects of stress are well known. Impacting on virtually every physical system as well as causing and maintaining emotional distress, the sequelae of stress easily spills over to interpersonal and job-related behaviors. The effect of chronic stress on the biological system is reviewed and examples given for physical disorders that must be monitored. The key factor to be discussed in this chapter will be the resilience and vulnerability of the LEO to effectively cope with stressors, of whatever the source and type.

Brandi Burque, Maj. Monty Baker, Vincent Van Hasselt and Judy Couwels expand on stress in law enforcement with a state of the science review of Critical Incident Stress Debriefing (CISD) in Chapter 5. Frequently called upon as a prime intervention subsequent to traumatic events, Critical Incident Stress Debriefing has been broadly studied, both as a stand-alone treatment and as a part of a comprehensive intervention strategy. The mixed research results will be considered and the present state of the model will be discussed along with recommendations and caveats for its use. The chapter includes a historical review of the psychological understanding of stress responses and will compare and contrast Critical Incident Stress Debriefing with Critical Incident Stress Management (CISM), an "integrated, multi-component crisis intervention system" (Mitchell and Everly, 1999).

Law enforcement officers often coexist and interact with current and former military members. In fact, many law enforcement officers once served in the military in some capacity. Most risk factors for violence such as suicide or violent crime are similar between these groups. In Chapter 6, Karen Kalmbach and Randy Garner provide a research-based overview of the relationship between these two warrior groups in order to provide a better understanding of the issues at home, and in the process of reintegration back into the civilian world.

Chapter 7 expands on the concepts above, however, it focuses on the LEOs that are currently in the military as a police officer. Deloria Wilson, John Price, and Brandi Burque bring their expertise from the Warrior Resilience programs and the San Antonio Police Department to introduce the reader to the roles and responsibilities of the military police officer, an area that has very little focus in both military and law enforcement research. This chapter focuses on both the current military and the veteran military officers' experiences and duties.

Chapter 8, by Andrea Brockman, Brandi Burque, Vincent Van Hasselt and Maj. Monty Baker bring the reader into the rarely seen, or discussed, world of law enforcement officers in correctional settings. Prisons are universally accepted as dangerous settings, for any job in that environment.

The authors provide us with an overview of specific areas of stress, danger, violence, and role strain in this highly specialized setting.

Laurence Miller provides practical information in Chapter 9 regarding officers who find themselves in trouble for a variety of reasons, including excessive force, abuse of authority, corruption, theft, and so on. He also provides recommendations for police officers who may find themselves in court as defendants, witnesses, or arresting officers. This chapter includes the most common psychological reactions to internal investigations or legal proceedings, with recommendations for the treating psychologist.

Dr. Miller continues in Chapter 10 with a review of special policing units that involve hostage negotiation, undercover officers, and sex crimes investigation. He separates out the fantasized world of *Miami Vice* or *Law and Order: SVU* with factual information regarding these officers' work environment and the stressors involved in a factual, informative manner. The role of the police psychologist in hostage crisis team training and operational assistance is described as well as selection procedures for LEOs working in these roles.

Chapter 11 delves further into the insular world of police officers and the effect that this separation from others has on them. Laurence Miller brings real-world examples of critical incidents of stress and the challenges of the law enforcement officer to "leave the job at the door." Symptoms such as domestic violence, sleep disorders, and reluctance to verbalize personal difficulties most relevant to LEOs is outlined and discussed by Laurence Miller in a matter of fact, yet compassionate manner. Recommendations for departmental support are discussed as well as recommendations for the police psychologist.

Perhaps one of the most frightening and least understood situations in police work involves individuals with mental illness. The mentally ill can be less predictable than the criminal suspects who are encountered, bringing additional complexity to an already difficult situation. Laurence Miller discusses management of the mentally ill individual and gives recommendations for police officers in Chapter 12.

LEOs will commonly be the first individual on the scene in auto accidents, building collapses, or bombings, as in the case of the Boston Marathon bombing in 2013. R. Trent Codd discusses one of the most difficult situations that police officers respond to in Chapter 13 on fatal crash investigations. Fatal crash investigations, especially those involving children, are some of the most stressful, with the highest likelihood of post-incident psychological trauma in law enforcement. As a matter of fact, this author asked a number of LEOs what they felt was the most traumatic or stressful situation they were required to respond to, and the majority stated "fatal crashes." Law enforcement officers are often the first ones to arrive at the scene, which may include a high negative emotional valence, yet are expected to be calm and pleasant after completion of their shift, or as they stop someone for speeding. These expectations of a human being are at odds with normal human responses, however, they are not examined in the literature very often.

Chapter 14 by Stephen Joseph, David Murphy, and Stephen Regel on growth in LEOs following trauma contains groundbreaking work on recovery from exposure to trauma in police work. Providing support, guidance, and therapy to LEOs following a traumatic incident is one of the most requested services of psychologists working with law enforcement.

We finish this book with law enforcement work from the perspective of the police chaplain. Robert Douglas, Christine Heiny, and Sharon Freeman Clevenger combine their personal experiences and, recommendations, with lessons learned over the years by a multitude of police chaplains.

2

THE LAW ENFORCEMENT OFFICER

Sharon M. Freeman Clevenger

> We sleep safely at night because rough men stand ready to visit
> violence on those who would harm us.
> — Winston Churchill

Police officers are always among the first responders to catastrophes such
as the September 11, 2001 attacks, Hurricane Katrina and the Sandy
Hook Elementary School massacre. Casualties in these horrific events
might include friends, family, neighbors, and coworkers. During periods
of high-intensity response, as in the Boston Marathon bombing incident,
first responders may work extremely long hours with little rest, often for
weeks, or even months after the crisis is over. There is little time for these
individuals to deal with their own feelings, much less their physical needs
or the impact of these traumatic situations on their own personal life.

For centuries, the law enforcement officer has carried major
responsibility in both maintaining peace and being in the first line when
regimes and power centers are overthrown. The Roman Centurion, the
Revolutionary Guard, and the local Sheriff's department all have carried
the burden of establishing, defending, and protecting both those in power
and those needing protection from those same political and powerful
elements. In fact, the idea of wearing a shield on the front of the uniform
is a carryover from times when the warrior carried a shield. The shield
distinguished the person as an authority, a soldier, and a protector.

Law enforcement officers (LEOs) will hopefully benefit from the
knowledge gained from research regarding post-traumatic stress disorder
(PTSD), shift work disorders, and other psychological problems associated
with exposure to trauma and high-stress situations. Due to the stigma

of disclosing a mental illness, or difficulty, LEOs become skilled at compartmentalizing their feelings, and just "sucking it up." Stigma refers to fears that disclosing a personal problem or concern will result in being perceived negatively by peers or supervisors, and may even harm one's career if seen as being weak. In addition, the concept of "sucking it up," which is the cultural norm of keeping silent about needing help after trauma, is clearly a negative protective factor (Sherman, 2005). Specifically, we may be able to apply research on resiliency factors, vulnerability factors, protective factors such as past personal experiences, targeted training experience, and even personality characteristics. The following chapters discuss these concepts and others as they apply to LEOs.

Personality Characteristics of a Successful Law Enforcement Officer

Interest in describing the "police personality" began with Robert W. Balch in 1972, and Jerome Skolnic's work in 1977, *A Sketch of the Policeman's Working Personality* (Skolnic, 1977). Skolnic felt that:

> Understanding the relationship between an officer's environment and cognitive and behavioral responses to that environment can lead to a deeper understanding of police behavior, isolation, and subsequent solidarity and cohesion. Specifically, exploration into the "working personality" of police, and the environment that helps to shape the working personality, can provide potential solutions for improving police/citizen relationships, and other serious challenges confronting police. Further, exploring the working personality and environment of police can highlight obstacles, and explain failures of, police initiatives and movements.
>
> (Skolnic, 1977: 1)

Stephen Curran expands upon the psychological assessment of LEOs in Chapter 3 of this book, however, in brief, a review of the literature includes many personality characteristics that describe the LEO, and also those characteristics that are most closely associated with career survival in law enforcement. Long-held civilian views of police officers were that they were bigoted, authoritarian, suspicious, and solitary figures (Balch, 1972; Skolnic, 1977). More recent characteristics describing LEOs are empathy, willingness to kill in order to protect, intelligence, ability to communicate clearly, courage, and integrity (Detrick & Chibnall, 2006; Josephson, 2009).

Once the characteristics of the LEO are established, the next challenge is to determine the best way to assess individuals for these traits. Establishing a standardized method of psychological screening has been a hotly debated topic however. In Chapter 3, Curran will outline the most recent recommendations (Dantzker, 2011).

Each officer has their own reason for becoming an LEO. The most common reason is to "help others" (Stone, 2007). The career choice and career path factors along with the impact of the LEO's responsibility and function on both immediate and extended family. In addition, there are implications of the LEO as a participant and member of the culture and the communities that the LEO is sworn to protect.

Women in Police Work

The term commonly used in the past was "policeman," as synonymous with a law enforcement office. That term can no longer be used inasmuch as national statistics estimate that less than 13 percent of LEOs are women (National Center for Women and Policing, n.d.). One might assume that the status and problems of being a minority within the law enforcement community has many facets, including possible issues of gender bias, trust, collaboration, and cooperative work. The National Center for Women and Policing's website reports that

> women police officers utilize a style of policing that relies less on physical force, and more on communication skills that defuse potentially violent situations. Women police officers are therefore much less likely to be involved in occurrences of police brutality, and are also much more likely to effectively respond to police calls regarding violence against women, which today remain the single largest category of calls to police agencies nationwide.
> (National Center for Women and Policing, n.d.)

In order to better understand the role and challenges facing policewomen, this author interviewed a number of female LEOs. One interview is summarized below.

Katrina, LEO Trainee for the Fort Walton Beach Police Department: Interview August 20, 2011

Katrina is a slightly built, attractive blonde woman approximately 22 years old. She has passed the classroom and practice components of law enforcement and has been placed with a Field Training Officer (FTO) for the final phase of training. The FTO will mentor her, train her in the nuances of police work, and finally evaluate her performance "on the street." The FTO will then make a recommendation as to whether or not Katrina should be hired as an officer.

SFC: Why did you choose to go into police work?
K: I wanted to do something with my life that would help people. In 6th grade we were given a project to talk about what we wanted

to do for a career. I investigated different choices for case workers, psychology and then law enforcement. After that I was pretty much set on becoming a police officer. That's all I wanted to do ever since. I wanted to make a difference, to do something that would really help people.

SFC: What differences, if any, did you experience as a woman when it came to the selection process and the training academy experience?

K: There is no difference when it comes to the selection process. As a woman we are expected to be able to perform physically the same as a man. We have to pass the same written exams and the same physical tests. The difference is at the Academy. They expect women to be more emotional, I think, so it seemed they were harder on the women. Most of the women in my class dropped out because of that. We actually had more women in our Academy class than they had ever had before. The final cut had more women in it than men. We started out with 13 and 5 finished. Three of the five that finished were women.

Law Enforcement Families

Law enforcement families face unique challenges on a daily basis. This author believes that one of the best descriptions of an LEO is one that was broadcast by Paul Harvey, date unknown. Paul Harvey, a well-known and popular radio icon, was born Paul Harvey Aurandt in Tulsa, Oklahoma on September 4, 1918 and died February 28, 2009. Apparently it is well known that Mr. Harvey's father was a police officer, and was killed in the line of duty when Harvey was about three years old. Harvey got his start at a Tulsa, Oklahoma radio station in 1933, and was heard nationally since 1951, when he began his *News and Comment* for ABC Radio Networks.

A transcript of Paul Harvey's broadcast *What is a Policeman?* is below:

> Don't credit me with the mongrel prose: it has many parents—at least 420,000 of them: Policemen.
>
> A policeman is a composite of what all men are, mingling of a saint and sinner, dust and deity.
>
> Gulled statistics wave the fan over the stinkers; underscore instances of dishonesty and brutality because they are "new." What they really mean is that they are exceptional, unusual, and not commonplace.
>
> Buried under the frost is the fact: Less than one-half of one percent of policemen misfit the uniform. That's a better average than you'd find among clergy!

What is a policeman made of? He, of all men, is once the most needed and the most unwanted. He's a strangely nameless creature who is "sir" to his face and "fuzz" to his back

He must be such a diplomat that he can settle differences between individuals so that each will think he won. But . . . if the policeman is neat, he's conceited; if he's careless, he's a bum. If he's pleasant, he's flirting; if not, he's a grouch.

He must make an instant decision which would require months for a lawyer to make.

But . . . if he hurries, he's careless; if he's deliberate, he's lazy. He must be first to an accident and infallible with his diagnosis. He must be able to start breathing, stop bleeding, tie splints and, above all, be sure the victim goes home without a limp. Or expect to be sued.

The police officer must know every gun, draw on the run, and hit where it doesn't hurt. He must be able to whip two men twice his size and half his age without damaging his uniform and without being "brutal." If you hit him, he's a coward. If he hits you, he's a bully.

A policeman must know everything—and not tell. He must know where all the sin is and not partake.

A policeman must, from a single strand of hair, be able to describe the crime, the weapon and the criminal—and tell you where the criminal is hiding.

But . . . if he catches the criminal, he's lucky; if he doesn't, he's a dunce. If he gets promoted, he has political pull; if he doesn't, he's a dullard. The policeman must chase a bum lead to a deadend, stake out ten nights to tag one witness who saw it happen—but refused to remember.

The policeman must be a minister, a social worker, a diplomat, a tough guy and a gentleman.

And, of course, he'd have to be genius . . . For he will have to feed a family on a policeman's salary.

(Paul Harvey, n.d., public domain)

Many of this author's friends and colleagues are LEOs, or LEO family members. Each day the LEO puts on body armor, holsters a weapon or two, and suits up to go into battle. They kiss their family goodbye and wish them a good day, or night. They go home after shifts that are brutal, and are expected to smile and attend the school play as if nothing has happened. Their wives/girlfriends/husbands/mothers say a prayer as they leave the door to "Please be safe today." There is no guarantee that the officer will return safely. On December 9, 2011, about a week after visiting a police wife friend of mine, Nancy, and her LEO husband, Bryan, Bryan's LEO brother, Steve, was shot in the face. (There is more on Nancy and Bryan's story below.) According to reports by the Okaloosa County Sheriff's Office, the suspect came out of a house and shot Okaloosa Sheriff's Deputy Seven Hough, once in the face and twice in the legs on Friday, December 9, 2011. Deputy Hough was working with the U.S. Marshals Service Regional Fugitive Task Force and was injured while trying to take the suspect into custody on multiple warrants. Colleagues drove Hough to a nearby hospital. He was then airlifted to Sacred Heart Hospital's trauma center. Steve has miraculously survived with facial reconstruction and nerve damage. His first thoughts upon awakening in ICU on December 10, 2011 were about others who might be worrying about him, rather than himself. He was unable to speak, so he wrote on a whiteboard "Facebook Update: Tell everyone I am doing OK." Incredibly, Steve Hough returned to full duty as a law enforcement officer ten months after the incident. Below are several photos depicting Steve's injury and recovery (all photos below courtesy of Steve and Tanya Hough, 2014).

Steve Hough's story is unfortunately not unusual in the fact that LEOs are injured in the line of duty at a rate of approximately 58,261 assaults against LEOs each year, resulting in approximately 15,658 injuries, according to the National Law Enforcement Memorial Fund website (www.nleomf.org). Law enforcement officers are not immune to the

Photo 2.1 Robert, Bryan and Steve Hough May 30, 2009.

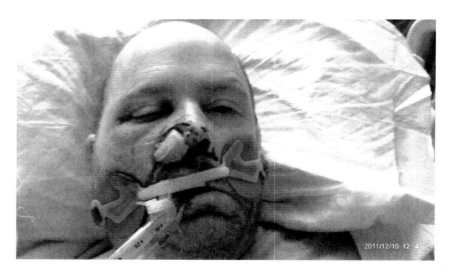

Photo 2.2 Steve Hough, December 10, 2011. Steve was shot in the face and leg in the line of duty.

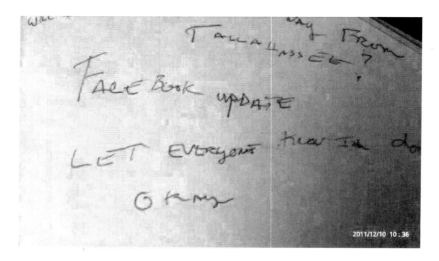

Photo 2.3 Steve Hough's first words in ICU, day two after the incident, December 12, 2011.

dangers that civilians face, in addition to the dangers of the job. Just six months before Steve's injury in the line of duty, Bryan Hough had been informed by one of his brothers in blue that his son, Geoff, had been killed in a motor vehicle crash at the age of 21 when a car pulled out in front of the vehicle in which he was a passenger.

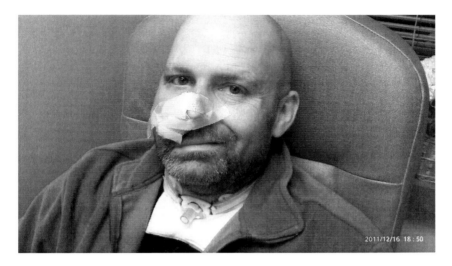

Photo 2.4 Steve Hough, first day out of ICU, December 16, 2011.

The news of Geoff's accident had a sense of horrible déjà vu for Bryan and Nancy because Geoff had previously been in a similar automobile accident, almost two years to the day, in 2009 at the age of 19. In that 2009 accident, Bryan was notified that Geoff had been in a serious accident and the highway patrol was working the scene as a fatality due to Geoff's severe head injury. Thankfully, Geoff was not killed in 2009, although no one had any idea how he survived the head injury. Two years

Photo 2.5 Robert, Steve (center), and Bryan Hough, August 4, 2012.

later, after a long stay in intensive care, multiple surgeries, and two full years of rehabilitation, he was well enough to enroll in emergency medical technician school. The future was bright for this wonderful young man, and then, almost two years later to the day in 2011, a car turned directly in front of the car that Goeff was riding in as a passenger, ending his life. This time the news was the worst a parent can hear, and Bryan's son was gone. What made things worse, if that is possible, for Bryan is that he was assigned to the vehicular homicide division and knew exactly what these types of accidents involve. Six months after Geoff's death, Bryan's brother Steve was involved in the gunfight that resulted in his being shot in the leg and face (described above). Despite experiencing these horrific events, each day Bryan and Steve suit up, kiss their wives goodbye, and head out for another shift. To see Steve "in person," the reader can access an interview conducted with him on YouTube (Nicholson, February 2, 2012, www.youtube.com/watch?v=9XoniA9dtvo).

Bryan's and Steve's stories are traumatic in nature. It is important to keep in mind that LEOs deploy each day into combat. Traumatic incidents related to "combat" situations are not limited to the military. Events that LEOs respond to include arriving at a domestic dispute and finding a child or adult dead; performing CPR at the scene of a car crash while the family looks on hoping the Hero will save their loved one, when that officer knows there is no hope; arriving as a first responder to a fatal car crash where there are scattered body parts of once beautiful teenagers; attending the autopsies of children beaten or abused; getting shot at, spat on, yelled at and dealing with body fluids of all kinds. How can these officers *not* experience combat stress reactions?

Combat stress is defined by the Department of Defense as: "The expected and predictable emotional, intellectual, physical and/or behavioral reactions of service members who have been exposed to stressful events in war or military operations other than war." According to the *Dictionary of Military and Associated Terms, U.S. Department of Defense* (2005), "combat stress reactions vary in quality and severity as a function of operational conditions, such as intensity, duration, rules of engagement, leadership, effective communication, unit morale, unit cohesion, and perceived importance of the mission."

According to the Officer Down Memorial page, the first recorded police death occurred in 1791 (www.odmp.org/search). Since that time, there have been over 19,000 LEOs killed in the line of duty. A total of 1,559 LEOs died in the line of duty during the past ten years, an average of one death every 56 hours, averaging 156 per year. There were 163 law enforcement officers killed in 2011. The deadliest day in law enforcement history was September 11, 2001, when 72 LEOs were killed while responding to the terrorist attacks on America. Of states in the United States, New York City has lost more officers in the line of duty than any

Table 2.1 LEO deaths, assaults and injuries, 2002–2011

Year	Deaths	Assaults	Injuries
2002	157	58,440	16,626
2003	149	58,278	16,412
2004	165	60,054	16,737
2005	162	59,428	16,072
2006	156	59,907	15,916
2007	190	60,851	15,736
2008	141	60,139	15,554
2009	122	57,268	14,985
2010	154	53,469	13,962
2011	163	54,774	14,578
2012	120	54,758	14,884

Source: National Law Enforcement Officers Memorial Fund and Federal Bureau of Investigation (n.d.), www.nleomf.org/facts/officer-fatalities-data/daifacts.html.

other department, with 695 deaths. Texas has lost 1,631 officers, more than any other state (National Law Enforcement Memorial Fund, n.d., www.nleomf.org).

Table 2.1 outlines ten-year statistics on LEO deaths, assaults and injuries.

The 1920s were the deadliest decade in law enforcement history, when a total of 2,318 officers died, or an average of almost 232 each year. The deadliest year in law enforcement history was 1930, when 290 officers were killed. That figure dropped dramatically in the 1990s, to an average of 161 per year. There are 257 female officers listed on the Memorial; 11 female officers were killed in 2011 (National Law Enforcement Officers Memorial Fund, n.d.).

It is amazing that men and women continue to choose careers in law enforcement: to basically seek a position that puts them into harm's way on a daily basis.

The Law Enforcement Couple

In describing the situation above in which Steve Hough was shot in the face in the line of duty, it would be remiss to not mention the fact that Steve is also a husband and father. The LEO is often viewed as a singular entity when they are working. However, each LEO has someone that knows, loves, and cares for them, even if it is "only" their brothers in blue. The issue of law enforcement families that support their LEO is similar to family members that support military members, with one huge difference. The LEO comes home and is required to "act normal," and then at the required time, suit up as a warrior, kiss the family goodbye, and head into harm's way on a daily basis. In order to better understand a functioning LEO family, the author has included an interview with Bryan and Nancy Hough (the interview was conducted one week before Steve's shooting incident).

Interview: Bryan and Nancy Hough

Bryan and Nancy are a couple in their forties, married for four years. Bryan is an officer with the Fort Walton Beach Florida Police Department. He was an enlisted sailor in the Navy and is now retired from the military and has been with the Fort Walton Police Department for 11 years. He is a Field Training Officer (FTO), which means that he trains and evaluate graduates from the Police Academy that want to be hired as officers in the Fort Walton Beach Florida Police Department. As an FTO, he acts as a mentor as well as an instructor. Nancy was raised in a military family (her father was in the Army) and prior to marrying Bryan was married to a military service member. They have seven children between them: Bryan has three and Nancy has four. The last child will be graduating from high school in nine months. They have experienced significant traumatic losses in these first years of marriage. Two colleagues from Bryan's small city were killed three years ago in the line of duty. One year later his son was in a horrible automobile accident and was at first thought to be dead. He was brain damaged and in intensive care for months before waking up and starting rehabilitation. The process included significant conflict issues with Geoff's mother, Bryan's former wife, which made the entire process even more stressful. Geoff recovered completely and was enrolled in college when he was involved in the second serious automobile accident in 2011. The second accident occurred almost exactly two years after the date of the first accident. In the 2011 accident, a driver pulled out in front of the car in which Geoff was a passenger. This time Geoff did not make it. One month after Geoff's death, Bryan's second son was also in an automobile accident; however, he escaped with no injuries.

SFC: What is the biggest challenge that the two of you face as a law enforcement couple?

Bryan: The hours are difficult

Nancy: Yes, the hours are pretty tough. There are sometimes weeks that will go by when we won't even see each other. He works second shift and I work day shift.

Bryan: She's sleeping when I get home and I'm sleeping when she gets up for work.

SFC: What is the most important marriage survival skill that the two of you use that keeps your marriage working?

Bryan: Flexibility. It's critical. You have to be able to change your plans at the last minute without it causing stress. Criminals don't work the same hours I do. I mean, they don't care that I might be on my lunch break and have just sat down to take a bite of [points to his sandwich] my dinner. If I get called, lunch is over. Nancy might have been planning an event all day, or all week, like a birthday party. I might get a call just before I'm supposed to be there and that's it, no Bryan at the party.

Nancy: [with a small laugh and a smile] That's right. You have to be flexible. I think it has been easier for me because I was raised in a military family and I was a prior military wife. I never knew when we would have to pick up and move, or when he would be deployed and would leave at the last minute. You have to learn how to be independent and take care of things as a single person. He loves his job. I want him to be happy and not to worry about me back at home. Then he can focus on what he is doing. That makes his job not only a little less stressful, it also means he's safer out there.

SFC: Is there anything else that you would recommend to other couples that are law enforcement families?

Bryan: Communicate, Communicate, and Communicate.

Nancy: Absolutely! That is the most important thing to do.

SFC: How do you communicate if you are working different shifts and sometimes don't see each other for weeks?

Nancy: He sends me a text when he leaves for work and again when he gets out of shift report. That's when I know that it is okay to text him. We send each other text messages (on our mobile phones) through the day, or emails that he can read on his phone. We have developed a routine about communicating and our own sets of code words. For example, I don't say "Hey I'm home!" I will say "Got the mail. Here's what might be important." He will answer "Open that one. That one will wait until I get home."

Bryan: Those texts and emails are really important. It keeps us connected during the day and we don't feel out of touch.

The Importance of Resiliency

Individuals that experience severe traumatic events have a variety of responses to the events, ranging from disabling PTSD to minimal or no discernible symptoms. The range of psychological responses has been hypothesized to be related to a number of factors, especially vulnerability to stress and resiliency to stress. Vulnerability factors can include genetic factors such as short/short serotonin transporter alleles, environmental factors such as prior experience with traumatic situations and personal factors such as limited coping skills. Increased vulnerability of PTSD has been associated with family instability (King et al., 1996), whereas good social support is associated with resilience to stress (Solomon et al., 1988). Resilience factors protect an individual from traumatic stress reactions. These factors are hypothesized to include successful prior exposure to traumatic situation, robust and varied coping skills, a positive general outlook and significant healthy support systems. Stress Inoculation Training (SIT) was developed by Don Meichenbaum in 1977 as one of the first therapies aimed at protection factors against the development of past and future coping responses to traumatic situation (Meichenbaum, 1986). Meichenbaum tailored a multifactorial process of response that includes three phases: a) a collaborative conceptualization phase aimed at the development of cognitive and behavioral problem-solving skills, b) a skills acquisition and rehearsal phase in which coping skills are developed and practiced, and c) application and follow-through phase where the client practices skills learned. Skills employed in SIT include imagery and imaginal exposure, behavioral rehearsal, modeling, role playing, and graded in vivo exposure in the form of "personal experiments" (Meichenbaum, 1985).

Dr. Meichenbaum created a workbook, *Roadmap to Resilience*, which is a masterful guide illustrating the process of SIT for individuals as a self-help manual, or as a manual to guide PTSD therapy in conjunction with a therapist. *Roadmap* walks the reader through reasonable, easy to follow action plans to understand the physical, psychological, and behavioral complexities of trauma. It includes easy-to-relate-to examples, numerous quotable quotes and "how to" examples that can be developed into a playbook for trauma victims, whether civilian or military (for more information, see www.roadmaptoresilience.org (Meichenbaum, 2012)).

Summary

Law Enforcement Officers are a tight knit group of men and woman who choose careers that place them in danger on a daily basis. Their families must adjust to the constant stress of not only shift work and long hours, but also the possibility that their loved one may not return. John Violanti describes the health consequences of stress and trauma on the LEO in Chapter 4. Additional consequences of stress and trauma take place within the family, or for the LEO that is in the minority, as in Katrina's example above. LEOs must therefore have the ability to compartmentalize their own emotions in order to function in the field, and then turn around and function "normally" at home, and in home situations. The psychological characteristics of these individuals must then include empathy, integrity, and

Table 2.2 Resources for Family Members of LEOs

Books	Kates, A. (1999). *CopShock: Surviving Post Traumatic Stress*. Tucson, AZ: Holbrook Street Press. (Contains an enormous list of support sources for PTSD and other mental health concerns). Kirschman, E. (1997). *I Love a Cop: What Police Families Need to Know*. New York: Guilford Publishing. Meichenbaum, D. (2012). *Roadmap to Resilience: A Guide for Military, Trauma Victims and Their Families*, available at www.roadmaptoresilience.com
Online support groups for wives, fiancées, or girlfriends of LEOs	Wives Behind the Badge: www.wivesbehindthebadge.org Policewives: www.policewives.org
For LEOs and their Families	Stone, V. (2007). *Cops Don't Cry: A Book of Help and Hope for Police Families*. Carp, Ontario: Creative Bound Books. Gilmartin, K. (2002). *Emotional Survival for Law Enforcement: A Guide for Officers and Their Families*. Tucson, AZ: E-S Press. Armstrong, K., Best, S., & Domenici, P. (2006). *Courage After Fire*. Berkeley, CA: Ulysses Press.

resilience. The remaining chapters in this book will give the reader a glimpse into the structure and process that make up a police officer. The mental health practitioner needs to be well versed in identifying both vulnerability and resilience factors that impact the development of PTSD. The resources listed in Table 2.2 may be useful to the mental health practitioner working with these unique warriors, and their family members.

Acknowledgment

A special thank you to Nancy, Bryan and Steve Hough for allowing me to include their experiences as a law enforcement family, and for sending me the photos of Steve's journey after being shot in the line of duty. Thank you also to my fellow sisters at www.policewives.org for your support and encouragement while writing this book. Without support such as yours, so many spouses of law enforcement officers would feel alone and lost.

References

Armstrong, K., Best, S., & Domenici, P. (2006). *Courage After Fire*. Berkeley, CA: Ulysses Press.

Balch. R.W. (1972). The police personality: Fact or fiction? *The Journal of Criminal Law, Criminology, and Police Science*, 63, 106.

Dantzker, M.L. (2011). Psychological preemployment screening for police candidates: Seeking consistency if not standardization. *Professional Psychology: Research and Practice*, 42(3), 276–283.

Detrick, P. & Chibnall, J.T. (2006). NEO PI-R personality characteristics of high-performing entry-level police officers. *John T. Psychological Services*, 3(4), 274–285.

Gilmartin, K. (2002). *Emotional Survival for Law Enforcement: A Guide for Officers and Their Families*. Tucson, AZ: E-S Press.

Harvey, P. "Address at Police Week 1992," National Law Enforcement Officers Memorial Fund Banquet.

Harvey, P. "What Are Policemen Made Of?" Law Enforcement Articles, http://www.lawenforcementarticles.com/what-are-policemen-made-of.

Josephson, M. (2009). *Becoming an Exemplary Peace Officer: The Guide to Ethical Decision-making*. California Commission on Peace Officer Standards and Training in Collaboration with the Josephson Institute of Ethics.

Kates, A. (1999). *CopShock: Surviving Post Traumatic Stress*. Tucson, AZ: Holbrook Street Press.

King, D.W., King, L.A., Foy, D.W., & Gudanowski, D.M. (1996). Prewar factors in combat-related post traumatic stress disorder: Structural equational modeling with a national sample of female and male Vietnam veterans. *Journal of Consulting and Clinical Psychology*, 64, 520–531.

Kirschman, E. (1997). *I Love a Cop: What Police Families Need to Know*. New York: Guilford Publishing.

The Law Enforcement Officers' Safety Act (LEOSA) 18 USC 926B.

Meichenbaum, D. (1985). *Stress Inoculation Training*. New York: Pergamon Press.

Meichenbaum, D. (1996). Stress inoculation training for coping with stressors. *The Clinical Psychologist*, 49, 4–7.

Meichenbaum, D. (2012). *Roadmap to Resilience: A Guide for Military, Trauma Victims and Their Families*. Clearwater, FL: Institute Press.

National Center for Women and Policing (n.d.). http://womenandpolicing.com/ (accessed January 11, 2013).

National Law Enforcement Officers Memorial Fund (n.d.). www.nleomf.org (accessed January 20, 2014).

National Law Enforcement Officers Memorial Fund and Federal Bureau of Investigation (n.d.). www.nleomf.org/facts/officer-fatalities-data/daifacts.html (accessed January 20, 2014).

Nicholson, P.M. (2012). Interview with Steven Hough for the Okaloosa Sheriff's Department. www.youtube.com/watch?v=9XoniA9dtvo (accessed January 2, 2013).

Sherman, N. (2005). *Stoic Warriors: The Ancient Philosophy Behind the Military Mind*. New York: Oxford University Press.

Skolnic, J.H. (1977). *A Sketch of the Policeman's Working Personality*. Upper Saddle, NJ: Pearson Education.

Solomon, Z., Mikulincer, M., & Avitzur, E. (1988). Coping, locus of control, social support, and combat-related posttraumatic stress disorder: A prospective study. *Journal of Personality and Social Psychology*, 55, 279–285.

Stone, V. (2007). *Cops Don't Cry: A Book of Help and Hope for Police Families*. Carp Ontario: Creative Bound Books.

3

ASSESSMENT AND EVALUATION

Collecting the Requisite Building Blocks for Treatment Planning

Stephen F. Curran

Introduction

The development of police psychological assessments has both a historical legal basis and a clinical practice background. The legal issues range from *Bonsignore* v. *City of New York* (1982) to the more recent Genetic Information Nondiscrimination Act (GINA) of 2008. During the 30-year window from the *Bonsignore* case to GINA, there have been numerous case law and federal regulations that have resulted in various degrees of impact on law enforcement assessments. This chapter will reference many, but not all, of the relevant case law that impacts psychological assessments. Among the cases that will be referenced are the Equal Employment Opportunity Commission (EEOC, 1995) and the Uniformed Services Employment and Re-employment Rights Act (USERRA, 1994).

The clinical origins of police psychology are rooted in the assessment domain. The history of police psychology will often cite the work of Lewis Terman, PhD, during the early 1900s in the development of intelligence testing. Terman is credited with applying his expertise to the selection of police officers for the San Jose Police Department in 1916.

Since then, the field of police psychology has sprouted in directions not foreseeable nearly a century ago. The growth was slow with a latency of about 50 years before flourishing. The near dormant phase from the early work of Termen to the 1960s was then followed by rapid growth.

During the 1960s, two areas of police psychology began to take hold and not because police agencies necessarily pushed for progress. This newfound growth of assessments was a response to the 1967 Presidential Commission on Law Enforcement and Administration of Justice (Kitaeff,

2011). This timeframe correlated with the Los Angeles Police Department selecting Dr. Martin Reiser as their in-house psychologist to head the assessment program. At the same time, the police agencies nationwide were experiencing a shift in attitudes toward professional counseling and became increasingly sensitive to the need to support and sustain police officers by having readily available counseling services (Gupton et al., 2011). James Shaw, PhD, in Olympia, Washington, then became the first full-time psychologist during 1963 for the King's County Sheriff's Department where he provided counseling and traumatic stress services. Weiss and Inwald (2010) provide an excellent review of the history about police pre-employment assessments over the past 100 years.

Recent Developments

The twenty-first century began with police psychology having advanced to become a recognized specialty. The American Psychological Association (APA) extended recognition of police psychology as a proficiency during 2008. This status was elevated to a recognized specialty in 2010 after exhaustive self-study by the major professional police psychological services organizations the Police Psychology Services Section of the International Association of Chiefs of Police (IACP), Police and Public Service Psychology (Division 18 of APA), and the Society for Police and Criminal Psychology). In 2010, the American Board of Professional Psychology (ABPP) recognized the specialty Police and Public Safety Psychology. In 2011, the first group of psychologists was granted board certification after a thorough credentialing review, written practice sample, and competency-based oral interview. The current field of police psychology proficiencies is across four domains: (1) assessment-related activities, (2) intervention services, (3) operational support, and (4) organizational/management consultation. The remainder of this chapter will address specifically the current issues in the assessment domain of police psychology.

The assessment area constitutes the greatest number of specific proficiencies in police psychology. These areas are identified along with a brief synopsis of the professional practice the psychologist performs. The reader is encouraged to review each with an eye to learning of areas previously not considered as an activity of a police psychologist. The assessment proficiencies[1] are:

- Job analysis—Identifying the essential psychological traits that are needed to perform duties of a law enforcement officer.
- Pre-employment, post-offer psychological evaluations of job candidates—The administration of one or more objective psychological tests along with an interview to assess the stability of a candidate and suitability to perform the essential job functions of the position. The

Police Psychological Services Section (IACP) has developed guidelines, revised every five years, which provide a comprehensive overview of the best practices for conducting the pre-employment evaluation (IACP, 2009a).

- Psychological fitness-for-duty evaluations of incumbents—The assessment of officers due to documented deficits in performance that are more likely than not due to psychological impairment. Similar to the pre-employment assessment, the IACP Police Psychological Services Section has developed guidelines, revised every five years, which provide a comprehensive overview of the best practices for conducting the fitness-for-duty evaluation (IACP, 2009b).
- Evaluations for FMLA eligibility—An employer-requested evaluation of an officer applying for leave under the Family and Medical Leave Act (FMLA).
- Evaluations for reasonable accommodation—Evaluation of employees seeking accommodations to their position as defined by the federal Americans with Disabilities Act (ADA).
- PEPSA (Psychological Evaluations for Police Special Assignments)—Assessments for special assignments such as tactical team (SWAT) and crisis negotiator.
- Direct threat assessments—A subset of the fitness-for-duty evaluation that specifically addresses direct threats to the officer or others.
- Workplace violence assessments—A subset of the fitness-for-duty evaluation to identify risk factors in the workplace for both employee and employer.
- Mental health hold evaluations and consultation—Evaluations conducted of citizens, either direct or indirect, who may pose a danger to self or others. This activity involves defusing a crisis and may include referral to a facility for further evaluation.
- Supervision of psychological assistants, residents, interns, or fellows—Assessment of trainees to meet American Psychological Association accreditation standards.
- Pre-offer suitability screening of job applicants (normal traits and competencies)—An assessment of candidate's personality traits through objective, validated tests that do not make "medical" inquiries about the applicant. Pre-offer personality testing does not replace the pre-employment psychological evaluation which may only be conducted after the conditional offer of employment.
- Promotional evaluations (normal traits and competencies)—Assessments conducted as part of assessing strengths and weaknesses of law enforcement personnel under consideration for promotion.
- Assessment center development and administration—These are standardized simulation exercises which may range from problem analysis, to role play, to in-basket tasks.

- Psychological autopsies—Assessments for contributing information from fields of suicidology and personality theory to develop hypotheses about the deceased's state of mind at time of death.
- Test development—Research and development of valid measures to assess specific job functions.
- Education and training—Programs that instruct a department's users of psychological assessment reports about psychological constructs employed in assessing prospective candidates and areas such as promotion and specialty team assignments.
- Research—Evaluating the assessment programs utilized by an agency and making recommendations based on results.
- Assessment-Related Consultation—Assisting in the design, modification, and research needs of an agency's assessment programs.

Review of Research: Civilian

The development of formal psychological assessment tools in the private, military and other government settings dates to the early 1900s with the application of structured interviews. The introduction of the formal mental status examination by Adolf Meyer, MD, in 1902 set the stage for using an assessment tool that could be validated against a criterion measure and is reliable upon re-testing (Groth-Marnat, 2009). As already noted, the work of Termen in testing intelligence was occurring around the same timeframe. Also, the field of industrial psychology was emerging during the early part of the twentieth century. When World War I began the National Academy of Sciences created the National Research Council for the purpose of developing tests to select and assign military personnel (Thomas and Scroggins, 2006). These advances soon were followed by expanded measures of intelligence testing (e.g., Wechsler scales) during the 1930s and personality testing (e.g., MMPI) in 1940.

Collectively, these measures were quickly applied across a variety of settings. Assessments of children and psychiatric patients grew in frequency. Similarly, the application to the private sector and positions of trust, among others, increased rapidly to the present. Today, the standard operating procedure for many organizations, both public and private, is for pre-placement assessment: cognitive or personality. Among examples is the clinical assessment requirement by the United States Department of Energy's National Nuclear Security Administration (2011) for determining eligibility for access to classified material.

Law Enforcement

An introductory overview has already been described in this chapter. The specific application of objective psychological measures to the selection of police officers started to emerge during the 1970s. Among the earliest research projects was a study conducted by Robert Hogan, PhD, in the use of the California Psychological Inventory (CPI). Dr. Hogan studied a sample of Maryland State Troopers to develop what would become the "Police Performance Quotient." The 1975 publication by Hogan was the precursor to current, generally accepted domains required of a police officer.

Another measure at the time that had become the most frequently used test was the original MMPI that was developed in 1939 (Butcher 2011). The first major revision of the MMPI was the MMPI-2, which was standardized on a new national sample of adults in the United States and released in 1989. Among advances to the MMPI-2 were restructured clinical (RC) scales which provided useful clinical information, in part because no items are contained in more than one RC scale.

More recently, the MMPI-2-Restructured Form (RF) provided further advancement in the assessment of police officers specifically but also other public safety positions (Ben-Porath & Tellegen, 2008). The research on the MMPI and its successors are voluminous. Sellbom et al. (2007) reported on a study of 291 male police officers of whom 40 percent had been on the job over seven years. The study examined internal affairs and related complaints. It found that the RC scales (RC3, RC4, RC6, and RC8) were the best predictors of police officer integrity and misconduct. Ben-Porath et al. (2011a) presented pre-hire MMPI-2-RF and outcome data at a level greater than the magnitude report by Sellbom. The strongest correlations were on measures of emotional dysfunction (RC2 and HLP) and interpersonal dysfunction (DSF and INTR-r). In addition, negative outcomes were associated with low scores on RC9/Activation, higher scores on the Aggression Scale, and higher scores on Cognitive Complaints, RC6, and the PSY-5 Psychoticism Scale. The CPI and MMPI-2/MMPI-2-RF are among the most frequently administered measures. There are others such as the Personality Assessment Inventory (PAI), Inwald Personality Inventory (IPI), and its recently released version, IPI-2, and the 16PF. Regardless of which measures an evaluating psychologist is using when conducting pre-employment, fitness for duty or specialty assignments the research and application for its use is essential to understand prior to incorporating a measure in a testing protocol. Figure 3.1 provides an overview of the continuum of psychological assessments conducted for a law enforcement agency.

Pre-employment Psychological Assessments

The pre-employment psychological assessment domain requires proficiency in the areas of assessment, employment law, and police functions, among others. These evaluations are the hallmark of the majority of services

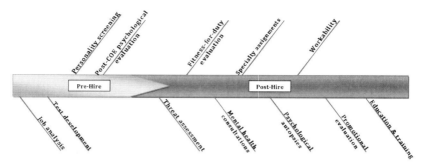

Figure 3.1 Continuum of police psychological assessments for the individual (top) and the organization (bottom).

rendered by psychologists to law enforcement agencies. The assessment protocols and practices have particularly evolved over the past 20 years. Among advances in psychometric assessment has been increased specificity about problematic behaviors and their impact upon performing essential job functions. This has led to normative data and measures specific to public safety candidates. In addition, the standards for recommended practices for psychologists continue to mature since the initial guidelines of the IACP Police Psychological Services Section were promulgated during the early 1990s (Ben-Porath et al., 2011b). These are not overwhelming areas to grasp but overlooking some of the basics can lead to conflicts. These conflicts may occur between the agency serving as the consultant, the potential candidate, and the licensing boards. A psychologist with a sharp eye on applying ethical standards will side-step the pitfalls.

Let's look at some of the prominent assessment practice errors to consider regardless of being a novice evaluator or experienced evaluator.

1 A police officer is a police officer is a police officer

This assumption is not even close to the realities among law enforcement agencies. This highlights the starting point of acquiring from the police agency their analyses of essential job functions: the assessment protocol and domains for evaluating a candidate will be closely linked to the essential job functions a potential candidate will be expected to perform. The reader may ask, "but aren't applicants all the same?" Visualize a Venn diagram (Figure 3.2) where there is a core that defines areas of stable emotional and behavioral functioning. These will be required for all positions. Agencies, however, have different missions, thus the psychological stability factor is but one area of the evaluation. Here the overlapping circles have a shared core but there are other factors present for one agency but less dominant at another agency. Let's look at some examples to demonstrate the point. Agency A is a small department of fewer than 15 officers providing calls for service responses within a community from 0700 hours to 2300 hours; Agency B is a federal law enforcement agency where Special Agents work around the world 24/7 with investigations in areas of civil, criminal, and international law; and Agency C is a transportation-related police agency (subways, light rail, interstate rail service). The overlapping circles for each agency share core attributes but the intersection with another agency may be small. Knowing the requirements for the position is important when providing an assessment that addresses the candidate's suitability as well as stability.

In addition, understanding the evolving nature of policing and the applicant pool deserves attention. A paper produced from Harvard's Executive Session, "Policing and Public Safety, Police Leadership Challenges in a Changing World" (Batts, Smoot, & Scrivner, 2012), hones in on issues that this author recommends psychologists consider when evaluating prospective candidates. The authors of the above paper provided a concise report on factors affecting the organizational structure and its adaptation to the world where crime fighting from the local to global arenas has had an impact. Similarly, the "contemporary" police

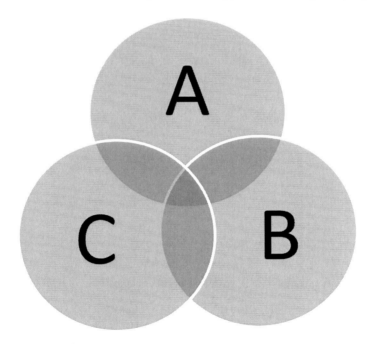

Figure 3.2 Venn diagram.

applicant is very different on many levels compared to those entering the field 20 to 30 or more years ago. The veteran officers now serve in leadership positions of the police agency, thus acknowledging the differences is important. The evaluating psychologist is recommended to have an understanding of the changes within police organizations as well as the cultural and personality differences among candidates. This understanding will provide context as well as enhance the quality of results provided to an agency.

2 Statement of Understanding (Informed Consent)

Nothing reduces a psychologists' risk more than having a clear, written Statement of Understanding. The disgruntled candidate not recommended even in part because of the psychological evaluation will run right through an open door to the licensing board. For example, if there is no written and signed document specifying the nature of evaluation, limitations of confidentiality, and defining the police agency as the client, the rejected candidate may file a complaint. Close that door proactively to prevent claims of "I thought you were my doctor" or "You have a duty to protect me but you gave the report to police agency xyz." Some psychologists exhibit what can be described as a cavalier attitude about obtaining a statement of understanding regarding an evaluation. This phenomenon is seen across many areas of forensic-oriented evaluations. The reader may be thinking, "Of course an informed consent is obtained." Good! This author estimates about one in ten do not document that the client has been defined through informed consent.

3 Pre-Employment Psychological Assessments are conducted after the Post-Conditional Offer of Employment

The pre-employment psychological assessment is defined as both psychological testing *and* an interview with a licensed psychologist or psychiatrist (IACP, 2009a). The pre-employment psychological evaluation is therefore a medical examination as defined by the EEOC (1995). The EEOC regulations implement the Americans with Disabilities Act and subsequent amendments (2008).

The responsible psychologist will want to clearly document with an agency for whom they are conducting an evaluation that the potential candidate for employment has been provided a COE letter. This does not absolve the psychologist completely because the agency must complete prior to the COE an agency-determined background investigation. Here is an example from a related occupation that highlights the problem. The decision from the Ninth Circuit U.S. Court of Appeals, *Leonel* v. *American Airlines, Inc.* (2005) best illustrates the confusion to Chiefs and Human Resources personnel in police and related public safety agencies. Often, in the rush to make hiring decisions, the agency wants background investigations done after the conditional offer is tendered. As demonstrated in the *Leonel* case, the employer did not provide sufficient justification why nonmedical inquiries were made after the conditional offer of employment. The responsible, risk-aversive psychologist will want to document that the police agency has conducted the background investigation prior to issuing a COE. This does not preclude an agency from receiving or learning about information post-COE that would have normally been obtained as part of the pre-COE background investigation. For example, a police agency may receive two of three prior employment reference letters that were favorable, thus, in conjunction with other favorable background elements, it issues the COE. Later, after the COE, the third reference letter is returned with negative and exclusionary information.

Special Police Populations

During the career of a psychologist consulting to public safety agencies, there are opportunities for assessments of officers who are not associated with issues of workability and/or fitness. Among examples are police officers under consideration for assignment to tactical units, crises (hostage) negotiators, child exploitation investigators, and undercover operations. These evaluations must be designed and implemented carefully. Similar to other evaluations, the police officer being evaluated must sign a statement of understanding about the purpose and use of the results. The recommendations to commanders from a specialized unit will need to be stated in a manner that does not suggest the officer is unfit to perform duties as a law enforcement officer. The findings are recommended to be stated in terms of suitability ranging from low, average, to high for the specialized assignment for which evaluated. Statements that refer to not recommended or unsuitable may have unintended consequences.

An example to illustrate the rationale for avoiding "not recommended" type statements is as follows. Five years post-evaluation, the officer not selected for the specialized assignment is named in a civil suit related to excessive use of force while performing duties of a police officer. The defense attorney, having subpoenaed the personnel file of the officer, asks the officer on the stand about being found unsuitable for a specialized assignment applied for several years ago. The repercussions may be great even if the assessment findings were not meant to imply an inability to perform police duties.

Another group, and growing number, of police officers within an agency have had combat experiences from military assignments in Iraq or Afghanistan in support of Operation Enduring Freedom (OEF) and

Operation Iraqi Freedom (OIF). There are several intervals across the continuum when the psychologist may be asked to evaluate a police officer or police officer candidate who has had combat experiences. Having knowledge about areas of in-country battles, legal rulings under the Uniformed Services Employment and Re-employment Rights Act (USERRA), Veterans Administration (VA) Compensation and psychometric assessment of Traumatic Brain Injury (TBI), and mental health conditions, such as post-traumatic stress (PTS), will be valuable. The pre-employment evaluation for some psychologists may be the most frequent type of contact an evaluating psychologist has with a veteran.

An assumption this author recommends to the psychologist with minimal Department of Defense or VA experience is to consider that the veteran brings a wealth of positive psychological strengths that are generalizable to effective performance of a police officer. These include resilience, teamwork, and a high level of performance orientation under a paramilitary structure of a police agency. At the same time, the evaluating psychologist cannot dismiss the potential negative effects causally related to combat experiences. Exposure to improvised explosive devices (IEDs), for example, may result in blast effects from direct projectile injury or air pressure changes that cause brain concussions and injury. These same IED incidents may be associated with injury and death to unit members. The pre-employment interview is recommended to ask about exposure to IEDs, mortar attacks, and firefights. An evaluator may want to consider administering the Combat Exposure Scale (Keane, Fairbank, Caddell, Zimering, Taylor, & Mora, 1989) as part of the assessment. Further, post-deployment adaptation to work and social functioning will be very important. Questions to consider are: Is the candidate with combat experience masking a depressive disorder with excessive alcohol use? Have the family dynamics deteriorated or improved since deployment? Incorporating these findings in conjunction with testing and interview data will be important in rendering an overall assessment of psychological stability and suitability. The literature contains emerging research concerning combat-related post-traumatic stress, of which the work of Castro and Adler (2011) is recommended reading.

The body of research on combat veterans is considerable, yet there are no research projects on combat veterans who become police officers. Furthermore, no rigorous research has been conducted on citizen soldier–police officers (Reserves and National Guard components) who have had deployment(s) (Curran, 2012). One factor that precludes evaluating a current police officer who returns from deployment is USERRA. The evaluating psychologist will want to be respectful about the implications of USERRA and work with a police agency wanting to evaluate formally a returning citizen soldier back to police duties.

The case of *Petty v. Metropolitan Government of Nashville-Davidson County* (2008) is representative of the issue. The police agency subjected the returning police officer to a fitness-for-duty-type assessment. The court ruled in favor of the officer, citing USERRA where the re-employment rights of the officer were violated. Thus, a police agency must restore the citizen soldier–police officer to full duty. This does not preclude subsequent evaluation of the officer when problems are documented regarding the performance of essential job functions. An indirect, retrospective study conducted by this author examined if there were differences between candidates seen for pre-employment evaluation with no current law enforcement employment but with combat experience (N = 87) compared to candidates with prior combat and who were current police officers of an agency but now under consideration for a prospective law enforcement agency (N = 27). This research provides a back door but best approximation of the psychological profile of police officers with prior combat. MMPI-2 differences on the RC Scale measuring Antisocial Behavior found significantly lower scores among current police officers (P = .028). The Inwald Personality Inventory (IPI) identified differences on the measures of Antisocial Attitudes (P = 0.17) and Phobic Personality (P = 0.49) where current police officers with combat experiences scored higher (Table 3.1). These are concerning data that suggest an observant analysis of psychometric data when evaluating combat veterans for public safety positions.

Police Officer Self-Assessment

A discussion about assessing police officers would not be complete without recognizing the ample opportunities occurring for assessment in the context of treatment planning or coaching. Two areas among others to consider are:

Table 3.1 Differences between current police officers and nonpolice officer candidates with both groups having prior combat experience

LEO		Antisocial Behavior $P = .028$	Antisocial Attitudes $P = .017$	Phobic Personality $P = .049$
Current	Mean ± SD	40.5 ± 7.1	48.4 ± 9.2	49.5 ± 9.8
	N	27	10	10
Not Current	Mean ± SD	44.0 ± 7.2	42.5 ± 6.4	44.6 ± 6.5
	N	87	49	49
Total	Mean ± SD	43.2 ± 7.3	43.5 ± 7.2	45.4 ± 7.3
	N	114	59	59

following when officers are involved in the use of weapon where a subject is injured or killed or related traumatic events, and during the course of a specialized assignment such as child exploitation investigations. Some background will lend support for the rationale to implement an assessment of officers in the context of supporting and sustaining an officer's career. Over 40 years ago (1967), Thomas Holmes and Richard Rahe determined a positive correlation (0.118) between life events and illnesses of medical patients examined. The results were published as the Social Readjustment Rating Scale (SRRS) (Holmes and Rahe, 1967), known more commonly as the Holmes–Rahe Stress Scale. Subsequent validation has supported the links between stress and illness. The SRRS provided the basis for adapting scales specific to law enforcement. For example, the Police Stress Survey (Spielberger et al., 1981) consists of 60 items corresponding to *perceived* stress. Findings from research indicate that physical threats was the most noted stressor among officers; the second most perceived stressor included a general lack of support experienced by officers; and the third most noted stressor involved perceptions of organizational pressure.

Another assessment tool is the Professional Quality of Life Scale (Stamm, 2012) for measuring compassion satisfaction and compassion fatigue. The 60-item self-assessment provides the police officer with feedback in the domains of compassion satisfaction, burnout, and secondary traumatic stress. This measure may be useful to establish a baseline for police officers entering a specialized assignment and then be re-administered during the course of the assignment. For example, regular meetings with a psychologist prior to and during the assignment for those assigned to child exploitation cases are recommended (Wolak and Mitchell, 2009). These meetings provide for an opportunity for self-assessment that the psychologist can incorporate in the support meetings.

Fitness-for-Duty/Workability Assessments

The importance of being a subject matter expert when conducting an assessment of a referred police officer to perform police duties cannot be overstated. The Fitness-for-Duty Evaluation (FFDE) is a specialized assessment. The seminal book by Stone (2000) and chapter by Corey (2011) provide information that an evaluating psychologist will want to review before considering conducting a FFDE. The FFDE is an infrequent assessment relative to other evaluations such as the pre-employment evaluation. The potential for restricting a police officer's source of income through this job jeopardizes assessment and immediately places the psychologist in an adversarial role. The psychologist can reasonably circumvent legal/administrative challenges through practical steps that incorporate following existing guidelines such as those proffered by the International Association of Chiefs of Police (IACP) Police Psychological

Services Section (2009). No matter how vigilant the ethical and responsible psychologist may be in attention to details, the nature of the FFDE may increase the risk for challenge by a police officer found unfit for duty.

Here are some considerations for the psychologist seeking to conduct the FFDE evaluation. These recommendations intertwine the best practices, survey data of practicing psychologists who conduct the FFDE, and examples from court decisions.

Is the referral reason a valid basis for conducting a FFDE?

Police chiefs have wide latitude in determining whether a police officer should be referred for a FFDE. The police chief, as the highest-ranking executive, has the responsibility to ensure officers are exhibiting stable emotional and behavioral functioning when performing essential job functions. A police chief is faced with considerable pressure to conduct a FFDE because the alternative is facing negligent retention-type claims or loss of community support when officers exhibit psychological impairments affecting job performance.

When would a FFDE not be recommended?

There are several reasons. A police shooting is an infrequent event yet totally consistent with an essential job function under the circumstance of serious risk of harm to the officer or public. The rationale for referring an officer for a FFDE after a shooting would then extend to conducting a FFDE on officers responding to motor vehicle crashes involving serious injury or death, responding to a homicide especially those involving a child, or similar infrequent yet potentially highly stressful police responses. Conducting the FFDE in these circumstances is not advised. The psychologist asked to conduct a FFDE following officer involved shootings is encouraged to educate the police chief including citing section 4.4 of the *IACP Guidelines for Fitness-for-Duty Evaluations*:

> In general, mental health professionals refrain from rendering fitness-for-duty opinions when they are not conducting an FFDE, such as when providing debriefings or similar services in the context of an officer-involved shooting or other critical incidents.

Another reason for not conducting the FFDE is in lieu of a police department taking disciplinary action. Again, the IACP offers guidance (4.2) that the FFDE is not a form of disciplinary action:

> FFDEs necessarily intrude on the personal privacy of the examinee and, therefore, are most appropriately conducted when the employer has determined that other options are inappropriate

or inadequate in light of the facts of a particular case. The FFDE is not to be used as a substitute for disciplinary action.

The FFDE as nondisciplinary may seem obvious to many psychologists but too often confused. The author conducted a survey of 105 psychologists nationwide on several assessment practice areas (Curran, 2008). The respondents to the survey were experienced public safety psychologists with membership in one or more of the following police psychological services-oriented professional groups: IACP PPSS, Consortium of Police Psychological Services (COPPS), and the Society of Police and Criminal Psychology.

The responding psychologists included 39 percent who reported conducting 10 or more FFDE annually. The 99 psychologists who responded to the question about ranking reasons for conducting a FFDE revealed 19 accepting the referral for disciplinary action as the primary reason, 20 as second most frequent reason and another 20 as the third most frequent reason (Table 3.2). Thus even seasoned psychologists would appear to expose themselves to risks by not conforming to the best practices in the field of police and public safety psychology.

Table 3.2 Psychologists' ranking of FFDE referral reasons

Answer options	Primary reason	Second most often	Third most often	Not a reason	Rating average	Response count
Disciplinary action	19	20	20	20	2.52	79
Concerns about suicide risk	11	19	26	15	2.63	71
Concerns about domestic violence	4	12	17	19	2.98	52
Supervisory concerns about mental health problems	57	22	8	6	1.60	93
Returning Iraq/ Afghanistan War Veteran	1	1	12	39	3.68	53
FMLA factors	2	6	8	33	3.47	49
Other	13	10	9	15	2.55	47
Answered question						99

Case example

Officer Smith is employed at a police department (A) and was interviewed by an officer from a nearby department (B) at the residence of Officer Smith and domestic partner. Officer B responded to a complaint called in by neighbors of arguing and banging noises in the residence of Officer Smith. Officer B interviewed Officer Smith and allowed the officer to leave the scene to stay with others. Officer B interviewed the domestic partner who while upset had no visible signs of injury. The domestic partner filed for and was granted a protective restraint order the following day, stating being fearful that Officer Smith would bring harm to the partner. Department A is made aware of the restraint order within a few days of the incident. The police chief or designate calls you, the contracted department psychologist, and asks for a FFDE on Officer Smith.

Here are a range of questions the psychologist may want to ask of themself and the referring department. First, clarify your relationship with the department.

1. REVIEW DECISION-MAKING STEPS

Are you, or others within your psychology practice, providing therapeutic or related services to Department A? Do you provide traumatic stress interventions to Department A? If yes to any of these questions, then the referral is recommended to be declined because of the conflicts. Second, has the department completed its own investigation of the complaint? If not, then is not a FFDE premature? If yes, then if the findings substantiated unbecoming conduct or worse, criminal conduct, then these need to be resolved. These are some, but not necessarily all, of the decision-making steps to consider prior to considering doing the FFDE.

2. WHAT IS A STATEMENT OF UNDERSTANDING?

Nothing reduces risk more than having a clear understanding about the nature of the FFDE, who is the client, and to whom the findings will be reported. This may appear obvious yet too frequently is overlooked. In the same survey referenced above, one in ten psychologists reported *not* having the evaluee sign an informed consent form.

3. WHERE ARE THE RESULTS REPORTED?

The psychologist evaluating a police officer for fitness for duty has been asked to render an opinion of "fit" or "not fit." Unless the police agency has specifically, in writing, asked the psychologist to address factors contributing to not being fit, then the psychologist is best advised to not provide commentary. Although this may, on the surface, appear straightforward, in the same survey already referenced above, the psychologists responded contrary to accepted standards, "If you provide more than a statement of fitness, has the requesting agency asked for more or do you feel compelled to provide more information?" A considerable number (54.7 percent, N = 47) affirmatively answered, "No matter what the Agency has asked, I will typically provide information about recommendations." This author suspects considerable confusion exists on this topic in part fueled by misinformation put forth in the literature. The psychologist conducting the FFDE is encouraged to consult with legal counsel for the public safety agency prior to the evaluation to clarify the scope of a fitness report and conclusions. Again, sticking to the statement of "fit" or "not fit" is the best course of action. The implications from recommending treatment may shift the burden of paying for the treatment services on the police agency.

The following case is illustrative. In *Sehie* v. *City of Aurora* (2005) the plaintiff, a police dispatcher, went home after an incident with the claim of a job-related injury. The plaintiff was sent for a FFDE. As a result of the FFDE, the employer required her to attend counseling sessions. Sehie later claimed the time for traveling to/from and during the sessions to be compensable. The Court of Appeals in the 7th Circuit ultimately agreed and concluded that the purpose of the required counseling sessions was to enable Sehie to perform her job duties better.

Respecting Personal Information

Another area for deliberate planning when doing an FFDE is being respectful of a police officer's personal, including medical, information. The report is recommended to provide only information that is relevant to assessing the current emotional and behavioral functioning of the police officer in response to the business necessity of the police agency that has requested the FFDE. The California case decision of *Pettus* v. *Cole* (1996) makes clear that certain background information in an employment report is not justified. In the *Pettus* case the issue was having reported the history of alcohol abuse that did not relate to the reason for the evaluation. The impact of the *Pettus* case upon the practice of police psychologists was another area probed in the already mentioned survey. More than ten years post-*Pettus* decision, which was highly publicized and a focus of police psychology presentations at several national meetings, approximately 40 percent of the psychologists surveyed gave more personal information in a report than may have been advisable.

The case of Eric Ostrov, PhD, Chicago area psychologist, reinforced similar principles; Ostrov released too much information in a report and

Table 3.3 Does your FFDE report provide a detailed developmental history of the employee including remote substance use history?

Answer options	Response Percentage	Response count
Yes	39.6	38
No	60.4	58
Answered question		96

the department was also in error in having released details of the report to others (*McGreal* v. *Ostrov*, 2004). The reporting of information is not the only concern a psychologist needs to be attentive to, but also the questions that are asked during the evaluation. The Genetic Information Nondiscrimination Act of 2008 (GINA) became effective on November 21, 2009 and applies to certain medical and psychological inquiries about the police officer and their family of origin. "Family medical history is included in the definition of genetic information because it is often used to determine whether someone has an increased risk of getting a disease, disorder, or condition in the future" (GINA, 2008). The implications from GINA are far-reaching in the manner of conducting psychological assessments.

In Sum

The above areas represent the core of issues which, if navigated ethically and responsibly, will help protect the evaluating psychologist from adverse actions in courts and a licensing board.

Future Directions in Police Psychological Assessments

The field of police psychology can be expected to grow during the next quarter century. Within the assessment domain of police psychology, the two prominent areas for research are related to evaluating current employee mental health and continued development of pre-employment psychological instruments.

The Fitness-for-Duty Evaluation (FFDE) continues to be reshaped in part due to legal decisions, but mostly because of evolving clinical practice standards. An aspect that will continue to mature is narrowing the cases of police officers referred for the FFDE. As already demonstrated in Table 3.2, many referrals lack an objective basis. An alternative evaluation conducted within an occupational medicine framework may meet the needs of police agencies, reduce adversarial proceedings, and complaints against the evaluating psychologist is the WorkAbility Evaluation.

The term is more than a relabeling and reframing of the FFDE but reconceptualizes the overall approach to employee health during the police career. The WorkAbility Evaluation is a repeated measure of both medical and psychological health with pre-hire assessments serving as baseline. Subsequent health factors that limit work attendance or are triggered by specific prescribed medications, FMLA requests, or nonwork injury are amenable to the WorkAbility approach rather than a FFDE.

Another area for future, ongoing research is refining psychometric predictions to reduce Type II errors in making pre-employment decisions, such as recommending a candidate because testing data is negative but in fact the candidate is poorly suited. Among factors is often the disconnect between consensus about essential psychological traits to be an effective police officer and direct, objective measures of these traits. For example, most of the currently used measures (MMPI-2, MMPI-2-RF, IPI, and 16PF) provide superb predictions about substance abuse and related risk-taking behaviors, social competence, and impulsiveness. These same measures are less robust in measuring decision-making however.

Future investigations using outcome measures continue to be needed to overcome weaknesses in psychometric assessment. Similarly, the evaluation of interview findings along with integrating testing data will be enhanced from rigorous research. Other research may expand the assessment tools used to measure a candidate's capacity to perform the essential job functions. Prospective studies will need to control for the variability of assessment programs across the spectrum of law enforcement agencies.

Police psychology has a rich history already described in this chapter yet researchers and practitioners will need to consider that many federal, state, and local law enforcement agencies do not employ psychological assessments of prospective candidates. This status further compounds the need not only for further research but also for education of the consumers of psychological services, such as state accreditation bodies and law enforcement agencies.

Note

1 The full description of these assessment proficiencies may be accessed at: www.theiacp.org/psych_services_section.

Resources

1 Discover Policing.org (http://discoverpolicing.org) is a nationwide police recruitment and career exploration resource featuring comprehensive information on job opportunities in law enforcement and a full-featured job board where agencies can browse résumés and post vacancies at no cost. This website is funded through a grant

from the Bureau of Justice Assistance, Office of Justice Programs, U.S. Department of Justice and through Cooperative Agreement Number 2010-CK-WX-K017 awarded by the Office of Community Oriented Policing Services, U.S. Department of Justice.

2   Police Psychological Services Section (PPSS), International Association of Chiefs of Police (IACP). Mission Statement: "This Section offers psychological solutions to the problems faced by police agencies in the areas of personnel assessment, individual as well as organizational intervention, consultation and operational assistance. The Section acts as a resource to the Association on psychological and behavioral issues. It promotes ethical and empirically based practices through education, training, consultation, research, and the publication of guidelines covering a variety of psychologically related topics."

3   Two guidelines developed by the PPSS and cited in this chapter are:

- Fitness For Duty Evaluation Guidelines (2009): http://theiacp.org/psych_services_section/pdfs/Psych-FitnessforDutyEvaluation.pdf
- IACP—Pre-employment Guidelines (2009): http://theiacp.org/psych_services_section/pdfs/Psych-PreemploymentPsychEval.pdf

References

Americans with Disabilities Act Amendments Act, 42 U.S.C. § 12101 (2008).

Batts, A.W., Smoot, S.M., & Scrivner, E. (2012). *Police Leadership Challenges in a Changing World* (NCJ 238338). Washington, DC: National Institute of Justice.

Ben-Porath, Y.S. & Tellegan, A. (2008). *The MMPI-2-RF Manual for Administration, Scoring and Interpretation*. Minneapolis, MN: University of Minnesota Press.

Ben-Porath, Y.S., Corey, D.M., & Stewart, C. (2011a). Predicting law enforcement officer performance outcomes using the MMPI-2-RF. Presentation at the International Association of Chiefs of Police, Police Psychological Services Section, Annual Meeting, October 23, Chicago, IL.

Ben-Porath, Y.S., Fico, J.M., Hibler, N.S., Inwald, R., Kruml, J., & Roberts, M.R. (2011b). Assessing the psychological suitability of candidates for law enforcement positions. *The Police Chief*, 78 (August), 64–70.

Bonsignore v. *City of New York*, 683 F.2d 635 (2d Cir. June 15, 1982).

Butcher, J.N. (2011). *A Beginner's Guide to the MMPI-2*, 3rd ed. Washington, DC: American Psychological Association.

Castro, C.A. & Adler, A.B. (2011). Reconceptualizing combat-related posttraumatic stress disorder as an occupational hazard. In Adler, A.B., Bliese, P.D., & Castro, C.A. (Eds.), *Deployment Psychology*, pp. 217–242. Washington, DC: American Psychological Association.

Corey, D.M. (2011). Principles of fitness-for-duty evaluations for police psychologists. In Kitaeff, J. (Ed.), *Handbook of Police Psychology*, pp. 263–293. New York, NY: Routledge.

Curran, S.F. (2008). Results and implications from a 2007 survey of police/forensic psychologists: fitness for duty assessment procedures. Presentation at the International Association of Chiefs of Police, Police Psychological Services Section, Annual Meeting, November 9, San Diego, CA.

Curran, S.F. (2012). Progress report: Effects from combat stress upon reintegration for citizen soldiers and on psychological profiles of police recruits with prior military experiences. Presentation at the International Association of Chiefs of Police, Police Psychological Services Section, Annual Meeting, September 29, San Diego, CA.

Equal Employment Opportunity Commission. (1995). ADA enforcement guidance: Preemployment disability-related questions and medical examinations. EEOC Notice Number 915.002, Date 10/10/95. www.eeoc.gov/policy/docs/preemp. html (accessed December 19, 2012).

Fulero, S.M. & Wrightsman, L.S. (2009). *Forensic Psychology*, 3rd ed. Belmont, CA: Wadsworth.

Genetic Information Nondiscrimination Act of 2008 (GINA, Publ.L. 110–223, 122 Stat. 881).

Groth-Marnat, G. (2009). *Handbook of Psychological Assessment*, 5th ed. Hoboken, NJ: John Wiley and Sons.

Gupton, H.M., Axelrod, E., Cornell, L., Curran, S.F., Hood, C.J., Kelly, J., & Moss, J. (2011). Psychological intervention for law enforcement personnel. *The Police Chief*, 78(8), August, 92–97.

Hogan, R. (1975). Personological correlates of police effectiveness. *Journal of Psychology*, 91(2), 289–295.

Holmes, T.H. & Rahe, R.H. (1967). The social readjustment rating scale. *Journal of Psychosomatic Research*, 11(2), 213–218.

International Association of Chiefs of Police. (2009a). *Pre-employment Psychological Evaluations*. Arlington, VA: International Association of Chiefs of Police. Retrieved December 19, 2012, from http://theiacp.org/psych_services_section/pdfs/Psych-PreemploymentPsychEval.pdf.

International Association of Chiefs of Police. (2009b). *Psychological Fitness-For-Duty Evaluation Guidelines*. Arlington, VA: International Association of Chiefs of Police. Retrieved December 19, 2012, from http://theiacp.org/psych_services_section/pdfs/Psych-FitnessforDutyEvaluation.pdf.

Keane, T.M., Fairbank, J.A., Caddell, J.M., Zimering, R.T., Taylor, K.L., & Mora, C.A. (1989). CES (Combat Exposure Scale). Retrieved December 19, 2012 from www.ptsd.va.gov/professional/pages/assessments/assessment-pdf/CES.pdf.

Keane, T.M., Fairbank, J.A., Caddell, J.M., Zimering, R.T., Taylor, K.L., & Mora, C.A. (1989). Clinical evaluation of a measure to assess combat exposure. *Psychological Assessment: A Journal of Consulting and Clinical Psychology*, 1(1), 53–55.

Kitaeff, J. (2011). History of police psychology. In Kitaeff, J. (Ed.), *Handbook of Police Psychology*, pp. 1–59. New York: Routledge.

Leonel v. American Airlines, Inc., 400 F.3d 702. (9th Cir. 2005).

McGreal v. Ostrov, 368 F. 3d 657. (7th Cir. May 10, 2004).

Pettus v. Cole, 57 Cal.Rptr.2d 46, 49 Cal#App. 4th 402. (Cal.App. Dist. 1996).

Petty v. Metropolitan Government of Nashville-Davidson County, 538 F.3d 431 (C.A.6, Aug. 18, 2008).

Sehie v. *City of Aurora*, 432 F.3d 749 (7th Cir. 2005).

Sellbom, M., Fischler, G.L., & Ben-Porath, Y.S. (2007). Identifying MMPI-2 predictors of police officer integrity and misconduct. *Criminal Justice and Behavior*, 34, 985–1004.

Spielberger, C.D., Westberry, L.G., Grier, K.S., & Greenfield, G. (1981). *The Police Stress Survey*. Final Report Submitted to Office of Criminal Justice Education Training, U.S. Department of Justice.

Stamm, B.H. (2012). *Professional Quality of Life: Compassion Satisfaction and Fatigue*. Version 5 (ProQOL). www.proqol.org.

Stone, A.V. (2000). *Fitness for Duty Principles, Methods, and Legal Issues*. Boca Raton, FL: CRC Press.

Thomas, S.L. & Scroggins, W.A. (2006). Psychological testing in personnel selection: contemporary issues in cognitive ability and personality testing. *Journal of Business Inquiry*, 5, 28–38.

Title 10 Code of Federal Regulations (CFR), Part 710, Criteria and Procedures for Determining Eligibility for Access to Classified Matter or Special Nuclear Material.

Uniformed Services Employment and Reemployment Rights Act, 38 U.S.C. 4301–4335 (1994).

Weiss, P.A. & Inwald, R. (2010). A brief history of personality assessment in police psychology. In *Personality Assessment in Police Psychology, A 21st Century Perspective*. Springfield, IL: Charles C. Thomas.

Wolak, J. & Mitchell, K.J. (2009). Work exposure to child pornography in ICAC task forces and affiliates. Retrieved December 19, 2012 from Crimes Against Children Research Center, www.unh.edu/ccrc/pdf/Law Enforcement Work Exposure to CP.pdf.

4

OF MIND AND BODY

Health Consequences of Stress and Trauma on Police Officers

John M. Violanti

Introduction

Stress

The term "stress" is a rubric generally used to describe a process brought about by environmental stimuli, individual psychological mediation, and physiological change. Individual perception and appraisal appear to play a part in what specific environmental demands initiate the stress process (Folkman & Lazarus, 1980). To gain a better understanding of how stress may be associated with disease outcome, one needs to consider both psychological and physiological factors.

Conceptualizing stress as a biosocial process allows for a systemic assessment of environmental stimuli, undue strain on an organism, and resultant psychological and biological changes that increase the risk for disease (Cohen, Kessler, & Gordon, 1997). Seyle (1950) was among the first to develop a model of stress based on physiological responses to external environmental stimuli. He proposed that disease states occur when the body can no longer adapt to external stressors and remains in a state of chemical imbalance. Stress was believed to produce a neuroendocrine response which, through nervous and endocrine systems, affected all body organs (Seyle, 1950).

The concept of homeostasis (steady state) is somewhat limited in describing the scope of physiological systems that activate during the stress response (McEwen & Seeman, 1999). Homeostasis applies to a limited number of systems, such as body temperature and oxygen regulation, that are essential to life and are controlled within a narrow range. These systems are not activated or varied in order to help the individual adapt to the environment. In contrast, systems that show variation to meet perceived/anticipated demands characterize the state of the organism in a changing world and reflect the operation of most body systems in meeting environmental challenges. Such stress mediators are not held constant and they lead to adaptation as well as damage when they are produced insufficiently or in excess, that is, outside of the normal range (McEwen & Seeman, 1999).

Sterling and Eyer (1999) formulated a concept to account for the more holistic nature of the stress response as it relates to stabilized bodily states— "allostasis"—which refers to the maintenance of physiological stability through change. The concept of "allostatic load," refers to the wear and tear that the body experiences due to repeated cycles of allostasis as well as the inefficient turning on or shutting off of physiological responses to stress (McEwen & Seeman, 1999; Sterling and Eyer, 1999). Seeman, McEwen, Rowe, and Singer (2001) reported an operational measure of allostatic load that reflects information on levels of physiologic activity across a range of important regulatory systems, including the HPA axis and sympathetic nervous systems as well as the cardiovascular system and metabolic processes. Over this 2.5-year follow-up study, higher baseline allostatic load scores were found to predict significant increased risk for incident cardiovascular disease (CVD), for decline in physical and cognitive functioning, and for mortality.

Allostatic load appears to be a more holistic way to describe stress as producing "wear and tear" on the body, across a variety of stressors which activate physiological systems (McEwen & Seeman, 1999). Hormones protect the body in the short run and promote adaptation, but in the long run, allostatic load causes changes in the body that lead to disease. Lifestyle factors such as diet, exercise, substance abuse, and social developmental experiences may also be involved in this process. All of these factors influence the turning on and off of the physiological mediators of stress (Seeman et al., 2001).

The most commonly studied physiological systems that respond to stress are the HPA (hypothalamic–pituitary adrenal axis) and the autonomic nervous system. The severity and impact of the stress response can be viewed by gauging physiological disruption and dysregulation of these systems (Chrousos & Gold, 1992; Black, 1994). The stress response is considered "adaptive" when it is in reaction to an acute situation and is of limited duration. It is considered "maladaptive" when the physiological reaction is not brought under control by the usual regulatory mechanisms. If a person cannot remove him/herself from the stressful encounter, the physiological response may become chronic and dysregulated (McEwen, 1998).

Cortisol is a primary hormone released by the adrenal glands as a result of the HPA axis response to stress, and is a frequently used biomarker of stress (Fischer, Calame, Dettling, Zeier, & Fanconi, 2000; Pruessner, Hellhammer, & Kirschbaum, 1999). Cortisol levels that are chronically elevated and hyper-reactivity of the HPA axis are associated with an increased risk for diabetes, hypertension, and CVD. Researchers have found cortisol levels to be 21.7 percent higher in persons reporting high job strain (Steptoe, Cropley, Griffith, & Kirschbaum, 2000). In addition, lower levels of cortisol output have been associated with higher psychological well-being (Lindfors & Lundberg, 2002). If prolonged stress suppresses immunity, more infectious diseases could result because of the longer cortisol secretion, which suppresses immunity below where it is effective. This impairs defense against disease and results in more illness (Sapolsky, 2002).

Cardiovascular effects of the HPA axis and sympathetic nervous system activity are diverse (Girod & Brotman, 2004; Curtis & O'Keefe, 2002). Both systems can potentially lead to harmful effects such as increased blood pressure (BP) and decreased insulin sensitivity (Brotman et al., 2006; von Kanel & Dimsdale, 2000). Some evidence suggests that both systems might precipitate endothelial dysfunction—an important early manifestation of atherosclerosis (Mangos, Walker, Kelly, Lawson, Webb, & Whitworth, 2000; Eisenach et al. 2002). During stress, these systems interact to form a complex pattern of cardiovascular adjustments involving neural, endocrine, and mechanical factors. Changes in any one component of the system necessarily affect other components of the system (Kessler, Sonnega, Bromet, Hughes, & Nelson, 1995).

Studies conducted on the rate of defibrillator firings among a sample of New York City residents during the month after the 2001 terrorist attacks on the World Trade Center in New York resulted in rates that were two to three times higher than normally observed (Steinberg et al., 2004; Shedd et al., 2004). In a study of work-related stressors, upcoming deadlines were associated with a six-fold increase in myocardial infarction (Johansen, Feychting, Moller, Arnsbo, Ahlbom, & Olsen, 2002). Other studies suggest that chronic work-related stress carries as much as two to three times higher risk of cardiac events, especially when employees perceive little control over their work environment (Kivimaki, Leino-Arjas, Luukkonen, Vahtera, & Kirjonen, 2002). In women with CVD, marital stress was associated with a risk of recurrent cardiac events that was three times higher than in women with no marital stress (Orth-Gomer, Wamala, Horsten, Schenck-Gustafsson, Schneiderman, & Mittleman, 2000). By contrast, with acute stress, which can trigger acute thrombotic, arrhythmic, or mechanical cardiovascular events, chronic daily stress seems to affect cardiovascular risk mainly by acceleration of the atherosclerotic process (Bonnet, Irving, Terra, Nony, Berthezene, & Moulin, 2005).

Post-Traumatic Stress

A specific type of stress is a severe form brought about by exposure to a traumatic event. Table 4.1 outlines the criterion for post-traumatic stress disorder (PTSD) as set forth by the American Psychiatric Association *Diagnostic and Statistical Manual*, fifth edition (DSM-V) (2013). PTSD involves several criteria; (1) exposure to or witnessing a traumatic event; (2) presence of distressing memories of the event, dissociative reactions, dreams, or marked physiological reactions; (3) avoidance of stimuli associated with a traumatic event; (4) negative alterations in cognition; and (5) alterations in arousal and reactivity. A diagnosis is made if these disturbances last for more than one month.

PTSD is a significant mental health issue and can be debilitating. The National Comorbidity Survey (NCS), a representative sample of 5,877 people in the United States aged 15–54, found a 7.8 percent lifetime prevalence of PTSD. Approximately 14 percent of people in the sample who had been exposed to trauma developed PTSD (Kessler et al., 1995). Individuals with a history of PTSD have demonstrated higher lifetime rates of endocrine disorders, major depression, medically explained and unexplained somatic complaints, and eating disorders. Neurobiologically, PTSD represents a dysregulated stress response and is characterized by neurochemical and neuroanatomic abnormalities.

Post-traumatic stress disorder (PTSD) may promote poor health through a complex interaction between biological and psychological mechanisms. Those who report PTSD symptoms are more likely to have a greater number of physical health problems. PTSD has also been found to be associated with greater medical service utilization for physical health problems (Friedman & Schnurr, 1995). Much of the research on the pathophysiology of PTSD has focused on dysregulation of the HPA axis. Evidence suggesting a role for HPA axis dysregulation in the development of PTSD is supported by clinical studies demonstrating decreased 24-hour urinary cortisol levels in subjects with PTSD. For example, Yehuda et al. examined 22 Holocaust survivors with PTSD and 25 without PTSD. Subjects with PTSD had an average cortisol level of 32.6 pg in their 24-hour urine sample, compared to a level of 62.7 pg of cortisol in those without PTSD (Yehuda, Teicher, Trestman, Levengood, & Siever, 1996). This finding has been replicated in other studies (Yehuda, 2002).

Individuals with a history of PTSD have demonstrated higher lifetime rates of endocrine disorders, major depression, medically explained and unexplained somatic complaints, and eating disorders. Evidence linking exposure to trauma with CVD has been found across different populations and various types of traumatic events. Military veterans diagnosed with PTSD, for example, were significantly more likely to have had abnormal electrocardiographic results, including a higher prevalence of myocardial infarctions (Boscarino & Chang, 1999; Boscarino, 2004). Civilian populations exposed to traumatic events also report increased cardiovascular health problems. A recent meta-analysis of cardiovascular status in persons with PTSD indicates that they have a higher resting heart rate (HR) and elevated blood pressure (BP) compared to individuals without PTSD. A subset analysis revealed that the effect sizes for comparisons of basal HR were greatest in studies with the most chronic PTSD samples (Buckley & Kaloupek, 2001). It has been suggested that lower cortisol levels in PTSD are associated with a down-regulated glucocorticoid system that may result in elevations in leukocyte counts and other immune inflammatory activities associated with CVD. Physiologic arousal during intrusive memories of traumatic events has been associated with alterations in neuroendocrine functions related to changes in the HPA axis (Freidman & McEwen, 2005).

The Police: Stress, PTSD, and Health Outcomes

Police work is routine in nature with episodic moments of intensive danger and stress. Officers are often placed in situations of severe emotional stress (Violanti & Paton, 1999). There is an ever-present perception of danger which leaves officers in a state of constant hypervigilance (Gilmartin, 1986). Previous research has identified two distinct sources of stress in police work (Spielberger, Grier, & Greenfield, 1982): (1) the inherent aspect, which involves danger and job risk; and (2) the police organization (Kop & Euwema, 2001; Bonnar, 2000).

In addition to chronic job stress, police officers are also exposed to traumatic work events. Such events may involve shootings (by oneself or other officers), riots, hostage situations, and other threatened or actual violence. PTSD risk factors among police officers include excessive difficulty in expressing emotions, lack of an outlet to vent feelings outside of work, and lack of diversion from the police role (Laufersweiler-Dwyer & Dwyer, 2000). Other trauma risk factors include inadequate social support networks, emotional exhaustion at the time of the traumatic event, and prior experience of traumatic incidents. Certain PTSD risk factors, such as insufficient time allowed for coping with traumatic incidents, dissatisfaction with the support provided, uncertain career prospects, and discontent about work, can also be present within the work environment of police officers (Violanti & Paton, 2007; Davidson & Foa, 1993; Carlier, 1999). Stephens, Long, and Flett (1999) discussed the impact of previous life trauma for those entering police work. Police recruits who have already suffered traumatic stress are, following exposure to subsequent distressing experiences, at increased risk of mental health problems and more likely to retire from police service early. Paton, Violanti, and Schmuckler (1999) discuss the long-term implications and consequences of repetitive exposure to high risk and duty-related traumatic incidents. They explore its implications for behavioral addiction and separation from active police duties. Figley (1999) developed a model of "police compassion fatigue," where he suggests that if police officers are empathic, have sufficient concern for others, and are exposed to traumatized people on a continuous basis, they may develop a debilitating psychological fatigue.

Police Stress and Cardiovascular Disease (CVD)

Persons who enter police work are generally part of a healthy work population, but appear to deteriorate physically and psychologically as years of police service increase (Violanti, Vena, & Petralia, 1998). A 22-year prospective study of the Helsinki Policemen (Pyörälä, Miettinen, Halonen, Laakso, & Pyörälä, 2000) hypothesized that complex clustering of risk factors related to insulin resistance could be predictive of coronary heart disease (CHD) and stroke risk. Factor analysis of ten risk variables produced three underlying factors: an insulin resistance factor, which comprised BMI, subscapular skinfold, insulin, glucose, maximal oxygen uptake, mean BP, and triglycerides; a lipid factor, which comprised cholesterol and triglycerides; and a lifestyle factor, which comprised physical activity and smoking. In this prospective study, the insulin resistance factor proved to be a statistically significant predictor of CHD. While metabolic syndrome was not specifically determined in this population, analysis of the 22-year risk of CHD by tertiles of insulin resistance showed that excess risk was confined to the highest tertile (Pyörälä et al., 2000). A cross-sectional study of metabolic syndrome in a sample of 84 adult male police officers in Texas found that prevalence of metabolic syndrome in male police officers may be higher than the American male population, and thus law enforcement officers may be at increased risk for future CVD morbidity and mortality (Humbarger, Crouse, Womack, & Green, 2004).

Similar patterns of CVD have historically been observed in other police cohort studies. Guralnick (1963) found mortality rates for policemen, sheriffs, and marshals to be significantly elevated for arteriosclerotic heart disease. Milham (1983) found increased rates for arteriosclerotic heart disease and pulmonary embolism in Washington state police officers. Age-specific proportionate mortality ratios for arteriosclerotic heart disease were highest for younger officers. Violanti, Vena, Marshall and Fiedler (1986) found city of Buffalo police officers had increased rates for arteriosclerotic heart disease. Feuer and Rosenman (1986) reported that police and firefighters in New Jersey had significant increased proportionate mortality ratios for arteriosclerotic heart disease. An inverse relationship was noted between arteriosclerotic heart disease and latency, indicating that police officers most susceptible to heart disease were affected early in their careers. Demers, Heyer, and Rosenstock (1992) compared police and firefighters in three cities in the United States and found police to have higher rates for all causes of death combined. Forastiere et al. (1994) studied a cohort of urban policemen in Rome, Italy and found increased rates for ischemic heart disease in officers less than 50 years of age. Additional studies have found police to have higher rates for heart disease, homicide, and suicide (Sardinas, Miller, & Hansen, 1986; Quire & Blount, 1990; Violanti, 2007; Violanti et al., 1998). A somewhat unexpected finding was that arteriosclerotic heart disease rates were higher in officers with fewer years of service. The average age of death for police officers in a mortality study was 66 years (Violanti et al., 1998) compared with the general population average of 75 years. Officers also died from heart disease at earlier ages than the general population. This is infrequently found in a healthy worker population (McMichael, 1976).

The low physical fitness level found among police officers may also be an indicator of the impact of stress. Williams (1987) found that a substantial number of officers in their sample were at elevated risk for atherosclerotic heart disease; 76 percent had elevated cholesterol, 26 percent had elevated triglycerides, and 60 percent elevated body fat composition. Price, Pollock, Gettman, and Kent (1978) concluded that middle-aged police officers had CVD risk above that of the general population. Franke and Anderson (1994) found that public safety officers had a higher probability of developing CHD than did the Framingham Heart Study population. Steinhardt, Greehow, and Stewart (1991) found an inverse association between cardiovascular fitness and medical claims among police officers.

Police Exposure to Traumatic Events and CVD

A recent study conducted by the Violanti et al. (2007) examined associations between PTSD symptoms and metabolic syndrome in police officers. The metabolic syndrome is a cluster of components believed to be associated with CVD. The National Cholesterol Education Program (NCEP) Expert Panel on Detection, Evaluation, and Treatment of High Blood Cholesterol in Adults (ATP III) (Expert Panel on Detection, Evaluation, and Treatment of High Blood Cholesterol in Adults, 1999) put forth guidelines for the proposed clinical definitions of the metabolic syndrome in adults to aid in diagnosis and recommended preventive interventions for this syndrome. Criteria for the metabolic syndrome include: (1) elevated waist circumference, >102cm in men, >88 in women; (2) elevated triglycerides, >150 mg/dL; (3) reduced high density lipids (HDL) cholesterol, <40 mg/DL for men, <50 mg/dL for women; (4) glucose intolerance, fasting glucose >100 mg/DL; and (5) hypertension, systolic BP >130 mm Hg or diastolic BP >85 mm Hg. Three or more of these five components fulfill the requirement for metabolic syndrome.

PTSD symptoms were measured with the Impact of Event scale (IES) (Horowitz, Wilner, & Alvarez, 1979), divided into categories of subclinical, mild, moderate, and severe symptom levels. This scale identifies

Table 4.1 Prevalence estimates and ratios for metabolic syndrome by PTSD severity category

PTSD category	N	Prevalence (%)	Unadjusted		Age-adjusted		Multivariable-adjusted[*]	
			PR	95% CI	PR	95% CI	PR	95% CI
Sub-clinical	59	15.1	1.00	referent	1.00	referent	1.00	referent
Mild	19	21.1	1.39	0.47–4.11	1.48	0.50–4.42	1.82	0.59–5.62
Moderate	23	4.4	0.29	0.04–2.17	0.28	0.04–2.14	0.37	0.04–3.17
Severe	6	50.0	3.31	1.19–9.22	3.12	1.15–8.50	2.69	0.79–9.13

Abbreviations: PTSD = Post-traumatic stress disorder; PR = prevalence ratio; CI = confidence interval

[*]Adjusted for age, education, smoking and alcohol intake.

Source: Violanti et al. (2007).

symptoms of PTSD. The metabolic syndrome was considered present if three or more constituent parameters of metabolic syndrome were present in each officer (obesity, BP, high-density lipoprotein cholesterol, triglycerides, and glucose levels). Table 4.1 provides prevalence estimates and ratios for metabolic syndrome by PTSD severity category.

Results indicated a slightly increased risk of metabolic syndrome for officers in the mild PTSD category (prevalence ratio (PR) = 1.39, 95 percent CI = 0.47– 4.11) and a significantly increased metabolic syndrome prevalence among those officers in the severe PTSD symptom category (PR = 3.31, 95 percent CI = 1.19–9.22; p = 0.021). Adjustment for age decreased risk in the severe category somewhat but the risk remained significantly elevated (PR = 3.12, 95 percent CI = 1.15–8.50, p = 0.0261). Adjustment of a combination of lifestyle factors (age, education, smoking, alcohol intake) reduced the prevalence ratio in the severe PTSD category (PR = 2.69, 95 percent CI = 0.79–9.13, p = 0.113), indicating the possible influence of these lifestyle factors.

Shift Work and Police CVD

Shift work is an integral part of law enforcement. Police officers report that shift work is among the most difficult and stressful requirement of their job (Vila, 2000; Charles et al., 2007).

Previous studies have suggested that shift work is associated with CVD. Knutsson and Boggild (2000) reported that shift work affects a number of metabolic components such as triglycerides, cholesterol, BMI, abdominal fat distribution, and coagulation. Karlsson, Knutsson and Lindahl (2001) found that obesity, high triglycerides, and low concentrations of HDL cholesterol seem to cluster together more often in shift workers than in day workers. Lasfargues, Sylvanie, and Caces (1996) found night shift workers to have significantly higher levels of triglycerides, smoking, and obesity than controls. Sookian, Gemma, and Fernandez-Gianotti (2007) concluded that shift workers had an increased risk of the metabolic syndrome independent of age and physical activity. In a review of the literature, Wolk and Somers (2007) found that the weight of evidence suggested that sleep deprivation and shift work independently lead to the development of both insulin resistance and individual components of the metabolic syndrome. Other studies found the metabolic effects of shift work to include abdominal obesity, lower HDL cholesterol and higher triglycerides, and changes in glucose intolerance (Hampton et al., 1996; Nagaya, Yoshida, Takahashi, & Kawai, 2002; Di Lorenzo, De Pergola, & Zocchetti, 2003).

Violanti et al. (2009) conducted a study examining the association between shift work and the metabolic syndrome. We used daily payroll records of the police officers to develop an objective measure of shift work and overtime. All shifts worked over the five-year period were categorized based on start times of 0400 to 1159 hours for the day shift, 1200 to 1959 hours for the afternoon shift, and 2000 to 0359 hours for the midnight shift. Taking into account the length of time the officer was working (i.e., from first date of work or the date when records were first available to date of exam at baseline), the computed hours were standardized on a weekly basis (hours worked per week), and the percentage of total hours worked on each shift was calculated. Officers were then classified into one of those three shifts based on whichever shift had the largest percentage of hours worked for a given officer. Officers' normal work shifts were ten-hours long. Thus, nearly all of the midnight shift workers were forced to sleep during the daylight hours, which would interfere with both the quality and the duration of sleep (Åkerstedt, 1995). Sleep duration was measured to address the extent to which work hours may have disrupted sleep patterns. Sleep duration was ascertained by questionnaires which asked for the average hours of sleep obtained each day during the past seven days. A dichotomous variable was created for sleep duration (< 6 vs. ≥ 6 hours/day), where poor sleep was considered as < 6 hours/day.

Metabolic syndrome component measures were based on the NCEP ATP III guidelines (Executive summary of the Third Report of the National Cholesterol Education Program (NCEP), 2001) with recent modifications from the American Heart Association and the National Heart, Lung, and Blood Institute (Grundy, Cleeman, & Daniels, 2005). Waist circumference was measured in centimeters (cm) as abdominal girth at the highest point of the iliac crest and the lowest part of the costal margin in the mid-axillary line (Violanti et al., 2006). Levels of triglycerides, HDL cholesterol, and glucose were measured from fasting blood specimens. The average of the second and third of three resting systolic and diastolic blood pressure readings were used. To satisfy the criteria for glucose intolerance and hypertension, the participant could either (1) have an elevated blood level based on set criteria or (2) report having the condition (hypertension or diabetes) and report being treated for that condition. The participant was considered to have metabolic syndrome if three or more of the five components were present. The number of syndrome components varied from 0 to 5 (0 = none present, 5 = all present).

As described in Table 4.2, our results suggested that police officers working midnight shifts may be at an increased risk for a higher mean number of metabolic syndrome components. The prevalence of metabolic syndrome among officers working the midnight shift was higher than that found in the National Health and Nutrition Examination Survey (NHANES III) 1988–1994 (Ford, Giles, & Dietz, 2002). NHANES III overall prevalence of metabolic syndrome was 21.8 percent, while officers in our sample working midnights had an overall prevalence of 30 percent. In addition, officers who worked the midnight shift were on average younger than those officers on the day shift (36.5 and 42.6 years

JOHN M. VIOLANTI

Table 4.2 Mean number of metabolic syndrome components by shift work

	Day (N = 46)	Afternoon (N = 32)	Midnight (N = 20)	p-value*
Unadjusted	0.97 (1.27)	1.25 (1.37)	1.70 (1.34)	0.127
Gender-adjusted	1.1 (0.19)	1.12 (0.23)	1.51 (0.29)	0.523
Age-and Gender-adjusted	1.0 (0.21)	1.20 (0.24)	1.62 (0.30)	0.328
Multivariable adjusted**	0.7 (0.26)	1.00 (0.28)	1.48 (0.34)	0.213

Values are means (SD) for unadjusted model and means (SE) for adjusted models.
* p-values for differences among the means.
** Adjusted for gender, age, smoking status, alcohol intake, education, marital status, rank, and physical activity score.

Source: Violanti et al. (2009).

of age respectively). The NHANES national prevalence of metabolic syndrome was 24 percent for those in this younger comparable age range (30–39 years). This slightly higher prevalence at a younger age coincides with police mortality cohort studies which found a higher risk of CVD among younger officers (Violanti et al., 1998), an infrequent result in healthy worker populations. Officers on the other two shifts had a lower prevalence of metabolic syndrome compared to NHANES data. One potential explanation for this unusual finding is that midnight shift officers were most likely to be sleep deprived because of difficulties associated with day sleeping (Åkerstedt, 1995) and sleep debt has been shown to have a harmful impact on carbohydrate metabolism and endocrine function that could contribute to metabolic disorders (Spiegel, Leproult, & Van Cauter, 1999).

The prevalence of an elevated waist circumference was nearly 50 percent and 30 percent respectively for females and males in NHANES III. In our police sample, the combined prevalence of elevated waist circumference was 55 percent for those working midnight shifts, higher than NHANES III levels and day or afternoon shift workers. Prevalence of low HDL cholesterol levels were approximately 38 percent in women and 35 percent in men in NHANES, while low HDL prevalence in our combined police sample was 50 percent among those working midnight shifts. Prevalence of hypertension and glucose intolerance for officers working midnights was also higher than found in NHANES (Ford et al., 2002; Meigs, 2002).

The significantly elevated prevalence ratio for abdominal obesity found when comparing midnight to day shifts in this study may be indicative of future health problems among officers. Ford et al. (2002) predicted that the increase in obesity in the United States since the NHANES data was collected (1988–1994) would lead to a higher prevalence estimate of metabolic syndrome. Ford further commented that even if obesity prevalence remained unchanged, the total number of individuals in the United States with metabolic syndrome would increase due to population growth in the 1990s (Ford et al., 2002).

Officers who worked midnights and had less than six hours sleep in our study had a significantly higher mean number of metabolic syndrome components than those who worked day shifts (multivariate-adjusted). This finding concurs with other research concerning sleep deprivation and shift work. Karlsson et al. (2001) found that sleep deprivation is a common denominator in most forms of shift work and has serious metabolic and cardiovascular consequences. Hall et al. (2008) found that adults between the ages of 30 and 54 years with six or fewer hours of sleep were at increased risk for cardiovascular disease and components of the metabolic syndrome (hypertension, weight increase and adverse changes in glucose metabolism). Sleep duration was significantly related to waist circumference, body mass index, percentage of body fat, serum levels of insulin and glucose, and insulin resistance.

PTSD, Neurological Processes, and Police Decision-making

Police work routinely engages officers in rapid decision-making situations in which the inhibition of a response may or may not result in a potentially detrimental if not catastrophic outcome. In spite of the repeated exposure of police officers to traumatic events, there are few studies that have examined the effects of trauma exposure on the neural basis of attention and decision-making in police officers. Only two studies have thus far examined brain structure and function in officers with PTSD using MRI. A structural imaging study of Dutch police officers by Lindauer et al. (2004b) found that hippocampal volume in officers with PTSD was significantly smaller in comparison with a trauma-exposed non-PTSD control group. A significant negative correlation was found between re-experiencing symptoms and hippocampal volume in the PTSD group. In a related study of police officers, Lindauer et al. (2004a) found that exposure to trauma-related scripts produced significantly less activation in the medial frontal gyms and more activation in the right cuneus in the PTSD group relative to the trauma-exposed control group. Neither of these studies examined attention and decision-making processes.

It is accepted that PTSD symptomatology is associated with a neurobiological dysregulation of the limbic system and its interrelation with the prefrontal cortex and the locus coeruleus (Bremner, Southwick, & Chaney, 1999, Bremner, 2003; Charney, Southwick, Krystal, Deutch, Nurburg, & Davis, 1994; Kimble & Kaufman, 2004; Liberzon & Martis, 2006; Pitman, Shin, & Rouch, 2001; Vermetten & Bremner, 2002).

A dysregulation of limbic/paralimbic system function, as a result of exposure to a traumatic stressor, can produce a state of hypersensitivity in which internal and external stimuli lead to heightened arousal (Kolb, 1987). Manifestations of PTSD can persist for years after the trauma and include attentional disturbances, hyperarousal, exaggerated startle response, hypervigilance, autonomic hyperactivity, and executive dysfunction (McFarlane, Weber, & Clark, 1993; Sutker, Vasterling, Brailey, & Allain, 1995; Wolfe & Charney, 1991).

Recent studies have demonstrated that traumatic experiences and subsequent PTSD symptoms have long-term effects on the structure and function of the brain (Bremner, 2003; Liberzon & Martis, 2006). Neuroimaging studies have shown that trauma-related stimuli activate brain areas associated with the stress response in individuals with PTSD and not in controls (see for review Liberzon & Martis, 2006). Hayes, LaBar, Petty, McCarthy, and Morey (2009) found that the separate neural circuitry involved in emotional and attentional processing were both altered in veterans with high PTSD symptomatology compared to those with low symptomatology. Interestingly, there is also evidence of different patterns of brain activation within the frontal and limbic circuitry for PTSD patients who fall into a re-experiencing/hyperarousal subtype versus a dissociative subtype (Lanius et al., 2005). Thus, relatively greater elevations of avoidance, emotional numbing, and dissociative symptoms may be associated with different patterns of brain function and structure than elevations of re-experiencing and hyperarousal.

The use of brain electrophysiological measures of attention (Event-related brain potentials—ERPs), along with speed of motor responding, provides converging information about the cognitive operations of attentional/response control systems. Event-related brain potentials are an excellent tool for assessing the timing and neuronal resources used in attention tasks. Thus, ERPs provide brain measures of the speed of processing of stimuli involved in decision-making tasks. ERPs have been widely examined in studies of PTSD because they provide temporal information about attentional processes such as the ability to detect a target, the salience of the target to the participant, and the response to novel or distractor stimuli (Polich, 2003).

Covey, Shucard, Violanti, Lee, and Shucard (2013) examined electrophysiological brain measures of response control processes using a visual "Go, No-Go" letter recognition task. "Go, No-Go" refers to a timed reaction task for recognition of stimuli presented to the officer on a screen. This task requires the officer to make rapid decisions whether to respond or not to certain letters. The effects of exposure to traumatic stress, in particular post-traumatic stress disorder (PTSD), was the focus of this work because police officers are at higher risk for PTSD given their traumatic work exposures.

The Covey et al. (2013) measured:

- PTSD and Psychological Symptomatology derived from the CAPS and SCID clinical assessments.
- Behavioral Measures: Accuracy (errors of omission and commission and an index of processing speed and neural efficiency).
- Electrophysiological Measures:
  - ERP amplitude and latency to all stimulus types (e.g., Go, No-Go, Task-Irrelevant stimuli).
  - 2-D topographical maps of ERP components.
  - Source localization of activity within the brain from specific time points in electrical events.

The Covey et al. (2013) study suggests that cognitive impairments in PTSD negatively compromise mechanisms associated with attention and decision-making in police officers (Shucard, McCabe, & Szymanski, 2008). ERPs associated with *irrelevant stimuli* were significantly higher in police officers with high levels of PTSD symptoms compared to officers with low PTSD symptoms and controls. Further, these cognitive difficulties are not confined to trauma-related stimuli, but are also seen with neutral stimuli that take away from the critical task at hand. *PTSD can thus lead to increased danger and poorer decision-making in critical police incidents.* When completed, this study can provide crucial information for consideration of police agency policy and care for police officers involved in critical incidents.

Conclusions

Empowering Resiliency; Depowering Stress

The presence of aversive health outcomes as described in this chapter suggests that stress may be a debilitating force in police work. This leads to the question of how to manage stress in police officers. According to Cooper (2004), stress management involves removing the individual from the stressful situation, changing the social situation, and/or strengthening the person's resilience to stress. It is likely not possible to remove stressors that are inherent in police work such as danger and exposure to traumatic situations. It is possible, however, to produce change both in the social environment (the police organization) and in the personal resiliency of the officer.

Protocols in stress management should consider the protective nature of resiliency—an ability to "bounce back" from adversity, stress, and trauma. Being able to bounce back is an important capability. However, because police officers are called upon *repeatedly* to deal with increasingly complex and threatening incidents, it is appropriate to expand the scope of this definition to include the development of one's capacity to deal with *future* events (Paton, Smith, Violanti, & Eranen, 2000). Therefore, resilience can provide support not only in the here and now but also in the future. This is the notion of "adaptive capacity" (Klein, Nicholls, & Thomalla, 2003). Police resiliency therefore includes the capacity of agencies and officers to draw upon individual, collective, and institutional resources to cope with demands, challenges, and changes encountered *during and after* critical incidents.

Recent research findings lend support to the notion that resiliency can be increased in individuals. For example, using a structured intervention program, Maddi (1987) successfully increased hardiness levels in corporate managers, and at the same time found that their physiological responses to stress were attenuated and healthier. Maddi and colleagues have followed up this work with a more refined "hardiness induction" program that appears to work quite well (Maddi, Khoshaba, & Pammenter, 1999). A key feature of hardiness training involves facilitating the adoption and application of new strategies for interpreting and making sense of experiences, especially highly stressful ones.

Changing the Social Environment: Police Organizational Resiliency

While typically investigated at the personality level of the individual, the comprehensive understanding of resilience must also integrate organizational perspectives, with the police organization exerting a greater influence in this process. The police organization defines the social context within which officers experience and interpret critical incidents and their sequelae and within which future capabilities are nurtured or restricted (Paton, 2006). There are three characteristics of a resilient organization to consider: (1) organizational climate; (2) trust; and (3) leadership.

Organizational Climate

Hart and Cooper (2001) proposed a conceptual model of organizational climate that predicts salutary outcomes. Organizational climate describes officers' perceptions of how their organization functions, and these perceptions influence both their well-being and their performance in their organizational role (Hart & Cooper, 2001). Burke and Paton (2006) tested the ability of this model to predict satisfaction in the context of emergency responders' experience of critical incidents. Organizational climate was the best single predictor of job satisfaction and represents a significant influence on officers' ability to render their critical incident experiences meaningful and manageable. Organizational climate had a direct positive influence on coping, resulting in an increase in positive work experiences. Organizational climate also demonstrated a direct negative influence on negative work experiences. The important role played by organizational climate indicates that police agencies have a key role in facilitating officer adaptability and resilience.

Trust

Police officers are noted for not trusting. This may be a result of occupational socialization which emphasizes that trusting can put one in danger on the street. Instead it is "safe" to be suspicious of everyone. Unfortunately, this lack of trust may impede the officer's ability to seek help in stressful situations. Trust is a prominent determinant of the effectiveness of interpersonal relationships, group processes, and organizational relationships (Barker & Camarata, 1998; Herriot, Hirch, & Reilly, 1998), and plays a crucial role in empowering officers (Spreitzer & Mishra, 1999). People functioning in trusting, reciprocal relationships are left feeling empowered, and more likely to experience meaning in their work. Trust has been identified as a predictor of people's ability to deal with complex, high-risk events (Siegrist & Cvetkovich, 2000), particularly when relying on others to provide information or assistance.

The resilient police organization is one where the officer can ask for help without reprise or hesitation. An officer is more willing to commit to acting cooperatively in high-risk situations when they believe those with whom they must collaborate or work under are competent, dependable, and likely to act with integrity as well as to care for their interests (Dirks, 1999). Organizations functioning with cultures that value openness and trust create opportunities for officers to engage in learning and growth, contributing to the development of officers' adaptive capacity (Barker & Camarata, 1998).

Leadership

Resilient police organizations have leaders who care about their people. Leaders play a central role in developing and sustaining empowering environments (Liden, Wayne, & Sparrow, 2000; Paton & Stephens, 1996). They have a major role to play in creating and sustaining a climate of trust as a result of their being responsible for translating organizational culture into the day-to-day values and procedures that sustain officers. Leadership practices such as positive reinforcement help create an empowering work environment (Paton, 1994).

Leaders are in a unique position to shape how members of the group understand stressful experiences. The leader who, through example and discussion, communicates a positive construction or re-construction of shared stressful experiences, may exert an influence on the entire group in the direction of his/her interpretation of experience. Thus, leaders who are high in resiliency will likely have a greater impact on their groups under high-stress conditions, when by their example as well as explanations they articulate to group members, they encourage an interpretation of stressful events as interesting challenges which they are capable of meeting, and in any event can learn and benefit from. This process itself, as well as the positive result of the process (a shared understanding of the event as something worthwhile and beneficial), could be expected to generate an increased sense of shared values, mutual respect, and cohesion (Bartone & Snook, 1999).

Supportive supervision is a crucial factor (Liden et al., 1997) because it enhances resiliency necessary for the feelings of competence. Support enables officers to find increased meaning in their work and perhaps their lives. In times of crisis, supervisory support can make the difference between life and death. Focusing on constructive discussion of work-related problems and how they can be resolved draws away from one's personal and psychological weaknesses in difficult situations and replaces it with an active approach to anticipating how to exercise control (Paton & Stephens, 1996). This can be valuable for suicide-prevention efforts.

In sum, police leaders need to communicate to officers a reaction and assessment that reinforces comprehensibility, manageability, and meaningfulness regarding their performance in stressful or traumatic events within the context of the organization. Cohen and Welch (2000) underscore the ability of the attitudes, beliefs, values, and culture of the organization and its members to mediate the effects of stress and trauma. Administrators must be aware of the messages they send that undercut workers' beliefs regarding their role in prevention, protection, intervention, mitigation, remediation, investigation, and resolution. Coworkers and peers, supervisors, and mental health caregivers must no longer ignore the importance of sociocultural context and group norms (Dunning, 2003).

Health Intervention

Police organizations would be well advised to establish worksite programs related to health. The workplace provides a unique opportunity for health intervention because most persons spend considerable time at work, and that amount of time has increased over the previous two decades (American Heart Association, 2008; Leaf, 1993; Linnan et al., 2008). Besides stress, lifestyle behaviors including physical activities, nutrition, smoking, and substance abuse have a significant impact on long-term health, including contributing to chronic diseases such as hypertension, obesity, heart disease, type 2 diabetes, strokes, and some forms of cancer. According to the Centers for Disease Control, factors such as obesity and smoking can be attributed to 40 percent of all deaths from heart disease or strokes (CDC Chronic Disease Prevention, 2004). In addition, behavioral disorders, including stress-related depression, have been shown to contribute significantly to the risk of heart disease, accounting for 33 percent of the population's attributable risk for development of myocardial infarction (Yusuf et al., 2004). That these and other risk factors are modifiable over the short term, and lead to long-term health benefits, has been demonstrated in numerous secondary prevention studies (Milani, Lavie, & Mehra, 2004).

The issues highlighted in this chapter deserve serious consideration in order to help reduce the sometimes devastating effects of chronic and traumatic stress. This chapter has discussed but one possible impact that stress has on police—their health. There are other effects related to police stress such as behavioral issues, excessive alcohol use, family disruption, and suicide (Violanti, 2007). All too often we emphasize the dangers of police work, but seem to neglect the hidden psychological danger of this profession. It is a clear indication of the strain placed on the police officer's work and life roles. In the least, we should adequately address these problems and provide methods to prevent such adverse outcomes in this unforgiving occupation.

References

Åkerstedt T. (1995). Work hours, sleepiness and the underlying mechanisms. *Journal of Sleep Research*, 4, 15–22.

American Heart Association. (2008). Position Statement on Effective Worksite Wellness Programs. Available at: www.americanheart.org/presenter.jhtml?identifier_305748.

American Psychiatric Association. (2013). *Diagnostic and Statistical Manual*, 5th ed. Arlington, VA: American Psychiatric Association.

Barker, R.T. & Camarata, M.R. (1998). The role of communication in creating and maintaining a learning organization: Preconditions, indicators, and disciplines. *The Journal of Business Communication*, 35, 443–467.

Bartone, P.T. & Snook, S.A. (2000). Gender differences in predictors of leader performance over time. Paper presented at the American Psychological Society convention, Miami, FL.

Black, P. (1994). Central nervous system interactions: Psychoneuroimmunology of stress and its immune consequences. *Antimicrobal Agents Chemotherapy*, 38, 1–6.

Bonnar A. (2000). Stress at work: The beliefs and experiences of police superintendents. *International Journal of Police Science Management*, 2, 285–302.

Bonnet F., Irving, K., Terra, J.L., Nony, P., Berthezene, F., & Moulin P. (2005). Anxiety and depression are associated with unhealthy lifestyle in patients at risk of cardiovascular disease. *Atherosclerosis*, 178, 339–344.

Boscarino J. (2004). Posttraumatic stress disorder and physical illness: Results from clinical and epidemiological studies. *Annals of the NY Academy of Science*, 1032, 141–153.

Boscarino J. & Chang J. (1999). Electrocardiogram abnormalities among men with stress related psychiatric disorders: implication for coronary heart disease and clinical research. *Annals of Behavioral Medicine*, 21, 227–234.

Bremner, J.D. (2003). Functional neuroanatomical correlates of traumatic stress revisited 7 years later, this time with data. *Psychopharmological Bulletin*, 37, 6–25.

Bremner, J.D., Southwick, S.M., & Charney, D.S. (1999). The neurobiology of posttraumatic stress disorder: An integration of animal and human research. In P.A. Saigh & J.D. Bremner (Eds.), *Posttraumatic Stress Disorder: A Comprehensive Text*, pp. 103–143. Needham Heights, MA: Allyn & Bacon.

Brotman, D.J., Girod, J.P., Posch, A., Jani, J.T., Patel, J.V., Gupta, M., Lip, G.Y., Reddy, S., & Kickler, T.S. (2006). Effects of short-term glucocorticoids on hemostatic factors in healthy volunteers. *Thrombosis Research*, 118, 247–252.

Buckley, T.C. & Kaloupek, D.G. (2001). A meta-analytic examination of basal cardiovascular activity in posttraumatic stress disorder. *Psychosomatic Medicine*, 63, 585–594.

Burke, K. & Paton, D. (2006). Well-being in protective services personnel: Organizational influences. *Australasian Journal of Disaster and Trauma Studies*, 2006–2. http://trauma.massey.ac.nz/issues/2006–2/burke.htm.

Carlier, I.V.E. (1999). Finding meaning in police trauma. In J.M. Violanti & D. Paton (Eds.), *Police Trauma: Psychological Aftermath of Civilian Combat*, pp. 227–239. Springfield, IL: Charles C. Thomas.

CDC Chronic Disease Prevention. (2004). *The Burden of Chronic Diseases and Their Risk Factors. National and State Perspectives*. Baltimore: US Department of Health and Human Services.

Charles, L.E., Burchfiel, C.M., Fekedulegn, D., Vila, B., Hartley, T.A., Slaven, J., Mnatsakanova, A., & Violanti, J.M. (2007). Shift work and sleep: The Buffalo police health study. *Policing: An International Journal of Police Strategic Management*, 30, 215–227.

Charney, D.S., Southwick, S.M., Krystal, J.H., Deutch, A.Y., Nurburg, M.M., & Davis, M. (1994). Neurobiological mechanisms of PTSD. In M.M. Nurburg, (Ed.), *Catecholamine Function in Posttraumatic Stress Disorder*, pp. 131–158. Washington, DC: American Psychiatric Press.

Chrousos, G. & Gold, P. (1992). The concepts of stress and stress system disorders: Overview of physical and behavioral homeostasis. *Journal of the American Medical Association*, 267, 1244–1252.

Cohen, S., Kessler, R.C., & Gordon, L.U. (1997). *Measuring Stress*. New York: Oxford University Press.

Cohen, J. & Welch, L. (2000). Attitudes, beliefs, values, cultures as mediators of stress. In V. Rice (Ed.), *Handbook of Stress, Coping and Health*. Thousand Oaks, CA: Sage.

Cooper, C.L. (2004). *Handbook of Stress Medicine and Health*, 2nd ed. Boca Raton, FL: CRC Press.

Covey, T.J., Shucard, J.L., Violanti, J.M., Lee, J., & Shucard, D.W. (2013). The effects of exposure to traumatic stressors on inhibitory control on police officers: A dense electrode array study using a go/nogo continuous performance task. *International Journal of Psychophysiology*, 87, 363–375. http://dx.doi.org/10.1016/j.ijpsycho.2013.03.009.

Curtis, B.M. & O'Keefe, J.H. Jr (2002). Autonomic tone as a cardiovascular risk factor: the dangers of chronic fight or flight. *Mayo Clinic Proceedings*, 77, 45–54.

Davidson, J.R.T. & Foa, E. (1993). *Posttraumatic Stress Disorder, DSM IV and Beyond.* Washington, DC: American Psychiatric Press.

Demers, P., Heyer, N., & Rosenstock, L. (1992). Mortality among firefighters from three northwestern United States cities. *British Journal of Industrial Medicine*, 49, 664–670.

Di Lorenzo, L., De Pergola, G., & Zocchetti, C. (2003). Effect of shift work on body mass index: results of a study performed in 319 glucose-tolerant men working in a southern Italian industry. *International Journal of Obesity Related Metabolic Disorders*, 27, 1353–1358.

Dirks, K.T. (1999). The effects of interpersonal trust on work group performance. *Journal of Applied Psychology,* 84, 445–455.

Dunning, C. (2003). Sense of coherence in managing trauma workers. In D. Paton, J.M. Violanti & L.M. Smith (Eds.), *Promoting Capabilities to Manage Posttraumatic Stress: Perspectives on Resilience.* Springfield, IL: Charles C. Thomas.

Eisenach, J.H., Clark, E.S., Charkoudian, N., Dinenno, F.A., Atkinson, J.L., Fealey, R.D., Dietz, N.M., & Joyner, M.J. (2002). Effects of chronic sympathectomy on vascular function in the human forearm. *Journal of Applied Physiology*, 92, 2019–2025.

Executive summary of the Third Report of the National Cholesterol Education Program (NCEP). (2001). Expert panel on detection, evaluation, and treatment of high blood cholesterol in adults (Adult Treatment Panel III). *JAMA*, 285, 2486–2497.

Expert Panel on Detection, Evaluation, and Treatment of High Blood Cholesterol in Adults. (1999). Executive Summary for the Third Report of the National Cholesterol Education Program (NCEP) Expert Panel on Detection, Evaluation, and Treatment of High Blood Cholesterol in Adults (Adult Treatment Panel III). *Journal of the American Medical Association*, 285, 2486–2497.

Figley, C.R. (1999). Police compassion fatigue (PCF): Theory, research, assessment, treatment, and prevention. In J.M. Violanti & D. Paton (Eds.), *Police Trauma: Psychological Aftermath of Civilian Combat*, pp. 37–53. Springfield, IL: Charles C. Thomas.

Fischer, J., Calame, A., Dettling, A., Zeier, H., & Fanconi, S. (2000). Objectifying psycho-mental stress in the workplace—an example. *International Archives of Occupational and Environmental Health*, 73(suppl), S46–S52.

Folkman, S. & Lazarus, R.S. (1980). An analysis of coping in a middle-aged community sample. *Journal of Health and Social Behavior*, 21, 219–239.

Forastiere, F., Perucci, C.A., Di Pietro, A., Miceli, M., Rapiti, E., Bargagli, A., & Borgia, P. (1994). Mortality among policemen in Rome. *American Journal of Industrial Medicine*, 26, 785–798.

Ford, E.S., Giles, W.H., & Dietz, W.H. (2002). Prevalence of the Metabolic Syndrome among US Adults: Findings from the Third National Health and Nutrition Examination Survey. *Journal of the American Medical Association*, 287, 356–359.

Franke, W.D., & Anderson, D.F. (1994). Relationship between physical activity and risk factors for cardiovascular disease among law enforcement officers. *Journal of Occupational Medicine*, 36, 1127–1132.

Friedman, M., & McEwen, B. (2005). Posttraumatic stress disorder, allostatic load, and medical illness. In P. Schnurr & B. Green (Eds.), *Trauma and Health*, pp. 157–188. Washington, DC: American Psychological Association.

Friedman, M. & Schnurr, P. (1995). The relationship between trauma, post-traumatic stress disorder, and physical health. In M. Friedman, D.S. Charney, & A.Y. Deutch (Eds.), *Neurobiological and Clinical Consequences of Stress: From Normal Adaption to PTSD*, pp. 507–524. Philadelphia: Lippincott-Raven.

Feuer, E., & Rosenman, K. (1986). Mortality in police and firefighters in New Jersey, *American Journal of Industrial Medicine*, 9, 309–322.

Gilmartin, K. (1986). Hypervigilance: A learned perceptual set and its consequences on police stress. In J. Reese & H. Goldstein (Eds.), *Psychological Services for Law Enforcement*, pp. 45–68. Washington, DC: US Government Printing Office.

Girod, J. & Brotman, D. (2004). Does altered glucocorticoid homeostasis increase cardiovascular risk? *Cardiovascular Research*, 64, 217–226.

Grundy, S.M., Cleeman, J.I., & Daniels, S.R. (2005). Diagnosis and management of the metabolic syndrome. An American Heart Association/National Heart, Lung, and Blood Institute scientific statement executive summary. *Critical Pathology Cardiology*, 4, 198–203.

Guralnick, L. (1963). Mortality by occupation and cause of death among men 20–64 years of age: 1950. In *Vital Statistics Special Reports*. Bethesda, MA: Department of Health, Education and Welfare.

Hall, M.H., Muldoon, M.F., Jennings, J.R., et al. (2008). Self-reported sleep duration is associated with the metabolic syndrome in midlife adults. *Sleep*, 31, 635–643.

Hampton, S.M., Morgan, L.M., Lawrence, N., et al. (1996). Postprandial hormone and metabolic responses in simulated shift work. *Journal of Endocrinology*, 151, 259–267.

Hart, P.M. & Cooper, C.L. (2001). Occupational stress: Toward a more integrated framework. In N. Anderson, D.S. Ones, H.K. Sinangil, & C. Viswesvaren (Eds.), *International Handbook of Work and Organizational Psychology, Vol.2: Organizational Psychology*. London: Sage.

Hayes, J.P, LaBar, K.S., Petty, C.M., McCarthy, G., & Morey, R.A. (2009). Alterations in the neural circuitry for emotion and attention associated with posttraumatic stress symptomatology. *Psychiatry Research: Neuroimaging*, 172, 7–15.

Herriot, P., Hirsh, W., & Reilly, P. (1998). *Trust and Transition: Managing Today's Employment Relationship*. New York: John Wiley & Sons.

Horowitz, M.J., Wilner, N., & Alvarez, W. (1979). Impact of event scale: a measure of subjective stress. *Psychosomatic Medicine*, 41, 209–218.

Humbarger, C., Crouse, S., Womack, J., & Green, J.S. (2004). Frequency of metabolic syndrome in police officers compared to NCEP III prevalence values. *Medicine & Science in Sports & Exercise*, 36, S161.

Johansen, C., Feychting, M., Moller, M., Arnsbo, P., Ahlbom, A., & Olsen, J.H. (2002). Risk of severe cardiac arrhythmia in male utility workers: A nationwide Danish cohort study. *American Journal of Epidemiology*, 156, 857–861.

Karlsson, B., Knutsson, A., & Lindahl, B. (2001). Is there an association between shift work and having a metabolic syndrome? Results from a population based study of 27,485 people. *Occupational and Environmental Medicine*, 58, 747–752.

Kessler, R.C., Sonnega, A., Bromet, E., Hughes, M., & Nelson, C. (1995). Posttraumatic stress disorder in the National Comorbidity Survey. *Archives of General Psychiatry*, 52, 1048–1060.

Kimble, M. & Kaufman, M. (2004). Clinical correlates of neurological change in posttraumatic stress disorder: An overview of critical systems. *Psychiatric Clinics of North America*, 27, 49–65.

Kivimaki, M., Leino-Arjas, P., Luukkonen, R.H., Vahtera, J., & Kirjonen, J. (2002). Work stress and risk of cardiovascular mortality: prospective cohort study of industrial employees. *British Medical Journal*, 325, 857.

Klein, R., Nicholls, R., & Thomalla, F. (2003). Resilience to natural hazards: How useful is this concept? *Environmental Hazards*, 5, 35–45.

Knutssen, A. & Boggild, H. (2000). Shiftwork and cardiovascular disease: Review of disease mechanisms. *Reviews of Environmental Health*, 15, 359–372.

Kolb, L. (1987). A neuropsychological hypothesis explaining posttraumatic stress disorder. *American Journal of Psychiatry*, 144, 989–995.

Kop, N. & Euwema, M. (2001). Occupational stress and the use of force by Dutch police officers. *Criminal Justice and Behavior*, 28, 631–652.

Lanius, R.A., Williamson, P.C., Bluhm, R.L., Densmore, M., Boksman, K., Neufeld, R.W., Gati, J.S., & Memon, R.S. (2005). Functional connectivity of dissociative responses in posttraumatic stress disorder. *Biological Psychiatry*, 57, 873–884.

Lasfargues, G., Sylvanie, V., & Caces, B. (1996). Relations among night work, dietary habits, biological measures, and health status. *International Journal of Behavioral Medicine*, 3, 123–134.

Laufersweiler-Dwyer, D. & Dwyer, R. (2000). Profiling those impacted by organizational stressors at the macro, intermediate and micro levels of several police agencies. *Justice Professionals*, 12, 443–469.

Leaf, A. (1993). Preventive medicine for our ailing health care system. *Journal of the American Medical Association*, 269, 616–618.

Liberzon, I. & Martis, B. (2006). Neuroimaging studies of emotional responses in PTSD. *Annals of the NY Academy of Sciences*, 1071, 87–109.

Liden, R.C., Wayne, S.J., & Sparrow, R.T. (2000). An examination of the mediating role of psychological empowerment on the relations between the job, interpersonal relationships, and work outcomes. *Journal of Applied Psychology*, 85, 407–416.

Lindauer, J.L., Booij, J., Habraken, J.B.A., Uylings, H.B.A., Olf, M., Carlier, I.V.E., den Heetan, G.J. van Eck-Smit, B.L.F., & Gersons, B. (2004a). Cerebral blood flow changes during script-driven imagery in police officers with posttraumatic stress disorder. *Biological Psychiatry*, 56, 853–861.

Lindauer, J.L., Vliegler, E.J., Jalink, M., Carlier, I.V., Majoie, C.B.L.M., den Heetan, G.J., & Gersons, B. (2004b). Smaller hippocampal volume in Dutch police officers with posttraumatic stress disorder. *Biological Psychiatry*, 56, 356–363.

Lindfors, P. & Lundberg, U. (2002). Is low cortisol release an indicator of positive health? *Stress and Health*, 18, 153–160.

Linnan, L., Bowling, M., Childress, J., Lindsay, G., Blakey, C., Pronk, S., Wieker, S., & Royall, P. (2008). Results of the 2004 National Worksite Health Promotion Survey. *American Journal of Public Health*, 9, 1503–1509.

Maddi, S.R. (1987). Hardiness training at Illinois Bell Telephone. In J.P. Opatz (Ed.), *Health Promotion Evaluation*. Stephens Point, WI: National Wellness Institute.

Maddi, S.R., Khoshaba, D.M., & Pammenter, A. (1999). The hardy organization: Success by turning change to advantage. *Consulting Psychology Journal*, 51, 117–124.

Mangos, G.J., Walker, B.R., Kelly, J.J., & Lawson, J.A., Webb, D.J., & Whitworth, J.A. (2000). Cortisol inhibits cholinergic vasodilation in the human forearm. *American Journal of Hypertension*, 13, 1155–1160.

McEwen, B. (1998). Protective and damaging effects of stress mediators. *New England Journal of Medicine*, 338, 171–179.

McEwen, B. & Seeman, T. (1999). Protective and damaging effects of mediators of stress: Elaborating and testing the concepts of allostasis and allostatic load. *Annals of the NY Academy of Science*, 896, 30–47.

McFarlane, A.C., Weber, D.L., & Clark, C.R. (1993). Abnormal stimulus processing in Posttraumatic Stress Disorder. *Biological Psychiatry*, 34, 311–320.

McMichael, A. (1976). Standardized mortality ratios and the healthy worker effect: scratching beneath the surface. *Journal of Occupational Medicine*, 18, 165–168.

Meigs, J.B. (2002). Epidemiology of the Metabolic Syndrome. *American Journal of Managed Care*, 8, S283–S292.

Milani, R.V., Lavie, C.J., & Mehra, M.R. (2004). Reduction in C-reactive protein through cardiac rehabilitation and exercise training. *Journal of the American College of Cardiology*, 43, 1056–1061.

Milham, S. (1983). *Occupational Mortality in Washington State*. DHEW Pub. 83–116. Washington, DC: US Government Printing Office.

Nagaya, T., Yoshida, H., Takahashi, H., & Kawai, M. (2002). Markers of insulin resistance in day and shift workers aged 30–59 years. *International Archives of Occupational and Environmental Health*, 7, 562–568.

Orth-Gomer, K., Wamala, S.P., Horsten, M., Schenck-Gustafsson, K., Schneiderman, N., & Mittleman, M.A. (2000). Marital stress worsens prognosis in women with coronary heart disease: The Stockholm Female Coronary Risk Study. *Journal of the American Medical Association*, 284, 3008–3014.

Paton, D. (1994). Disaster relief work: An assessment of training effectiveness. *Journal of Traumatic Stress*, 7, 275–288.

Paton, D. (2006). Posttraumatic growth in emergency professionals. In. L. Calhoun and R. Tedeschi (Eds.), *Handbook of Posttraumatic Growth: Research and Practice*. Mahwah, NJ: Lawrence Erlbaum Assoc.

Paton, D. & Stephens, C. (1996). Training and support for emergency responders. In D. Paton & J.M. Violanti (Eds.), *Traumatic Stress in Critical Occupations: Recognition, Consequences and Treatment*. Springfield, IL: Charles C. Thomas.

Paton, D., Smith, L.M., Violanti, J., & Eranen, L. (2000). Work-related traumatic stress: Risk, vulnerability and resilience. In D. Paton, J.M. Violanti, & C. Dunning (Eds.), *Posttraumatic Stress Intervention: Challenges, Issues and Perspectives*, pp. 187–204. Springfield, IL: Charles C. Thomas.

Paton, D., Violanti, J.M., & Schmuckler, G. (1999). Chronic exposure to risk and trauma: Addiction and separation issues in police officers. In J.M. Violanti & D. Paton (Eds.), *Police Trauma: Psychological Aftermath of Civilian Combat*, pp. 78–87. Springfield, IL: Charles C. Thomas.

Pitman, R.K., Shin, L.M., & Rauch, S.L. (2001). Investigating the pathogenesis of posttraumatic stress disorder with neuroimaging. *Journal of Clinical Psychiatry*, 62, 47–54.

Polich, J. (2003). Theoretical overview of P3a and P3b. In J. Polich (Ed.), *Detection of Change: Event-related Potential and fMRI Findings*, pp. 83–98. Boston, MA: Kluwer Academic Press.

Price, C.S., Pollock, M.L., Gettman, L.R., & Kent, D.A. (1978). *Physical Fitness Programs for Law Enforcement Officers: A Manual for Police Administrators.* Washington, DC: U.S. Department of Justice, 1978.

Pruessner, J., Hellhammer, D., & Kirschbaum, C. (1999). Burnout, perceived stress, and cortisol responses to awakening. *Psychosomatic Medicine*, 6, 197–204.

Pyörälä, M., Miettinen, H., Halonen, P., Laakso, M., & Pyörälä, K. (2000). Insulin Resistance Syndrome predicts the risk of coronary heart disease and stroke in healthy middle-aged men. The 22 year follow-up results of the Helsinki Policemen Study. *Thrombosis Vascular Biology*, 20, 538–544.

Quire, D. & Blount, W. (1990). A coronary risk profile study of male police officers: Focus on cholesterol. *Journal of Police Science and Administration*, 17, 89–94.

Sapolsky R. (2002). Endocrinology of the stress-response, in J. Becker, R. Breedlove, & M. McCarthy (Eds.), *Behavioral Endocrinology*, pp. 409–450. Boston, MA: MIT Press.

Sardinas A., Miller C., & Hansen H. (1986). Ischemic heart disease mortality of fireman and policemen. *American Journal of Public Health*, 76, 1140–1141.

Seeman, T., McEwen, B., Rowe, J., & Singer, B. (2001). Allostatic load as a marker of cumulative biological risk: MacArthur studies of successful aging. *Proceedings of the National Academy of Sciences*, 98, 4770–4775.

Seyle, H. (1950). *Stress.* Montreal, Canada: Acta

Shedd, O.L., Sears, S.F. Jr, Harvill, J.L., Arshad, A., Conti, J.B., Steinberg, J.S., & Curtis, A.B. (2004). The World Trade Center attack: Increased frequency of defibrillator shocks for ventricular arrhythmias in patients living remotely from New York City. *Journal of the American College of Cardiology*, 44, 1265–1267.

Shucard, J.L., McCabe, D.C., & Szymanski, H. (2008). An event-related potential study of attention deficits in posttraumatic stress disorder during auditory and visual go/nogo continuous performance tasks. *Biological Psychology*, 79, 223–233.

Siegrist, M. & Cvetkovich, G. (2000). Perception of hazards: The role of social trust and knowledge. *Risk Analysis*, 20, 713–719.

Sookian, S., Gemma, C., & Fernandez-Gianotti, T., et al. (2007). Effects of rotating shift work on biomarkers of metabolic syndrome and inflammation. *Journal of Internal Medicine*, 261, 285–292.

Spielberger, C., Grier, K., & Greenfield G. (1982). Major dimensions of stress in law enforcement. *Florida Fraternal Order of Police Journal*, Spring, 10–12.

Spiegel, K., Leproult, R., & Van Cauter, E. (1999). Impact of sleep debt on metabolic and endocrine function. *Lancet*, 354, 1435–1439.

Spreitzer, G.M. & Mishra, A.K. (1999). Giving up control without losing control: Trust and its substitutes' effect on managers involving employees in decision-making. *Group & Organization Management*, 24, 155–187.

Steinberg, J.S., Arshad, A., Kowalski, M., Kukar, A., Suma, V., Vloka, M., Ehlert, F., Herweg B., Donnelly, J., Philip, J., Reed, G., & Rozanski, A. (2004). Increased incidence of life-threatening ventricular arrhythmias in implantable defibrillator patients after the World Trade Center attack. *Journal of the American College of Cardiology*, 44, 1261–1264.

Steinhardt, M., Greehow, L., & Stewart, J. (1991). The relationship of physical activity and cardiovascular fitness to absenteeism and medical care claims among law enforcement officers. *American Journal of Health Promotion*, 5,455–460.

Stephens, C., Long, N., & Flett, R. (1999). Vulnerability to psychological disorder: Previous trauma in police recruits. In J.M. Violanti & D. Paton (Eds.), *Police Trauma: Psychological Aftermath of Civilian Combat*, pp. 65–77. Springfield, IL: Charles C. Thomas.

Steptoe, A., Cropley, M., Griffith, J., & Kirschbaum, C. (2000) Job strain and anger expression predict early morning elevations in salivary cortisol. *Psychomatic Medicine*, 62, 286–292.

Sterling, P. & Eyer, J. (1999). Allostatsis: A new paradigm to explain arousal pathology. In S. Fisher & J. Reason (Eds.), *Handbook of Life Stress, Cognition and Health*, pp. 629–649. New York: Wiley.

Sutker, P. B., Vasterling, J.J., Brailey, K., & Allain, A.N. (1995). Memory, attention, and executive deficits in POW survivors: Contributing biological and psychological factors. *Neuropsychology*, 9, 118–125.

Vermetten, E., & Bremner, J.D. (2002). Circuits and systems in stress II: Applications to Neurobiology and Treatment of PTSD. *Anxiety and Depression*, 16, 14–38.

Vila, B. (2000). *Tired Cops*. Washington, DC: The Police Foundation.

Violanti, J.M. (2007). *Police Suicide: Epidemic in Blue*, 2nd ed. Springfield, IL: Charles C. Thomas.

Violanti, J.M. & Paton, D. (1999). *Police Trauma: Psychological Aftermath of Civilian Combat*. Springfield, IL: Charles C. Thomas.

Violanti, J.M., & Paton, D. (2007). *Who gets PTSD? Issues of Posttraumatic Stress Vulnerability*. Springfield, IL: Charles C. Thomas.

Violanti, J.M., Vena, J.E., & Petralia, S. (1998). Mortality of a police cohort: 1950–1990. *American Journal of Industrial Medicine*, 3, 366–373.

Violanti, J.M, Vena, J.E., Marshall, J.R., Fiedler, R. (1986). Disease risk and mortality among police officers: New evidence and contributing factors. *Journal of Police Science and Administration*, 14, 17–23.

Violanti, J.M., Burchfiel, C.M., Miller, D.B., et al. (2006). The Buffalo Cardiometabolic Occupational Police Stress (BCOPS) pilot study: Methods and participants characteristics. *Annals of Epidemiology*, 16, 148–156.

Violanti, J.M., Fekeduklgen, D., Hartley, T., Andrew, M., Charles, L., Mnatsakanova, A., & Burchfiel, C.M. (2007). Police trauma and cardiovascular disease: Association between PTSD symptoms and metabolic syndrome. *International Journal of Emergency Mental Health*, 8, 227–238.

Violanti, J.M., Burchfiel, C.M., Hartley, T.A., Mnatsakanova, A., Fekedulegn, D., Andrew, M.E, Charles, L.E., & Vila, B.J. (2009). Atypical work hours and metabolic syndrome among police officers. *Archives of Environmental and Occupational Health*, 64, 194–201.

von Kanel, R. & Dimsdale, J.E. (2000). Effects of sympathetic activation by adrenergic infusions on hemostasis in vivo. *European Journal of Haematology*, 65, 357–369.

Williams, C. (1987). Peacetime combat: Treating and preventing delayed stress reactions in police officers. In T. Williams (Ed.), *Post-traumatic Stress Disorders: A Handbook for Clinicians*. Cincinnati, OH: Disabled American Veterans.

Wolfe, J., & Charney, D.S. (1991). Use of neuropsychological assessment in posttraumatic stress disorder. *Psychological Assessment: A Journal of Consulting and Clinical Psychology*, 3, 573–580.

Wolk R. & Somers V.K. (2007). Sleep and the metabolic syndrome. *Experimental Physiology*, 92, 67–78.

Yehuda R. (2002). Post-Traumatic Stress Disorder. *New England Journal of Medicine*, 346, 108–114.

Yehuda, R., Teicher, M., Trestman, R., Levengood, R., & Siever, L. (1996). Cortisol regulation in PTSD and major depression: A chronological analysis. *Biological Psychiatry*, 40, 79–88.

Yusuf, S., Hawken, S., Ounpuu, S., Dans, T., Avezum, A., Lanas, F., McQueen, M., Budaj, A., Pais, P., Varigos, J., & Lisheng, L. (2004). Effect of potentially modifiable risk factors associated with myocardial infarction in 52 countries (the INTERHEART study): case-control study. *Lancet*, 364, 937–952.

5

CRITICAL INCIDENT STRESS DEBRIEFING

What is the State of the Science?

*Brandi Burque, Monty T. Baker, Vincent
B. Van Hasselt, and Judy Couwels*

Introduction

Officers are called upon to handle situations that civilians do not expect to
encounter in their daily lives. The job entails responding to calls in which
distress, misery, and human suffering are readily apparent. Indeed, stressors
are present across the board for the officer, from organizational practices,
the daily calls for service, to personal and family life (Finn & Tomz, 1996).
Not surprisingly, first responder populations, in general, are at a higher risk
for stress-related physical and psychological disorders. Therefore, developing
and implementing stress management programs are important steps toward
mitigating stress reactions and facilitating recovery. This chapter will focus on
the rationale for crisis intervention in law enforcement and the extant literature
on the issue. Specifically this chapter will provide: (1) a brief overview of
law enforcement stress, (2) a presentation of terminology associated with the
field of crisis intervention, (3) a review of the literature on the use of crisis
intervention in victim populations and law enforcement, (4) a discussion of
the key issues in this area, and (5) a presentation of factors associated with
stress resiliency, with case examples.

Law Enforcement Stress

Besides dealing with their own organization and the daily calls, officers
may also encounter: (1) criticism from the media and the citizens with
whom they interact, (2) conflicts with the judicial and political systems,
and (3) problems in dealing with the mental health system due to the

stigma of such involvement (Blau, 1994; Miller, 2006). The nature of police culture has a major impact on stress, as it is often seen as a sign of weakness to seek help when needed, complicated by the notion that "outsiders," or civilians, are not capable of understanding what the officers endure on a daily basis (Miller, 2006).

Police officers handle their stress in a variety of ways, some more adaptive than others. However, there may come a time when stressors become overwhelming. This may be caused by cumulative stress over time, or the result of a critical incident, such as a line-of-duty death, an event involving children, an officer-involved shooting, etc. There are indications that a significant number of officers experience moderate to severe problems including sleep disturbances, feelings of guilt, anger, depression and anxiety, and post-traumatic stress disorder (PTSD) after being involved in a critical incident (Miller, 2006; Sewell, Ellison, & Hurrell, 1988; Solomon, 1995).

The physical health consequences of such stress are well understood. Severe PTSD symptoms have been linked to obesity, high blood pressure and cholesterol, and glucose abnormalities in police officers (Violanti et al., 2006). Violanti (2004) found that certain police encounters may increase the risk of the development of PTSD and are associated with alcohol abuse and suicidal ideation. Further, it is clear that negative life events are correlated with depression. Consequently, the need for organizations and programs that can help officers handle distress caused by these events has been underscored (Hartley, Fekedulegn, Violanti, Andrew, & Burchfiel, 2007).

Review of Crisis Intervention Terminology

Much work in the field of crisis intervention has been directed toward mitigating stress reactions and restoring individual and group adaptive functioning. It is important to review key concepts and terminology, as these are often overlooked and misinterpreted in the literature. First, a *crisis* is a response to an event that is demonstrated by: (1) the interruption of one's psychological balance, or homeostasis, (2) overwhelming of one's usual coping mechanisms, and (3) impairment or distress that is readily apparent (Caplan, 1961, 1964; Everly & Mitchell, 1999, 2000). Second, a *critical incident* is any event that is outside the realm of ordinary human experience and has the potential to overwhelm one's usual coping skills (Everly & Mitchell, 2000). As a result, *crisis intervention* is defined as "the provision of emergency psychological care to victims as to assist those victims in returning to an adaptive level of functioning and to prevent or mitigate the potential negative impact of psychological trauma" (Everly & Mitchell, 1999; Flannery & Everly, 2000, p. 120). It is psychological first aid, not therapy; therefore, by its nature, it is brief and temporary.

Crisis intervention is based partly on principles developed in the military (Kardiner & Spiegel, 1947), namely immediacy, proximity, and expectancy (Flannery & Everly, 2000). In other words, any intervention during a crisis should be immediate, close to the time and location of the event, and should instill a sense of expectancy of recovery (Everly, Flannery, & Mitchell, 2000; Flannery & Everly, 2000). This sense of expectancy is very important, in light of evidence showing that those individuals who perceive that they will persevere through the crisis and return to a level of adaptive functioning tend to fare better than those who do not.

For example, in World War II, the British and French had a different way of treating their "combat stress" casualties. When an individual was identified as having symptoms, the British sent the person away from the front line in order to be treated in hospitals in another country. It was found that the majority of those soldiers did not return to duty. However, the French treated their soldiers closer to the front and subsequently returned their soldiers to duty faster and more frequently. The British later started labeling those individuals who exhibited post-traumatic stress symptoms as "Not Yet Diagnosed Nervous" or "NYDN," and found those labeled this way, instead of "combat stress casualty" on Field Medical Cards, were more likely to return to duty.

This sense of expectancy is apparent in training as well. Cornum, Matthews, and Seligman (2011) cited a study that surveyed 100 West Point Academy cadets in their junior and senior years about their understanding of PTSD and Post-Traumatic Growth (PTG). PTG is conceptualized as the transformation that can occur after enduring a critical incident, whereby an individual transcends his/her previous normal level of functioning. The person may have a new appreciation of life, have different priorities, more spiritual growth and personal strength, stronger relationships and recognize new possibilities for themselves (Tedeschi & Calhoun, 2004). The study demonstrated 80 percent of those surveyed indicated they understood PTSD, but only 2 percent were confident in their understanding of PTG. Surprisingly, only 22 percent of the participants believed that they would not develop PTSD at some point in their careers. Since the literature suggests that the majority of people recover from critical incidents (Bonanno, 2004), enhanced pre-crisis training for those populations that are more likely to be exposed to trauma (i.e., first responders and military personnel) might serve as a preventive measure. Further, crisis intervention techniques are of paramount importance to facilitate this understanding and recovery process.

Caplan (1961, 1964) conceptualized the goals of crisis intervention to include stabilization, mitigation of acute symptomatology, and restoration of adaptive function, or most importantly, facilitation of access to another level of care when needed (i.e., triage) (Everly & Mitchell, 1999, 2000; Flannery & Everly, 2000). In addition, other basic principles are important in crisis intervention. These include: (1) assisting the individual and group in understanding the event that occurred, (2) instilling problem-solving skills and resources, and (3) facilitating reliance on the self (Everly & Mitchell, 1999; Flannery, 1998; Flannery & Everly, 2000; Robinson & Mitchell, 1995; Wollman, 1993). These strategies have been identified as integral components of building resiliency (Antonovksy, 1990), specifically, police officer resiliency (Paton et al., 2008), as well as comprising a significant component of evidence-based treatments for PTSD, such as Cognitive Processing Therapy (CPT; Resick, Monson, & Chard, 2008). One of the bases for CPT is that during a trauma, a person's memory of the event becomes fragmented. As a result, key details are omitted or rendered incoherent, thus complicating a true understanding of the event. Through exercises developed in CPT (e.g., writing the Impact Statement, reviewing it in session, and ABC worksheets), the individual starts to make sense of the event and the memories become more cohesive.

The next logical step is to ascertain the manner in which crisis intervention is supposed to accomplish its goals. It has been posited that group dynamics in therapy (Yalom, 1985) are mechanisms of change. These dynamics include cohesion, sharing of information, and catharsis. In other words, through the group process, individuals develop a sharing of ideas and information, become more cohesive over time, and openly discuss events in their lives. This is very similar to what occurs in crisis intervention, particularly in such group interventions as Critical Incident Stress Debriefing (CISD). The opportunity to discuss both positive and negative reactions to an incident has been identified as critical for recovery and resiliency (Everly, Smith, & Welzant, 2008). Further, providing a platform for social support, especially in cultures such as law enforcement and the military, where this is solidified in their identity, assists in the facilitation of recovery (Carver & Connor-Smith, 2010; Seligman & Csikszentmihalyi, 2000; Solomon, Mikulincer, & Hobfoll, 1987; Yates & Masten, 2004). Additionally, it allows the sharing of information with others and promotes unit cohesion. Finally, psychoeducation is a key component of crisis intervention and provides individuals and groups with the opportunity to learn and practice adaptive coping skills.

It is important to note where crisis intervention can be involved in the spectrum of intervention. Primary intervention consists of strategies aimed at reducing the possibility of symptoms. The individuals targeted for these types of interventions have not experienced any risk factors for symptoms. For example, smoking cessation campaigns targeted at teenagers who have not started smoking are considered primary interventions. Secondary intervention consists of strategies aimed at reducing symptoms and/or mitigating any further risk in a population of individuals or groups already experiencing early symptomatology. Further education on lung cancer and providing early smoking cessation classes to teenagers already smoking can be beneficial secondary intervention practices. Finally, tertiary intervention consists of strategies aimed at a population or group already experiencing symptomatology and attempting treatment. Psychotherapy tends to be a prime example of tertiary intervention. CISM is the foundation of secondary intervention, where risk (e.g., those exposed to a critical incident) has already been identified and skills are implemented to mitigate symptom severity. When primary intervention is practiced, individuals receive information on warning signs of developing issues and coping skills; however, the information may become lost in times of crisis. Secondary intervention affords people the opportunity to understand and implement those coping skills learned in primary intervention and allows them to find what works for them, especially when it is likely they will encounter additional critical incidents in the future.

Critical Incident Stress Management (CISM)

Critical Incident Stress Management (CISM) is the umbrella term to describe the various interventions offered in this model of crisis intervention. CISM is a "comprehensive crisis intervention system consisting of multiple crisis intervention components which functionally span the entire temporal spectrum of a crisis" (Flannery & Everly, 2000, p. 4). In other words, depending on the reaction and the time since the event, different crisis intervention strategies can be implemented. The other interventions comprising CISM include: pre-incident preparation, large-group/disaster interventions (demobilizations, crisis management briefings), small group crisis intervention (defusing and CISD), one-on-one crisis intervention, pastoral crisis intervention, family crisis intervention, and follow-up care (see Everly & Mitchell, 2000). Pre-incident preparation enables an organization to provide education on critical incidents and stress management. Demobilizations and Crisis Management Briefings (CMBs) are large group interventions whereby individuals and groups receive information about the incident and stress management to deal with the acute crisis, and facilitate "psychological decompression" (Everly & Mitchell, 1999). These large group interventions are typically conducted following large-scale events, such as natural disaster, terrorism, and school violence. Both of these large group interventions can be conducted any time after crisis, with demobilizations recommended to be utilized when people are leaving their shift. Further, Everly and Mitchell (1999) define them as "event driven," meaning as a result of the event, these interventions are provided.

Defusings are classified as a small group intervention, typically performed within 12 hours after a crisis, and are "symptom driven," meaning if a group is reporting symptoms, this intervention can be implemented.

The main focus of a defusing is triage and "symptom mitigation" (Everly & Mitchell, 1999). The individual crisis intervention ("1:1") and family CISM can be conducted at any point post-critical incident and consist of the same goals and focus as outlined above. Finally, it is always recommended to conduct follow-up care and referrals (if needed) in order to "check-in" and triage.

Critical Incident Stress Debriefing (CISD)

CISM has been frequently confused in the literature with Critical Incident Stress Debriefing (CISD), which is only one component of the entire CISM model, and should never be used as a "stand-alone intervention" (Mitchell & Everly, 1997). The CISD is a group crisis intervention strategy that is highly structured, consisting of seven stages and is typically performed 2–14 days after a critical incident (Mitchell, 1983; Mitchell & Everly, 1997). The seven stages include introduction, fact, thought, reaction, symptom, teaching, and re-entry phases (Table 5.1).

The purpose of the introduction and fact phases is to allow CISM team members to explain the use of the CISD and for the participants to explain the critical incident from their own perspective. When moving through the thought and reaction phases, participants are asked to describe the cognitive and emotional reactions that they experienced and to identify the most difficult aspects of the incident. Afterwards, there is a transition to

Table 5.1 The seven stages of CISM

Phase	Goals
Introduction	Explain intervention process, introduce members, set goals for the intervention
Fact	Gather details from the event from each individual's point of view
Thought	Individuals are provided with the opportunity to discuss their cognitive "thoughts" about the incident, both during and after the event
Reaction	Individuals discuss the most difficult part of the incident and are provided the opportunity to discuss emotional reactions
Symptom	Individuals are able to discuss the distress they may be experiencing since the incident
Teaching	Psychoeducation
Re-Entry	Closing remarks, discuss reintegration

Note: Above is summary only, see Mitchell and Everly (2001).

the symptom and teaching phases where participants discuss their level of distress and functioning and psychoeducation is provided on what experiences to expect, how to cope and where to find further services. Finally, in the re-entry phase, team members prepare for "closure," answer any questions, and facilitate return-to-duty. Throughout this process, triage remains an invaluable component to assess who may need additional services. One of the interesting facets of the CISD is that it is designed to facilitate "closure" for those involved. Further, besides the other mechanisms of change described above, an important component of such an intervention (and any intervention in the CISM system) is to allow for triage to identify those needing additional resources and care (Everly & Mitchell, 2000).

Review of Research

History

The ever-evolving field of crisis intervention has had a significant history, as the foundational principles are not new. As previously mentioned, many of these principles were derived from work with the military. The effects of war have been duly noted since the mid-17th century, if not earlier. At this point in time, the symptoms of depression and anxiety exhibited by soldiers were known as "nostalgia," based on the belief that the cause of these symptoms was simply homesickness. In the Civil War, the term "soldier's heart" was used to delineate the cardiac symptoms presented by combat soldiers. However, it was in 1905 that the Russian Army started noticing significant losses due to a "neuropsychiatric illness," also known as "battle fatigue." It was then that the development of treatment close to the front lines emerged. In World War I, soldiers were presenting with strange symptoms including confusion, blindness, muteness, and at times, paralysis. Termed "shell shock," it was apparent that these symptoms were not necessarily associated with concussion but with a mental breakdown; therefore, the name was more aptly changed to "war neurosis." When soldiers presented with these symptoms, they were sent to Britain, far away from the front lines. However, the French started treating their "combat stress casualties" (as they called them) close to the front lines in rest camps, resulting in higher return-to-duty rates than the British. It was also in WWI where it was recognized that providing early psychological interventions could mitigate psychiatric symptoms (Everly, 1999; Salmon, 1919). Treatment close to the front lines included rest, reassurance, and the expectation that individuals would return to duty.

Artiss (1963) discussed the ideas of immediacy, proximity, and expectancy in dealing with soldiers in acute crisis in World War II. However, lessons from WWI were lost when those labeled "psychoneurosis" were sent away from front lines for treatment. However, soldiers presenting with traumatic stress symptoms were later labeled as suffering from "combat exhaustion" and were then treated near the front lines in "exhaustion centers," resulting in 70 percent return-to-duty rates within 72 hours and 20 percent returning to limited duty. Additionally, Historical Group Debriefings (HGD) were developed by Brigadier General Marshall with the purpose of obtaining a historical account of combat. Marshall believed that discussing the events in detail and in chronological order was helpful in facilitating an understanding of events from others' perspectives, and in building unit morale. A similar rationale is linked to modern CISM concepts, in particular, CISD. However, the HGD was not psychoeducational, and, therefore, was missing a key component useful for fostering adaptive coping strategies to critical incidents. Further, Lindemann (1944) noted that the use of early psychological intervention for grief symptoms may be beneficial based on his work in the tragedy of the Cocoanut Grove Night Club fire in 1945. His ideas "marked the beginning of the 'modern age' of crisis intervention" (see discussion by Everly, 1999, p. 3).

The evidence for forward intervention (i.e., treating stress reactions near the front lines and in close time proximity from the event) in the military continued during the Korean War, which saw better post-trauma return-to-duty rates than WWII. Poor record-keeping during the Vietnam War, combined with difficulties in treatment, reintegration, and public perception, caused problems in assessing return-to-duty rates and psychiatric morbidity. However, from the 1950s through the 1970s in America, suicide prevention and crisis intervention proliferated. Additionally, the use of nonphysicians, such as paraprofessionals or peer counselors, emerged as a new trend which has had a profound impact on mental health crisis intervention today in law enforcement (Carkhuff & Truax, 1965; Durlak, 1979; Levenson & Dwyer, 2003).

It was not until 1980 that PTSD was first recognized as a distinct syndrome in the third edition of *the Diagnostic and Statistical Manual of Mental Disorders* (DSM-III). And it was in 1982 that CISD was first used for emergency responders as a result of the Air Florida 90 crash in the Potomac River (Everly, 1999). In the early 1990s, the American Red Cross established their role in disaster mental health. Later in the decade, the Occupational Safety and Health Administration (OSHA) made the recommendation that employers should start providing crisis intervention and violence prevention programs for their employees (Everly, 1999). Since then, a whole host of events, including both man-made and natural disasters, have provided an opportunity for early psychological intervention (EPI) to be utilized and studied. The crisis intervention models have been adapted to various settings to include law enforcement, military, health services, airlines, schools, and even private companies (Robinson, 2008). And the controversy over its use and effectiveness, particularly over the CISM and CISD models, has continued for over two decades.

The Research and Controversy, Part I: The Positive Reviews

There have been numerous reports of the utility and efficacy of CISM and the CISD process. It is the objective here to report on some of these articles, discuss the methodological challenges in investigating such a model, and then review aspects that should be considered when examining research and implementing the interventions.

The utilization of crisis intervention strategies has been demonstrated in a variety of settings. Researchers initially demonstrated effectiveness in psychiatric populations with a reduction in psychiatric symptoms and need for more intensive services, and an increase in coping strategies (Decker & Stubblebine, 1972; Langsley, Machotka, & Flomenhaft, 1971; Parad & Parad, 1968). In one meta-analytic study, Stapleton, Lating, Kirkhart, and Everly (2006) noted positive results in medical patients. They found that crisis intervention had a significant impact on anxiety and posttraumatic stress symptoms, and that the focus should be on providing multiple-session intervention conducted by trained personnel. Supportive counseling has been associated with decreased levels of anxiety, compared to controls, in relatives of hospital patients (Bunn & Clarke, 1979). More recently, in the disaster mental health literature, it was demonstrated that crisis intervention strategies provided by employers after the World Trade Center disaster on September 11, 2001 reduced impairment indicators, such as binge drinking, alcohol dependence, symptoms of PTSD, depression, anxiety, and physical complaints (Boscarino, Adams, & Figley, 2005). In this particular study, crisis intervention included brief sessions based on psychoeducation to include information about stress, coping resources, relaxation techniques, as well as a cognitive component (i.e., negative thoughts, positive thoughts) and how to handle difficult emotions. Most individuals reported attending one to three sessions conducted by a mental health professional. The crisis intervention strategies utilized in these studies include providing "directive support" (Everly, 1999) and psychoeducation.

A notable programmatic effort focusing on CISM was conducted by Flannery and colleagues as part of the Assaulted Staff Action Program (ASAP), a comprehensive, multi-component model designed to assist staff victims of patient assaults, that includes pre-crisis preparation. The program has demonstrated success as indicated by decreases in assaults on staff, disability claims, turnover rates, and use of sick time (Flannery, 1998, 1999, 2000; Flannery, Penk, & Corrigan, 1999). The ASAP's utilization of a more comprehensive and integrated intervention model has been associated with better outcomes than use of a single intervention alone, like that of CISM (Richards, 2001).

The impact of CISD was studied in a randomized controlled trial (RCT) for a group of bank robbery victims (Campfield & Hills, 2001).

One group of bank employees received a CISD less than ten hours after the event, while others had the intervention more than 48 hours later. Results indicated that those who received the early CISD had a reduction in stress symptoms over the course of two weeks. In a similar study, Leeman-Conley (1990) evaluated Australian bank employees after receiving one year without and one year with a CISM program. This program was a comprehensive, multi-intervention CISM program, entitled the "Post Hold-Up Support Program." The comprehensive nature of such a program is one that has been advocated by CISM proponents for years. In the year with the CISM program, there were more robberies than the prior year. However, there was an approximate 60 percent reduction of sick day usage and worker compensation claims.

There is compelling evidence for the use of CISD for disaster workers and first responders (e.g., law enforcement, firefighters, EMTs). In a study conducted with police officers (Bohl, 1991), those who received a CISD within 24 hours were compared to a group of officers who did not. Compared to controls, the CISD officers reported less depression, anger, anxiety, and fewer post-traumatic stress symptoms three months post-incident. Bohl (1995) conducted a follow-up assessment on the cohort in the previous 1991 study and found symptoms of anxiety and stress remained at lower levels in the CISD group relative to controls. Similar results were obtained with EMS personnel receiving CISD after a mass shooting incident (Jenkins, 1996). After a CISD was provided within 24 hours post-incident, semi-structured interviews and surveys assessing symptom report (SCL-90-R) and distress were administered to 36 workers. These individuals were assessed eight to ten days after the shooting and a month post-shooting. It was noted that after the first assessment, those in the CISD group indicated a decrease in feelings of helplessness, depression, and anxiety compared to controls. The Los Angeles County Fire Department conducted surveys of their personnel receiving the CISD program and found that individuals reported faster recoveries from events when they were debriefed than when they were not (Hokanson & Wirth, 2000). Specifically, 39 percent of those debriefed indicated a reduction in symptoms within 24 hours of receiving a debriefing. Comparatively, it was indicated that only 29 percent of nondebriefed respondents reported a symptom reduction within 24 hours. Further, 18 percent of those not debriefed indicated that their symptoms lasted three to six months, and 17 percent still reported symptoms over six months after the incident.

Crisis intervention strategies, such as CISD, have been implemented and studied in military populations around the world. In a randomized control study of British soldiers, Deahl et al. (2000) observed that those participating in the CISD group demonstrated significantly less anxiety and depression, fewer symptoms of PTSD, and a lower prevalence of alcohol abuse. The soldiers not only received CISD, but also a complete "Operational Stress Training Package," which included pre-crisis preparation. Deahl et al. (2001) also found less alcohol use in another CISD-treated cohort of British soldiers on a mission in Bosnia. A complete package including debriefing not only for soldiers, but also for family members has yielded positive results as reflected by a reduced marital discord (Ford et al., 1993). Meehan (1996) found that after implementing CISD with Navy personnel, participants tended to view these interventions as helpful in sharing information related to the critical incident with each other. During the debriefing process, important details about the critical incident is shared and clarified.

In a series of studies, Adler and colleagues (2009) developed and implemented early intervention protocols for the debriefing of U.S. military personnel. Adler et al. (2009) compared soldiers who participated in Battlemind debriefings with those who took part in small or group Battlemind Training, and those only receiving post-deployment stress education on outcomes such as depression, post-traumatic symptoms, sleep problems, and stigma. Battlemind Training is composed of both cognitive and skills education about the transition from combat to home. Specifically, soldiers learn how combat-related skills can be related and translated to their home environment. Additionally, soldiers are taught about common psychological, social, and physical reactions for combat and how to build safety and foster relationships when they return home. Battlemind debriefings are similar to CISD; however, the language and stages are adapted for the military culture. These groups were compared to individuals who only received a post-deployment stress education session. Results showed that those who attended the debriefing reported less depression and sleep difficulties and fewer post-traumatic stress symptoms. Lower levels of post-traumatic symptoms and sleep problems were evident in the small-group Battlemind Training participants. Finally, attendance at the large-group Battlemind Training was associated with a reduction in stigma beliefs (e.g., beliefs that seeking help would harm their career, worries about how others would treat them (Adler et al., 2009)). However, Adler et al. (2008) found different results in a randomized controlled trial of U.S. Peacekeepers. Compared to a stress management class, the effect of participating in CISD was minimally related to decreases in post-traumatic stress and aggression. Compared to a survey-only condition, those receiving CISD reported a higher degree of organizational support.

The CISM literature is replete with meta-analytic studies and literature reviews. The National Institute for Mental Health (NIMH, 2002) reviewed 17 studies that were identified to demonstrate the use of group crisis intervention, or debriefings. The papers included samples of law enforcement, medical patients, and robbery or disaster settings. Additionally, the studies were divided into individual and group debriefing. Most studies that were based on first responder populations and utilized a group format were favorable, compared to those that utilized an individual debriefing with medical and surgical patients. Roberts and Everly (2006) also conducted a meta-analysis of 36 crisis intervention studies. They concluded that crisis intervention, especially home-based interventions and multi-component models, such as CISM, is demonstrably effective. Specifically, it was found that crisis intervention that is focused on family issues was effective in reducing childhood neglect and abuse. The importance of follow-up or "booster sessions" were also underscored in this review. In other meta-analytic reviews, authors have demonstrated modest-to-large positive effect sizes for the effectiveness of CISM (Everly & Boyle, 1999; Everly, Boyle, & Lating, 1999).

Overall, numerous studies indicate that participants attending a CISD feel that it is "helpful" and/or that it contributes to a reduction in symptoms (Burns & Harm, 1993; Chemtob, Tomas, Law, & Cremniter, 1997; Dyregrov & Mitchell, 1992; Hanneman, 1994; Hokanson, 1997; Lanning, 1987; North et al., 2002; Nurmi, 1999; Ott & Henry, 1997; Richards, 2001; Robinson & Mitchell, 1993; Robinson, 1994; Rogers, 1992; Wee, Mills, & Koehler, 1999; Young, 2003).

The Research and Controversy, Part II: The Negative Reviews

There are a number of studies that do not demonstrate a positive effect on those who participate in psychological debriefings. One methodological problem is that "debriefing" is not standardized across studies. Some results indicate no effect, whereas others claim that there was a worsening of symptoms caused by the debriefing. One of the most significant criticisms of debriefings is that they have not prevented the development of PTSD (Harris, Baloglu, & Stacks, 2002). Bisson, Jenkins, Alexander, and Bannister (1997) conducted a randomized controlled trial of individual debriefing with medical patients with burn injuries. After 13 months, those who received a debriefing reported higher scores on anxiety, depression, and even PTSD. In another trial of road traffic accidents, Hobbs, Mayou, Harrison, and Worlock (1996) concluded that individual debriefings were harmful to participants as a result of an increase in reported symptoms. In a follow-up study, participants were assessed again and remained symptomatic (Mayou, Ehlers, & Hobbs, 2000).

Further studies replicate the finding that one-on-one, individual "debriefings" are not effective, and in some cases, may be harmful (Lee, Slade, & Lygo, 1996; Rose, Berwin, Andrews, & Kirk, 1999; Small, Lumley, Donohue, Potter, & Waldenstrom, 2000). Van Emmerik, Kamphuis, Hulsbosch, and Emmelkamp (2002) further provided a meta-analytic review of single-session debriefings and included studies that have reported a poor response. The authors concluded that single-session debriefings are not effective. Kenardy et al. (1996) investigated the use of stress debriefings on 195 first responders in Australia after an earthquake and were unable to demonstrate better recovery rates for those who were debriefed.

A widely cited review article purporting to demonstrate the ineffectiveness of crisis debriefings was the first Cochrane Report (Wessely, Rose, & Bison, 1998). This effort was designed to be an independent review of the use of debriefing as a means to treat trauma symptoms and prevent PTSD. The articles included in the review were single-session, one-on-one "debriefings" on mostly a medical population. However, the authors indicate that they were unable to generalize the results of this review to group debriefings or the use of this technique after a mass trauma. This is an important point, since this article has been cited as "proof" that CISDs are ineffective. In a follow-up publication, the Cochrane Report (Rose, Bisson, & Wessely, 2002) once again concluded that single-session, one-on-one debriefings should not be a part of a crisis intervention model, but they were unable to make generalizations to the group CISD format. Based upon their meta-analysis of 11 randomized controlled trials of single-session, individual/couple debriefings, Rose, Bisson, and Wessely (2003) concluded that the routine use of debriefings should cease and that more research on group debriefings is needed. Once again, this 2003 report is cited to support the cessation of CISD despite the fact that the studies only developed conclusions based on a single-session, one-on-one "debriefing," and cannot be utilized to draw the same conclusions about the CISM or CISD format.

Methodological Concerns

There are several methodological shortcomings in the research on crisis intervention. Several articles discuss the methodological flaws on both sides of the CISM controversy and argue for continued research (Bledsoe, 2002; Everly, Flannery, & Mitchell, 2000; Litz, Gray, Bryant, & Adler, 2002; Malcolm et al., 2005). Methodological issues include the use of randomized controlled trials (RCTs), reliance on self-report data, adequacy of sample sizes and control groups, lack of consistency in definitions, and the lack of understanding of what CISD, CISM, or any crisis intervention model is designed to accomplish. Further, law enforcement culture needs to be taken into consideration when implementing CISM and conducting research because the way in which officers view the intervention and the structure of their work schedules and tasks can have an impact on the efficacy of the interventions and research outcomes.

Proponents of randomized controlled trials (RCTs) argue that this is how the impact of psychological techniques should be determined. This approach is undoubtedly the gold standard in such research. However, while RCTs may be preferred, the subject matter of interest must be considered. For example, it can be very difficult to conduct a true RCT when what is being studied (e.g., critical incidents and the subsequent intervention) is highly unpredictable and requires flexibility in its application. By their nature, critical incidents vary considerably. Therefore, implementation and content of crisis intervention techniques will not be the same across events. Further, as Everly, Flannery, and Mitchell (2000) point out, more research is needed to ascertain the impact of different critical incidents (i.e., child drowning, line-of-duty death) and the way these may affect different groups (i.e., law enforcement versus civilians). Also, in order for a study to be empirically validated, the use of a control group and group randomization is needed. Some investigations have failed to achieve appropriate randomization. For example, it was found that participants debriefed in the Bisson et al. (1997) study had more severe burns than the control group. This would affect the nature and validity of results. Ethical concerns are raised when using control groups, such as withholding an intervention in order to do a comparison. Measures have been taken in order to ensure the ethical viability for participants and to ensure sound scientific research. These measures tend to include offering another standard-of-care intervention such as supportive counseling or a psychoeducation group to the control sample. Although adaptations to the CISM model may be warranted in a crisis situation to assist those affected by the critical incident, this may dramatically alter a research study (Everly et al., 2000); clearly, many kinds of crisis intervention research cannot be carried out in a laboratory. However, where RCTs are being conducted, preparation and care need to be taken in order to adequately design and implement research protocols in this area.

In addition, many studies have failed to obtain baseline data, including a history of prior psychiatric conditions (see reviews by: Everly et al., 2000; Malcolm et al., 2005; Robinson, 2008). This is important in order to ascertain the proportional effects of the crucial incident itself versus premorbid personality on post-incident symptomatology. Baseline data may be easier to collect with some populations, such as law enforcement agencies, which typically collect data on officers' pre-employment, academy, and on-the-job performance. Examples of such data include self-report, personality tests administered prior to the start of the police academy; performance scores at the academy, tardiness/absenteeism rates, and civilian complaints post-academy.

It has been argued that there is an over-reliance on self-report and subjective measures as outcome variables in CISM and debriefings research (Malcolm et al., 2005; NIMH, 2002; Robinson, 2008). Further, there is a concern that people may not accurately respond to these instruments because the critical incident is obviously more important than the assessment due to having to handle the various impacts of a crisis (Everly et al., 2000). In other words, their "minds are elsewhere" and focused on other priorities. Although some assessments may be useful in a clinical setting (e.g., Beck Depression Inventory), these instruments may not be useful in assessing an intervention in which the goal is to return an individual, or group, to a pre-existing level of functioning. Instead, behavioral indicators may be more appropriate to evaluate the effectiveness of CISM and CISD. Some examples of behavioral indicators include return-to-duty rates, substance use, and use of sick leave. Deahl et al. (2001) suggested that group morale and motivation could also be used as indices of the efficacy of debriefing. Although there is some evidence of a decrease in post-traumatic symptoms (e.g., re-experiencing, avoidance, and arousal) following some debriefings, it should be noted that CISD was not designed to prevent PTSD. Moreover, assessing psychiatric symptomatology violates the main tenets of CISM, which is that it is "psychological first aid" and not psychotherapy. The goal of crisis intervention is to "stabilize, reduce impairment, and return to function or move to next level of care" (Everly, 1999). The general goals of psychotherapy are symptom reduction, exploring affect, and possibly gaining insight and awareness into symptomatology. Assessing psychotherapy outcomes with an intervention that is not considered psychotherapy is not a valid or useful practice (Robinson, 2008), much the same as measuring the usefulness of a hammer in its ability to saw a piece of wood in half.

Another methodological concern is that numerous studies have focused on one-on-one single-session debriefings and concluded, based upon their results, that psychological debriefings, including group debriefings that were not directly studied, are ineffective and, therefore, should not be utilized. Further, such results have been erroneously generalized to CISM and CISD. First, as previously noted, CISM is a comprehensive, multi-component model that includes services from pre-incident preparation to follow-up care. Researchers studying "single-shot" debriefings are not evaluating a comprehensive system. Second, CISD is an intervention that consists of phases (Mitchell & Everly, 1997). Further, it is a group intervention and should only be used with groups. Therefore, the group intervention should be the research focus, rather than one-on-one single-session "debriefings." Unfortunately, this has not been the case in this area, where results of evaluations of single-session, one-on-one interventions have been generalized to the multiphase group protocol of CISD. Further, it is often difficult to ascertain the specific type of interventions that have been utilized in these studies, and there has been a high level of inconsistency in their definitions of debriefing. Not all debriefing models are the same. For example, the National Organization for Victim's Assistance (NOVA) model of debriefing utilizes the skills of a scribe whose responsibility is to document for the group what has been discussed (NOVA, 1997). Those who work with law enforcement know that this would not be appropriate for that culture given the frequent distrust of providers in general, and concerns about confidentiality in particular, not to mention the legal issues involved.

Further, Robinson (2008) noted that some studies have utilized a debriefing model with primary victims (e.g., burn victims in a hospital) without a needs assessment. Given the fact that CISM is a comprehensive model, and strategic planning is of paramount importance when implementing a care plan, the lack of assessment is in direct violation of this model. Additionally, there are models of debriefing other than CISM that may be more appropriate for nonfirst responders. Further, a comprehensive model has been demonstrated to be more effective than a single-session intervention (Busuttil et al., 1995; Dyregrov, 1998; Flannery, 1998). Also, it has been recommended that CISD be conducted when some level of closure is possible. The CISD may act as a facilitator of "psychological closure and reconstruction" (Everly & Langlieb, 2003). Therefore, conducting a CISD prior to when it is most likely to be of value is contrary to what it is designed to do.

The CISD was also designed to be used as a form of triage, noting when some individuals or groups may need additional resources. This is a goal of crisis intervention and does not negate the use or utility of CISM or other strategies comprising the model. Therefore, it is a violation of practice to conduct any crisis intervention technique, including CISD, without preparation and knowledge of symptoms needing additional care. And, it is crucial in this model to provide follow-up intervention when indicated. When facilitators are trained in the use of CISD procedures, they tend to be more comfortable and implement the protocol with more success than when they are not trained (Blackwelder, 1995).

Certain concerns regarding the utilization of groups also warrant mention. For example, Dyregrov (1999) outlined the "helpful" and "hurtful" aspects of groups that should be taken into consideration when using a group intervention. These issues were described by Yalom (1985) in his work on group psychotherapy. Despite the fact that Yalom was addressing more formal, long-term psychotherapeutic components, some of these same principles and group dynamics, such as group cohesion and catharsis, occur in groups of all types, whether they be conceptualized as crisis intervention or therapy. For example, it has been observed that group members tend to benefit from the processing of emotions and thoughts to the point that it encourages emotional support, the dissemination of information about the event, and subsequent coping resources. Additionally, participants may realize that they are "not alone" and may experience some of the same reactions as someone else in the group. It has also been argued that conducting a debriefing in a group format may be more beneficial for an insular culture, such as law enforcement, where an inherent "brotherhood" is more likely to emerge (Dyregrov, 1999). By contrast, negative aspects of group formats include the possible encouragement of a "victim mentality" and an over-abundance of self-disclosure which may trigger negative reactions in others, thus increasing the risk of secondary traumatization.

To counter these possible negative effects, several suggestions have been made. First, training and leadership are important when dealing with sensitive topics, such as what may arise in a critical incident. Leaders and group facilitators should be well trained in: (1) understanding the group process, (2) determining when to move from one topic to another, and (3) how to manage excessive emotionality. The ability to balance the appropriate expression of such emotion and to determine when additional resources (i.e., referrals) are needed is essential in order to properly facilitate a CISD. Homogenous groups are, indeed, crucial to minimize the risk of secondary traumatization. For example, a CISM team may choose to not include dispatchers in a CISD for those officers who were on the scene of a line-of-duty death because each group not only has its own needs, but also was exposed to different aspects of the event. The officers may disclose details that may not be necessary or appropriate for dispatchers to hear, and which may cause stress later.

Review of Issues

CISD critics contend that this intervention interferes with a person's, or unit's, normal coping mechanisms, pathologizes stress reactions, and fails to prevent PTSD. Much of this criticism is based on faulty research methodology, which is due in part to the nature of this field and content of study (e.g., it is impossible to predict when a critical incident will occur, the ethical problem of not offering services to a control group, and the inconsistent definition of terms, procedures, and outcome measures). Further, some of the frequently cited investigations do not specify the actual intervention used or apply a group intervention procedure (CISD) to an individual, an improper application of the technique. It is important to note that a crisis intervention system, such as CISM, includes a psychoeducational component, which serves to de-pathologize stress reactions to critical incidents. Further, in the full CISM model, there is a wide range of interventions in a comprehensive system, and the selection of a particular technique is based on the individual's or group's response to the event. Not every critical incident will call for a CISD. This intervention may be selected if the needs of the group will be assisted by its use. An additional problem arises from inadequately trained personnel providing the intervention.

Finally, it has been recommended that outcome measures should be redefined in order to fit the goals of crisis intervention (Malcolm et al., 2005; Robinson, 2008). If the goals are to increase stabilization, decrease acute symptoms, restore adaptive functioning (i.e., return-to-work), and facilitate access to care, then the appropriate outcome variables should include adaptability, coping skills acquisition and use, return-to-work, and other behavioral indicators instead of solely preventing PTSD. Again, psychological first aid is not psychotherapy. Could a byproduct of the utilization of a crisis intervention model be a decrease in PTSD symptomatology? This is possible, especially if we consider the fact that it helps decrease stress, increase coping skills, and for those that are experiencing a more severe reaction, facilitate access to more comprehensive services to reduce subsequent PTSD symptoms. It is suggested (Robinson, 2008) that basing the use of a crisis intervention system solely on a decrease in PTSD symptoms may be missing the point and goals of crisis intervention.

There are several considerations in the implementation of a multi-component crisis intervention model such as CISM. First, one must examine the first responder (police and firefighter) culture in general, and within the agency in which it will be used. There are advantages to using a system like CISM, which emphasizes development of a peer support network, within the law enforcement community. The benefits of utilizing trained peer personnel (paraprofessionals) has been underscored (see Sheehan, Everly, & Langlieb, 2004), especially in a culture where seeking formal, clinical mental health support is viewed as a weakness (Castellano & Plionis, 2006). Further, mental health professionals may be viewed as "outsiders" who do not understand the nature and challenges of police work. However, peers can provide initial support, thus serving as a liaison between officers and the mental health provider system. The first time an officer may be in contact with mental health could be after a critical incident. Therefore, it is important to establish a strong network of care, to include both professionals and paraprofessionals, to increase the likelihood that officers will utilize available services in the future.

Mitchell (2004) delineated elements of a successful CISM intervention program. For example, when establishing a crisis intervention team, there must be a well-established and defined operational plan, to include the team's capabilities, when the team is to be deployed, and how it will function. This may vary across teams. This plan must be well established and practiced to reduce the likelihood of disorganization or chaos when a critical incident occurs. A strategic plan should also be developed to assist the team in selecting the most efficacious intervention(s) to be used in response to the critical incident. Further, Mitchell (2004) recommends that teams meet frequently to role play strategic responses to different types of incidents that are likely to occur. If these skills are trained and rehearsed regularly, team members will be better prepared, confident, and effective when real-world events occur. Adequately trained personnel are crucial to providing effective leadership, innovation, and flexibility when needed. Mitchell (2004) also suggests that teams meet after a critical incident to provide support to their own personnel. These "debrief the debriefer" sessions can be very beneficial in maintaining the well-being of the team. Finally, networking with other local CISM teams is recommended in order to have additional or backup teams available to assist if needed.

An agency's command staff should be educated on the use and rationale for crisis intervention and be prepared to encourage and support the team's function. Education should include the various types of interventions that are available within CISM (e.g., CISD, defusing, Crisis Management Briefings) and how they can be strategically implemented in order to maximize beneficial and adaptive results for those involved. A frequently cited controversy is whether a CISD intervention should be "mandatory." Members of first-responder populations tend to deny any difficulties after a critical incident. If the intervention is made voluntary, it is likely that many officers will choose not to participate. Therefore, the utilization of peer support and educating command can be beneficial in fostering an environment where the implementation of crisis intervention strategies, such as CISD, is seen as positive and helpful. Hokanson and Wirth (2000) addressed this issue by calling debriefings "automatic" instead of "mandatory," implying that the intervention is associated as an "automatic part of operational procedures." Although a change in wording can effect perceptions, it is ultimately a cultural climate change that needs to be addressed and this process can be supported with professionally trained peers to bolster the use of such crisis intervention techniques within their organization.

Resiliency in a Law Enforcement Organization: The Role of CISM

Availability of a crisis intervention strategy that can foster and enhance resiliency is crucial in a profession like law enforcement that is often faced with critical incidents. Kaminsky, McCabe, Langlieb, and Everly. (2007) proposed that disaster mental health services could develop and implement strategies that integrate the concepts of resistance, resiliency, and recovery. *Resistance* is defined as an individual's or group's capability to defend against symptoms of distress and functional impairment. Law enforcement officer pre-incident training is an illustration of how this capability is fostered. And pre-incident preparation is a component of the CISM model. Pre-incident training could be implemented at the police academy level. Specifically, cadets can be trained in skills that are helpful in enhancing their performance and resilience. Asken (2005) identified several key tactical skills that are commonly utilized in sports psychology to build optimal performance in police officers. Some of these include: muscle control, mental practice, attention management, tactical breathing, and self-talk procedures. These skills are not only useful when an officer must respond to a critical incident; they can be practiced in other contexts (e.g., at home) as well. If these skills are rehearsed and implemented in both didactic and live training scenarios, they become more crystallized in an officer's repertoire of adaptive coping skills. This can help an officer build resistance to the stress and distress of a critical incident.

Kaminsky et al. (2007) define *resiliency* as the ability to "bounce back" or "rebound" from an incident. It is important to understand that it does not necessarily refer to an absence of symptoms; it is common to experience a wide range of responses to a critical incident. However, a person's or unit's functioning may not be completely disrupted, and they are able to handle the situation quite well despite some negative reactions. Crisis intervention techniques can promote these characteristics of resiliency. Finally, according to Kaminsky et al. (2007), the idea of *recovery* is the regaining of full adaptability and functioning, even when there has been a disruption and the presence of symptomatology. Crisis intervention techniques, as well as more traditional forms of therapy, can hasten recovery efforts for a quicker return to duty, especially since triage is a main goal of crisis intervention and part of the CISM model, and is included in each of its interventions such as CISD. Lating and Bono (2008) note that many of the "mechanisms of action" of crisis intervention are included under the rubric of CISM. These include information on stress management techniques, group cohesion, and social support. In many respects, the CISM model and its specific interventions (e.g., CISD) can facilitate a manageable understanding of an event in order for a person to integrate more effectively into their job and home life, which is a cornerstone of resiliency. This has been promoted in a model of police resiliency and expanded upon to include other factors regarding the law enforcement culture (Paton et al., 2008; Paton & Violanti, 2008). The utility of CISM for not only helping in times of crisis but also for establishing and fostering an environment of resiliency is a topic warranting further research.

Case Examples

The crisis intervention and CISM literature has showcased several case scenarios and their subsequent outcomes. Some key take-home points will be discussed here to provide a demonstration of essential elements that must be taken into consideration when employing an intervention program for the purposes of crisis intervention.

Tucker, Spaulding, Henry, and Van Hasselt (2008) provided an example of an "in-house" crisis intervention team based upon the CISM model with a local law enforcement department in South Florida. The Pembroke Pines Police Department (PPPD) joined forces with the Federal Bureau of Investigation (FBI) Miami Field Office for the development, training, and implementation of a crisis intervention team comprising PPPD crisis negotiators. The purpose of which was to develop a team that was solidified in peer support and able to be trained both as negotiators and as CISM paraprofessionals. In one incident, an officer in the agency was killed when she was hit by a truck while off-duty. Crisis Management Briefing (CMB) is an intervention within CISM designed to provide information on the event and stress management techniques as well as serve as a means for triage. The PPPD peer support network attended regular roll calls for a week, conducting these CMBs. A challenge for the officers, however, was the lack of officers in other agencies trained in the same manner to help in times of a critical incident affecting the officers on the team. Inter-agency training may be a key component in ensuring a network of peer support to be utilized when necessary.

The CISM model was utilized by the "cop-to-cop" program by the New Jersey Port Authority Police Department (New Jersey PAPD). Six components of the program were outlined by Castellano and Plionis (2006) as (1) acute crisis counseling conducted by trained peer personnel, (2) Executive Leadership Program, (3) the use of a multi-disciplinary team, (4) Acute Traumatic Stress Group Training Sessions, (5) the provision of a hotline, and (6) a Re-entry Program. The authors noted that the implementation of CISM was used only after assessing the needs of the officers and conducting a thorough review of the risks and benefits of CISM and CISD. There was a collaboration of mental health professional and paraprofessionals who offered one-on-one crisis intervention (not debriefings) and information on stress management, and who conducted triage over a three month period. In the Executive Leadership Program, a two-hour lecture was provided to management and staff of the PAPD to provide information and facilitate support for future assistance. A multi-disciplinary team, consisting of mental health professionals, was formed to assist workers 24/7 at ground zero and provide crisis intervention services, called "training" so as to reduce the stigma associated with such services for first responders. Two-day psychoeducational training sessions were provided (Acute Traumatic Stress Group Training Sessions) to help officers understand and recognize the signs of stress and coping resources with an emphasis on cop culture. Additionally, a 24/7 hotline was established to assist with further information and outreach. Finally, a re-entry program was performed in order to help those return to more "routine" calls on the job and their families. This program as outlined in this article demonstrated a comprehensive, multicomponent system of crisis intervention that was innovative and flexible. It is notable that a strict CISD protocol was not used; however, other crisis intervention techniques of CISM were modeled and adapted for the needs of the workers at that time.

It is also important to highlight the importance of strategic planning in developing and implementing a crisis management plan. The response is always based upon the needs of those involved and not necessarily the event. In other words, just because a critical incident has occurred, that does not mean a CISD is the only intervention that should be applied. As the Tucker et al. (2008) article demonstrated, CMBs were employed by peer-trained officers of the agency at roll calls. Additionally, "ride-alongs," where a mental health professional or peer support rides with an officer on patrol, can be a manner in which officers are contacted to ascertain the effects of events. One-on-one techniques can be utilized on-scene to let officers know that there is assistance when needed so as to not interfere with the normal recovery process. And the manner of success can be dependent upon the reputation of those involved in crisis intervention. Mental health providers need to become actively involved in the departments they serve so as to not only "show up" when something "bad" happens. Peer personnel can help facilitate credibility, but providers can continue to reduce stigma by becoming involved with all aspects of the department, not just when a critical incident occurs. Finally, all those involved in developing and implementing a crisis intervention plan need to be trained in the specific model they will be deploying. All organizations that are involved in crisis intervention have their own specific training (e.g., International Critical Incident Stress Foundation provides training in the CISM model) and those on the team need to be well trained, prepared and practiced to intervene appropriately. Proper supervision is essential.

Conclusion

Law enforcement and emergency personnel may be exposed to a wide variety of stressful and potentially traumatic events on the job. Crisis intervention techniques are a cornerstone of any program designed to assist first responders and their families. Critical Incident Stress Management (CISM) and Critical Incident Stress Debriefing (CISD), its subcomponent, have been among the most researched crisis intervention methodologies. This model has been applied in medical settings, with first responders, with military populations, and with a wide range of critical incidents, including mass disasters, assaults, and line-of-duty-death. It is important to consider that CISM is an "integrated, multi-component crisis intervention system" (Mitchell & Everly, 1999) which has been confused with CISD, which is only one component (or intervention) of the comprehensive system. The term "multi-component" in this context means that there are a wide variety of services that are offered to span the spectrum of care to include pre-crisis training and preparation, crisis intervention, assessment, and triage, and follow-up care. Any crisis intervention program has several main goals: (1) stabilization, (2) reduction or mitigation of acute signs and symptoms of distress, (3) restoration of adaptive functioning, and (4) triage (determination of need for access to higher level of care) (Everly & Mitchell, 2000). A crisis intervention system should employ characteristics of immediacy, proximity, expectancy, brevity, and simplicity. In other words, interventions should be early, brief, simple, innovative, and facilitate an expectation of restoration of functioning (and normalization of symptom presentation) (Caplan, 1961, 1964). These principles and ideas must be kept in mind when developing and implementing a model of crisis intervention for a police agency.

References

Adler, A.B., Bliese, P.D., McGurk, D., Hoge, C.W., & Castro, C.A. (2009). Battlemind Debriefing and Battlemind Training as early interventions with soldiers returning from Iraq: Randomization by platoon. *Journal of Consulting and Clinical Psychology*, 77(5), 928–940.

Adler, A.B., Litz, B.T., Castro, C.A., Suvak, M., Thomas, J.L, Burrel, L., & Bliese, P.D. (2008). A group randomized trial of Critical Incident Stress Debriefing provided to U.S. Peacekeepers. *Journal of Traumatic Stress*, 21(3), 253–263.

Antonovksy, A. (1990). A somewhat personal odyssey in studying the stress process. *Stress Medicine*, 6, 71–80.

Artiss, K. (1963). Human behavior under stress: From combat to social psychiatry. *Military Medicine*, 128, 1011–1015.

Asken, M. (2005). *Mindsighting: Mental Toughness Skills for Police Officers in High Stress Situations*. Camphill, PA: www.mindsighting.org.

Bisson, J.L., Jenkins, P., Alexander, J., & Bannister, C. (1997). Randomized controlled trial of psychological debriefings for victims of acute burn trauma. *British Journal of Psychiatry*, 171, 78–81.

Blackwelder, N.L. (1995). *Critical Incident Stress Debriefing for School Employees*. Ann Arbor, MI: UMI Dissertation Services.

Blau, T.H. (1994). *Psychological Services for Law Enforcement*. New York: Wiley.

Bledsoe, B.E. (2002). Critical Incident Stress Management (CISM): Benefit for risk for emergency services? *Journal Best Practices in Emergency Services*, 5, 66–67.

Bohl, N. (1991). Measuring the effectiveness of CISD. *Fire Engineering*, 125–126.

Bohl, N. (1995). The effectiveness of brief psychological interventions in police officers after critical incidents. In J.T. Reese, J. Horn, & C. Dunning (Eds.), *Critical Incidents in Policing, Revised*. Washington, DC: Department of Justice.

Bonnano, G.A. (2004). Loss, trauma, and human resistance: Have we underestimated the human capacity to thrive after extremely aversive events? *American Psychologist*, 59(1), 20–28.

Boscarino, J.A., Adams, R.E., & Figley, C.R. (2005). A prospective cohort study of the effectiveness of employer-sponsored crisis interventions after a major disaster. *International Journal of Emergency Mental Health*, 7(1), 9–22.

Bunn, T.A. & Clarke, A.M. (1979). Crisis intervention: An experimental study of the effects of a brief period of counseling on the anxiety of relatives of seriously injured or ill hospital patients. *British Journal of Medical Psychology*, 52(2), 191–195.

Burns, C. & Harm, I. (1993). Emergency nurses perceptions of critical incidents and stress debriefing. *Journal of Emergency Nursing*, 19(5), 431–436.

Busuttil, W., Turnbull, G.J., Nal, L.A., Rollins, J., West, A.G., Blanc, N., & Herepath, R. (1995). Incorporating psychological debriefing techniques within a brief group psychotherapy programme for the treatment of post-traumatic stress disorder. *British Journal of Psychiatry*, 167, 495–502.

Campfield, K. & Hills, A. (2001). Effect of timing of Critical Incident Stress Debriefing (CISD) on posttraumatic symptoms. *Journal of Traumatic Stress*, 14, 327–340.

Caplan, G. (1961). *An Approach to Community Mental Health*. New York: Grune & Stratton.

Caplan, G. (1964). *Principles of Preventative Psychiatry*. New York: Basic Books.

Carkhuff, R.R. & Truax, C.B. (1965). Lay mental health counseling: The effects of lay group counseling. *Journal of Counseling Psychology*, 29(5), 426–431.

Carver, C.S. & Connor-Smith, J.K. (2010). Personality and Coping. *Annual Review of Psychology*, 61, 679–704.

Castellano, C. & Plionis, E. (2006). Comparative analysis of three crisis intervention models applied to law enforcement first responders during 9/11 and Hurricane Katrina. *Brief Treatment and Crisis Intervention*, 6, 326–336.

Chemtob, C., Tomas, S., Law, W., & Cremniter, D. (1997). Post disaster psychosocial intervention. *American Journal of Psychiatry*, 134, 415–417.

Cornum, R., Matthews, M.D., & Seligman, M.E.P. (2011). Comprehensive Soldier Fitness: Building resilience in a challenging institutional context. *American Psychologist*, 66(1), 4–9.

Deahl, M., Srinivasan, M., Jones, N., Neblett, C., & Jolly, A. (2001). Evaluating psychological debriefings: Are we measuring the right outcomes? *Journal of Traumatic Stress*, 14, 527–529.

Deahl, M., Srinivasan, M., Jones, N., Thomas, J., Neblett, C., & Jolly, A. (2000). Preventing psychological trauma in soldiers: The role of operational stress training and psychological debriefing. *British Journal of Medical Psychology*, 73, 77–85.

Decker, J.B. & Stubblebine, J.M. (1972). Crisis intervention and prevention of psychiatric disability: A follow-up study. *The American Journal of Psychiatry*, 129(6), 725–729.

Durlak, J.A. (1979). Comparative effectiveness of paraprofessional and professional helpers. *Psychological Bulletin*, 86(1), 80–92.

Dyregrov, A. (1998). Psychological debriefing: An effective method? *Traumatology*, 4(2), Article 1.

Dyregrov, A. (1999). Helpful and hurtful aspects of psychological debriefing groups. *International Journal of Emergency Mental Health*, 3, 175–181.

Dyregrov, A. & Mitchell, J. (1992). Work with traumatized children— Psychological effects and coping strategies. *Journal of Traumatic Stress*, 5, 5–17.

Everly, G.S., Jr. (1999). Emergency mental health: An overview. *International Journal of Emergency Mental Health*, 1, 3–7.

Everly, G.S., Jr. & Boyle, S. (1999). Critical Incident Stress Debriefing (CISD): A meta-analysis. *International Journal of Emergency Mental Health*, 1, 165–168.

Everly, G.S., Jr., & Langlieb, A. (2003). The evolving nature of disaster mental health services. *International Journal of Emergency Mental Health*, 5(3), 109–115.

Everly, G.S., Jr. & Mitchell, J.T. (1999). *Critical Incident Stress Management (CISM): A New Era and Standard of Care in Crisis Intervention.* Ellicot City, MD: Chevron Publishing.

Everly, G.S., Jr. & Mitchell, J.T. (2000). The debriefing "controversy" and crisis intervention: A review of lexical and substantive issues. *International Journal of Emergency Mental Health*, 2(4), 211–225.

Everly, G.S., Jr., Boyle, S., & Lating, J.M. (1999). Effectiveness of psychological debriefing with vicarious trauma: A meta-analysis. *Stress Medicine*, 15, 229–233.

Everly, G.S, Jr., Flannery, R.B., & Mitchell, J.T. (2000). Critical Incident Stress Management (CISM): A review of the literature. *Aggression and Violent Behavior*, 5(1), 23–40.

Everly, G.S, Jr., Smith, K.J., & Welzant, V. (2008). Cognitive-affective resilience indicia as predictors of burnout and job-related outcome. *International Journal of Emergency Mental Health*, 10(3), 185–190.

Finn, P. & Tomz, J.E. (1996). *Developing a Law Enforcement Stress Program for Officers and Their Families.* National Institute of Justice Issues and Practices: U.S. Department of Justice.

Flannery, R.B., Jr. (1998). *The Assaulted Staff Action Program (ASAP): Coping with the Psychological Aftermath of Violence.* Ellicot City, MD: Chevron Publishing Corporation.

Flannery, R.B, Jr. (1999). Critical Incident Stress Management and the Assaulted Staff Action Program. *International Journal of Emergency Mental Health*, 1(2), 103–108.

Flannery, R.B., Jr. & Everly, G.S., Jr. (2000). Crisis intervention: A review. *International Journal of Emergency Mental Health*, 2(2), 119–125.

Flannery, R.B., Jr., Penk, W., & Corrigan, M. (1999). Assaulted Staff Action Program (ASAP) and a decline in assault rate: Community based replication. *International Journal of Emergency Mental Health*, 1, 19–22.

Ford, J.D., Shaw, D., Sennhauser, S., Greaves, D., Thacker, B., Chandler, P., Scwarta, L., & McClain, V. (1993). Psychological debriefing after operation desert storm: Marital and family assessment and intervention. *Journal of Social Issues*, 49, 73–10.

Hanneman, M.F. (1994). *Evaluation of Critical Incident Stress Debriefings as Perceived by Volunteer Firefighters in Nova Scotia.* Ann Arbor, MI: UMI Dissertation Services.

Harris, M.B., Baloglu, M., & Stacks, J.R. (2002). Mental health of trauma-exposed firefighters and Critical Incident Stress Debriefing. *Journal of Loss and Trauma*, 7, 223–238.

Hartley, T.A., Violanti, J.M., Fekedulegn, D., Andrew, M.E., & Burchfiel, C.M. (2007). Associations between life events, traumatic incidents, and depression among Buffalo police officers. *International Journal of Emergency Mental Health*, 9(1), 25–35.

Hobbs, M., Mayou, R., Harrison, B., & Worlock, P. (1996). A randomized controlled trial of psychological debriefing for victims of road traffic accidents. *British Medical Journal*, 313, 1438–1439.

Hokanson, M. (1997). *Evaluation of the Effectiveness of the Critical Incident Stress Management Program for the Los Angeles County Fire Department.* Emmitsburg, MD: Executive Fire Officer Program, NFA.

Hokanson, M. & Wirth, B. (2000). The Critical Incident Stress Debriefing process for the Los Angeles County Fire Department: Automatic and effective. *International Journal of Emergency Mental Health*, 2(4), 249–257.

Jenkins, S.R. (1996). Social support and debriefing efficacy among emergency medical workers after a mass shooting incident. *Journal of Social Behavior and Personality*, 11, 447–492.

Kaminsky, M., McCabe, O., Langlieb, A.M., & Everly, G.S. (2007). An evidence-informed model of human resistance, resiliency and recovery: The Johns Hopkins Outcome-driven paradigm for disaster mental health services. *Brief Treatment and Crisis Intervention*, 7, 1–11.

Kardiner, A. & Spiegel, H. (1947). *War, Stress and Neurotic Illness*. New York: Paul Hoeber.

Kenardy, J.A., Webster, R.A., Lewin, T.J., Carr, V.J., Hazell, P.L., & Carter, G.L. (1996). Stress debriefing and patterns of recover following a natural disaster. *Journal of Traumatic Stress*, 9, 37–49.

Langsley, D.G., Machotka, P., & Flomenhaft, K. (1971). Avoiding mental health hospital admission: A follow-up study. *The American Journal of Psychiatry*, 127(10), 1391–1394.

Lanning, J.K.S. (1987). *Post Trauma Recovery of Public Safety Workers for the Delta 191 Crash: Debriefing, Personal Characteristics and Social Systems*. Ann Arbor, MI: UMI Dissertation Services.

Lating, J.M. & Bono, S.F. (2008). Crisis intervention and fostering resiliency. *International Journal of Emergency Mental Health*, 10(2), 87–94.

Lee, C., Slade, P., & Lygo, V. (1996). The influence of psychological debriefing on emotional adaptation in women following early miscarriage. *British Journal of Psychiatry*, 69, 47–58.

Leeman-Conley (1990). After a violent robbery. *Criminology Australia*, April/May, 4–6.

Levenson, R.L., Jr. & Dwyer, L.A. (2003). Peer support in law enforcement: Past, present and future. *International Journal of Emergency Mental Health*, 5(3), 147–152.

Lindemann, E. (1944). Symptomatology and management of acute grief. *American Journal of Psychiatry*, 101, 141–148

Litz, B.T., Gray, M.J., Bryant, R. A., & Adler, A.B. (2002). Early interventions for trauma: Current status and future directions. *Clinical Psychology*, 9(2), 112–133.

Malcolm, A.S., Seaton, J., Perrera, A., Sheehan, D.C., & Van Hasselt, V.B. (2005). Critical Incident Stress Debriefing and law enforcement: An evaluative review. *Brief Treatment and Crisis Intervention*, 5, 261–278.

Mayou, R.A., Ehlers, A., & Hobbs, M. (2000). Psychological debriefing for road traffic accident victims: Three-year follow-up of a randomized controlled trial. *British Journal of Psychiatry*, 176, 589–593.

Meehan, D. (1996). Critical Incident Stress Debriefing. *Navy Medicine*, 35, 4–7.

Miller, L. (2006). *Practical Police Psychology: Stress Management and Crisis Intervention for Law Enforcement*. Springfield, IL: Charles C. Thomas Publisher, Ltd.

Mitchell, J.T. (1983). When disaster strikes: The Critical Incident Stress Debriefing process. *Journal of Emergency Medical Services*, 8(1), 36–39.

Mitchell, J.T. (2004). Characteristics of successful early intervention programs. *International Journal of Emergency Mental Health*, 6(4), 175–184.

Mitchell, J.T. & Everly, G.S., Jr. (1997). *Critical Incident Stress Debriefing: An Operations Manual for the Prevention of Traumatic Stress Among Emergency Services and Disaster Workers*, 2nd ed. Ellicot City, MD: Chevron Publishing.

National Institute of Mental Health. (2002). Mental health and mass violence: Evidence-based early psychological intervention for victims/survivors of mass violence. A Workshop to Reach Consensus on Best Practices. Washington, DC: NIMH

National Organization for Victim Assistance (NOVA). (1997). *Community Crisis Response Team Manual*, 2nd ed. Washington, DC: www.try-nova.org.

North, C.S., Tivis, L., McMillan, J.C., Pfefferbaum, B., Cox, J., Spitznagel, E.L., & Smith, E.M. (2002). Coping, functioning, and adjustment of rescue workers after the Oklahoma City Bombing. *Journal of Traumatic Stress*, 15(3), 171–175.

Nurmi, L. (1999). The sinking of the Estonia: The effects of Critical Incident Stress Debriefing on rescuers. *International Journal of Emergency Mental Health*, 1, 23–32.

Ott, K. & Henry, P. (1997). *Critical Incident Stress Management at Goulburn Correctional Centre: A Report.* Goulburn, NSW, Australia: NSW Department of Corrective Services.

Parad, L. & Parad, H. (1968). A study of crisis-oriented planned short-term treatment: Part II. *Social Casework*, 49, 418–426.

Paton, D. & Violanti, J.M. (2008). Law enforcement respond to terrorism: The role of the resilient police organization. *International Journal of Emergency Mental Health*, 10(2), 125–136.

Paton, D., Violanti, J.M., Johnston, P., Burke, K.J., Clarke, J., & Keenan, D. (2008). Stress shield: A model of police resiliency. *International Journal of Emergency Mental Health*, 10(2), 95–108.

Resick, P.A., Monson, C.M., & Chard, K.M. (2008). *Cognitive Processing Therapy: Veteran/Military Version.* Washington, DC: Department of Veterans' Affairs.

Richards, D. (2001). A field study of Critical Incident Stress Debriefing versus Critical Incident Stress Management. *Journal of Mental Health*, 10, 351–362.

Roberts, A.R. & Everly, G.S. (2006). A meta-analysis of 36 crisis intervention studies. *Brief Treatment and Crisis Intervention*, 6, 10–21.

Robinson, R.C. (1994). *Follow-up Study of Health and Stress in Ambulance Services, Victoria, Australia.* Melbourne, Australia: Victorian Ambulance Crisis Counseling Unit.

Robinson, R. (2008). Reflections on the debriefing debate. *International Journal of Emergency Mental Health*, 10(4), 253–260.

Robinson, R.C. & Mitchell, J.T. (1993). Evaluation of psychological debriefings. *Journal of Traumatic Stress*, 6(3), 367–382.

Robinson, R.C. and Mitchell, J.T. (1995) Getting some balance back into the debriefing debate. *The Bulletin of the Australian Psychological Society*, October, 5–10.

Rogers, O.W. (1992). *An Examination of Critical Incident Stress Debriefing for Emergency Services Providers: A Quasi Experimental Field Study.* Ann Arbor, MI: UMI Dissertation Services.

Rose, S., Bisson, J., & Wessely, S. (2002). Psychological debriefing for preventing post traumatic stress disorder (PTSD). *The Cochrane Library*, 1. Oxford: Update Software.

Rose, S., Bisson, J., & Wessely, S. (2003). A systematic review of single-session psychological interventions ("debriefing") following trauma. *Psychotherapy and Psychosomatics*, 72, 176–184.

Rose, S., Berwin, C., Andrews, B., & Kirk, M. (1999). A randomized controlled trial of individual psychological debriefing for victims of violent crime. *Psychological Medicine*, 29, 793–799.

Salmon, T.W. (1919). War neuroses and their lesson. *New York Medical Journal*, 59, 993–994.

Seligman, M. & Csikszentmihalyi, M. (2000). Positive psychology: An introduction. *American Psychologist*, 55, 5–14.

Sewell, J.D., Ellison, K.W., & Hurrell, J.J. (1988). Stress management in law enforcement: Where do we go from here? *The Police Chief*, October, 94–98.

Sheehan, D.C., Everly, G.S., Jr., & Langlieb, A.M. (2004). Current best practices: Coping with major critical incidents. *FBI Law Enforcement Bulletin*, 73(9), 1–13.

Small, R., Lumley, J., Donohue, L., Potter, A., & Waldenstrom, U. (2000). Randomized controlled trial of midwife led debriefing to reduce maternal depression after operative childbirth. *British Medical Journal*, 321, 1043–1047.

Solomon, Z., Mikulincer, M., & Hobfoll, S.E. (1987). The effects of social support and battle intensity on loneliness and breakdown during combat. *Journal of Personality and Social Psychology*, 51, 1269–1276.

Solomon, R.M. (1995). Critical incident stress management in law enforcement. In G.S. Everly (Ed.), *Innovations in Disaster and Trauma Psychology: Applications in Emergency Medical Services*. Ellicot City, MD: Chevron Publishing.

Stapleton, A.B., Lating, J., Kirkhart, M., & Everly, G.S., Jr. (2006). Effects of medical crisis intervention on anxiety, depression, and posttraumatic stress symptoms: A meta-analysis. *Psychiatric Quarterly*, 77, 231–238.

Tedeschi, R.G. & Calhoun, L.G. (2004). Posttraumatic growth: Conceptual foundations and empirical evidence. *Psychological Inquiry*, 15(1), 1–18.

Tucker, A.S., Spaulding, T., Henry, J., & Van Hasselt, V.B. (2008). Critical Incident Stress Management in a mid-size police department: A case illustration. *International Journal of Emergency Mental Health*, 9(4), 299–304.

Van Emmerik, A.A.P., Kamphuis, J.H., Hulsbosch, A.M., & Emmelkamp, P.M.G. (2002). Single session debriefing after psychological trauma: A meta-analysis. *Lancet*, 360, 766–771.

Violanti, J.M. (2004). Predictors of police suicide ideation. *Suicide and Life-Threatening Behavior*, 34(3), 277–283.

Violanti, J.M., Fekedulegn, D., Hartley, T.A., Andrew, M.E., Charles L.E., Mnatsakanova, A., & Burchfiel, C.M. (2006). Police trauma and cardiovascular disease: Association between PTSD symptoms and metabolic syndrome. *International Journal of Emergency Mental Health*, 8(4), 227–238.

Wee, D.F., Mills, D.M., & Koelher, G. (1999). The effects of Critical Incident Stress Debriefing on emergency medical services personnel following the Los Angeles civil disturbance. *International Journal of Emergency Mental Health*, 1, 33–38.

Wessely, S., Rose, S., & Bisson, J. (1998). A systematic review of brief psychological interventions (debriefing) for the treatment of immediate trauma related symptoms and the prevention of post traumatic stress disorder. *Cochrane Library*, 3. Oxford: Update Software.

Wollman, D. (1993). Critical Incident Stress Debriefing and crisis groups: A review of the literature. *Group*, 17, 70–83.

Yalom, I.D. (1985). *The Theory and Practice of Group Psychotherapy*, 3rd ed. New York: Basic Books.

Yates, T.M. & Masten, A.S. (2004). Fostering the future: Resilience theory and the practice of positive psychology. In P.A. Linley & S. Joseph (Eds.), *Positive Psychology in Practice*, pp. 521–539. Hoboken, NJ: Wiley.

Young, A.T. (2003). An examination of the effectiveness of period stress debriefing with law enforcement personnel. *Dissertation Abstracts International: Section B: The Sciences & Engineering*, 64, 2902.

6

LAW ENFORCEMENT AND MILITARY MEMBERS

Engaging in the Community

Karen C. Kalmbach and Randy Garner

Military Members in the Community

Two things happened in the summer of 2012 that crystallized a nation's long-standing concern about military members in the community.[1] In July, the Pentagon released a report acknowledging military suicide rates had increased significantly and were continuing to climb. Every major news outlet reported military suicides had officially surpassed those of the civilian population; more service members had taken their own lives than were killed in combat in Iraq and Afghanistan combined. Then, in August, Army veteran Wade Michael Page walked into a Wisconsin temple parking lot and shot dead seven congregants as they prepared for morning services. Most Americans had access to these news stories within minutes; frequent updates posted daily. Media coverage of the temple shooting was so immediate, law enforcement was forced to beg helicopter news crews *not* to broadcast images until the scene was secured. Military suicide and "violent veterans" quickly became the most popular topics on blogs, television and radio, dominating news cycles for the next two weeks. The public was treated to a mixture of facts, political rhetoric, outraged grief and editorializing—conflated to produce an alarming profile of military members in the community.

These stories perfectly highlighted two extreme stereotypes of service members (especially combat veterans): unpredictably violent or emotionally unstable. "[T]he soldier," some have noted, "is being framed contemporarily, first as a 'criminal,' then as a 'victim'" (McGarry & Walklate, 2011, p. 900). The reality, of course, is that the vast majority of U.S. military members are neither. Bombarded daily with sensational news reports, the public, including law enforcement, is poorly informed about the real challenges of service members returning home, and the relative risk posed to the community.

How does such media coverage impact fear of violence and crime? More to the point—have reported events changed how law enforcement evaluate and respond to a call if a veteran or service member is involved? Putting aside sensational news stories about statistically rare events, what do we know—empirically—about the relationship between military service and mental health problems or violence?

Military culture is highly unifying and unique, yet members can differ widely in important ways (e.g., branch of service, era and length of service, deployment history, combat experience, and military occupational specialty [MOS]) (see Strom et al., 2012). With tens of thousands of service members returning to communities across the nation, the importance of providing accurate information to the public cannot be overstated. Particularly critical is the role of law enforcement; no other entity has such a broad mandate and so few resources. Police are indeed the "street corner" psychologists, social workers, protectors, and mediators—daily filling a role unlike any other in society.

This chapter seeks to assist law enforcement by providing an empirical review of research on the relationship between military service and risk of dangerousness—to self (suicide) or others (violent crime). The risks posed by military members are poorly understood and largely overstated by media reports. The following discussion will reveal that—notwithstanding the unique aspects of military culture and service—most risk factors for violence (toward self and others) *are similar for both military members and nonmilitary alike*. However, some aspects of military service (e.g., combat exposure) may impact the behavior and thought processes of service members who come into contact with law enforcement in the community. A better informed approach to the issues can assist officers in handling incidents, resulting in safer and more effective outcomes for all involved.

Military Members Returning Home

After exiting a highly structured and unique institution and lifestyle, veterans must successfully reintegrate back into their communities. Most, but not all, are successful. National estimates suggest that veterans comprise between 26 and 40 percent of the homeless population, despite making up only 7 percent of the current U.S. demographic (Copeland et al., 2009; Martinez & Bingham, 2011; National Law Center on Homelessness and Poverty, 2007). Mental health problems are a chronic concern and rates of some disorders in the military are three to four times that of the civilian population (Hoge et al., 2004; Tanielian & Jaycox, 2008). Homelessness, mental illness, and incarceration are strongly correlated in populations served by the U.S. Department of Veterans Affairs (VA). These conditions often result from other factors such as lack of access to treatment, medication noncompliance, substance abuse, and employment instability (Copeland et al., 2009; Erickson, Rosenheck, Trestman, Ford & Desai, 2008; MacLean & Elder, 2007; Pandiani, Ochs, & Pomerantz, 2010; Siegal, Li, & Rapp, 2002).

Many service members struggle to find gainful employment, sometimes facing the same unspoken fear and prejudice from potential employers that they often face in the community.[2] As might be expected, the presence of mental illness can greatly increase risk of unemployment and related financial problems (Elbogen, Johnson, Wagner, Newton & Beckham, 2012a). Post-Vietnam-era veterans have had higher unemployment rates on average than that of nonveterans, despite many government initiatives designed to promote the hiring of veterans. Recently, younger veterans appear to fare the worst (Humensky, Jordan, Stroupe, & Hynes, 2012). In June 2012, for example, unemployment among 18–24-year-old service members was reportedly as high as 30 percent (Rieckhoff, 2012). The importance of stable housing and employment is highlighted by a recent national study. Outcome data revealed that employment, stable living circumstances, having enough money to cover basic expenses, social support, and the perception of having control over one's life significantly reduced risk of violence toward others in a veteran sample (Elbogen et al., 2012a).

> I was pretty lucky. He could have arrested me. I was pretty belligerent, obnoxious . . . my friend told me later. I don't remember much about it to be honest. I was drunk, had been drinking all day. Unemployed for over a year. And then her idiot nephew starts setting off firecrackers right behind me. Like it was funny or something. Kid's lucky he runs fast. But that cop, you know, he sat down on the curb beside me. He knew. He'd been over there too. All I remember him saying was "You need to pull it together man, get some help. You need to fix this." He was right.
>
> A.J.

A Legacy of Trauma

Some have suggested that the violent and traumatic experiences of war produce troubled individuals, uniquely dangerous to their own communities upon return (see Bucher, 2011; Hayes, 2012; Holowka et al., 2012). Is this a valid general assumption? It is the case that some military members will return home with mental health problems. What is often overlooked, however, is the fact that some went *into* the military with problems. Research reveals a significant number of military recruits come from troubled and abusive backgrounds (see Benda, Rodell, & Rodell, 2003; Patrick, Critchfield, Vaccaro, & Campbell, 2011). For example, a large-scale study conducted by the Walter Reed Army Institute of Research found half of all soldiers surveyed reported physical abuse as children. A history of sexual abuse was reported by half of the female soldiers and one-sixth of the male soldiers. Some 34 percent of female soldiers and 11 percent of male soldiers reported a pre-service history of *multiple* forms of abuse (Rosen & Martin, 1996).

A history of early abuse has been long associated with later mental health and behavioral problems. Further, recent research has revealed that female veterans are three to four times more likely to become homeless and are victimized at higher rates than nonveteran females (Washington et al., 2010); both of these factors are known to increase the risk of acting out aggressively (increasing the likelihood of coming into contact with law enforcement). Additionally, some veterans may be struggling with the legacy of sexual trauma that occurred while in the military (Ellison, 2011; Kimerling et al., 2010). Recent government data reflects disturbing numbers of female (and male) service members reporting sexual assault in service.[3] A history of abuse or maltreatment is just one factor that has been consistently linked to later criminal justice system involvement as well as mental health problems.

> There's about a dozen of us heading to the gate. My friend and me, we're joking about the night before, how it was just like when we were in high school—we all had got messed up on some Hennessey the VIPs had flown in. And he just drops. He crumples like his legs lost power or something. I'm confused, I reach down for him—It's all happening so fast. I swing around, and this f**er has his rifle up under the chin of my Captain. This guy he had been walking beside, a National, puts his AK right here and pulls the f**ing trigger. My boy's down and now my Captain's helmet blows back, his face is . . . I can see inside his head . . . but he's still standing. Then he starts to fall. It's like slow motion, everything is happening so fast, but it's in slow motion. And everybody is shouting and pulling their weapons and pointing at each other and nobody knows who to shoot— these are the guys we spent four months training, eating with, living with . . . And I'm staring at him, this ANA guy, and I swear to God he smiles, and he looks just like my old man used to look after he'd beat the crap out of us, and this rage comes over me, hot, and the last thing I remember I'm running at him, screaming, firing, and I can feel his bullets as they go past my face . . . Been deployed five times now . . . Everywhere, anywhere, anytime. When you least expect it. You better be ready for it, if you plan to stay alive. Like that shooting in Colorado. If I'd have been there, I'd have taken him out. No doubt. S**t like that don't need to live.
>
> S.C.

The Wounds of War

The Rand Corporation has drawn attention to the "invisible wounds of war" in a study on the prevalence of post-traumatic stress disorder (PTSD), traumatic brain injury (TBI), and depression, in troops who served during Operation Enduring Freedom (OEF; Afghanistan) and Operation Iraqi Freedom (OIF) (Tanielian & Jaycox, 2008). Government data reflects increasing rates of these three diagnoses over a decade of mission eras (OEF/OIF and Operation New Dawn (OND)). Both PTSD and TBI diagnoses show a spike in 2007 (Fischer, 2010), interestingly, paralleling suicide rates (US Armed Forces, 2010). Anxiety disorders and substance abuse are also known to be elevated in combat-exposed military members (Wright, Carter, & Cullen, 2005).

Since 2001, more than two million U.S. troops have been called into the service of ongoing wars (Exec. Order No. 13625, 2012). Additionally, in a recent nationwide study of OIF/OEF/OND veterans, 27 percent reported more than one deployment (Elbogen et al., 2012b).[4] The current all volunteer force (AVF) faces a new and different kind of warfare. For those who have deployed to war zones, unlike any prior conflict, the pace, number, and duration of deployments is much greater than ever before. Operations involve smaller forces in combat theaters that are unconventional, unpredictable, and intense. The Centers for Disease Control and Prevention (CDC) and other agencies have devoted considerable resources to the rapid up-training of medical professionals, most of whom had no prior experience with the type of injuries sustained in OEF/OIF/OND (CDC, n.d.). Repeated exposure to improvised explosive devices (IEDs) and other high-order explosives has resulted in multisystem polytrauma injuries seldom seen outside of combat and which challenge the very reach of modern medicine and clinical knowledge. Nonetheless, due in great part to medical and technological advances, current casualty rates are much *lower* than those of any prior prolonged conflict (Fischer, 2010).

But surviving combat may be only half the battle. Some service members return home with invisible injuries—psychological and cognitive trauma not immediately apparent to others. The Rand Corp found much higher rates of major depressive disorders (14 percent) and PTSD (14 percent) in a veteran survey when compared to community rates; almost half (47 percent) had never sought treatment. Approximately one in five (19 percent) veterans reported experiencing TBI; more than half (57 percent) had never been evaluated for the condition by a physician. In 2008, these rates translated into more than 300,000 veterans with serious mental health or cognitive problems—fully half of which went undiagnosed and untreated. The picture is even worse for service members who have deployed numerous times—one-third were reported to have at least one disorder, and one in 20 reported all three (PTSD, depression, and TBI)

(Tanielian & Jaycox, 2008). Other research suggests rates of PTSD may be *double* those of survey data (i.e., closer to 30 percent) when multiple deployments and delayed-onset symptoms are considered (Atkinson, Guetz, & Wein, 2009).

Understanding Risk Factors

Researchers and mental health professionals refer to *risk factors* (or risk predictors) when calculating the likelihood of an event happening (e.g., suicide, violence). Risk is a dynamic probability estimate, subject to change across time and situation (see Monahan, 1996). A risk factor, present or absent in an individual's life, does not definitively determine an outcome. Rather, it is simply a factor that has been found to be reliably associated (or correlated) with certain outcomes more times than not. Some risk factors attain strong predictive power only when combined with another (e.g., serious mental illness *with* substance abuse; see Monahan & Arnold, 1996). Others, such as a history of violence, are consistently powerful predictors on their own. Indeed, past behavior alone may be the single best predictor of future behavior (see Elbogen et al., 2010; Monahan, 1996; Mossman, 1994). However, not all persons with a history of violence or suicide attempts will be violent or suicidal in the future; they simply have *a greater likelihood* of being so, compared to others with no such history.

Not all risk factors are equally powerful (or useful). Some predictors are weak or indirect, and others are only useful when combined with a number of risk factors in a multivariate group model. However, in general, the more risk factors an individual possesses (relative to protective factors), the greater the likelihood of adverse outcomes. Responding to any call, law enforcement must be able to accurately judge the situation and appropriately assess for risk factors that may be present. A better understanding of empirically validated risk factors will assist officers in making this critical determination.

Evaluating Risk—Avoiding Pitfalls

For law enforcement tasked with responding to real-time threat—often in the absence of any quality information—reliance upon *heuristics* is imperative. *Heuristics* are mental shortcuts, or rules, that are employed instead of inspecting every new situation and evaluating it on its own merits. This latter approach would simply take too long. Instead, we wisely learn rules: If the back door is ajar upon arriving home, we assume an unauthorized entrance. Heuristics may be thought of as rules that operate largely in our unconscious but are sometimes attributed to "intuition" or "gut instinct." For law enforcement, the use of heuristics may sometimes be the difference between life and death. But can such mental shortcuts ever backfire? Can the unconscious operation of heuristics be detrimental?

When citizens watch a sensational news story about violent crime, without realizing it, many come to believe their own risk of being victimized is suddenly higher than before (or more than crime statistics would predict) (Gilliam & Iyengar, 2000). Modern media has increased our instant access to, and awareness of, the wider world. Yet some events require background knowledge and a larger context to place the event within. Without this larger frame, events can be perceived as more dangerous, more frequent, or more pervasive than they actually are. In the early 1970s, two researchers noted an unconscious strategy that individuals employ when asked to make predictions about the likelihood or probability of an event occurring. In simple terms, *we are more likely to overestimate how frequent an event is, if we can easily bring to mind memories of similar events* (i.e., if such memories are more "available"). This is especially true for events that are dramatic, frightening, or in some way out of the ordinary. *Events that are remembered more easily are believed to be more common, and accurate, than they actually are.* This phenomenon was called the *availability heuristic* (Tversky & Kahneman, 1973).

The news stories reported at the beginning of this chapter are the kind that will live in the public mind for a long time and perhaps rightly so. The August shooting in Wisconsin was the fourth mass shooting incident of 2012—the public was rightly concerned (Lynch, 2012). However, very few, if any, reports placed these events within the larger statistical context. To do so would lessen the dramatic impact of the news story. Reports of crime and violence increase newscasts' ratings. The problem, of course, is that the same violent stories the public craves simultaneously increases their fear of violence and convinces them crime is far more prevalent and imminent than it is in reality (Gilliam & Iyengar, 2000). This is a phenomenon of which law enforcement is intuitively aware. Scholars have used it to explain why Americans persist in believing crime rates are high or increasing, despite data showing violent crime steadily dropping for four decades (FBI, 2011; Romer, Jamieson, & Aday, 2003).[5] Can professionals also be subject to the same biased thinking? The research would suggest so.

The vast majority of our 23 million military members are neither violent nor suicidal. Military members return home, reunite with family, struggle to reintegrate, find work or go to school, and pay taxes like their neighbors. But these everyday stories are not reported—a nonevent is not a reportable event. However, without the larger context, and based on nothing more than sensational news reports of statistically rare events, the public will be primed to fear military members as potential "time bombs" just waiting to "go off."

Although such violent and tragic incidents are rare, the viewing public does not have the larger context in mind when recalling the stories they have seen in the news. Nor do most citizens pause to calculate the odds of one act of violence relative to the total number of law abiding and peaceful military members across the nation. Additionally, because news stories typically settle quickly on one background factor—military service—the public is often not aware that many other (weightier) risk factors existed in the life histories of many offenders. Law enforcement, whose encounters with military members might be in less than ideal circumstances, may be likewise primed to think immediately of military members as higher risk or more dangerous than they actually are. This perception may unduly influence the handling of incidents involving military members. In some cases military members may pose a greater threat than a nonmilitary community member; however, in the large majority of cases, research suggests they are *not* more dangerous.

Risk Factors for Violence, Arrest, and Incarceration

General Population Risk factors

A considerable amount of violence risk research of increasing sophistication and scientific rigor has been conducted over the past four decades. Some studies have focused on correctional or psychiatric populations while others include only community members. Results suggest that many risk factors are shared in common: history of prior arrest/violence/criminality, substance abuse, history of childhood abuse (physical and/or sexual), deviant/criminal/incarcerated caregivers (especially drug using fathers), unemployment or employment instability, lower socioeconomic status, living in a high crime neighborhood, psychopathy, antisocial traits, young age at first offense/arrest, early maladjustment, high levels of anger/impulsivity/hostility and prior community supervision failure (see Table 6.1). Interestingly, serious mental illness alone (e.g., major depression, schizophrenia, bipolar disorder)—long considered to be a risk factor in itself—is actually sometimes found to be negatively correlated with violence, or elevated only when *comorbid with substance abuse or an angry/irritable/delusional* presentation. In general, simply having a mental illness does not increase one's risk of violence significantly; however, when combined with substance abuse, risk of violence can increase considerably (Benda et al., 2003; Douglas, Cox, & Webster, 1999; Monahan, 2002; Monahan & Arnold, 1996).

Risk Factors Unique to Military Populations

Exposure to combat and wartime atrocities has been associated with increased threat sensitivity, hypervigilance (Anaki, Brezniak, & Shalom, 2012), marital and family problems (Gimbel & Booth, 1994), aggression, PTSD symptoms (Beckham, Feldman, & Kirby, 1998), and risk of violent offending (see Bouffard, 2005; MacLean & Elder, 2007; White,

Mulvey, Fox, & Choate, 2012). Three possible links are explored in the literature: any military service and violence; combat exposure and violence; and mental illness and violence. The research is equivocal; no one factor emerges strongly. However, one relatively consistent finding over three decades seems to be *a small but significant relationship between combat exposure and increased risk of violence* in some military members (MacLean & Elder, 2007).

Current research shows higher rates of certain mental disorders (notably depression, PTSD, TBI) and related problems (e.g., substance abuse) in the military when compared to the general population (Hoge et al., 2004; Tanielian & Jaycox, 2008). Some studies have found these mental disorders, in turn, to be associated with increased intimate partner violence, general aggression, poor health, and interpersonal problems (Fontana & Rosenheck, 2005; Freeman & Roca, 2001; Rabenhorst et al., 2012; Taft et al., 2005). However, other research has found that risk of incarceration and interpersonal violence is better predicted by antisocial personality disorder (present *prior to* service), than by PTSD (Shaw, Churchill, Noyes, & Loeffelholz, 1987; Taft et al., 2012). Research with psychiatric patients found that it was the *co-occurrence of substance abuse* with a major mental disorder that significantly increased risk of violence (Monahan, 2002), and this finding was confirmed in a recent large-scale study of veterans with PTSD (Elbogen, 2012).

The Mischaracterization of PTSD in the Media

Although research does exist linking PTSD with a slightly increased risk of violence (see Byrne & Riggs, 1996), it is not consistently found to be a primary risk factor. *Many other risk factors often demonstrate a far more robust relationship with violence* (e.g., history of violence, prior arrests, history of physical abuse, substance abuse, psychopathy and antisocial traits) (see Monahan, 2002; Steadman et al., 2000). Nonetheless, much public concern centers on the condition of PTSD and the presumed tendency of those diagnosed with PTSD to "act out."

The defining core of PTSD is the experiencing of extreme trauma which is subsequently re-experienced psychologically and/or physiologically, with symptoms of persistent hyperarousal, and avoidance of recollection of the trauma (APA, 2000, p. 468). These features have been frequently misinterpreted and distorted by the media. For example, "One of the symptoms of PTSD," a *Huffington Post* blogger writes, "is uncontrollable violence" (Benedict, 2009). Unfortunately, this statement is both factually incorrect and grossly irresponsible. Nowhere in the definition of PTSD is there a criterion of "uncontrollable violence." Presumably the blogger is referring to one of 19 possible symptoms, namely, "irritability or outbursts of anger." This particular criterion is neither required for a

KAREN C. KALMBACH AND RANDY GARNER

diagnosis of PTSD nor universally experienced by individuals with PTSD. Equating irritability or outbursts of anger with "uncontrollable violence" is just one way PTSD is mischaracterized in the media, adding to the public's confusion and fear. The vast majority of individuals diagnosed with PTSD, whether military members or not, are neither violent nor unstable (see Appendix A at end of chapter for discussion).

A recent national study revealed that it was only when PTSD presented *with high levels of anger/irritability*, or, was comorbid *with substance abuse*, that risk was significantly elevated (Elbogen, 2012). Researchers hypothesized that veterans with PTSD who also report high levels of anger/irritability would have higher arrest rates than other veterans. This hypothesis was confirmed in simple bivariate analyses. However, when all risk factors were statistically entered into the analysis, overall probability of arrest was linked *more strongly to substance abuse and criminal history* than to PTSD or other mental illness. Interestingly, the authors discovered that, contrary to prior research, it was *not* combat exposure, nor PTSD or TBI alone that best predicted arrests. Instead, researchers found some of the *same risk factors as in nonmilitary populations* including prior arrest history, younger age, male gender, alcohol/drug abuse, history of family violence, and recent homelessness (see Elbogen, 2012; Elbogen & Johnson, 2009; Elbogen et al., 2012b; Skeem, Manchak, & Peterson, 2011).

These and other findings suggest that military service (particularly combat exposure) and related mental health problems *may* play a role in the increased risk of violence, arrest, and/or incarceration for a small minority of veterans. However, results also highlight the fact that most risk factors for most individuals are the *same for both veterans and nonveterans alike*.

Digging Deeper: A Case in Point

On a beautiful Sunday morning in August, Oak Creek Police Department in Wisconsin received an active shooter call. An unidentified male had launched an assault on a group of Sikh worshipers as they assembled for morning services. Ultimately, 40-year-old Wade Michael Page would take several bullets to the torso from officers before raising his own weapon and discharging it into his head, ending the siege which would ultimately leave seven dead and others wounded (Nelson, 2012). By the afternoon, the FBI assumed jurisdiction; news updates began featuring the term *domestic terrorism* (CNN Wire Staff, 2012). Within 12 hours, the shooter had been identified as an Army veteran (Associated Press, 2012). Tensions ran high. Just two weeks earlier the nation had reeled under the news of a lone shooter calmly opening fire on an audience in a darkened theater in Colorado, ultimately killing 12 and wounding 58. Many wondered aloud, on blogs and in interviews, whether he might be a veteran. He was not. Unfortunately for the family, his grandfather *was* a veteran, and the *Contra Costa Times* was quick to report this fact as though it were somehow relevant (Hennessey, 2012).

When a perpetrator is found to be a military member, this fact dominates. Many important questions related to other more important risk factors are not asked, and these critical details are often presented secondarily if at all. However, utilizing nothing but news reports, it becomes quickly apparent that a host of other common, and far more powerful risk factors for violence, are often present in the backgrounds of offenders who happen to be military members.

According to *The Army Times*[6] and many other news reports, Page served for six years, was never deployed to combat (although he is said to have told "war stories" to neighbors), and was demoted and discharged from the Army following a "pattern of misconduct" including substance abuse and being absent without leave (AWOL). Additionally, Page had criminal histories in at least two states (and possibly four)[7] primarily for impaired driving. He did not complete his mandatory drug treatment sentence in Colorado. A charge for impaired driving in North Carolina was dropped in 2010,[8] but he was fired from at least one job for operating a truck while impaired,[9] and is reported to have been frequently unemployed due to heavy drinking.[10] Page was also reported to have undergone recent property foreclosure, had a troubled relationship with a convicted felon,[11] and lost his mother at an early age. Perhaps most importantly, we now know that he was long affiliated with neo-Nazi hate groups. According to many interviews Page gave to Dr. Peter Simi,[12] (a "hate rock" music researcher at the University of Nebraska), Page began to endorse increasingly racist ideology after being exposed to the diversity he encountered in the military (CNN, 2012).

In the information found in news reports alone, Page's history reveals a handful of the most powerful predictors of violence and criminal offending— *none of which are related to military service*. Despite these clearly delineated and well-known risk factors for violence—news reports continued to highlight Page's veteran status. Similarly, when individuals with military experience take their own lives, news reports will often note veteran status first, before identifying other relevant risk factors in the deceased's background. In the case of suicide, as with acts of violence toward others, the *majority of risk predictors are similar for military and nonmilitary community members alike*. However, as the next section will address, based on emerging research, we now know that *a few variables uniquely related to military experience appear to elevate risk* in some service members (see Ilgen et al., 2012).

Risk Factors for Suicide

Law enforcement is in the unenviable position of being the only public entity which cannot say "no" to any call for help. Although not trained in a wide

Table 6.1 Risk factors for violence, arrest, incarceration

General population	Unique to military
• Past history of violence or arrests	• Exposure to combat/wartime atrocities**
• Substance use/abuse	• PTSD (with high anger/irritability)
• Younger age/young age at first arrest	• PTSD + substance abuse
• Male gender	• TBI (with aggression manifested)
• Lower socioeconomic status (SES)	• TBI + PTSD + substance abuse
• Lower education level	
• History of childhood maltreatment/abuse	
• History of witnessing domestic violence	
• Psychopathy/Antisocial traits	
• Parental criminality (esp. father's drug use)	
• High Anger/Hostility/Suspiciousness	
• Major mental illness* (with substance abuse)	
• Unemployment and/or Employment Instability	

* Major mental illness *not* found consistently to elevate risk; in some cases the inverse was found. Substance abuse in combination with major mental illness reliably increases risk of violence.
** *Not* consistently found across studies.
Compiled sources: Douglas et al., 1999; Elbogen et al., 2010; Elbogen et al., 2012b; Otto & Douglas, 2009; Steadman et al., 2000.

range of social services, they must nonetheless respond to all such emergencies. Currently, many agencies are beginning to implement mandatory mental health training or specialized response teams. Of the myriad of situations an officer can find himself or herself in (from the bizarre to the terrifying), one of the most personally challenging is a potential suicide incident.

In June 2012, a Pentagon report confirmed what many had feared—the overall rate of active duty military suicides had risen to an unprecedented level and was averaging nearly one per day—the greatest number and fastest growing statistic since such data had begun to be collected (Associated Press, Fishel, Leveine, & Winter, 2012). Confirmed suicides outpaced the number of troops killed in action. "While suicide remains a relatively rare event . . . it is increasing at an unprecedented rate and, unlike any other time in history, U.S. military suicide rates now appear to have surpassed those among comparable civilian populations. It is therefore critical that we address this emerging public-health problem," warned a doctor who works with veterans (Castillo, 2012).

Approximately 34,000 Americans take their own lives annually (94 per day) in the United States (CDC, 2010). According to VA estimates, 18 veterans commit suicide per day, totaling a disproportionate 20 percent of all suicides annually (Shinseki, 2010). Adding active duty suicides to this number, it becomes clear why the president himself has called for action issuing an executive order directing the VA to immediately expand suicide prevention programs and improve mental health services (Exec. Order No. 13625, August 2012).

Risk Factors in the General Population

Experts have identified a number of important risk factors for suicide in the general population (Pope & Vasquez, 2011). Historically, the highest rate of suicide in America was for elderly Caucasian males (36 per 100,000 in the 75 years of age and older group), although we are beginning to note disturbing trends in younger and racial/ethnic minority groups (i.e., 31 per 100,000 in 15–34-year-old American Indian and Alaskan Natives) (CDC, 2010). Compared to younger Americans, suicide attempts by older individuals tend to be more successful, having been more carefully planned and executed. For many elderly persons, long-term or chronic mental health problems such as depression or cognitive decline are suspected to be one important causal factor.

Lack of resources and physical illness, in addition to losing loved ones over time, are also thought to contribute to the high risk of this demographic. The top risk factors for suicide in the general population include: a history of suicide attempts, evidence or articulation of a specific suicide plan, and a pervasive sense of hopelessness (often a feature of major depression). Ill health, job loss or financial difficulty, as well as a history of mental illness or psychiatric hospitalization are risk factors that also contribute to suicide in the general population. Substance abuse plays a role, just as it does in the commission of violent acts, by reducing impulse control and long-term consequence assessment. Although females attempt suicide more often, males are much more likely to complete the act, typically using more lethal means. *Interestingly, some military suicide statistics stand in contrast to this general population suicide profile.*

Risk Factors Unique to Military Populations

Historically, military suicide rates have long been *lower* than that of the general population (Harrell & Berglass, 2011; White, Barber, Azrael, Mukamal, & Miller, 2011). Prior to 2007, there were proportionally more suicides in the general population than in the military; beginning in 2007 that pattern reversed. The Army, for example, saw suicides spike in 2004 and rates have continued to climb—from 9 per 100,000 (2001), to more than 24 in 100,000 (2011) (Black, Gallaway, Bell, & Ritchie, 2011). Any increase in suicide rates is of concern. However, are military suicide rates dramatically higher than comparable civilian populations as widely reported? Or is this yet another example of media-fueled misinformation?

Problems with Military Suicide Data

Military suicide data is often incomplete and opaque. Not all suicides are captured or identified. Not all branches of service report data or calculate trends in the same manner. Complicating the issue further is the fact that there exists no coordinated reporting process between the Department of Defense (DoD) and the VA (Harrell & Berglass, 2011). Furthermore, the majority of news reports tend to compare military suicide rates to general population rates *with no adjustment or statistical correction for the very different sex and age ratio makeup of the military*. Therefore, it is important to note that when *adjusted* general population rates are used, most branches of the military *continue to have rates modestly lower than or comparable to the civilian population* with only one exception: the Army (see Figure 6.1).

Young Males: A High-Risk Group

Males—especially young males—are at higher risk for many things, including violent crime, auto accidents, homicide, suicide, and substance abuse (Brooks, 2012; Park, Mulye, Adams, Brindis, & Irwin, 2006; Snyder, 2011). In the United States, males comprise nearly 50 percent of the population; however, in the military, 80–95 percent of service members are male. Young adult males (18–24 years) make up 10 percent of the general U.S. population. Of military members, more than two-thirds (67 percent) are under 30 years of age. Specifically, 18–21 year olds comprise 20 percent of active duty forces with an additional 47 percent aged 22–30 years. There is variation across branches. Marines are the youngest of all: 37 percent are 17–22 years of age (83 percent of troops are younger than 30). The average Marine, in 2011, was a 25-year-old Caucasian male (29 in the Army and Navy; 30 in the Air Force and Coast Guard). Caucasians comprised 75 percent of active duty troops (Howden & Meyer, 2011; Defense Manpower Data Center, 2011).

This dramatic difference in sex and age representation between the general population and military is important and becomes highly relevant when discussing the potential risk posed by military members. Apart from any other factor, a large portion of the military comprise a group with pre-existing qualities that place them in a higher risk group, *simply by virtue of being young and male*. Indeed, notwithstanding current concerns, given the overrepresentation of self-selected, risk-tolerant young males in the military, one might even say it is surprising that the rate of adverse outcomes is not greater.

With respect to suicide, males are four to five times more likely to complete a suicide compared to females (although females attempt more often). In other words, if the general population comprised 80–95 percent males (as in the military), the general population suicide rates would be much higher than reported. If age and race/ethnicity were factored in, rates might shift again (suicide rates are higher for Caucasians than minority group members). The importance of statistically corrected population estimates is addressed by some (e.g., Bruenig, 2012; United States Armed Forces, 2010) but typically overlooked by most media reports. The difference between demographically corrected general population suicide rates and noncorrected data is significant (see Figure 6.1). While there is no doubt that military suicide is a serious problem and worthy of directed resources, it is equally important to note that current trends *have effectively increased the averaged rate to that of the corrected civilian population.* Only one branch—the Army—remains above the rate for the general population.

Nonetheless, based on data from the past five years, it is clear that, for at least three branches (Army, Marines, and Air Force), suicides have increased. What factors contribute to these suicide statistics? Does the self-selection of primarily young males who choose to enter the military, especially during wartime, predict something about risk-tolerance or risk-taking behavior? Do the personal histories of service members contain risk factors unknown to official investigators?

Suicide by Branch of Service and Demographic

Suicide rates for the Marine Corps, historically the highest of all branches, more than doubled between 2006 and 2009 before dropping back down in 2010. Army suicides, the largest group in absolute numbers, spiked in 2004 and have climbed relentlessly since that time (Harrell & Berglass, 2011; Maurer & Watson, 2010). The Army comprises the majority (38 percent) of current active-duty military members, and, along with the Marine Corps (14 percent), are most likely to be "boots-on-the-ground" combat weary and bearing the greatest casualties (Fischer, 2010; Office of the Under Secretary of Defense, Personnel and Readiness, 2010; Statistic Brain, 2011). Although Air Force pilots and the Navy's Construction Battalions (Seabees) and Medical Corps also deploy in-country, typically, the Air Force, Navy, and Coast Guard provide supportive functions during wartime. Seemingly consistent with this, the Marine Corps and Army service members have the highest rates of suicide.

However, suicide data can be puzzling. For example, rates for members of the National Guard and Reserve units *who have never deployed* also increased. This pattern is also true for the other branches: in 2009, 52 Marines killed themselves; 31 percent (16) had never deployed. In 2007, a similar pattern was noted for the Army; of 115 confirmed suicides, 26 percent (30) had never deployed (Center for Deployment Psychology, n.d.). Increases in suicides in Guard and Reserve units may be the result of difficulty adjusting to "full-time" military service, but explaining increased rates in the never-deployed is more challenging. The reason has yet to be determined. "'Suicides have increased across the military,' Defense Secretary Leon Panetta told Congress . . . 'service members of all branches are killing themselves at the rate of about one per day. That is an epidemic,' he testified. 'Something's wrong'" (Zoroya, 2012). What risk factors are driving the increase in military suicides, and how do they compare to those found in the community?

Statistically, a majority of military members are very young (approximately half are 17–25 years of age), Caucasian (75 percent) and male (85 percent). *This is also the demographic which is currently at highest risk for suicide in the military.* However, even before the 2007 spike in suicide rates, between 1993 and 2002 suicide was the first and second leading cause of death for female and male veterans respectively (Center for Deployment Psychology, n.d.; Lutz, 2008; Martin, Ghahramanlou-Holloway, Lou, & Tucciarone, 2009; Office of the Under Secretary for Defense, Personnel and Readiness, 2010).

Many of the general population risk factors for suicide apply to both military and nonmilitary community members alike (Griffith, 2012). However, research has identified factors *unique to military service which appear to increase suicide risk.* The military risk demographic is much younger although still Caucasian. Recent evidence suggests that it may be military service itself—including *frequent deployment, combat trauma/violence, PTSD/ TBI, loss of colleagues, stigmatization/avoidance of help seeking, alcohol abuse, and greater firearm availability*—that are more proximate predictors of suicide in the military (Barnes, Walter, & Chard, 2012; Black, Gallaway, Bell, & Ritchie, 2011; Bryan & Cukrowicz, 2011; Harrell & Berglass, 2011; Mansfield, Bender, Hourani, & Larson, 2011; Martin et al., 2009).

Suicide in the Army

In 2007, the prototypical Army suicide completer was a young, unmarried, junior, enlisted Caucasian male. At that time, approximately 96 percent of military suicides were males and 81 percent were active duty; half had a *recently failed relationship* but the majority had *no documented psychiatric history* (6 percent had a PTSD diagnosis). Approximately 30 percent of suicides involved *drug or alcohol abuse*, and the most common method of suicide was a *firearm* (CDC, 2010; Center for Deployment Psychology, n.d.). In addition to major depression, both PTSD and

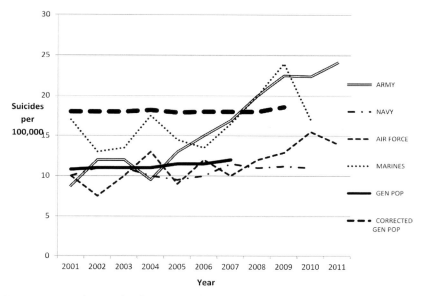

Figure 6.1 Civilian and military suicides by branch of service 2001– 2011.

Source: Reconstructed from multiple print and online data sources including Harrell & Berglass, 2011; US Armed Forces, 2010; US Census Bureau, 2012.

TBI are known to *independently* increase risk of suicide; other disorders are often co-occurring for those with a TBI diagnosis (Barnes, Walter, & Chard, 2012).

For law enforcement responding to a potential suicide incident, it is important to know that, for military members, *suicide risk factors may be more complex than those of the civilian population.* The stressful lifestyles of many service members (deployment, combat, financial issues, separation from loved ones) may exacerbate mental health problems which, absent military stressors, would otherwise be manageable. In some cases, the typical protective factors do not mitigate risk in a military population. For example, in the general population, close relationships such as marriage can be a protective factor; however, marriage has *not* emerged as a protective factor in the military (possibly because of the stress of distance, frequent relocations, and separation).

Certain jobs or occupations (MOS) within the military may expose service members to greater levels of trauma. For example, combat medics are often tasked with traumatic life-saving duties under severely compromised conditions and with limited supplies; many must deliver life-saving care even while in hot zones with no protection for themselves. Mortuary affairs and remains recovery personnel are required to handle dead and disfigured bodies and body parts on a regular basis. Death notification can take a toll on service members even when stateside. Infantry soldiers are often asked to perform a range of duties sometimes far outside their training, in unfamiliar regions and cultures, while taking the brunt of explosive-related trauma and other physical injuries which can result in long-term medical conditions or chronic pain and disability (see CDC, n.d.). Military police are often required to serve in dangerous and inhospitable regions, sometimes in close supervision of detainees who may pose a chronic, imminent, and dynamic risk of violence toward the military member.

A Dangerous Barrier: Stigma

Law enforcement must be mindful of the fact that many military members in the community may have no connections to mental health care providers or hospitals. Indeed, the majority are likely to have no record of mental health care documented while in service. For many service members, a visit to the Chaplain is the only acceptable, nonstigmatized route for seeking help. This avoidance of mental health providers is regrettable; with appropriate, timely and compassionate intervention, even challenging symptoms can be mitigated. However, the greatest obstacle to receiving assistance may be that military culture is not conducive to help-seeking of any kind. Indeed, many military members are reportedly advised that answering "Yes" to any post-deployment mental health questions will delay them from going home with their unit (a mandated psychiatric evaluation will be triggered). Even less appealing is the reporting of mental health concerns during service or deployment. Even in distress, most service members will avoid visiting mental or behavioral health services for fear of becoming socially ostracized or negatively viewed in terms of career advancement. In fact "concern about stigma was disproportionately greatest among those most in need of help from mental health services" (Hoge et al., 2004).

The prevalence of this widespread stigma virtually ensures minimal incentive exists for military members to answer truthfully when given mental health screens or questionnaires. As a result, many veterans may have no service records indicating the presence of mental health problems. Currently, stigmatization has been characterized by the military as the "biggest deterrent to seeking help"; a public commitment to reducing stigma and increasing awareness is now part of the mandate for all branches of service (e.g., U.S. Armed Forces, 2010).

> Do you know what it's like to hold a child in your arms that you've run over—on orders? But here she is, four, maybe five years old. Same as my daughter back home. Long brown hair, brown eyes staring up at me. Her legs are missing. Blood everywhere. Sgt is yelling at me to get my ass back in the Humvee, and the father or brother or someone runs toward us—he's screaming and crying, holding his arms out for her, and they open fire on him. Next thing

I know, I'm covered in his brains and blood, and his daughter's or sister's blood and the whole family goes insane. Howling, wailing, asking me "Why? Why did you do this?" It's chaos, and all I can think is that I can't put her down and I can't keep holding her. It's been four years. I still see her face every night I close my eyes.

J.S.

Law enforcement must approach each situation without prejudice, cognizant that situations involving service members vary widely and are impacted by individual circumstances. As a general matter, the vast majority of current and former service members are not dangerous to themselves or others. However, as noted previously, in certain situations, *especially if substance abuse or a mental health problem is involved*, the officer should attempt to assess for all risk factors including those that may be unique to military service. In the case of suicide, these *unique factors* may include: violence/combat exposure, repeated deployments, violent loss of comrades/repeated bereavement, stigmatization of help-seeking, greater firearm availability, legal or administrative problems, poor social support network/relationship problems (due to military lifestyle), and mental health problems (substance abuse PTSD, TBI, depression) (Table 6.2).

Engaging Military Members in the Community

Military culture is unique yet similar to law enforcement culture in many ways. In fact, this similarity may account for the attractiveness of policing as a career for many exiting service members. The rigorous training, intense camaraderie fostered by shared experiences in dangerous situations, and the hierarchical organizational structure is familiar to both law enforcement and military members. Law enforcement officers are encouraged to be aware of and to leverage those similarities to engage effectively with military members, especially in crisis situations. As discussed previously, much research has identified the impact of the "hidden wounds of war." Importantly for law enforcement, this has resulted in an abundance of information suggesting that some service members are returning home with problems which, if left untreated, can result in depression, suicide, substance abuse, or relational problems. In turn, these issues can lead to involvement with law enforcement and ultimately the criminal justice system.

Responding to the Need: Compassion and Training

Police agencies are gaining greater awareness of emerging issues when responding to incidents that involve a military member. Many officers themselves know the stress associated with witnessing terrifying or life-threatening events, death, and traumatic injury. The aftermath of such

Table 6.2 Risk factors for suicide

General population	Unique to military
• History of suicide attempts	• Frequent/extended deployment/ stoploss
• Specific plan; lethal means	• Violent bereavement/loss of colleagues
• Statement of intent	• Combat intensity/violence exposure
• Mental illness/history of hospitalization	• Greater firearm availability
• Depression/hopelessness	• PTSD; TBI; depression*
• Substance abuse (esp. alcohol)	• Alcohol abuse
• Multiple stressful events	• Stigmatization/avoidance of help-seeking
• Health problems	• Chronic pain/injury
• Single/Divorced/No children	• Poor social support/relationship problems**
• Lack of belonging (social/family)	• Legal problems
• Bereavement/Loss of loved one	• Disciplinary/performance problems
• Unemployment	• Medical/administrative discharge
• Older age (75yrs+)	• Younger age
• Male/Caucasian	• Male/Caucasian

* Although mental illness, including PTSD, is a risk factor for suicide, the majority had no documented psychiatric history or diagnosis (only 6 percent had a formal PTSD diagnosis).
** Marriage does *not* appear to be a protective factor in military populations.

Sources: Barnes et al., 2012; Black et al., 2011; Griffith, 2012; Harrell & Berglass, 2011; Martin et al., 2009; Pope & Vasquez, 2011; U.S. Armed Forces, 2010.

exposure can have long-ranging, consequential effects on an officer. Emotional numbing, heightened arousal, sleep disturbance, recurring visualizations or memories, and avoidance may occur (Hoge et al., 2004). An officer's typical coping mechanism can be impacted, resulting in behavior that is seemingly inconsistent with the situation. This shared experience can be invaluable in developing rapport with military members who may be in crisis. However, law enforcement should not ever presume to understand a military member's experience; it is much more effective to garner as much as information as possible from collateral sources and then seek to query the veteran himself or herself. In this way, careful and respectful communication can assist in the development of trust and credibility.

As first responders, police officers and law enforcement professionals are now being better trained and prepared to recognize signs of mental health problems in order to help military members receive needed assistance (Ritchie, 2012; Weaver, Joseph, Dongon, Fairweather, & Ruzek, 2013). Additionally, given the disturbing suicide data on service members, many agencies are providing officers with resource lists, including referral agencies and crisis hotlines. Several police training and intervention programs have been developed using scenario-based training, role playing, and group discussion to supplement other fact-based or resourced-based information. Such programs also include other emergency services personnel such as dispatchers, paramedics, and firefighters (Etter, McCarthy, & Asken, 2011). Law enforcement who themselves are veterans can be invaluable in assisting other department personnel understand and more effectively respond to incidents involving military members in the community.

Law enforcement officers responding to a call involving a military member may encounter an individual who has witnessed events that few others could fathom—except perhaps—a police officer. The training internalized by military personnel involves survival in a combat or hostile environment—not something that is typically encountered in the community, and not a skill set that translates well in the civilian population. In some cases, officers may be asked to intervene with individuals who have been in a near constant state of hypervigilance, have been trained to rely on weapons for defense, and have been taught to respond immediately to imminent or perceived threat. Additionally, issues of social isolation, separation, and disconnectedness from family or other support abound. Many military members have missed the birth or graduation of a child, wedding anniversaries, or funerals of loved ones back home. Conversely, some have become all too acquainted with death on the battlefield but cannot talk about it with civilians. Coupled with the stress of returning to a less regimented and structured life while facing the uncertainty of post-service employment, it is easy to see how incidents involving some military members have the potential to become volatile.

Effective Incident Management

Most law enforcement officers strive to engage all community members with respect and dignity; however, this is particularly important for veterans, who often feel like alienated strangers in their own communities. Although there may not be clear early information about veteran status, when law enforcement arrive and begin speaking with individuals on the scene, that information will often surface. If possible, the dispatcher may inquire about the military status of the individual when taking the initial call and relay that to the responding officers. Depending on the situation, if there exists some reason to believe that a community member might be former military, officers may ask initial questions such as "Have you served in the military?" or "What was your branch of service [or 'MOS' if Army]?" Depending on the response, officers can gain additional information by asking questions related to deployment and length of service. If such questions are not possible, other indications may be present such as the presence of "dog tag" identification, military tattoos, military-style clothing or footwear, and so forth. Additionally, manner of bearing or demeanor as well as speech can help identify those with past military service. Many expressions, for example, "That's when I got my weapon and I told him to stand down!" can provide clues. The use of military time in the conversation may be an additional indicator (e.g., "I told you I returned home at 1800 hours!"). Awareness is crucial.

Once it becomes apparent that law enforcement is engaging a person with a military background, content-specific training and heightened sensitivity comes into play. While remaining vigilant about personal and public safety, officers can view the current situation within the context of an individual who may be suffering from an injury. The military member may not be entirely functional or able to understand or optimally control their behavior. For example, in addition to mental health problems, the military member may be suffering from hearing loss (due to repeated blast or gunfire exposure) or other physical injuries that result in chronic pain or mood lability which could affect his or her thinking, judgment and behavior.

If possible, law enforcement will want to help the military member regain a sense of safety and reduce any perceived imminent threat. This is not the time to rush toward resolution or unnecessarily encroach upon personal space. Military members may have been in positions where personal safety, autonomy, and control have been repeatedly threatened or violated. It is imperative that law enforcement officers avoid being perceived as similarly threatening. If the situation allows, a slower, supportive, calm and confident tone and demeanor can help to de-escalate the situation. Respect is crucial. The military fosters a culture rich in tradition and strong on values such as bravery, loyalty, honor, and strength. If possible, the service member should be treated in a manner that communicates respect and avoids suggesting they are weak or cowardly.

Abrupt or furtive movements should be avoided if possible. A service member's military training might flag these actions as threatening. If an officer is going to reach into a pocket or duty bag, it may be best to first describe this action (i.e., "I'm going to reach into my pocket to get my notebook" or "I'm going to answer the dispatcher to tell them everything is OK."). External stressors such as unnecessary noise: sirens, radio traffic, crying/yelling/arguing of other individuals or family members should be minimized. If an officer is attempting to build rapport with an individual, those who might adversely impact the development of that relationship (such as an irritated relative or an upset child) should be directed to another location.

As law enforcement works to establish rapport with the military member, they must remain ever cognizant that, as in any incident, the situation could deteriorate quickly. If the individual begins acting erratically or dangerously, officers must be prepared to respond appropriately in defense of public and personal safety. As always, the ultimate goal is to provide a positive and successful resolution to the problem with minimal harm incurred. If possible, once the immediate situation has been resolved, the military member (or family members) should be referred to appropriate service agencies to receive the kind of care needed to mitigate the likelihood of such events in the future. All responding officers should have readily available a list of local VA hospitals, clinics, emergency rooms, or crisis line contacts.

Conclusion

Following each major foreign conflict, the American public has voiced concern about the danger posed by returning military members (see, for example, Bennett, 1954). Following more than a decade of ongoing wars (OIF/OEF/OND), both civilian and military populations are currently exhausted by the effort and cost. Estimates by the Institute of Medicine (IOM) suggest that the maximum cost load of caring for these veterans will not hit until the year 2040 (IOM, 2010). In the intervening years, the public will need to adjust to the reassimilation of hundreds of thousands of young and middle-aged military members. There is no question that military service—especially combat exposure—can impact the mental health and functioning of service members. However, after decades of research, findings consistently indicate *the majority of risk factors for both suicide and violent offending are primarily the same in both military and nonmilitary populations.*

Law enforcement responding to calls involving military members are advised to consider such individuals *in a holistic manner* and not automatically over-weight the influence of a military history. Military service is but one background factor that may or may not play a role in the behavior of community members. Law enforcement should first familiarize themselves with general risk factors for harm to self and others, as these factors tend to be the weightiest in any assessment regardless of military status. They should next consider the unique aspects of military service which may or may not play a role in any given incident. A well-informed and skillful approach to engaging with military members in the community can improve outcomes and increase the likelihood of a successful incident resolution with no harm occurring to any party.

Appendix A

Rob Ulrey is an Army veteran, federal law enforcement officer, fledgling blogger, media critic and writer. Interviewed by NBC following publicization of the below post, he shares his thoughts on living with PTSD. He

121

hopes that his experience may help educate the public and address media misinformation. Reproduced with permission.

I have PTSD . . . So what?

I have PTSD. We all know what it is, post-traumatic stress disorder. I am one of millions who are affected by it each and every day. Millions of men and women who have varying symptoms yet manage to maintain a normal lifestyle. I, along with my cohorts, have been classified as a potential powder keg just waiting on that spark to set us off into a murderous explosion of ire. This is not the case as I am just as normal as you.

At the end of every day I lay my head down in an attempt to sleep. That in itself is no different than you. But when my eyes close and I should be drifting off into a peaceful bliss, my mind takes over and I am tormented in my dreams with a vivid and exaggerated version of every combat encounter witnessed. There has been nary a night that I do not have this, and have not had an uninterrupted night of sleep for years. Yet in the morning, I rise with the consistency of the sun, roll out of my sweat soaked bed, and shake off the remnants of the nightly battles and start my day . . . just like you.

I am functional in society, but I am a little more vigilant than you, always on the look-out for danger, avoiding large crowds and loud places. But somehow, I can still manage to go out to eat, shop for my clothes and drive my car. I pay close attention to those around me, see the drug deal that just took place on my right and notice the people who just don't belong in a certain situation. You may not have evil intentions, but I will notice nonetheless.

I have guns. As a matter of fact I just about always have one on me. You see, even though I have PTSD, I am still a Sheepdog watching out for my flock. I don't brandish my weapon and most of the time you won't even know I have it on my body, but it is there. I also carry a large knife in my pocket, one that could cause serious injury or death if used improperly. I have never used any of my weapons in a malicious manner and never will, but in my duties as a Sheepdog I will not hesitate to draw down on you should the circumstance warrant it. I am armed, but I am not dangerous.

There are times that I am medicated. My PTSD comes in cycles and when things get bad I need that extra chemical push to regulate me. I accept this and because of it I do not drink. I have other physical problems that could easily warrant an addiction to pain killers, but just like most of us with PTSD, I avoid it.

I have never committed violence in the workplace, just like the vast majority of those who suffer with me. My coworkers know I spent time in the military but they do not know of my daily struggles, and they won't. I can still communicate with my subordinates and supervisors in a clear manner. I have never physically assaulted anyone out of anger or rage.

It pains me when I listen to the news and every time a veteran commits a crime (or commits suicide); it is automatically linked to and blamed on PTSD. Yes, there are some who cannot control their actions due to this imbalance in our heads, but don't put a label on us that we are all incorrigible. Very few of us are bad. There are more of us out there that are trying harder to do good than the lesser alternative.

Do not pity me. I know who I am and recognize the journey that has shaped me into what I am. I have no regrets about anything that I have done in the past and look forward to many wonderful years in the future. I freely take every step of life during the day knowing that there is something that will haunt me at night.

For those who are like me, there is help. Seek it out. You were strong enough to make it this far, don't give up. Dig a little deeper and make that final push. If you do not know where to go or have fallen astray, contact me. I will help. We are all brothers and sisters in this battle that will rage invariably for eternity and the one constant is that we have each other.

To the rest of society and particularly the media: I have PTSD!

"RU Rob"

February 5, 2012

Available at http://rhinoden.rangerup.com/i-have-ptsd-so-what/

Notes

Correspondence concerning this chapter should be addressed to Karen C. Kalmbach, PhD, Department of Psychology, Texas A&M University-San Antonio, One University Way, San Antonio, TX 78224. Email: Karen.Kalmbach@tamusa.tamus.edu

1 The U.S. Armed Forces during wartime comprises five branches: Army, Navy, Air Force, Marine Corps, and Coast Guard. For simplicity, the terms *military member* or *service member* is used herein to include all the foregoing categories of individuals who are now or have ever been in any branch of the military. A distinction is made, when necessary, between a) active duty, b) deployed, c) combat-deployed, d) reserve, e) conscripted vs. all volunteer force (AVF), and f) veterans of current or former wars.

2 See for example, www.usatoday.com/story/news/nation/2013/04/06/recent-war-vets-face-hiring-obstacle-ptsd-bias/2057857.

3 See for example www.csmonitor.com/USA/Military/2012/0119/Pentagon-report-Sexual-assault-in-the-military-up-dramatically as well as Department of Defense, Sexual Assault Prevention and Response Annual Report 2011–2012 at www.defense.gov/news/sexualassaultannualreportfactsheet.pdf.

4 Of the total active duty military population, typically less than two-thirds (60 percent) ever deploy; 40 percent are never deployed, and not all deployed service members are deployed to combat zones (Defense Business Board, 2010).

5 *Cultivation Theory* suggests that prime time and news programming depicts a world far more dangerous and violent than reality would support. Mass

consumption of this material produces citizens who are more afraid and who believe their risk of victimization is far greater than the data would suggest.

6 See www.armytimes.com/news/2012/08/ap-sikh-temple-shooting-army-veteran-080 612.
7 See http://video.msnbc.msn.com/nightly-news/48539422#48539422.
8 See http://latino.foxnews.com/latino/news/2012/08/07/sihk-temple-shooter-michael-wade-urged-fellow-white-supremacist-to-get-involved.
9 See www.businesswire.com/news/home/20120806006418/en/Barr-Nunn-Issues-Statement-Wade-Michael-Page.
10 See www.huffingtonpost.com/brian-levin-jd/exclusive-interview-with_b_1751181.html.
11 See http://abcnews.go.com/US/wisconsin-gunman-wade-michael-pages-girlfriend-arrested/ story?id=16954183.
12 See www.huffingtonpost.com/brian-levin-jd/exclusive-interview-with_b_1751181.html.

References

American Psychiatric Association (APA). (2000). *Diagnostic and Statistical Manual of mental Disorders,* 4th ed., text rev. Washington, DC: Author.

Anaki, D., Brezniak, T., & Shalom, L. (2012). Faces in the face of death: Effects of exposure to life-threatening events and mortality salience on facial expression recognition in combat and noncombat military veterans. *Emotion,* 12(4), 860–867.

Associated Press. (2012). U.S. military averaging a suicide a day in 2012. *CBS News,* June 7. Retrieved from www.cbsnews.com/8301–201_162–57449214/u.s-military-averaging-a-suicide-a-day-in-2012.

Associated Press with Fishel, J., Levine, M., & Winter, J. (2012). Gunman in Sikh temple shooting identified as ex-army soldier Wade Michael Page. *FOX News,* August 6. Retrieved from www.foxnews.com/us/2012/08/06/authorities-search-for-motive-in-deadly-shooting-at-wisconsin-sikh-temple.

Atkinson, M., Guetz, A., & Wein, L. (2009). A dynamic model for posttraumatic stress disorder among U.S. troops in Operation Iraqi Freedom. *Management Science,* 55(9), 1454–1468.

Barnes, S.M., Walter, K.H., & Chard, K.M. (2012). Does a history of mild traumatic brain injury increase suicide risk in veterans with PTSD? *Rehabilitation Psychology,* 57(1), 18–26.

Beckham, J.C., Feldman, M.E., & Kirby, A.C. (1998). Atrocities exposure in Vietnam combat veterans with chronic posttraumatic stress disorder: Relationship to combat exposure, symptom severity, guilt, and interpersonal violence. *Journal of Traumatic Stress,* 11(4), 777–785.

Benda, B.B., Rodell, D.E., & Rodell, L. (2003). Crime among homeless military veterans who abuse substances. *Psychiatric Rehabilitation Journal,* 26(4), 332–345.

Benedict, H. (2009). Violent veterans, the big picture. *Huffington Post,* January 14. Retrieved from www.huffingtonpost.com/helen-benedict/violent-veterans-the-big_b_157937.html.

Bennett, J.V. (1954). The criminality of veterans. *Federal Probation,* 18(29), 40–42.

Black, S., Gallaway, M.S., Bell, M.R., & Ritchie, E.C. (2011). Prevalence and risk factors associated with suicides of Army soldiers 2001–2009. *Military Psychology,* 23, 433–451.

Bouffard, L. (2005). The military as a bridging environment in criminal careers: Differential outcomes of the military experience. *Armed Forces & Society*, 31(2), 273–295.

Brooks, R. (2012). No army for young men. *Foreign Policy*, September 27. Retrieved from www.foreignpolicy.com/articles/2012/09/27/no_army_for_young_men.

Bruenig, M. (2012). *Military suicide rate and the importance of demographic controls*. June 12 (web log post). Retrieved from http://mattbruenig.com/2012/06/12/military-suicide-rate-and-the-importance-of-demographic-controls.

Bryan, C.J. & Cukrowicz, K.C. (2011). Associations between types of combat violence and the acquired capability for suicide. *Suicide and Life-Threatening Behavior*, 41(2), 126–136.

Bucher, J. (2011). General issue (GI) strain: Applying strain theory to military offending. *Deviant Behavior*, 32, 846–875.

Byrne, C.A. & Riggs, D.S. (1996). The cycle of trauma: Relationship aggression in male Vietnam veterans with symptoms of posttraumatic stress disorder. *Violence and Victims*, 11(3), 213–225.

Cable News Network (CNN) (2012). Military, music marked temple suspect's path to Wisconsin. *CNN*, August 7. Retrieved from www.cnn.com/2012/08/06/us/wisconsin-shooting-suspect/index.html.

Cable News Network Wire Staff. (2012). Gunman, six others dead at Wisconsin Sikh temple. *CNN*, August 5. Retrieved from www.cnn.com/2012/08/05/us/wisconsin-temple-shooting/index.html.

Castillo, M. (2012). Study: Suicide rates among army soldiers up 80 percent. *CBS News*, July 10. Retrieved from www.cbsnews.com/8301–504763_162–57394452–10391704/study-suicide-rates-among-army-soldiers-up-80-percent.

Center for Deployment Psychology. (n.d.). *Addressing the Psychological Health of Warriors and Their Families*. (Training Manual for Civilian Providers) Training provided in Houston, TX, October 3–7, 2011. Author.

Centers for Disease Control and Prevention (CDC) (n.d.). *Explosions and Blast Injuries: A Primer for Clinicians*. Retrieved September 25, 2012 from www.bt.cdc.gov/masscasualties/pdf/explosions-blast-injuries.pdf.

Centers for Disease Control and Prevention. (2010) *Suicide: Facts at a glance*. Summer. Retrieved from www.cdc.gov/ViolencePrevention/pdf/Suicide_Data Sheet-a.pdf.

Copeland, L.A., Miller, A.L., Welsh, D.E., McCarthy, J.F., Zeber, J.E., & Kilbourne, A.M. (2009). Clinical and demographic factors associated with homelessness and incarceration among VA patients with bipolar disorder. *American Journal of Public Health*, 99(5), 871–877.

Defense Business Board. (2010). *Reducing Overhead and Improving Business Operations: Initial Observations*. (Presentation). July 22. Retrieved from http://timemilitary.files.wordpress.com/2012/03/punaro-brf.pdf.

Defense Manpower Data Center (2011). *Demographics of U.S. Active Duty Military*. (Reported by Statistic Brain). Aug 8. Retrieved September 25, 2012 from www.statisticbrain.com/demographics-of-active-duty-u-s-military/.

Douglas, K., Cox, D., & Webster, C. (1999). Violence risk assessment: Science and practice. *Legal and Criminological Psychology*, 4(2), 149–184.

Elbogen, E. (2012). *Criminal Justice Involvement Among Iraq and Afghanistan War Veterans: Risk Factors and Barriers to Care.* (Webinar/PowerPoint presentation/UNC Chapel Hill). April 4. http://www.pacenterofexcellence. pitt.edu/documents/Elbogen%20Criminal%20Justice%20Webinar%204%20 2012.pptx.

Elbogen, E. & Johnson S. (2009). The intricate link between violence and mental disorder: Results from the national epidemiologic survey on alcohol and related conditions. *Archives of General Psychiatry*, 66, 152–161.

Elbogen, E., Johnson, S., Wagner, R., Newton, V., & Beckham, J. (2012a). Financial well-being and postdeployment adjustment among Iraq and Afghanistan war veterans. *Military Medicine*, 177(6), 669–675.

Elbogen, E., Fuller, S., Johnson, S., Brooks, S., Kinneer, P., Calhoun, P., & Beckham, J. (2010). Improving risk assessment of violence among military Veterans: An evidence-based approach for clinical decision-making. *Clinical Psychology Review*, 30, 595–607.

Elbogen, E., Johnson, S., Newton, V., Straits-Troster, K., Vasterling, J., Wagner, H., & Beckham, J. (2012b). Criminal justice involvement, trauma, and negative affect in Iraq and Afghanistan war era veterans. *Journal of Consulting and Clinical Psychology*, October 1. Advance online publication. DOI: 10.1037/a0029967.

Ellison, J. (2011). The military's secret shame. *Newsweek Magazine*, April 3. Retrieved from www.thedailybeast.com/newsweek/2011/04/03/the-military-s-secret-shame.html.

Erickson, S.K., Rosenheck, R.A., Trestman, R.L., Ford, J.D., & Desai, R.A. (2008). Risk of incarceration between cohorts of Veterans with and without mental illness discharged from inpatient units. *Psychiatric Services*, 59(2), 178–183.

Etter, D., McCarthy, L., & Asken, M. (2011) Police negotiations with war veterans: Seeing through the residual fog of war. *FBI Law Enforcement Bulletin*, July.

Exec. Order No. 13625 (2012). *Executive Order—Improving Access to Mental Health Services for Veterans, Service Members, and Military Families.* August 31. Retrieved from www.whitehouse.gov/the-press-office/2012/08/31/ executive-order-improving-access-mental-health-services-veterans-service.

Federal Bureau of Investigation (FBI) (2011). *Preliminary Annual Uniform Crime Report: January–December* 2011. Retrieved from www.fbi.gov/about-us/cjis/ ucr/crime-in-the-u.s/2011/preliminary-annual-ucr-jan-dec-2011.

Fischer, Hannah. (2010). *U.S. Military Casualty Statistics: Operation New Dawn, Operation Iraqi Freedom, and Operation Enduring Freedom* (RS22452). Report for Congress, September 28. Washington, DC: Congressional Research Service. Retrieved from www.fas.org/sgp/crs/natsec/RS22452.pdf.

Fontana, A. & Rosenheck, R. (2005). The role of war-zone trauma and PTSD in the etiology of antisocial behavior. *The Journal of Nervous and Mental Disease*, 193(3), 203–209.

Freeman, T.W & Roca, V. (2001). Gun use, attitudes toward violence, and aggression among combat veterans with posttraumatic stress disorder. *The Journal of Nervous and Mental Disease*, 189(5), 317–320.

Gilliam, F. & Iyengar, S. (2000). Prime suspects: The influence of local television news on the viewing public. *American Journal of Political Science*, 44(3), 560–573.

Gimbel, C. & Booth, A. (1994). Why does military combat experience adversely affect marital relations? *Journal of Marriage and the Family*, 56, 691–703.

Griffith, J. (2012). Suicide in the Army National Guard: An empirical enquiry. *Suicide and Life-Threatening Behavior*, 42(1), 104–119.

Harrell, M. & Berglass, N. (2011). *Losing the battle: The challenge of military suicide*. (Policy Brief). October. Washington, DC: Center for a New American Security. Retrieved from www.cnas.org/files/documents/publications/CNAS_LosingTheBattle_HarrellBerglass.pdf.

Hayes, A. (2012). Experts: Vets' PTSD, violence a growing problem. *Cable News Network (CNN)*, January 17. Retrieved from http://articles.cnn.com/2012–01–17/us/us_veterans-violence_1_iraq-war-vet-face-death-penalty-homeless-men.

Hennessey, V. (2012). James Holmes: Accused Colorado shooter is grandson of decorated veteran, has family roots in Monterey County. *Contra Costa Times*, July 20. Retrieved from www.contracostatimes.com/rss/ci_21124710?source=rss.

Hoge, C., Castro, C., Messer, S., McGurk, D., Cotting, D., & Koffman, R. (2004). Combat duty in Iraq and Afghanistan, mental health problems, and barriers to care. *The New England Journal of Medicine*, 351, 13–22.

Holowka, D.W., Wolf, E.J., Marx, B.P., Foley, K.M., Kaloupek, D.G., & Keane, T. (2012). Associations among personality, combat exposure and wartime atrocities. *Psychology of Violence*, 2(3), 260–272.

Howden, L. & Meyer, J. (2011). *Age and Sex Composition*–2010. 2010 *Census Briefs*. May. United States Census Bureau. Retrieved from www.census.gov/prod/cen2010/briefs/c2010br-03.pdf.

Humensky, J., Jordan, N., Stroupe, K., & Hynes, D. (2012). How are Iraq/Afghanistan-Era Veterans Faring in the Labor Market? *Armed Forces & Society*, 0095327X12449433, 1–26. First published online June 19 as DOI: 10.1177/0095327X12449433.

Ilgen, M.A., McCarthy, J.F., Ignacio, R.V., Bohnert, A., Valenstein, M., Blow, F.C., & Katz, I.R. (2012). Psychopathology, Iraq and Afghanistan service, and suicide among Veterans Health Administration patients. *Journal of Consulting and Clinical Psychology*, 80(3), 323–330.

Institute of Medicine (IOM). (2010). *Returning Home from Iraq and Afghanistan: Preliminary Assessment of Readjustment Needs of Veterans, Service Members, and Their Families*. Washington, DC: The National Academies Press.

Kimerling, R., Street, A., Pavao, J., Smith, M., Cronkite, R., Holmes, T., & Frayne, S. (2010). Military-related sexual trauma among Veterans Health Administration patients returning from Afghanistan and Iraq. *American Journal of Public Health*, 100(8), 1409–1412.

Lutz, A. (2008). Who joins the military? A look at race, class, and immigration status. *Journal of Political and Military Sociology*, 36(2), 167–188.

Lynch, R. (2012). Sikh temple rampage: List of mass shootings grows—and grows. *Los Angeles Times*, August 6. Retrieved from http://articles.latimes.com/2012/aug/06/nation/la-na-nn-sikh-temple-rampage-20120806.

MacLean, A. & Elder, G. (2007). Military service in the life course. *Annual Review of Sociology*, 33, 175–196.

Mansfield, A.J., Bender, R.H., Hourani, L.L., & Larson, G. E. (2011). Suicidal or self-harming ideation in military personnel transitioning to civilian life. *Suicide and Life-Threatening Behavior*, 41(4), 392–405.

Martin, J., Ghahramanlou-Holloway, M., Lou, K., & Tucciarone, P. (2009). A comparative review of U.S. military and civilian suicide behavior: Implications for OEF/OIF suicide prevention efforts. *Journal of Mental Health Counseling*, 31(2), 101–118.

Martinez, L. & Bingham, A. (2011). U.S. Veterans: By the numbers. *ABC News*, November 11. Retrieved from http://abcnews.go.com/Politics/us-veterans-numbers/story?id=14928136 #all.

Maurer, K. & Watson, J. (2010). Marine's suicide rate highest in the military, report says. *My SA*, August 26. Retrieved from www.mysanantonio.com/news/military/article/Marines-suicide-rate-highest-in-the-military-785337.php.

McGarry, R. & Walklate, S. (2011). The soldier as victim: Peering through the looking glass. *British Journal of Criminology*, 51, 900–917.

Monahan, J. (1996). Violence prediction: The past twenty and the next twenty years. *Criminal Justice and Behavior*, 23(1), 107–120.

Monahan, J. (2002). The MacArthur studies of violence risk. *Criminal Behavior and Mental Health*, 12, S67–S72.

Monahan, J. & Arnold, J. (1996). Violence by people with mental illness: A consensus statement by advocates and researchers. *Psychiatric Rehabilitation Journal*, 19(4), 67–70.

Mossman, D. (1994). Assessing predictions of violence: Being accurate about accuracy. *Journal of Consulting and Clinical Psychology*, 62(4), 783–792.

National Law Center on Homelessness and Poverty (2007). *2007 Annual Report: Changing Laws, Changing Lives*. Washington, DC: Author. Retrieved from www.nlchp.org /content/pubs/2007_Annual_Report2.pdf.

Nelson, L. (2012). Officer critically injured in Sikh temple shooting leaves hospital. *Los Angeles Times*, August 22. Retrieved from www.latimes.com/news/nation/nationnow/la-na-nn-officer-temple-shooting-leaves-hospital-20120822,0,1363010.story.

Office of the Under Secretary of Defense, Personnel and Readiness (2010). *Population Representation in the Military Services*. Retrieved from http://prhome.defense.gov/RFM/MPP/ACCESSION%20POLICY/PopRep2010/contents/contents.html.

Otto, R. & Douglas, K. (Eds.). (2009). *Handbook of Violence Risk Assessment Tools*. Milton Park, UK: Routledge.

Pandiani, J.A., Ochs, W.R., & Pomerantz, A.S. (2010). Criminal justice involvement of armed forces veterans in two systems of care. *Psychiatric Services*, 61(8), 835–837.

Park, M., Mulye, T., Adams, S., Brindis, C., & Irwin, C. (2006). The health status of young adults in the United States. *Journal of Adolescent Health*, 39, 305–317.

Patrick, V., Critchfield, E., Vaccaro, T., & Campbell, J. (2011). The relationship of childhood abuse and early separation from the military among Army advanced individual trainees. *Military Medicine*, 176(2), 182–185.

Pope, K.S. & Vasquez, M.J.T. (2011). Recognizing, assessing, and responding to suicidal risk. *Ethics in Psychotherapy and Counseling: A Practical Guide*, 4th ed., pp. 292–314. Hoboken, NJ: John Wiley & Sons, Inc.

Rabenhorst, M.M., Thomsen, C.J., Milner, J.S, Foster, R.E., Linkh, D.J., & Copeland, C.W. (2012). Spouse abuse and combat-related deployments in active duty air force couples. *Psychology of Violence*, 2(3), 273–284.

Rieckhoff, P. (2012). Solving the riddle of veteran unemployment. *Forbes*, June 22. Retrieved from www.forbes.com/sites/paulrieckhoff/2012/06/22/solving-the-riddle-of-veteran-unemployment.

Ritchie, E. (2012). How cops can best deal with vets. *Time*, August 27. Retrieved from http://nation.time.com/2012/08/27/how-cops-can-best-deal-with-vets/#comments.

Romer, D., Jamieson, K.H., & Aday, S. (March, 2003). Television news and the cultivation of fear of crime. *Journal of Communication*, 88–104.

Rosen, L. & Martin, L. (1996). The measurement of childhood trauma among male and female soldiers in the U.S. Army. *Military Medicine*, 161(6), 342–345.

Shaw, D.M., Churchill, C.M., Noyes, R., & Loeffelholz, P.L. (1987). Criminal behavior and post-traumatic stress disorder in Vietnam veterans. *Comprehensive Psychiatry*, 28(5), 403–411.

Shinseki, E. (2010). *Remarks by Secretary Eric K. Shinseki*. Department of Defense-Veterans Affairs. Suicide Prevention Conference, January, 11. Retrieved from www.va.gov/opa/speeches/2010/10_0111hold.asp.

Siegal, H.A., Li, L., & Rapp, R.C. (2002). Case management as a therapeutic enhancement: Impact on post-treatment criminality. *Journal of Addictive Diseases*, 21(4), 37–46.

Skeem, J., Manchak, S., & Peterson, J. (2011). Correctional policy for offenders with mental illness: Creating a new paradigm for recidivism reduction. *Law and Human Behavior*, 35, 110–126.

Snyder, H. (2011). *Arrest in the United States*, 1980–2009 (NCJ 234319). Bureau of Justice Statistics. Retrieved from http://bjs.ojp.usdoj.gov/content/pub/pdf/aus8009.pdf.

Statistic Brain. (2011). Demographics of active duty U.S. military. Retrieved from www.statisticbrain.com/demographics-of-active-duty-u-s-military.

Steadman, H., Silver, E., Monahan, J., Appelbaum, P., Clark Robbins, P., Mulvey, E., Grisso, T., Roth, L., & Banks, S. (2000). A classification tree approach to the development of actuarial violence risk assessment tools. *Law and Human Behavior*, 24(1), 83–100.

Strom, T.Q., Leskela, J., Gavian, M.E., Possis, E., Loughlin, J., Bui, T., Linardatos, E., & Siegel, W. (2012). Cultural and ethical considerations when working with military personnel and veterans: A primer for VA training programs. *Training and Education in Professional Psychology*, 6(2), 67–75.

Taft, C.T., Pless, A.P., Stalans, L.J., Koenen, K.C., King, L.A., & King, D.W. (2005). Risk factors for partner violence among a national sample of combat veterans. *Journal of Consulting and Clinical Psychology*, 73(1), 151–159.

Taft, C.T., Kachaduorian, L.K., Suvak, M.K., Pinto, L.A., Miller, M.M., Knight, J.A., & Marx, B.P. (2012). Examining impelling and disinhibiting factors for intimate partner violence in veterans. *Journal of Family Psychology*, 26(2), 285–289.

Tanielian, T. & Jaycox, L.H. (2008). *Invisible Wounds of War: Psychological and Cognitive Injuries, Their Consequences, and Services to Assist Recovery.*

Santa Monica, CA: Rand Corp. Retrieved from www.rand.org/multi/military/veterans.html.

Tversky, A. & Kahneman, D. (1973). Availability: A heuristic for judging frequency and probability. *Cognitive Psychology* 5(2), 207–232.

United States Armed Forces. (2010). *Army Health Promotion, Risk Reduction, Suicide Prevention Report 2010.* Retrieved from http://csf.army.mil/downloads/HP-RR-SPReport2010.pdf.

United States Census Bureau (2012). *Table 516. Active duty military deaths by manner of death:* 1980–2010. Statistical Abstract of the United States: 2012. Retrieved from www.census.gov/compendia/statab/2012/tables/12s0516.pdf.

Washington, D.L., Yano, E.M., McGuire, J., Hines, V., Lee, M., & Gelberg, L. (2010). Risk factors for homelessness among women veterans. *Journal of Health Care for the Poor and Underserved*, 21, 81–91.

Weaver, C., Joseph, D., Dongon, S., Fairweather, A., and Ruzek, J. (2013). Enhancing services response to crisis incidents involving veterans: A role for law enforcement and mental health collaboration. *Psychological Services*, 10(1), 66–72.

White, M.D., Mulvey, P., Fox, A.M., & Choate, D. (2012). A hero's welcome? Exploring the prevalence and problems of military veterans in the arrestee population. *Justice Quarterly*, 29(2), 258–286.

White, R., Barber, C., Azrael, D., Mukamal, K.J., & Miller, M. (2011). History of military service and the risk of suicidal ideation: Findings from the 2008 National Survey on Drug Use and Health. *Suicide and Life-Threatening Behavior*, 41(5), 554–561.

Wright, J.P., Carter, D.E., & Cullen, F.T. (2005). A life-course analysis of military service in Vietnam. *Journal of Research in Crime and Delinquency*, 42(1), 55–83.

Zoroya, G. (2012). Army suicide rate hits record in July. *The Voice of Tucson*, August 16. Retrieved from http://tucsoncitizen.com/usa-today-news/2012/08/16/army-suicide-rate-hits-record-in-july.

7

SPECIAL ISSUES WITH MILITARY LAW ENFORCEMENT OFFICERS

Deloria Wilson, John Price, and Brandi Burque

Overview

There is a paucity of research regarding law enforcement officers in the military as well as on military veterans who work in a civilian law enforcement capacity. The majority of the literature focuses on general military service members, their stressors, and interventions. Further, there is an abundance of research on civilian law enforcement officers. However, a purview of the research of civilian officers combined with military service reveals very little about the military law enforcement officer (MLEO). Therefore, this chapter will provide an introduction to the roles and responsibilities of the military police officer and continue with a discussion of special issues related to their work. Further, special attention will be made toward military veterans who are also law enforcement officers in municipal, state, and federal law enforcement agencies or seeking employment as a police officer for the first time.

A MLEO must be able to enforce state and federal laws on a military base or post with millions of dollars of federal assets to protect. Officers may be involved in a wide variety of tasks, including writing tickets, guarding planes or ships, or investigating crimes on base. MLEOs must also be prepared for humanitarian missions, such as in Haiti after the earthquake in 2010, or combat operations, such as those in Iraq or Afghanistan.

The career field of a MLEO is diverse and requires flexibility unlike many other military occupations. In essence, the military law enforcement officer duties are first and foremost to provide combat capability as an Airman, Soldier, Marine, or Sailor, coupled with policing responsibility, which may present unique challenges and opportunities for the MLEO.

MLEO Duties

Common culture has often referred to law enforcement officers in the military as "military policemen," and even more commonly as, MPs. However, the terms used to describe a military law enforcement officer can vary depending on the service in which they are located. For instance, the Army and Marines typically call their MLEOs military policemen or MPs. The Air Force MLEOs are known as the Security Forces (SF) defined by the motto of "Defensor Fortis" or "Defenders the Force." They often refer to themselves as Defenders and not MPs. Finally, the Navy refers to its law enforcement officer as a "Master of Arms." These differences are subtle but important as each service takes great pride in its unique role in the defense of the nation. It is also important to note that there are investigative agencies, such as the Air Force Office of Special Investigations (AFOSI), the Naval Criminal Investigation Service (NCIS), and the Army's Criminal Investigation Command (CID) that also have law enforcement duties and work with military police though they may be under separate command structures. Finally each of the four major sister services may now also have a civilian law enforcement component (CP) that work side by side with the MLEO.

Each service's law enforcement arm shares a number of aspects in regards to role, responsibilities, and training, and although some of these may look similar to community law enforcement, it is the combat capability that these law enforcement officers bring to bear that is the most central part of their duties. The main duties of the MLEO are in the performance of force protection of both civilian and military members, general physical security, antiterrorism, and law enforcement. These duties may be accomplished on land and sea, in both foreign and domestic environments. MLEOs authority spectrum ranges from enforcement of traffic laws to the resolution of criminal investigation ranging from crimes such as shoplifting to murder. Therefore, their primary purpose is to respond to both inside and outside threats to the safety and well-being of the military and civilian members of that community. The MLEO may serve on a hostage negotiation team, a critical incident team, be involved in base community events, and crime prevention programs. They may also conduct preliminary investigations into domestic violence and child abuse issues, or around violations of the Uniformed Code of Military Justice (UCMJ). The MLEO sometimes serve as correctional officers and are responsible for operating the jails or brigs on post for military members that must serve confinement. Some MLEOs also serve as part of working dog teams with duties similar to civilian law enforcement teams. Additionally, the MLEO must be prepared for deployment to overseas locations for combat and humanitarian operations.

Operational contingencies in a deployed environment can vary depending on location. In some cases, MLEOs may be guarding and protecting airstrips or providing base and port security for deployed bases. They may be conducting checkpoint duties, assisting in the safety of convoy operations, running detainee operations or training host nation police recruits among others. Expectedly, the type and amount of stress experienced in these operations can vary considerably. Boredom and complacency can be coupled with instantaneous fear during a critical incident. Although this cycle of boredom to crisis may not be so different than what nondeployed or general municipal and state agencies may experience, it tends to happen more often due to the nature of the combat environment. Humanitarian missions can be equally stressful. MLEOs may be part of a humanitarian mission to provide general security or to protect the medical personnel and supplies providing aid. Depending on the mission, stressors may include less fear for one's own personal safety and more about the stress of being helpless to alleviate the suffering of victims.

Training

There are several levels of training for the MLEO. They first attend their military entry-level training, commonly known as basic training, for the enlisted members. All enlisted members, regardless of what job they will do, attend this basic training course, which can last from eight to twelve weeks, depending on the service department. After an enlisted member completes basic military training, they then move on to their technical school, or the training where they learn the job that they are to perform in the military. It is important to note that for the most part MLEOs, unless chosen for a special duty, do not undergo systematic psychological screening or assessment as part of a selection process to becoming a MLEO. It is assumed for at least a basic MLEO, the rigors of basic training are enough. All service members undergo a basic background check and physical screening before entering the military. Training to become a MLEO can last another 12 or more weeks. The prior level of education for an enlisted member varies from high school to a bachelor's degree.

Officers often enter the military law enforcement career field in a different manner and it may vary based on the service. Generally, an officer earns a commission either through attending one of the nation's service academies (e.g., West Point, Air Force Academy, Naval Academy), through a Reserve Officer Training program, or a direct commissioning through a service's officer training school. The latter requires that a commissioned officer MLEO already have at least a bachelor's degree. It is also possible for an enlisted member to be selected for officer school through various programs in the military.

Training at these law enforcement schools or academies can be quite rigorous and the training encompasses both general law enforcement curriculum and curriculum for deployed operations. Both officers and enlisted learn basic general policing techniques, such as search and seizure, addressing domestic issues, patrolling, hand-cuffing, hand-to-hand combat, and appropriate use of force, among others. Accordingly, there are some parallels to what civilian law enforcement officers will learn at their police academies. MLEOs also learn the use of basic weapons, similar to civilian police, however, their exposure and training is usually to a larger assortment as they may encounter in the deployed setting. Further, training that is more "militaristic" is conducted on antiterrorism, land navigation, patrolling, urban operations, and convoy operations. Although there is a significant amount of classroom training, a great deal of the training is "hands-on" and scenario based. For example, a scenario may include that, while on patrol, they encounter a simulated stalled vehicle that may or may not be carrying a vehicle improvised explosive device and the passengers may be friendly civilians or terrorists. Similar to civilian law enforcement training, MLEOs may participate in "Hogan's Alley" scenarios with mock villages that have realistic smells, simulated weapons fire, as well as role players as "bad guys." This initial academy training is meant to provide a foundation and familiarization, but training continues throughout the MLEO's career.

Once the initial academy is completed and an MLEO embarks on their first assignment, advanced on-the-job training begins. There may also be specialized training if the MLEO is assigned to unique situations, such as an assignment to submarines or placed on military working dog teams. Both enlisted and officers are expected to continue to hone their skills at their home station and also with advanced training. For example, in the Air Force, the enlisted MLEO must take Career Development Courses (CDCs). Passing the End of Course (EOC) tests is required for further advancement in duties and promotion. The path of the enlisted member including training is more vocational in nature as it is for most enlisted jobs in the military.

The path for the officer who is an MLEO can be quite different than the enlisted MLEO. MLEOs who are officers are foremost trained in leadership and direct troop leading as well as some of the vocational aspects of being an MLEO. For example, in the Air Force, there is a separate enlisted and officer academy to learn their job as a Security Forces Officer. Although there may be some general leadership aspects of the academy training for the enlisted members, how to lead and move troops and care for their needs are more strongly emphasized in the officer school. The officers will continue with on-the-job training, with an emphasis on both general and duty-specific training, as they advance in rank and this training will continue.

There are some parallels between enlisted and officer training and knowledge, but officers are expected to lead from early in their career. This may include managing people and equipment, planning missions, and running operations. Enlisted members' leadership responsibilities grow as they are promoted in rank, and they often play the role of mentor for a younger officer. A close working relationship and a reliance on enlisted leadership is crucial for a commissioned officer. This structure may be quite different than civilian law enforcement agencies as the civilian structures, though hierarchical, do not have the parallel hierarchies of enlisted and officer as exists in military law enforcement structures.

Since 2001, many of the armed services now possess a civilian law enforcement component that works closely with military police. Although civilian and military law enforcement officers have worked together and trained together for contingencies affecting the post and surrounding community, it was atypical to have a civilian police component assigned to the base, and this is unique to the military. These civilian officers rarely deploy and are most visible at the entry gates to a base or post. The civilian police (CP) play a vital role in force and property protection. Each service may utilize the CP differently, but training may often look very much like a municipal, state or federal police agency academy. In many ways, the civilian police component bridges both the military and the civilian law enforcement world.

Special Issues Affecting Military Law Enforcement Officers

As previously indicated, there is a relative lack of literature focusing on the stressors specific to military law enforcement. However, there is an abundance of research and current efforts to ascertain the variables involved in operational stress for general service members, especially those deployed in a combat environment. The Mental Health Advisory Team (MHAT VI) gathered data from December 2008 to March 2009 of Operation Iraqi Freedom (OIF) soldiers addressing issues related to behavioral health concerns. The team indicated that mental health issues, such as anxiety, depression, and acute stress, were approximately 12 percent ($N = 2442$). Divorce and separation rates were presented as a steady increase, with similar rates in both types of unit. The MHAT VI (2009) also delineated risk and resiliency factors for the units surveyed. Specifically, a shorter time frame between deployments was associated with higher reported mental health issues and even low morale. In contrast, the perception of positive leadership was noted as a significant factor in soldier resilience, with an emphasis on fostering the importance of the junior officer's role in the process.

The MHAT surveys demonstrate important factors associated with deployment and mental health concerns. Although these are specific to general military units in combative and supportive roles, the conclusions may shed some light on the deployed operational impact to military law enforcement since they operate in the same environment with similar stressors. Overall, some of these stressors include separation from family, long deployments, extended combat missions coupled with periods of boredom, and sleep deprivation (Warner, Appenzeller, Breitbach, Mobbs, & Lange, 2011). The reactions to these stressors vary widely among individuals and units, just as it is seen in civilian law enforcement. Previous MHAT reports (MHAT V, 2008) have indicated a positive association between combat stress symptoms and the number of deployments; an increase in deployments is linked with an increase in stress reactions.

Undoubtedly, the role of a service member will impact his/her family life. Matsch, Sachau, Gertz and Englert (2009) conducted a study with 170 Air Force Office of Special Investigations (OSI) agents and found that these service members reported a bidirectional conflict between both family and work. In other words, work interfered with their family roles and their family roles interfered with their work roles. However, both agents and their spouses attributed less support from the working organization than from their closer supervisors. Further, social support has been identified as a strong protective factor in resilience. Individuals who possess a strong social support network tend to be considered better prepared for handling a crisis event and issues in their life. Stetz, Stetz, and Bliese (2006) found that self-efficacy is a moderator variable for the relationship of social support and how stressors impact an individual in a study of United States Military Police. It was indicated that individual self-efficacy should be taken into consideration when leaders attempt to build and promote social support.

Studies on civilian law enforcement stress may assist in completing the picture of special issues of military law enforcement, especially when general military stress has been considered. It has been noted that stressors for civilian law enforcement include the nature of the job (e.g., the calls to which they respond on a daily basis), role ambiguity, organizational stressors such as perceived lack of administrative support, threat and dangerousness of the job, and being away from their families (Miller, 2006; Sheehan & Van Hasselt, 2003). The overlap between military and law enforcement stressors is indeed palpable and having an understanding of these commonalities assists in gathering information about the MLEO.

Military Veteran Law Enforcement Officers (MVLEO)

The purpose of this section is to focus on the military veteran law enforcement officer (MVLEO), which for the purposes of this chapter is defined as any military veteran who served or is serving either as a military law enforcement officer or other specialty. This MVLEO may be retired, separated, or a current member of the National Guard (NG) or Reserve Component (RC).

Military service members and first responders share many commonalities. They both endure vigorous training programs and indoctrination, which often creates a sense of organizational belonging. They both follow a hierarchal structure, and their professions offer unique challenges and opportunities that can expose them to a variety of extreme and unique stressors that put them at risk of both physical and psychological injury. Therefore, it is not uncommon that military members would be drawn to the profession of law enforcement. The cultural similarities between the military and the law enforcement agencies create an opportunity for veterans to apply abilities and skill sets they developed while serving within a military organization. These include, but are not limited to, the experience and seasoning that military structure and operations can bring, such as managing critical incidents, appropriately using force in ambiguous situations, confidence in handling unusual and/or deadly encounters, knowledge of firearms, and the ability to work independently or as a team. Many also have leadership skills far beyond their years. Although there are a number of similarities between the military and law enforcement environments, there are enough differences where one cannot assume that the transition between the military to civilian law enforcement will be smooth. Providing support for issues specific to veterans may enhance their ability to transition from military service to civilian law enforcement or move between both worlds if they are in the NG or RC.

To date there is no published study to understand the effects that serving in military operations, such as in combat or in humanitarian efforts, have on the subsequent performance of police officers once they return from deployment, whether they are retired, separated, or still currently serving in the guard or reserve. The impact may be quite different for those who may have separated from the military for months or years before joining a civilian law enforcement agency versus those who are in a reserve unit and have recently de-mobilized and must re-integrate back to their civilian job duties.

Support for the MVLEO is likely to depend on a number of factors, such as the length of deployment, the level of support sustained both at the deployed setting and at home station, and the amount of exposure to critical incidents while on deployment. Undoubtedly some transition regardless of the type of deployment is expected and civilian departments must determine with their available resources what type of support they can offer. From an organizational perspective, there are three main areas for consideration: training, support during deployment, and reintegration into law enforcement duties. For service members who have completed their service obligation, academy training will be important for them to learn how their military experience can help them with the functions of being a police officer. If they had prior deployed experience, they likely will have higher confidence and ability to cope with the stressors of training. However, there could possibly be a negative transfer of skills. In other words, what may have been standard operating procedure in the military, particularly in the deployed environment, will not be acceptable in civilian law enforcement. For instance, because of the ambiguity of the role of civilians in the deployed setting, a more aggressive approach with higher vigilance may be called for even if the civilians pose no obvious threat. The same response in the community would likely result in a complaint or something more severe. Training that focuses on positive aspects of prior military experiences, as well as differences and how to navigate them, could help service members make a more effective transition.

It would be beneficial at the police academy level training for both military and nonmilitary cadets to learn and gain an appreciation for what the other brings to the table. It could be easy for someone who has been in combat to have less empathy for those who have not yet faced similar challenges. Additionally, there may be stereotypes of the military veteran with certain unrealistic expectations in regards to physical and mental toughness. Training in the academy could include discussions on how expectations for use of force and interacting with civilians could be quite different. In order to bridge the gap, taking a strengths-based approach may be beneficial. Examples can be provided to those with prior military service on how mental toughness helped them in various situations during deployed operations. And for those without the same experience, examples can be provided on how mental toughness assisted them during athletic challenges or how they overcame various struggles.

Integrating veteran issues within academy training is a way to address concerns that both the veteran and the department may have. Training of supervisors on veteran issues is also important. Many leaders may be unaware of what to expect and how to support returning veterans, especially if they themselves have not had prior military experience. Training for the returning veteran should also be considered to allow for further transition to civilian law enforcement. Field Training Officers (FTOs) who are aware of typical transition and re-integration issues for veterans can address those as they review and practice driving procedures and weapons qualifications. Finally, training supervisors and commanders informed of the normal transitional issues for veterans and available resources are an essential component for assisting in that transition and early identification and referral of veterans who may be having difficulty.

A second key area to consider is for the veteran who is still serving a commitment through the NG or RC. Many of the larger departments have begun peer and organizational support programs for service members before, during, and after deployment. The focus of some of these programs is to provide support of the family members back home, and keep officers informed of departmental information and changes so that they maintain some contact with changes while they deploy. This may ease the transition when they return. Although there is little research in any of these areas, a report conducted by the International Association for Chiefs of Police (IACP, 2009) provides a good overview of what the MVLEO may need depending where they may be in the deployment cycle.

Return-to-Duty Programs (RTDs)

For police departments, the question of returning officers who have been away from duty for extended periods of time has been a long-standing problem. Most departments have dealt with sick or injured officers by returning them to duty once they were released by their physicians. Officers who have been away for other reasons were put back to work upon their return. This has not always worked out well, but the relatively small number of officers effected, and the fact that they returned to duty one at a time, brought little notice by departments.

The wars in Iraq and Afghanistan have lead police departments to focus more attention on this problem. Estimates from Ritchie and Curran (2006) noted that 10 percent of NG and RC consist of first responders. Although this number may be negligible for some departments, in others the number of police officers who are in the NG and RC has impacted some police departments in regards to the amount of officers on active duty and concern for the impact of combat on the officer's ability to return to civilian police work.

Law enforcement faces a unique challenge when returning Reserve and Guard members to their civilian jobs. Departments must balance the right of their military members to return to civilian position with the obligation to ensure officers are fit to perform their duties. Understanding the importance of considering resources and departmental needs, one strategy that balances the needs of officers, the department and the public, may be for agencies to establish return-to-duty programs. The details of these programs may vary depending on the nature of the organization, but should have certain core components. These include psychological screening, assessment of critical skills, familiarization with changes in policies, procedures and the laws. The final component is a period of reintegration in which officers performs their normal duties while being monitored.

Organizations may need to vary their approach depending on their size and deployment of resources. For example, a big city department with all of its personnel deployed in a relatively small geographic area may be able to easily move staff from academy training to having officers make calls with a Field Training Officer. However, a state-wide agency may be more dependent on assets in field offices.

Before a department institutes a program to place officers back to work after deployment, the elements of the program, and even the name, need to be carefully considered. A neutral or positive title such as "Return-to-Duty Program" (RTD) creates the impression that the individual is expected to return to a law enforcement setting. Rather than setting up a RTD program based on military deployment or injury, an alternate model would be to initiate inclusion in a RTD program based on time away from civilian police work. For example, any officer away from duty for 90 days or longer would automatically be placed in the return-to-duty program. This would avoid any one group from being stigmatized or not included.

It is recommended that RTD programs have core elements that are consistent and the options to include unique elements are based on the individual needs of the officer. Core elements should include screening by psychological services, providing updates to changes in department, policies, and procedures, as well as any changes in states laws. Critical skills, such as driving and shooting, need to be assessed to ensure officers meet a minimum level of competence. For patrol officers, an opportunity to ride with a FTO will allow for assessment of the officer's ability to perform in a fields environment. For officers assigned to investigative or special units, job performance may best be evaluated by their supervisor in their parent unit. If officers demonstrate problems in the core areas, then the program can be individually tailored to address these deficits.

Questions of confidentiality and inclusion in the program should be dealt with by establishing RTD program policies and procedures. When officers enter the program, they should be provided a description of the program. If the triggering mechanism for inclusion in a RTD program is based on time away from duty, then inclusion is universal. The majority of referrals will tend to consist of those officers who have been sick, injured, or returning from military duties. However, officers who have been suspended or fired, who are reinstated but have been off beyond the allowed time, will also be included in the program.

Return-to-duty programs should be designed to reintegrate officers back to full duty. If the officer demonstrates problems in the core elements, a plan to improve performance needs to be developed. Officers should understand that their return to full duty is dependent upon demonstrating the ability to function at the level of competence expected of officers in their duty assignment. Officers who have been sick or severely injured may benefit from contact with peer support, family assistance officers, and psychological services. In that case, psychological assessment should be conducted by a psychologist not involved in the officer's treatment.

Officers in the RC or NG facing deployment may benefit from contact from peer support officers to assist with transition and to ensure that the officer's family members have support from department personnel during the member's deployment. This proactive approach should be considered part of the RTD program as it helps to set up an environment in which the officer is more likely to view the department as supportive and concerned.

Education of department members assisting with the RTD program regarding the normal pattern of adjustment from combat to civilian life is essential in assisting the veteran in adapting to police work. If the returning combat veteran is not demonstrating a common pattern of adjustment, department personnel should be aware that a problem may exist and assist the veteran with obtaining appropriate services.

Psychological assessment of police cadet applicants generally involves a review of background history, interview, and psychological testing. Combat veterans applying to be police cadets may face a unique set of challenges. If the psychologist does not understand the normal pattern of readjustment, some of the veterans' behavior may be misunderstood. For those individuals who have been diagnosed with PTSD, the chances of being found psychologically unfit are much greater. An individual who currently meets criteria for PTSD should not be cleared to attend a police academy. However, subjects who are asymptomatic but have a PTSD diagnosis in their record are often rejected because of lack of understanding of PTSD and its treatment, or out of concern that a PTSD diagnosis may represent a future liability problem. Efforts to better educate police psychologists hopefully will lead to veterans being assessed on their individual merit rather than assumptions about the impact of combat and the diagnosis of PTSD. It is imperative for police psychologists to become educated on military culture, the deployment cycle, and its impact on service members. It may be beneficial to consider the impact on officers of dealing with demands of police work over time. Questions regarding the differences between the combat veteran and the veteran of the police department, their diagnosis of PTSD, and how that impacts the department, may be important to consider. Is the development and symptom presentation of PTSD in the police officer holistically different than what is experienced in the combat veteran? Is the treatment and impact on the department significantly different? Each case should be reviewed individually for the most efficacious treatment and recommendations. It is recognized that some departments have strict legal requirements and very little can be accomplished in terms of navigating the system. This is understandable and hopefully future education can help modify legal requirements to reflect changes in the growing scientific literature on the matter. Finally, it is essential to consider and consult legal and police union assets when developing RTD or other support programs.

Future Directions

Research in military police and subsequent transition from military to civilian law enforcement is a burgeoning field of scientific study. Little is known about the differences in stress of those in military law enforcement versus those in other military occupations. Much of the information that is generated is garnered through literature on general service in the military and civilian law enforcement. Future directions of research are imperative, as this will inform approaches to training and selection, treatment, and integration.

First, the most obvious research arena is analyzing the differences between military law enforcement and those in other specialty fields within the military. Developing a deeper understanding of the unique stressors for the MLEO can be beneficial in establishing selection, training, and intervention programs for these officers. Given the unique job description and the needed flexibility of job role, MLEO stress is a growing area of research that will yield invaluable information for the law enforcement population, both civilian and military. Second, although training is highly specialized in both military and civilian law enforcement, some advancement in psychological skills training has been identified as crucial elements. The skills taught are nothing new to the field, as they are derived from the sports psychology literature and based upon critical coping skills developed in the clinician's office. Asken (2005) outlined these skills as critical Mental Toughness Skills. Miller (2010) further delineated the purpose and these skills in training and rationale. These skills include tactical breathing (aka diaphragmatic breathing), self-talk, performance imagery, concentration and attention management, and the understanding of how physiological arousal can impact performance. Taken individually, the skills have been utilized in clinical psychology work for decades to help with anxiety and depression, and to boost performance. The skills are incorporated in military and law enforcement training on many different levels, however, the acquisition, maintenance, and impact of these skills has yet to be thoroughly studied in these populations and in these specific contexts. For example, it may be possible to assess these skills in military and law enforcement selection and ascertain the differences in skill levels between those with prior military experience versus those with none.

Further, based upon the ideas in performance enhancement and the trainings that tend to be provided to both military and civilian law enforcement on psychological health, stress, and disorders, there is a relatively small percentage of studies devoted to measuring their effectiveness. There are many training initiatives that have been and are currently being developed to enhance performance and resiliency for at-risk populations. Models of police resilience are beginning to be further elaborated (Paton et al., 2008). Psycho-educational programs for the military and first responder populations have demonstrated some efficacy, however, results tend to be inconsistent (Mulligan, Fear, Jones, Wessely, & Greenberg, 2011). Studying their efficacy and effectiveness can be a beneficial area of research, especially for specialized populations within the military. These trainings can be invaluable sources of information and serve as a basis for those with prior military experience entering, or re-entering, the civilian law enforcement.

Another area for investigation would be on return-to-duty programs. This may be helpful in the reintegration process to civilian law enforcement for those with prior military experience. In 2009, the International Association of Chiefs of Police (ICPA, 2009) put forward recommendations on reintegrating military personnel back into civilian law enforcement. While RTD programs appear to have good face validity, there is little research on the efficacy of these programs.

Finally, research should begin to focus on the effects of operational stress, specifically a diagnosis of PTSD, on the potential employability of veterans in civilian law enforcement. This can inform best practice models for departments, from both a psychological and a legal viewpoint. Anecdotal evidence may not be enough in terms of developing the right protocols to handle these situations, especially when a certain percentage of those are joining or returning to the civilian law enforcement community.

Conclusion

Military law enforcement officers, whether serving in one of the services as an MLEO or CP, or whether as a NG or RC member, play a unique and vital role in the protection of our nation and its assets. Little research has been conducted to understand their unique stressors and if or how they are different from civilian law enforcement officers. MLEOs have unique cultures within their services though they share a great deal in regards to training and mission. The balance between law enforcement duties back home and abroad, particularly while deployed in combat zones, can be challenging not only for the MLEO, but also for the family and the unit. Reintegration concerns for the RC or NG member are a challenge for civilian agencies as they determine how to best leverage the skills of their former or current military members to fulfill their civilian duties while assisting them in the transition back to community and civilian law enforcement. The individual who chooses the field of law enforcement is a unique individual and they have earned every effort to enhance their well-being whether as MLEOs or military veterans serving at municipal, state or federal agencies.

Note

The views expressed herein are those of the authors, and do not necessarily reflect the official policy position of the Department of Defense (DOD); the Department of Justice (DOJ); any government agency including police departments; or, the United States Army, Navy, or Air Force.

References

Asken, M.J. (2005). *Mindsighting: Mental Toughness Skills for Police Officers in High Stress Situations.* Camp Hill, PA: www.mindsighting.com.

International Association for Chiefs of Police. (2009). *Employing Returning Combat Veterans as Law Enforcement Officers: Supporting the Integration or Re-Integration of Military Personnel into Federal, State, Local and Tribal Law Enforcement.* Alexandria, VA: IACP.

Matsch, M.A., Sachau, D.A., Gertz, J., & Englert, D.R. (2009). Perceptions of work-life balance among military law enforcement personnel and their spouses. *Journal of Criminal Psychology,* 24, 113–119.

Mental Health Advisory Team V. (2008). *Mental Health Advisory Team (MHAT) V Operation Iraqi Freedom 06–08: Iraq, Operation Enduring Freedom 8: Afghanistan.* Retrieved from: www.armymedicine.army.mil/reports/mhat/mhat_v/mhat-v.cfm.

Mental Health Advisory Team VI. (2009). *Mental Health Advisory Team (MHAT) VI Operation Iraqi Freedom 07–09.* Retrieved from www.armymedicine.army.mil/reports/mhat/mhat_vi/mhat-vi.cfm.

Miller, L. (2006). *Practical Police Psychology: Stress Management and Crisis Intervention for Law Enforcement.* Springfield, IL: Charles C. Thomas Publisher, Ltd.

Miller, L. (2010). *METTLE: Mental Toughness Training for Law Enforcement.* Flushing, NY: Looseleaf Law Publications.

Mulligan, K., Fear, N.T., Jones, N., Wessely, S., & Greenberg, N. (2010). Psycho-educational interventions designed to prevent deployment-related psychological ill-health in Armed Forces personnel: A review. *Psychological Medicine,* 41(4) 673–686.

Paton, D., Violanti, J., Johnston, P., Burke, K.J., Clarke, J., & Keenan, D. (2008). Stress shield: A model of police resiliency. *International Journal of Emergency Mental Health,* 10, 95–107.

Ritchie, E.C. & Curran, S. (2006). *Warrior Transition by Army Reserve and National Guard Personnel from Combat Operations in Iraq to Policing in the United States.* Presented to the International Association of Chiefs of Police, Police Psychological Services Section, Boston.

Sheehan, D.C. & Van Hasselt, V.B. (2003). Identifying Law Enforcement Stress Reactions Early. *FBI Law Enforcement Bulletin,* 72(9), 12–17.

Stetz, T.A., Stetz, M.C., & Bliese, P.D. (2006). The importance of self-efficacy in the moderating effects of social support on stressor-strain relationships. *Work & Stress,* 20(1), 49–59.

Warner, C.H., Appenzeller, G.N., Breitbach, J.E., Mobbs, A., & Lange, J.T. (2011). *The CARE Framework: The Broadening of Mental Health Services in a Deployed Environment.* In Adler, A.B., Bliese, P.D., & Castro, C.A. (Eds.) *Deployment Psychology: Evidence-Based Strategies to Promote Mental Health in the Military.* Washington, DC: American Psychological Association.

8

LAW ENFORCEMENT IN CORRECTIONS

*Andrea M. Brockman, Brandi Burque,
Vincent B. Van Hasselt, and Monty T. Baker*

Introduction

Research on stress in police and correctional officers has proliferated over the past several years. Investigative efforts addressing police stress is expansive and includes its causes, consequences, and assessment (Sheehan & Van Hasselt, 2003; Van Hasselt, Sheehan, Sellers, Baker, & Feiner, 2003). However, correctional officer stress research is limited in its extent and scope, focusing primarily on the identification of the sources of stress (Cheek & Miller, 1983; Finn, 1998; Grossi, Keil, & Gennaro, 1996). The deleterious consequences of stress in the field of corrections are well documented and include: extended use of sick leave, job turnover, understaffing, hostility and violence by officers (Dowden & Tellier, 2004; Finn, 1998). Further, institutional liability may increase due to incidents of officer-to-inmate violence. The implications of stress at home are also important to understand with regard to both marriages and families. It is important to determine the various causes of stress, especially those that are unique to the field of corrections, and the effects on both the individual and the institution. Such information is needed to identify and implement stress assessments and interventions for this unique population.

Causes of Correctional Officer Stress

Work Stress

Stress is a response to one's environment which results in physiological, psychological, and behavioral changes (Frazier & Chapman, 2000; Pollak & Singer, 1998). In high-risk occupations, stress leads to a decrease in job satisfaction, increased rates of burnout, and physical and/or mental

145

symptoms (Dvoskin & Spiers, 2004). One survey of correctional officers revealed that the most frequent stress reactions encountered were over-irritability, anger outbursts, and headaches (Keinan & Malach-Pines, 2007).

Task-Related Stressors

Correctional officers are required to maintain order, security, and control (Castle & Martin, 2006; Jurik & Halemba, 1984). Throughout the day, their responsibilities vary as they are faced with an ever-changing environment. Researchers have identified task-related stressors which impact the officer's ability to adequately respond to their fast-paced environment. These include: workload, role problems, role ambiguity (Keinan & Malach-Pines, 2007; Lambert, Hogan, Barton, Jiang, & Baker, 2008; Morgan, 2009; Schaufeli & Bakker, 2004; Tewksbury & Higgins, 2006; Triplett & Mullings, 1999), and dangerousness (Black, 2001; Castle & Martin, 2006; Cullen, Link, Wolfe, & Frank, 1985b; Dowden & Tellier, 2004; Keinan & Malach-Pines, 2007; Triplett & Mullings, 1999). Dowden and Tellier (2004) found that the strongest predictive variables of stress in correctional officers were related to work tasks, lack of participation in decision-making, low job satisfaction, low commitment, and high turnover.

Understaffing has historically been an issue in correctional settings (Finn, 2000). The inability to complete assigned tasks is often a function of departmental expectations and understaffing. Although the inmate population in the United States continues to grow, hiring of correctional officers has consistently decreased, impacting the time needed to complete required tasks (i.e., head counts, searches, paperwork) (Finn, 2000). Further, inadequate staffing leads to situations in which one officer may be in charge of a large number of inmates, causing high levels of anxiety.

Prisons are universally recognized as dangerous (Black, 2001; Dowden & Tellier, 2004) for those working in these environments. When understaffed, the response time for additional or backup officers to arrive following a violent act will increase, leaving the first responders feeling isolated and at risk (Finn, 2000). And, an officer's perception of danger significantly impacts occupational stress, which, in turn, affects job satisfaction (Black, 2001; Castle & Martin, 2006; Dowden & Tellier, 2004; Cullen et al., 1985b; Triplett & Mullings, 1999). Finn (1998) noted that hostage-taking, assaults, riots, and inmate suicides are all sources of stress for officers. However, it is not always merely the incident that is the source of stress, but also lack of confidence and feelings of uncertainty concerning their responsibilities. Cheek and Miller (1983) reported that, in crises, officers felt they did not receive appropriate training to handle the situation properly, and were fearful that they would do something wrong. In general, an officer may lack confidence in their role as inmate supervisor (Black, 1982). Further, the unpredictability of assaults is an ongoing danger and stressor for correctional officers. Some officers may have more difficulty dealing with this unpredictability than the event itself (Cullen et al., 1985b).

Dangerousness also is associated with role conflict and ambiguity, as well as family conflict (Lambert, Hogan, & Barton, 2002). Both role conflict and ambiguity could be potential causes of perceived dangerousness of the job. Officers suffering from role strain may have more difficulty and feel that their safety is at greater risk (Castle & Martin, 2006). Additionally, perceived dangerousness may also cause family conflict (Lambert et al., 2002). However, contrary to previous research (Black, 2001; Castle & Martin, 2006; Cullen et al., 1985b; Dowden & Tellier, 2004; Triplett & Mullings, 1999), Finn (2000) and Tewksbury and Higgins (2006) observed a decrease in work stress as time spent with inmates increased.

Communication is an essential feature in correctional settings. Communication problems, such as providing limited instructions, make completing tasks difficult, leading to frustration and stress. Similarly, a lack of input into decision-making has a significant negative affect on job stress (Morgan, 2009). Limiting staff input leads to feelings of frustration, especially when related to their duties. With constant changes in one's work activities and work roles, officers are often faced with conflicting directions, causing ambiguity (Glazier & Chapman, 2000). On their survey of correctional officers in an area of the Southeast United States, Lambert and Paoline (2008) found that both organizational and job characteristics are important factors in shaping job stress, job satisfaction, and level of organizational commitment for correctional workers. It is often the supervisors' attitudes that can cause tension among their staff. For example, Jacobs (1978) found that 44 percent of officers agreed that their supervisors are more sympathetic to inmates than to them. Conversely, when officers work in an environment in which they feel their supervisors are supportive and attuned with their concerns, job satisfaction increases. Indeed, in a study of stress in police officers, Cullen, Lemming, Link, and Wozniak (1985a) reported that supervisory support alleviated work stress, and family support helped mitigate general life stress.

Organizational Stress

An organizational structure is identified by the centralization, instrumental communication, and integration within an establishment, referring specifically to the management and operations of the department (Lambert, Hogan & Allen, 2006). Due to the impact it has on the general environment within the workplace, the "organization is a major source of stress for many officers" (Finn, 2000, p. 12). Sources of organizational stress include problems with: supervisory support, peer support, administration policies and actions, and job satisfaction (Castle & Martin, 2006; Keinan & Malach-Pines, 2007; McVey & McVey, 2005) – the most relevant predictors of negative job attitudes being institutional and management variables (Glazier & Chapman, 2000; Patenaude & Golden, 2000). Correctional officers are faced with a number of responsibilities which cannot be ignored. However, role conflict and role ambiguity often lead to confusion, which in turn requires officers to make decisions on a whim, ultimately resulting in work stress (Tewksbury & Higgins, 2006). As a result of the contradictory directives and lack of uniform evaluation criteria, promotional opportunities may be slowed (Black, 1982).

Role conflict is recognized as an individual's inability to identify their assigned duties and responsibilities due to conflicting information (Black, 2001; Castle & Martin, 2006; Finn, 2000; Glazier & Chapman, 2000; Rogers, 2001; Tewksbury & Higgins, 2006). This has been found to be a common occurrence in corrections as supervisors often require contact prior to decision-making (Lambert et al., 2008; Tewksbury & Higgins, 2006). Although similar, *role ambiguity* is identified as a lack in information regarding the employee's assigned position which leads to a greater source of stress as the officer is unable to identify the expectations, duties, and responsibilities of their position (Black, 2001; Finn, 2000; Glazier & Chapman, 2000; Lambert, Hogan, & Barton, 2002; Rogers, 2001). As correctional staff perceive conflict existing within their assigned duties and perceive a lack in control over their tasks, work stress often results (Tewksbury & Higgins, 2006). Stress and burnout are also associated with tensions inherent in correctional officer work. The organizational norms that structure correctional environments have as much to do with stress and burnout as do individual differences in officers (Ray, 2001).

A strong predictor of job satisfaction and psychological well-being is related to supervisor support (Brough & Williams, 2007; Tewksbury & Higgins, 2006), which can function as a buffer between encountered organizational stress and psychological disturbance. Essentially, when provided with strong supervisor support, the daily stressors are not as likely to become internalized, thus potentially increasing the likelihood of job satisfaction. Further, it appears that, as input into decision-making decreases, correctional officers indicate greater amounts of work stress (Lambert, Hogan, & Allen, 2006; Slate, Vogel, & Johnson, 2001). In other words, when officers must seek permission prior to completing a task or making a decision, greater tension and frustration develop. Further, when there is a breakdown in communication, officers experience an increase in job stress. Correctional employees therefore appear to want concrete information related to their assigned duties, regulations, and procedures (Lambert et al., 2006).

Although several organizational factors play a role in job stress, when officers are provided with supervisory support or work resources their level of stress decreases. Specifically, those correctional settings that emphasize involvement, coworker cohesion, and managerial support can reduce stress levels (Waters, 1999). In one study, when officers perceived the organization to be running well, they reported less occupational stress (Castle & Martin, 2006). One of the greatest mediators of stress is social support, that is, the greatest support often comes from coworkers. The importance of employee orientation, introducing employees to the goals and responsibilities of their position, lies in its potential influence on the work environment and, conversely, in its ability to be influenced by organizational variables (Anonymous, 2004).

External Stressors

External stressors are identified as conflicts, problems, or issues that are not directly related to stressors within the organization. However, the impact of the outside source of stress may affect correctional officers' work performance and/or their organizational commitment. Correctional officers encounter community suspicion (Keinan & Malach-Pines, 2007), while being portrayed as "stupid, animalistic, and senseless abusers" by the media (Finn, 2000, p. 15). Unfortunately, the accompanying feelings become internalized and the resulting stress interferes with their ability to complete their job tasks: "When such problems at work spill over to the worker's home life, not only does the home life of this person suffer, but the bond with the organization suffers as well" (Lambert et al., 2008, p. 94).

Strained family relationships also become a factor in correctional officer stress. Family members may find that the officer begins displacing his/her frustrations on them. When under stress, the officer may be unable to separate work from home and may treat his/her family members as inmates by issuing commands and behaving in an overly controlling manner (Gillan, 2001; Lambert et al., 2002). In addition, as stress mounts, the officer may withhold information about his/her job due to a fear of being misunderstood (Gillan, 2001). While the stress begins in the workplace, it generalizes and impacts the family, which, in turn, further affects the officer's perception of their home life. Thus, role ambiguities lead to stress both on and off the job.

Demographics

Correctional officer demographics have been identified as a factor in burnout, job satisfaction, and work stress. For example, one study examined age, experience, and education, and found that older officers with more education reported higher levels of personal accomplishment

149

(Applegate & Paoline, 2006; Lambert & Paoline, 2008; Morgan, Van Haveren, & Pearson, 2002). Officers with less education and experience reported lower levels of personal accomplishment and this deteriorated further with increasing levels of job responsibility (Morgan et al., 2002). Conversely, in another sample, Applegate and Paoline (2006) observed that more-experienced officers identified their work as routine, less satisfying, and stressful. Further, a higher education level was associated with greater role-ambiguity (Applegate & Paoline, 2006; Robinson, Proporino, & Simourd, 1997). However, Robinson et al. (1997) found that a correctional officer's level of post-secondary education does not impact job performance, job involvement, or career development.

While much of the emphasis in this area has been on male correctional officers, a significant number of females serve in this role as well. It has been reported that female correctional officers are more likely than male officers to have a higher educational background (e.g., a bachelor's degree), a professional employment history, and a greater likelihood of being divorced (Jurik & Halemba, 1984). In one study, female officers stated that they perceived themselves as having a great sense of autonomy (Applegate & Paoline, 2006). When examining work–home conflict, both female and male officers have been found to experience a high amount of work-related stress (Jurik & Halemba, 1984; Tiplett & Mullings, 1999). Further, officers of both sexes identified a lack of job variety, and of promotional or training opportunities.

Just as age and education impact job satisfaction, race also impacts work stress and satisfaction. For example, there are indications that minority officers show higher levels of effectiveness regardless of institutional context and are generally less affected by the racial composition of the inmate population with which they work than white officers (Applegate & Paoline, 2006; Britton, 1997; Patenaude & Golden, 2000). For black and Hispanic male officers, value in their work with inmates is the most important element; those who report more effectiveness are also more satisfied and experience less stress (Britton, 1997). White female officers do not perceive the work environment more negatively than do white male officers. Their positive evaluation of supervision reportedly leads to significantly higher levels of work satisfaction (Britton, 1997; Jurik & Halemba, 1984). However, a meta-analysis found that nonwhite officers, female officers, younger officers, and officers with more education held more negative attitudes toward their job (Maahs & Pratt, 2001).

Effects of Stress for Correctional Officers and Institutions

The effect of stress on correctional officers and their institutions has been duly noted by various studies. Extended use of sick leave, hostility, and violence by officers have been identified as evidence of the negative impact of stress on officers. Further, early retirement and absenteeism are other effects of stress in correctional officer work (Gardner, 1981). Job turnover rates are high, often resulting in understaffing (Dowden & Tellier, 2004; Finn, 1998). Additionally, treatment of inmates is often compromised in times of stress, thereby increasing institutional liability. The implications of stress at home are also important to understand, especially when considering that divorce rates among correctional officers have been reported to be twice the average in the general population (Huckabee, 1992). Most often, communication between intimate partners is low and very few officers seek counseling or professional help for their stress (Marston, 1993). Officers engage in what Black (1982) terms "selective communication." This communication style is used by correctional officers to determine what they will and will not disclose about their work experiences to others. This lack of communication with family members may produce marital problems which only serve to add more stress to the officer's life. Another phenomenon that was demonstrated in Cullen et al.'s (1985a) study of police officers was that stressors, such as shift changes and court problems, were significantly related to general life stress, not work stress. They indicated that most officers were able to adjust to the stressors while engaged in work duties; however, there was a significant impact on their psychological health.

Symptoms of stress experienced by correctional officers can be quite diverse. Marston (1993) found that the five most prominent symptoms reported by correctional officers were irritability, emotional tension, insomnia, headaches, and upset stomach. This study also reported that officers with a low stress tolerance often engage in self-destructive behavior such as heavy drinking and even suicide attempts. Black (1982) described additional symptoms observed in correctional officers, including moodiness, indigestion, depression, hypertension, heart palpitations, mouth and gum disease, and abrupt behavioral changes. The latter took the form of over-hostility, frequent illnesses, defensiveness, heightened suspiciousness, obsessiveness, or accident-proneness. These symptoms of stress usually result in chronic stress, fatigue, and even burnout (Black, 1982). Gerstein, Topp, and Correll (1987) support the definition of burnout as emotional and/or physical exhaustion, over-depersonalization, and lowered job productivity. Burnout results in psychological effects and manifests itself in alienation, apathy, dissatisfaction, and lack of enthusiasm and concern in the workplace.

Lindquist and Whitehead's (1986) survey of Alabama correctional officers found that about one-third reported emotional exhaustion; one-fifth stated that they treat inmates in an impersonal manner, and approximately one-fourth endorsed negative self-evaluation. Black (1982) noted that the fight-or-flight response is often repressed when dealing with inmates, since the two options are not feasible in the correctional setting. This repeated suppression can result in reduced stress tolerance, as the amount of the body's energy to handle such situations decreases. When muscle work is suppressed, possible harmful effects include muscle contraction, ulcers, and increased blood pressure, and coronary heart disease (Black, 1982). Increased and steady hyperarousal of the nervous system can result in anxiety, depression, and symptoms of post-traumatic stress disorder (PTSD) (Taylor, 2006).

Organizational Commitment, Absenteeism, and Burnout

Correctional officers' organizational commitment has been examined in relation to working conditions. For example, it has been found that perceived promotional opportunities, organizational fairness, and constructive job performance feedback are positively related to organizational commitment (Lambert et al., 2002). However, role strain and ambiguity are linked to decreased commitment (Castle & Martin, 2006). Views on punishment and rehabilitation have also been identified as significant predictors of organizational commitment (Castle & Martin, 2006; Mitchell, Mackenzie, Styve, & Gover, 2000). Employees who support the rehabilitation model are more likely to have completed post-secondary education (Robinson et al., 1997) and to identify with an organization whose major goal is treatment to achieve behavior change (Castle & Martin, 2006). In these settings, employees who adhere to punitive models may find it difficult to identify with an organization dedicated to intervention as a focus, thus leading to decreased organization commitment.

Several reasons for the difficulty in retaining correctional personnel have been identified. These include: demanding hours and shift work, inadequate pay and benefits, stress and burnout, and inaccurate or inadequate initial selection leading to the hiring of employees not suited to the job (Mitchell et al., 2000). Several surveys have evaluated organizational commitment in relation to absenteeism and turnover (Lambert et al., 2008; Tewksbury & Higgins, 2006). In one study, the most powerful predictor of turnover and absenteeism was organizational stress (Lambert et al., 2002), with absenteeism defined as the nonattendance of employees for scheduled work, and is a chronic problem. As officers experience greater stress, they report diminished job satisfaction, and are more likely to consider terminating employment (Lambert, 2001b).

Workers with lower levels of commitment are less inclined to put forth extra effort or to make sacrifices for the sake of the organization (Lambert, 2001a). According to Udechukwu (2009), the unmet needs of the correctional officer lead to dissonance between job satisfaction and job challenges. Satisfaction is based on *motivators* (intrinsic factors), which are internal factors motivated by enjoyment in the task, while dissatisfaction is due to *hygiene factors* (extrinsic factors), which are activities that are performed to achieve an outcome. Thus, when faced with inadequate supervision, poor working conditions, and strained interpersonal relationships, workers experience decreased job satisfaction. However, intrinsic aspects of the work environment lead to higher levels of job satisfaction (e.g., promotion, achievement, responsibility, and recognition). In one study, both individual characteristics (e.g., race, gender) and organizational attributes (e.g., roles, communication) were significant predictors of turnover intentions (Mitchell et al., 2000). In contrast to some of the above findings, other studies have found that dangerousness (Black, 2001; Castle & Martin, 2006; Cullen et al., 1985; Dowden & Tellier, 2004; Triplett & Mullings, 1999), gender, and tenure are not related to staff turnover (Mitchell et al., 2000).

Job burnout often occurs in those who continuously work with difficult or challenging individuals, and is characterized by physical fatigue, a sense of helplessness or hopelessness, emotional dissonance, and development of negative self-concepts and attitudes toward work, life, and others (Garland, 2002; Zapf, Seifert, Schumutte, Mertinia, & Holz, 2001). Burnout is a work-related syndrome that stems from an individual's perception of a significant discrepancy between effort and reward (Schaeufeli & Bakker, 2004). This syndrome is marked by withdrawal from and cynicism toward those persons, emotional and physical exhaustion, and irritability, anxiety, sadness, and lowered self-esteem (Frazier & Chapman, 2000; Schaeufeli & Bakker, 2004). Burnout weakens self-esteem, drains enthusiasm and motivation, evokes feelings of helplessness/hopelessness, and generates anger. In some cases, burned-out employees deal with their troubles through misuse of drugs and/or alcohol (Garland, 2002).

Insufficient clarification of roles and responsibilities has emerged as a source of stress and burnout in many studies (Keinan & Malach-Pines, 2007; Lambert et al., 2008; Morgan, 2009; Schaufeli & Bakker, 2004; Tewksbury & Higgins, 2006; Triplett & Mullings, 1996). Not surprisingly, personnel feel "caught in a bind" when: (1) conflicting messages are sent by separate supervisors; (2) assignments exceed their resources or capabilities; or (3) when tasks do not coincide with their training or skill level. Restrictions on staff autonomy and decision-making are two more ways that correctional administrations contribute to burnout (Garland, 2002). Burned-out officers may believe that coworkers will refuse to back them, that their peers are too experienced to want to help out, or that they do not have the physical or emotional strength to be effective. Burned-out correctional officers may be more willing to engage in inappropriate behavior with inmates, such as bringing in contraband, getting too friendly (e.g., calling them by their first name), or using unnecessary force (Finn, 2000).

Job Satisfaction

Job satisfaction involves the interaction between personal and organizational characteristics (Crews & Bonham, 2007). Personal characteristics include those things which employees bring with them to the organization (e.g., education, age, gender, and race). Organizational characteristics are factors associated with the work environment, such as stress, conflict, job variety, decision-making, salary, and promotion. For both men and women, perceptions of opportunities for advancement within the department have been found to be associated with higher levels of job satisfaction. Despite their demographic differences (higher education, more diverse background, professional families, and divorced/separated), women and men have been found to exhibit the same attitudes toward their work. However, in these studies, women were more likely to indicate intrinsic reasons for becoming correctional officers; men entered for the reason of job security, benefits, and/or salary (Jurik & Halemba, 1984; Tang & Gilbert, 1995).

While these stressors have effects on correctional staff, role ambiguity is most strongly associated with lowered job satisfaction (Glazier & Chapman, 2000; Lambert et al., 2002), that is, as ambiguity increases, job satisfaction decreases. Dangerousness of the position and one's supervisor were also found to be significantly related to job dissatisfaction (Applegate & Paoline, 2006). Unfortunately, as employees become dissatisfied with their position, they are likely to leave the department. To better understand job satisfaction and workplace stress, the Bureau of Prisons has developed and utilized the Prison Social Climate Survey for over 20 years (Saylor, Gilman, & Camp, 1996; Whiteacre, 2006), focusing upon quality of supervision, effectiveness of training, and working with inmates (Saylor et al., 1996).

Using the prison Social Climate Survey, employee stressors included increased involvement with inmates, lack of respect, and decreased job satisfaction and commitment (Whiteacre, 2006). With less job satisfaction there is more occupational and general stress. It is thus possible that low job satisfaction is one of the first indicators of job stress (Castle & Martin, 2006). As expected, it has been indicated that job satisfaction leads to greater organizational commitment (Lambert & Paoline, 2008). Job stress is inversely related to job satisfaction. Workers who report job stress tend to be less satisfied with their jobs (Cullen et al., 1985). Conversely, when officers believed that the possibility of advancement was available and could be achieved by demonstrating high-quality job performance, they tended to view other aspects of jail work positively as well (Whiteacre, 2006).

It is obvious that job burnout in the field of corrections can have deleterious effects. Particularly, in social service situations such as corrections, burnout can result from being overstressed and feeling

154

under-challenged (Gerstein et al., 1987). As previously mentioned, officer boredom, periods of inactivity, and lack of perceived participation in institutional decision-making have been identified as major stressors in work of correctional officers. The more powerlessness an officer experienced, the more physically exhausted and emotionally unfulfilled he felt (Saylor et al., 1996). Further, those who possessed more "bad" workdays believed that their jobs were limiting and rigid in terms of their own creativity. Griffin, Hogan, Lambert, Tucker-Gail, and Baker (2010) found that variables such as job stress, job satisfaction, and job involvement were better predictors of burnout than any demographic variable. Their findings also supported Maslach and Jackson's (1984) conclusions that the dimensions of job burnout include depersonalization, exhaustion and lack of personal accomplishment in the work setting. Satisfaction with, involvement with, and commitment to the organization are also correlated with turnover rates (Lambert & Paoline, 2010). And, as with many other fields, job satisfaction in correctional officers has been significantly correlated with life satisfaction (Lambert, Hogan, Elechi, Jiang, Laux, Dupuy & Morris, 2009).

In summary, the results of stress lead to detrimental effects for not only the individual officer, but also the institution as a whole. Ongoing stress symptoms result in chronic stress which impact one's psychological and physiological well-being. Additionally, the stress that is felt individually causes difficulties within the institution. This is manifested in sick leave, absenteeism, turn-over rates, and poor job performance, which not only jeopardize the safety of others, but also impairs the efficiency of the institution.

Correctional Officer Stress Survey

In an attempt to identify stress in corrections, past studies have utilized surveys which primarily focus upon those stressors directly related to organizational structure and demographics, ignoring the emotions, feelings, and behaviors expressed by the officers. Unlike previous researchers, Senol-Durak, Durak, and Gencoz (2006) developed a Work Stress Scale for Correctional Officers (WSSCO). This scale was developed based upon an interview format, but only included the responses of 15 correctional officers, thus limiting the available information. Open-ended questions were used to probe for information related to stressful conditions and work environment. Those items that had a high frequency were included in the scale. The content identified for inclusion included items related to work overload, role conflict and role ambiguity, inadequacies in physical conditions of prison, threat perception, and general problems.

As indicated, an early screening tool is needed to prevent the negative effects of stress in correctional settings. To address this, an ongoing research project focuses on the development of the Correctional Officer Stress Survey (CrOSS) which has been designed to extend research on a brief, early warning screening measure of stress among correctional officers. CrOSS is modeled after the development of the Law Enforcement Officer Stress Survey (Van Hasselt, Sheehan, Malcolm, Sellers, Baker, & Couwels, 2008). As seen throughout the law enforcement arena, 38 percent of correctional officers interviewed reported having experienced extremely difficult events during their work (Rogers, 2001). Of that number, 40 percent experienced an intense response to things that bring to mind the event, 38 percent reported reliving the event, and 36 percent reported feelings of alertness and jumpiness (Keinan & Malach-Pines, 2007). The purpose of developing the CrOSS is to give correctional facility administrators a tool that can be utilized for early detection of stress-related psychological, physiological, and/or behavioral changes in their employees. In this way, it is hoped that reduction and management of stress in the correctional workplace may avert the numerous consequences that are likely to arise from a highly stressed environment and staff (Tewksbury & Higgins, 2006).

The development of the CrOSS will contribute to the literature on correctional officer stress and be useful to the officers who are working in correctional institutions by providing them with a stress measure that can: (1) identify officers who may be experiencing significant stress in their lives currently; and (2) provide early detection of stress before it escalates into more serious stress-related psychological and/or physiological problems. One of their most immediate needs is to better understand the job-related stressors that detrimentally affect correctional deputies.

Current Use of Stress Management Programs in Corrections

Indeed, intervention is crucial for mitigating the impact of stress. Given the fact that there are various causes of stress for correctional officers, and that the effects have consequences for both the individual and the institution, a public health approach to stress intervention could be beneficial. Prevention is the key concept in the field of public health and it has been providing preventative recommendations for various health issues and chronic diseases. The Institute of Medicine (1994) published a document that reviewed the state of the science of preventing mental disorders and recommended new policies and programs and definitions of prevention as applied to mental and behavioral health. Accordingly, prevention programs are categorized into three categories: primary, secondary and tertiary intervention.

Primary intervention refers to a set of measures that can reduce the probability of development of a disease or disorder. Programs that provide psychoeducation and skills development and that strengthen social support systems are primary intervention strategies. *Secondary prevention* includes programs and activities that are focused on decreasing the rate of progression of a disease or disorder once it has begun, often at the stage before the symptoms are clinically obvious. These efforts can help an individual return to his/her previous state of functioning. In essence, it is the process of identifying those at greater potential risk (e.g., first responders) and applying appropriate intervention or prevention measures. Finally, *tertiary interventions* are aimed at individuals or groups whose symptoms are clinically significant, and the focus is on treatment and rehabilitation. It is suggested that the earlier the intervention, the more likely it is that an individual or institution will avoid the most deleterious consequences of the disease or disorder.

Finn (2000) identified the rationale for stress management programs, including saving administrators money by reducing overtime pay that is utilized when other officers use their sick time or leave their jobs because of stress, as well as improving officer performance and increasing institutional safety. Further, this author noted that a solid stress program can improve the morale and image of the administration by demonstrating that the department cares about its employees, as well improving relations with the union (Finn, 2000). Interestingly, Finn argues that supervisors also benefit from the program because, instead of writing up or disciplining an officer, they may have the option of referring them to the stress management program.

Initially, it should be decided whether the particular correctional facility program will be an in-house program, independent program, or a combination of both. Police stress management programs are distinguished in the same manner (Finn, 1997). An in-house program is a unit within the actual agency. An independent or, external, program uses private service providers through contracts with the agency. Hybrid programs are a combination of in-house and private practices or agencies. Of course, there are advantages and disadvantages to all three and the most important aspect for success is how they are operated and viewed by the actual officers and users of the programs. In the case studies Finn (1997) presented, each agency provided services in a successful and efficient manner. Each had components that were crucial to a stress management program, including Critical Incident Stress Management (CISM), substance abuse counseling, and family counseling. For example, one corrections agency utilizes a private counseling team of 13 full-time and three part-time counselors who not only serve the officers and their families, but also train peer counselors to be liaisons. Another department utilizes a peer support program which possesses three distinct teams to provide interventions: drug abuse team, a trauma team, and a debriefing team. The program operates in manner in which members of each team refer individuals to the chaplain. The chaplain, in turn, refers individuals, if needed, to one of the five psychologists who are contracted to treat public service personnel (Finn, 2000).

Stress management programs may be successfully applied with either a peer or professionally guided format. Peers give credence and validity to those who are professional psychologists, which may encourage more officers to seek mental health services when needed. Often, simple in-house programs which are staffed mostly by agency employees are often viewed as "tools of management," and officers may be suspicious of these programs. However, in-house programs have the advantage of utilizing familiar staff members, which increases visibility among the officers and provides the opportunity for officers to talk to someone who is part of their culture. Therefore, the hybrid programs supply the best of both worlds, however, disadvantages of the individual programs are not completely eliminated (Finn, 2000).

Indeed, these types of programs are important during varying phases of the careers of correctional officers. Referral to intervention programs are typically made once mental health or behavioral issues have already manifested themselves in problems on the job. However, what also needs to be considered is the training that is provided in the Police Academy before an officer begins his/her career. According to the *Occupational Outlook Handbook* provided by the U.S. Department of Labor (2005), the American Correctional Association and the American Jail Association provide formal instruction that includes legal restrictions, firearms proficiency, and self-defense training. Further, officers receive training on institutional policies and regulations, and in security procedures. They receive 120 hours of formal training while being employed in their first year and 120 hours of specialized training within 60 days after appointment at the U.S. Federal Bureau of Prisons. However, very little is mentioned about stress management training. Marston (1993) found that, although officers in one agency received initial stress management training, staff had not received continuing education in this area within the past 12 months.

In the academy, officers are trained in a wide array of important policies and procedures, however, they may receive only a few days of training in stress management. Some programs may outline the definition of stress, how the body reacts to stress, and various coping skills such as removing the actual stressor, removing oneself from the stressful situation, and learning stress-coping techniques. The stress-coping techniques include communication skills, attitude change, biofeedback, time management, relaxation, and exercise. These topics are covered within a limited time frame, without continual practice or reminders as the deputy's career progresses. Ongoing stress management training is crucial and could be supported by corrections personnel if presented well and endorsed by their peers. Marston (1993) found that 64 percent of officers surveyed stated that they would be interested in attending ongoing stress training if given the opportunity. Furthermore, the way in which the information is presented can mean the difference between tuning out the valuable information or actually adhering and utilizing the skills learned.

The Future of Stress Management in Corrections

Many authorities offer various opinions on what will reduce stress, especially when given the causes and effects of stress within the field of corrections. Huckabee (1992) proposes that strategies for reducing stress should be addressed in three categories: training, individual coping, and administrative change.

Training should begin at the Police Academy level and continue throughout the officer's career. Initial training should be focused on defining stress and identifying the stressors that are often encountered on the job (Gardner, 1981). In the police stress management modules employed by Amaranto, Steinberg, Castellano, and Mitchell (2003), the stress management component in training addresses types of stress, defines the human stress response, and describes the impact of stress on different aspects of the lives of officers. A PTSD module and modules covering substance abuse and domestic violence could also be implemented (Amaranto et al., 2003). Further, it would be important to address the stressors that are specific to correctional officers, as identified by research. This will provide a proper introduction and initial preview of what will be expected on the job. Rosefield (1981) suggests that management be involved in teaching the officers the proper role that they should adhere to and associated work-related duties, whether it be custodial, treatment oriented, or a combination of both.

A cognitive behavioral stress management (CBSM) approach could be utilized not only in the initial training, but also in ongoing "booster" sessions. Research regarding CBSM has shown promising results in health and sports populations (Antoni et al., 2000). CBSM uses interventions from a cognitive-behavioral approach, specifically, relaxation training, assertiveness training, problem-solving, and cognitive restructuring. In a randomized clinical trial of athletes, it was found that those exposed to a CBSM intervention experienced fewer illnesses and injuries, as well as fewer visits to a health care center (Perna, Antoni, Baum, Gordon, & Schneiderman, 2003). Further, in a ten-week CBSM program for HIV-infected gay men, it was found that those in the experimental group experienced less self-reported anxiety, anger, and mood disturbances (Antoni et al., 2000).

In applying CBSM to correctional officers, specifically in the initial training, a block of time should be devoted to illustrating the specific techniques of CBSM. Relaxation training is a key component. Hymen,

Feldman, Harris, Levin, and Mallow (1989) demonstrated that relaxation techniques, such as progressive muscle relaxation, breathing, and imagery, alleviate clinical symptom of headaches, insomnia, and hypertension. Officers who understand the physiological mechanisms of action underlying the stress response will help lend credence to physiologically based interventions. Problem-solving, as it relates not only to work-related situations, but also to financial and work strains, are also critical in the in-service training of officers. Finally, assertiveness training and social skills training would be useful in the initial phases of training.

The structure in which these issues are presented is crucial to the adherence of the learned coping skills. Providing officers and deputies with strictly psychologically and medically based programs, especially using the technical terms attached to such disciplines, can detract from the key points and individuals may "tune out" the message. One recommendation is to utilize information from sports psychology to frame stress management programs. This essentially shifts the focus from "stress management" to managing an officer's "optimal response," both on the job and at home. Providing didactic-style training and subsequent in-vivo use of the learned skills can maximize the knowledge and utility of the skills, as well as enhance an officer's performance. Asken (2005) outlined several key skills that can be taught to officers, including tactical breathing, tactical self-talk, concentration and attention skills, performance imagery, and an open discussion on stress, fear, and arousal and its impact on an individual's optimal response. "Mental toughness training," or MTT, can be divided into pre-incident training, which can be utilized with practice for real situations, and post-incident reinforcement to consolidate gains (Miller, 2009). As such, these skills can be utilized throughout the cycle of events that can occur on the job from academy training, to scenario practice, to use during an incident, to reinforcement after an incident via various interventions such as event debriefings.

Additionally, utilizing the methods demonstrated by Tomaka, Blascovich, Kelsey, and Leitten (1993) and Folkman et al. (1986) and teaching officers how to approach certain incidents that may occur on the job can be helpful. Their research focuses on how our appraisals of events, such as viewing it as a challenge or viewing it as a threat, have a direct impact on our performance. In *challenge appraisals*, the individual believes there is a possibility of mastery in the situation, whereas in *threat appraisals*, harm or loss is believed to be an inevitable consequence of the situation (Folkman et al., 1986). In a study conducted by Tomaka et al. (1993), challenge appraisals resulted in greater physiological reactivity, that is, more energy was mobilized for action. Specifically, cardiac activity increased and vascular resistance decreased. In contrast, threat appraisals were correlated with poorer task performance and negative beliefs about abilities. The series of studies conducted by Tomaka et al. (1993) demonstrated that a cognitive appraisal model can predict subjective, physiological, and behavioral reactions to stressful stimuli. Tomaka, Blascovich, Kibler, and Ernst (1997) found that manipulating the instructions on how a task is presented directly influences the use of challenge and threat appraisals.

Training should also have a crisis management and critical incident component. Teaching correctional officers how to handle a variety of inmate situations, such as suicide and violence, could build their confidence and alleviate some of the fear of uncertainty they experience. Garcia (2004) reported that crisis negotiations are incredibly important in correctional settings as a result of the number and composition of the inmate population, as well as the "litigious climate" surrounding corrections. He suggests training and utilizing the Special Emergency Response Team (SERT) that are developed for corrections facilities, since most often, institutions use outside Special Weapons and Tactical (SWAT) teams. Further, given the rise in the number of mentally ill inmates in the U.S. prison system, it is also suggested that mental health training and negotiations be a major part of the training of correctional officers (Mandeville, 2003). Parker (2009) studied the utility of a mental health training course for correctional officers within a special housing unit. This involved a ten-hour mental health training seminar conducted by the National Alliance on Mental Illness (NAMI) which was distributed among five weekly sessions, followed by additional training 15 months after the initial meeting. Although the mechanisms of change are not readily understood, the implementation of this training program was associated with a reduction in correctional officers' use of force, as well as in a reduction of inmate violence toward officers.

Romano (2003) outlined specific areas of interest in training for successful negotiations in corrections. Officers should be required to attend the FBI school of hostage negotiations as well be trained in hostage survival techniques since it is possible that in hostage situations officers will be taken hostage as evidenced in the 1971 Attica prison riot. The skills learned can not only be utilized during a critical incident, but also in dealing with inmates on a daily basis. A correctional officer in Vermont's Northern State Correctional Facility has pointed out that any time you interact with an inmate, whether it is positive or negative, you are making a connection (Corrections Forum, 1998). As a result, learning skills to better interact with inmates will increase confidence and reduce anger, hostility, and the probability of violence. Wittenberg (1996) reported that institutional disturbances could be decreased or eliminated if officers could communicate more effectively about inmates' concerns before they escalate to crisis level. Hutchinson, Keller, and Reid (2005) purport that increased staff interaction with inmates serves to encourage positive behavior and compliance with the institutional rules. Further, it enables officers to detect and often resolve issues before they elevate to crisis level. Reducing stress levels correlates with decreases in the number of critical incidents because of better problem-solving skills, enhanced communication, and lowered perception of threats. Crisis communication training could reduce correctional officer stress by decreasing role ambiguity and role conflict. It may also enable correctional officers to gain a new sense of job satisfaction and increased self-confidence to deal with perceived and actual threats. Further, it could reduce burnout and officers feeling under-challenged at work. All of the stress-management covered in the initial Academy training should also be offered as continuing education seminars throughout their careers, as well as utilized as tools in counseling and therapy.

Finally, in the realm of administration, supervisors should be trained and required to attend ongoing seminars in the topics delineated above. Supervisors should be aware of the significance of allowing their officers the opportunity for open communication and of providing officers some opportunities to participate in the decision-making process. Cullen et al. (1985a) found that supportive supervisors helped alleviate the pressure and stress at work experienced by correctional officers. Further, if officers are given the opportunity to feel more in control of their environment and also are given time to engage in stimulating activities, they tend to feel less job dissatisfaction and stress (Gerstein et al., 1987). Lambert et al. (2009) indicates that officers who are provided with decision-making opportunities, job autonomy, and organizational justice have higher levels of job satisfaction among officers. Finally, crisis negotiation training (CNT) should be offered and required by supervisory staff in order to gain support for officers who are trained in this module, as well to promote the actual use of these techniques.

Coping resources are a main focus of training. Instructing officers about the various types of coping that individuals can employ, as illustrated by Folkman et al. (1986), provides officers with an idea of what are the normal ranges of feelings when faced with a variety of stressful situations, as well as instructing them in the most effective coping strategies. Emphasis should be placed on social supports through administration, peers, and family, with instruction on maintaining open communication with all types of relationships (Keinan & Malach-Pines, 2007). These skills should continue to be reinforced throughout their training and after any incident that occurs. Through framing these skills in such a manner, it may be easier to change the stigma associated with behavioral health and increase the use of these techniques when faced with difficulties on the home front.

Future Directions

Although a part of the law enforcement community, the field of corrections entails unique stressors for the officer. Understanding the different environment and the stressors involved can guide the clinician in formulating effective strategies for assessment, training, and intervention. Further research in this field addressing new training initiatives would be beneficial in order to ascertain training techniques that would be effective in reducing stress rates for correctional officers. Current research is being conducted on the development and norming of a population-specific stress assessment measure, the Correctional Officer Stress Survey (CrOSS). This assessment tool may be invaluable in identifying and addressing officer-specific stressors for training and intervention. Finally, future research should also focus on developing intervention programs to include both secondary and tertiary interventions and measures to study their efficacy on stress-related disorders in this population.

References

Amaranto, E., Steinberg, J., Castellano, C., & Mitchell, R. (2003). Police stress interventions. *Brief Treatment and Crisis Intervention*, 2003(3), 47–53.

Anonymous (2004). Correctional officers. *Corrections Compendium*, 29(4), 10–25.

Antoni, M., Cruess, D., Cruess, St., Lutgendorf, S., Kumar, M., Ironson, G., Klimas, N. et. al. (2000). Cognitive behavioral stress management intervention effects on anxiety, 24-hr urinary norepinephrine output, and T-cytotoxic/suppressor cells over time among symptomatic HIV-infected gay men. *Journal of Consulting and Clinical Psychology*, 68(1), 31–45.

Applegate, B. & Paoline, E. (2006). Jail officers' perceptions of the work environment in traditional versus new generation facilities. *American Journal of Criminal Justice*, 31(2), 64–80.

Asken, M.J. (2005). *Mindsighting: Mental Toughness Skills for Police Officers in High Stress Situations*. Camp Hill, PA: www.mindsighting.com.

Black, R. (1982). Stress and the Correctional Officer. *Police Stress*, February, 10–16.

Black, S. (2001). Correctional employee stress & strain. *Corrections Today*, 63(6), 82–85.

Britton, D.M. (1997). Perceptions of the work environment among correctional officers: Do race and sex matter? *Criminology*, 35(1), 85–105.

Brough, P. & Williams, J. (2007). Managing occupation stress in a high-risk industry: Measuring the job demands of correctional officers. *Criminal Justice and Behavior*, 34(4), 555–567.

Castle, T.L., & Martin, J.S. (2006). Occupational hazard: Predictors of stress among jail correctional officers. *American Journal of Criminal Justice*, 31(1), 65–80.

Cheek, F., & Miller, M. (1983). The experience of stress for correction officers: A double-blind theory of correctional stress. *Journal of Criminal Justice*, 11, 105–120.

Crews, R., & Bonham, G. (2007). Strategies for employee retention in corrections. *Corrections Compendium*, 32(3), 7–29.

Cullen, F., Lemming, T., Link, B., & Wozniak, J. (1985a). The impact of social supports on police stress. *Criminology*, 23(3), 503–522.

Cullen, F.T., Link, B.G., Wolfe, N.T., & Frank, J. (1985b). The social dimensions of correctional officer stress. *Justice Quarterly*, 2(4), 505–532.

Dowden, C. & Tellier, C. (2004). Predicting work-related stress in correctional officers: A meta-analysis. *Journal of Criminal Justice*, 32, 31–47.

Dvoskin, J.A. & Spiers, E.M. (2004). On the role of correctional officers in prison mental health. *Psychiatric Quarterly*, 75(1), 41–59.

Finn, P. (1997). Developing a law enforcement stress program for officers and their families. *National Institute of Justice Issues and Practices*, 1–217.

Finn, P. (1998). Correctional officer stress: A cause for concern and additional help. *Federal Probation*, 62(2), 65–74.

Finn, P. (2000). Addressing correctional officer stress: Programs and strategies. *National Institute of Justice Issues and Practices*, 1–126.

Folkman, S., Lazarus, R.S., Dunkel-Schetter, C., DeLongis, A., & Gruen, R., (1986). The dynamics of a stressful encounter: Cognitive appraisal, coping and encounter outcomes. *Journal of Personality and Social Psychology*, 50, 992–1003.

Garcia, J. (2004). Are correctional emergency response teams prepared for the new generation of correctional facilities? Retrieved from www.corrections.com on March 1, 2009.

Gardner, R. (1981). Guard Stress. *Corrections Magazine*, October, 7–14.

Garland, B. (2002). Prison treatment staff burnout: Consequences, causes and prevention. *Corrections Today*, 64(7), 116–121.

Gerstein, L., Topp, C., & Correll, G. (1987). The role of the environment and person when predicting burnout among correctional personnel. *Criminal Justice and Behavior*, 14(3), 352–369.

Gillan, T. (2001). The correctional officer: One of law enforcement's toughest positions. *Corrections Today*, 63(6), 112–115.

Glazier, B. & Chapman, B. (2000). *Stomp Out Stress: Summary Report*. National Institute of Justice, Corrections and Law Enforcement Family Support Program.

Griffin, M., Hogan, N., Lambert, E.G., Tucker-Gail, K.A., & Baker, D.N. (2010). Job involvement, job stress, job satisfaction, and organizational commitment and the burnout of correctional staff. *Criminal Justice and Behavior*, 37(2), 239–255.

Grossi, E.L., Keil, T.J., and Vito, G.F. (1996). Surviving the joint: Mitigating factors of correctional officer stress. *Journal of Crime and Justice*, 19(2), 103–120.

Huckabee, R. (1992). Stress in corrections: An overview of the issues. *Journal of Criminal Justice*, 20, 479–486.

Hutchinson, V., Keller, K., & Reid, T. (2005). Inmate Behavior Management. *American Jails*, May/June, 9–13.

Hymen, R., Feldman, H., Harris, R., Levin, R., & Mallow, G. (1989). The effects of relaxation training on clinical symptoms: A meta-analysis. *Nursing Research*, 38, 216–220.

Institute of Medicine. (1994). Reducing risks for mental disorders: Frontiers for preventative intervention research. Washington, DC: National Academy Press.

Jacobs, J. (1978). What prison guards think: A profile of the Illinois force. *Crime & Delinquency*, 24(2), 185–196.

Jurik, N.C. & Halemba, G.J. (1984). Gender, working conditions, and the job satisfaction of women in a non-traditional occupation: Female correctional officers in men's prisons. *Sociological Quarterly*, 25(4), 551–566.

Keinan, G. & Malach-Pines, A. (2007). Stress and burnout among prison personnel: Sources, outcomes, and intervention strategies. *Criminal Justice and Behavior*, 34(3), 380–398.

Lambert, E.G. (2001a). Absent correctional staff: A discussion of the issue and recommendations for future research. *American Journal of Criminal Justice*, 25(2), 279–292.

Lambert, E.G. (2001b). To stay or quit: A review of the literature on correctional staff turnover. *American Journal of Criminal Justice*, 26(1), 61–76.

Lambert, E.G. & Paoline, E.A. (2008). The influence of individual, job, and organizational characteristics on correctional staff job stress, job satisfaction, and organizational commitment. *Criminal Justice Review*, 33(4), 541–564.

Lambert, E., Hogan, N., & Allen, R. (2006). Correlates of correctional officer job stress: The impact of organizational structure. *American Journal of Criminal Justice*, 30(2), 227–246.

Lambert, E.G., Hogan, N.L., & Barton, S.M. (2002). The impact of work-family conflict on correctional staff job satisfaction: An exploratory study. *American Journal of Criminal Justice*, 27(1), 35–52.

Lambert, E., Hogan, N., Barton, S.M., Jiang, S., & Baker, D.N. (2008). The impact of punishment and rehabilitation views on organizational commitment among correctional staff: A preliminary study. *American Journal of Criminal Justice*, 33(1), 85–98.

Lambert, E.G., Hogan, N.L., Elechi, O.O., Jiang, S., Laux, J.M., Dupuy, P., & Morris, A. (2009). A further examination of antecedents of correctional staff life satisfaction. *The Social Science Journal*, 46(4), 689–706.

Lambert, E.G., Hogan, N.L., Moore, B., Tucker, K., Jenkins, M., Stevenson, M., & Jiang, S. (2009). The impact of work environment on prison staff: The issue of consideration, structure, job variety, and training. *American Journal of Criminal Justice*, 34, 166–180.

Lindquist, C. & Whitehead, J. (1986). Burnout, job stress and job satisfaction among southern correctional officers: Perceptions and causal factors. *Journal of Offender Counseling, Services and Rehabilitation*, 10(4), 5–26.

Maahs, J. & Pratt, T. (2001). Uncovering the predictors of correctional officers' attitudes and behaviors: A meta-analysis. *Corrections Management Quarterly*, 5(2), 13–19.

Mandeville, M. (2003). Improving mental health services in the nations prisons. Retrieved from http://www.corrections.com/articles/515-improving-mental-health-services-in-the-nations-prisons August 18, 2014.

Marston, J.L. (1993). Stress and Stressors: Inmate and staff perceptions. *American Jails*, September/October, 21–30.

Maslach, C. & Jackson, S. (1984). Burnout in organizational settings. In S. Oskamp (Ed.), *Applied Social Psychology Annual*, 5. Beverly Hills, CA: Sage.

McVey, C.C. & McVey, R.T. (2005). Responding to today's work force: Attracting, retaining, and developing the new generation of workers. *Corrections Today*, 67(7), 80–83, 108.

Miller, L. (2009). *METTLE: Mental Toughness Training for Law Enforcement*. Flushing, NY: Looseleaf Law Publications.

Mitchell, O., Mackenzie, D.L., Styve, G.J., & Gover, A.R. (2000). The impact of individual organizational, and environmental attribute on voluntary turnover among juvenile correctional staff members. *Justice Quarterly*, 17(2), 333–357.

Morgan, R.D., Van Haveren, R.A., & Pearson, C.A. (2002). Correctional officer burnout: Further analysis. *Criminal Justice Behavior*, 29(2), 144–160.

Morgan, W.J. (2009). Correctional officer stress: A review of the literature 1977–2007. *American Jails*, 23(2), 33–43.

Parker, G.F. (2009). Impact of mental health training course for correctional officers on a special housing unit. *Psychiatric Services*, 60(5), 640–645.

Patenaude, A.L. & Golden, J.W. (2000). Is race a factor in saying "I ain't working here no more": Exploring retention among Arkansas correctional officers. *Corrections Management Quarterly*, 4(1), 64–74.

Perna, F., Antoni, M., Baum, A., Gordon, P., & Schneiderman, N. (2003). Cognitive behavioral stress management effects on injury and illness among competitive athletes: A randomized clinical trial. *Annals of Behavioral Medicine*, 25(1), 66–73.

Pollak, C. & Singer, R. (1998). Low levels of stress among Canadian correctional officers in the northern region of Ontario. *Journal of Criminal Justice*, 26(2), 117–128.

Ray, G. (2001). The emotions hidden behind the badge. *Corrections Today*, 63(6), 9–105.

Robinson, D., Proporino, F.J., & Simourd, L. (1997). The influence of educational attainment on the attitudes and job performance of correctional officers. *Crime and Delinquency*, 43(1), 35–52. www.ncjrs.gov/pdffiles1/nij/grants/188094.pdf

Rogers, J.B. (2001). *FOCUS I Survey and Final Report: A summary of findings: Families officers and corrections understanding stress.* U.S. Department of Justice.

Romano, S.J. (2003). Achieving successful negotiations in a correctional setting. *Corrections Today*, 65(2), 114–118.

Rosefield, H.A. (1981). Self-identified stressors among correctional officers. Dissertations Abstracts.

Saylor, W., Gilman, E., & Camp, S. (1996). *Prison Social Climate Survey: Reliability and validity analyses of the work environment constructs.* Office of Research and Evaluation: Federal Bureau of Prisons. http://www.bop.gov/resources/research_projects/published_reports/cond_envir/oresaylor_pscsrv.pdf

Schaufeli, W.B. & Bakker, A.B. (2004). Job demands, job resources, and their relationship with burnout and engagement: A multi-sample study. *Journal of Organizational Behavior*, 25(3), 293–315.

Senol-Durak, E., Durak, M., & Gencoz, T. (2006). Development of work stress scale correctional officers. *Journal of Occupational Rehabilitation*, 16(1), 157–165.

Sheehan, D.C., & Van Hasselt, V.B. (2003). Identifying law enforcement stress reactions early. *FBI Law Enforcement Bulletin*, 72, 12–17.

Slate, R.N., Vogel, R.E., & Johnson, W.W. (2001). To quit or not to quit: Perceptions of participation in correctional decision-making and the impact of organizational stress. *Corrections Management Quarterly*, 5(2), 68–78.

Tang, T.L.P., & Gilbert, P.R. (1995). Attitudes toward money as related to intrinsic and extrinsic job satisfaction, stress and work-related attitudes. *Person Individual Differences*, 19(3), 327–332.

Taylor, S. (2006). *Clinician's Guide to PTSD*. New York: Guilford Press.

Tewksbury, R. & Higgins, G. (2006). Prison staff and work stress: The role of organizational and emotional influences. *American Journal of Criminal Justice*, 30(2), 247–266.

Tomaka, J., Blascovich, J., Kelsey, R., & Leitten, C. (1993). Subjective, physiological, and behavioral effects of threat and challenge appraisal. *Journal of Personality and Social Psychology*, 65(2), 248–260.

Tomaka, J., Blascovich, J., Kibler, J., & Ernst, J. (1997). Cognitive and physiological antecedents of threat and challenge appraisal. *Journal of Personality and Social Psychology*, 73(1), 63–72.

Tracy, S.J. (2003). Correctional contradictions: A structural approach to addressing officer burnout. *Corrections Today*, 65(2), 90–95.

Triplett, R. & Mullings, J.L. (1999). Examining the effect of work-home conflict on work- related stress among correctional officers. *Journal of Criminal Justice*, 27(4), 371–385.

Udechukwu, I.I. (2009). Correctional officer turnover: Of maslow's needs hierarchy and herzberg's motivation theory. *Public Personnel Management*, 38(2), 69–82.

U.S. Department of Labor. (2005). *Occupational Outlook Handbook* 2004–2005 *Edition*. Qualifications and Training of Correctional Officers. Washington, DC: U.S. Government Printing Office.

Van Hasselt, V.B., Sheehan, D.C., Malcolm, A.S., Seller, A.H., Baker, M.T., & Couwels, J. (2008). The law enforcement officer stress survey (LEOSS): Evaluation of psychometric properties. *Behavior Modification*, 32(1), 133–151.

Van Hasselt, V.B., Sheehan, D.C., Sellers, A.H., Baker, M.T., & Feiner, C. (2003). A behavioral-analytic model for assessing stress in police officers: Phase I. Development of the Law Enforcement Officer Stress Survey (LEOSS). *International Journal of Emergency Mental Health*, 5, 77–84.

Waters, J.E. (1999). The impact of work resources on job stress among correctional treatment staff. *Journal of Addictions & Offender Counseling*, 20(1), 26–34.

Whitecare, W.K. (2006). Measuring job satisfaction and stress at a community corrections center: An evidence-based study. *Corrections Today*, 68(3), 70–73.

Wittenberg, P. (1996). Crisis communication. *American Jails*, January/February, 82–83.

Zapf, D., Seifert, C., Schmutte, B., Mertini, H., & Holz, M. (2001). Emotion work and job stressors and their effects on burnout. *Psychology and Health*, 16, 527–545.

Part II

SPECIAL TOPICS FOR LAW ENFORCEMENT OFFICERS

9

POLICE OFFICERS IN THE LEGAL SYSTEM

Laurence Miller

It is every police officer's nightmare: they receive notice that they are being subject to an Internal Affairs investigation, disciplinary proceeding, administrative action, or legal charge. Some officers are caught by surprise by these actions; for others, it is the culmination of a long period of problems within the department.

The purpose of this chapter is not to provide legal advice, nor to second-guess the decisions of law enforcement, public safety, and mental health administrators, but to provide practical information on two related areas: (1) for officers who find themselves in trouble, coping with the psychological stress of an internal investigation, disciplinary action, legal charge, and their aftermath; and (2) whether as a defendant, witness, or arresting officer, how an officer can make his or her best presentation in court.

Reasons for an Internal Investigation or Other Action

Law enforcement officers may find themselves under the microscope for a variety of reasons. The following list is not exhaustive, but represents the most common factors (Miller, 2004, 2006b, 2009): excessive force, abuse of authority, substandard performance, corruption, theft, drug dealing, domestic battery, intoxication on duty, misuse of weapons or other equipment, racial bias or insensitivity, sexual harassment, perjury in court, or conduct unbecoming an officer on or off-duty.

Police officers are not alone. Other professionals who may come under administrative, disciplinary, or legal action include firefighters, paramedics, medical doctors, psychologists and other mental health clinicians, attorneys and judges, teachers, clergy, airline or other transportation crew, corporate or government executives, and political figures.

What these professionals all have in common is that they occupy positions of high public authority and trust. Like law enforcement officers, society places great power and responsibility in their hands and so we hold them to a higher standard of personal and professional conduct than other types of workers. That is why supervisors in these fields take the position that tolerating even a few bad apples can have devastating repercussions on the department and the profession as a whole. And that is why investigators may seem especially zealous in pursuing those who are suspected of breaking the rules.

Possible Consequences of an Internal Investigation

Although there can be several kinds of administrative and legal actions stemming from a particular incident or pattern of behavior, probably the one that is feared and loathed the most by law enforcement officers is the departmental internal investigation, because this comes from inside the tribe, from one's fellows and professional compatriots, from the folks who should *understand*. While the details vary from agency to agency, there are several possible outcomes of a departmental internal investigation.

Exoneration. The charges are found to have an insufficient basis to sustain them, the officer is thanked for his/her cooperation, and is returned to duty.

Discipline. The investigating panel concludes that the officer did do something wrong, but not severe enough to be terminated, so he/she may be subject to a range of sanctions, from suspension with or without pay, to demotion in rank, reassignment to other duties, removal from a special unit, verbal or written reprimand, or other measures.

Termination. The charges are either serious enough in themselves, or they occur following a string of prior violations, to warrant the officer being fired from the department.

Criminal prosecution. The case is serious enough to be turned over to local or federal prosecutors for further investigation that may lead to criminal charges being brought against the officer, most commonly in excessive force cases, violation of a suspect's civil rights, or where the officer was involved in outright criminal activity.

Civil lawsuit. This is an action that may be taken by a third party who sues the officer—and typically the department and the municipality as well—for physical, emotional, financial, or other damages. Most commonly, the plaintiff is the subject (or the surviving family member of a deceased subject) of an allegedly excessive action or of an insufficient or negligent action on the officer's part. Even if the department or agency is not directly involved in this lawsuit, the worker's personnel file and other records may be subpoenaed by plaintiff or defense counsel for use in the case.

Personal damage. Ruined reputation, family crisis, financial disruption, reduced employment prospects, media intrusion, and personal mental health and substance abuse problems are all possible sequelae to the stress of being investigated, charged, and/or sued.

Psychological Reactions to an Internal Investigation or Other Legal or Administrative Action

While each officer will respond individually, based on his or her unique personality, temperament, and personal history, certain reaction patterns occur fairly commonly.

Fear. Suddenly, the officer's career is on the line and, with it, his/her whole sense of personal and professional identity. There may be good moments, when the officer is able to put it out of his/her mind and hope for the best, and bad moments when he/she is close to panic.

Anger. "I can't believe this is how I get treated for doing my job!" If the officer feels that the actions in question were justified or that the department is overzealously pursuing this case because of political pressure, a personal vendetta, or just an unwillingness to understand the officer's point of view, anger may be the result. Even worse is when they believe that the discipline was meted out unfairly; in some cases, the officer knows of other personnel who have done the same thing, or worse, and got away with it.

Hopelessness/helplessness. Many officers facing administrative or legal action go through periods where they just crash and succumb to demoralization and defeat. If something this awful can happen, they tell themselves, then what's the point of anything? They may walk around feeling drained of energy and motivation until a swell of panic or anger hits again, propelling an emotional roller-coaster that may lead some officers to suspect that they are going crazy.

Recklessless/revenge. Sometimes, as a reaction against feeling like an impotent victim, the officer will get the urge to act out in some way: "Okay, if they think I'm such a criminal, I'll show them how bad I can really be." This is probably a subset of the angry response discussed above and highlights the importance of officers keeping the big picture in mind and not sabotaging their own efforts (see below).

Guilt. Nobody's perfect and, as much as they hate to admit it, maybe there was some way that the officer did contribute to their own plight. Perhaps the officer really did not believe that their actions violated departmental policy or the law. Or maybe the situation was ambiguous and the officer made a judgment call which turned out to be the wrong one. Or maybe the officer did know they were doing something wrong but never thought they would get caught because everybody does it and gets away with it. In such cases, fear, guilt ("How could I have been so stupid?"), anger ("Everybody does it and I get nailed!"), and paranoia ("I'll bet this was a set-up—they've had it in for me for a long time!") may all percolate and magnify the officer's distress.

Clinical syndromes. These disturbances may be physical, such as headaches, stomach problems, or sleep disruption; or psychological, including panic disorder, depression, or sometimes full-blown post-traumatic stress disorder (PTSD). Alcohol or substance abuse is a distinct risk, further compounding the problem.

Psychological Coping Strategies for Dealing with an Internal Investigation or Other Legal Action

Some of these recommendations for officers come from other officers who have gone through this type of ordeal, while some have been suggested by police psychologists and other mental health professionals who work with law enforcement officers (Miller, 2006a, 2006b, 2007, 2008a, 2008b, and 2009).

Don't panic. Some amount of worry is unavoidable, given the seriousness of the situation. But try to maintain perspective and not become overwhelmed with worst-case scenarios. Since anxiety tends to rush in and fill any unoccupied mental space, keeping a balanced view will be aided by the next recommendation.

Strategize. At some point, sit down and figure out what you are going to do. Review the actions that led to the investigation. Be clear about what is being charged and what your options are. The game plan you develop may be modified multiple times as new information comes in and contingencies change, but at least you will *have* a game plan, which will give you a little bit more feeling of control to counteract ruminative anxiety.

Get legal help. Retain competent, qualified legal representation, whether it be your departmental legal rep or private counsel that you independently hire. Once you have representation, the rule of thumb before you take any action on your own behalf is "ask your lawyer first." You can disagree with your attorney, you can argue with him or her and, ultimately, you can choose not to take his or her advice, but use this person's knowledge and experience to guide your efforts so that they help you, not hurt you.

Keep a low profile. Feeling that you have got no one on your side, you may be tempted to publicize your travails through phone calls, e-mails, blogs, letters to the editor of local newspapers, contact with the media, and so on. Don't do it. Except for a few close, sympathetic family members and allies, most people's reaction will range from indifference to "better you than me." Additionally, in most cases, turning your case into a crusade will only further alienate those who are in the process of deliberating critical decisions about your career and your life and who might be prepared to show a little flexibility if you provide them a face-saving way of doing so. But turning your case into an us-versus-them contest of wills, and proclaiming it to the world, will usually only encourage them to defensively dig in their heels and redouble their efforts to expunge you.

Keeping a low profile also means staying out of further trouble. During a suspension, with too much free time on your hands and growing sick of the worried waiting that consumes each passing day, you may be tempted to go out, have some fun, and raise a little hell while you still can. Don't. From now until this case is resolved, behave as if there is a surveillance camera on you 24/7. It is not fair, but again, think of the larger picture. You do not want the decision-makers in your case to be teetering on the brink of exonerating you, only to suddenly learn that you were just pulled over for a DUI, were involved in a domestic violence call, got into a bar fight, made threatening phone calls to an obnoxious neighbor or former supervisor, or were seen out partying as if this whole affair were just one big joke to you. Save your celebrating for when your case is over.

Work your case. This is a far more productive way to utilize all that pent-up nervous energy. Even the best attorney cannot do everything by him- or herself, so you may have to be the point-man/woman on your case and start doing some research. With your lawyer's assent, offer to create a card or disk file and keep it organized. If clerical or computer work is not your strong suit, get help. The more information you can glean that is helpful to your case, and the more clearly you organize it, the easier time your representative will have punching it up into a form that will get your point across to those who will make the ultimate decisions in your case. Just remember to check everything with your lawyer first, so you will be a helper, not a pest.

Don't lie. One attorney I know put it this way: "All you need is one tiny speck of bullshit to stink up the whole room." Translation: If I think you're lying to me once, what are the chances of me ever believing anything you say again? This goes for what you tell your attorney, the investigators, or testify to at any review board hearing, deposition, or court trial; in the latter case, you risk being charged with perjury. Work the legitimate points of your case to the max, but understand that if you are caught lying, you have just handed your adversaries the shovel to bury you with.

Seek mental health counseling. If you feel you can deal on your own with the stresses of having your life dissected, then all power to you. But the right mental health counselor can make a tremendous difference at those times when it looks like it's all going downhill and there's no one else you can vent to, either because your usual sounding boards and support systems are getting tired of hearing about it or you don't want to further burden them. On a practical level, having a mental health clinician in your back pocket is not only a source of emotional support, but can provide essential reality-checks that keep you from acting like a jerk and sabotaging your own case. As with all such actions, if you seek the services of a mental health counselor, let your attorney know and, if you want the two professionals to communicate, be sure to sign the appropriate release documents.

Have a Plan B. And, preferably, a Plan C and D, too. If, despite your best efforts, worse comes to worst and it looks like your professional career in this department, or in law enforcement generally, is over, then it is vital to have some contingency plans made ahead of time for what you are going to do in your new life. Understandably, this kind of advance planning is especially hard because the mere acknowledgment of alternative plans may seem like you are jinxing yourself or giving in to the possibility of your first choice—that is, keeping your present job—going down in flames. But these contingency plans should be made for the same reason people buy health or disaster insurance: you hope the big illness or hurricane one does not hit, but if it does, you want to be prepared.

Again, this type of planning may also be a productive way to keep your mind focused while you are waiting. Check out alternative employment opportunities, get some additional training, finish that degree you always promised you would complete, call up some old contacts and call in some old favors, and so on. Acting rationally, constructively, and courageously on your own behalf can be one of the most stress-reducing and self-empowering actions you can take.

Testifying in Court for Law Enforcement Officers

Whether as a defendant in an internal investigatory or legal hearing related to one's own charges of misconduct, or as an arresting officer in a criminal case, testifying in court can be one of the most stressful aspects of the job for many officers, a venue where they are not the ones in charge, but may be subject to the wiles and manipulation of clever attorneys during aggressive cross-examination. Whether for purposes of your own case, or as a witness in another case, this section of the chapter provides practical recommendations for testifying in court based on a survey of literature, the practical experience of my law enforcement colleagues, and my own experience as an expert witness in forensic psychology (Miller, 1996, 1997, 2006, in press).

Types of Witnesses and Testimony

A *fact witness* is someone who has personal knowledge of events pertaining to the case and can only testify to things he or she has personally observed.

A fact witness may not offer *opinions*, which are interpretations of facts they have observed or that they have learned about through third parties. Opinions are the province of the *expert witness*, who is retained by an attorney or appointed by the court precisely to assist the factfinders (judge or jury) in understanding specialized technical knowledge that would otherwise be beyond their expertise. Expert witnesses are typically credentialed specialists in forensically related fields, such as a medical examiner, crime lab expert, firearms specialist, or forensic psychologist. Although experts are typically allowed more latitude in testimony than fact witnesses, the content of their testimony is also carefully vetted by the court for admissibility.

Police officers may find that their testimony sometimes spans the domains of fact and expert witness. For example, an officer may be queried about what he/she did and what the defendant did, like a fact witness, and then asked to state an opinion like an expert witness. Or he/she may state such an opinion, which the opposing attorney may challenge, and the judge must decide whether or not to allow it to be admitted into the record.

Attorney:	Officer Jackson, can you tell us how you first approached the defendant while undercover?
Officer:	Well, actually, he first approached me.
A:	What do you mean?
O:	I was undercover as a local high school student, and the defendant came over and asked me if I "needed directions."
A:	And what did you answer?
O:	That I was "going uptown."
A:	Can you explain to this court what that conversation means?
O:	Well, in that neighborhood, "needing directions" means if you want to buy drugs, and "uptown" is coke or sometimes crystal meth—some kind of stimulant drug.
A:	But at no time did the defendant actually ask you if you, quote–unquote, "wanted to buy drugs," did he?
O:	Not in those words.
A:	So you don't know for sure if he really intended to sell you drugs or was just trying to help out.
O:	Of course I knew. That's the language they use.
A:	Officer Jackson, are you an expert in linguistics?
O:	No, but I'm an expert on that neighborhood—I've worked undercover there for five years.

Preparing for Testimony

Police officers should understand the importance of proper record keeping and strive to develop a well-organized, standardized, and readable style for writing reports—not just because these may be read by probing, critical eyes, but because writing out one's thoughts in words is an excellent way to clarify, organize, and remember the points you will want to get across, should this case come to trial.

There is no such thing as too much preparation and officers should review their case as often as necessary. The more thoroughly an officer knows their facts and theories about the case, the easier it will be to answer questions thrown from "left field" because the officer will not be relying on rote memorization of individual answers to different questions, but will rather be in command of an organic, holistic, automatic process that is hard to trip up by clever cross-examination. When the case involves the officer him- or herself, they will probably have one or more meetings with their attorney to go over the planned testimony and to anticipate any challenges from the other side. In a regular, job-related criminal case, the officer may have met with the prosecutor or may sometimes walk into the courtroom cold.

On the Stand

Certainly, most important aspects of courtroom demeanor cannot be programmed; every witness brings his or her own unique style to the stand. Nevertheless, there are a few principles of effective testimony that all witnesses can productively apply (Anderson, Swenson, & Clay, 1995; Mogil, 1989; Posey & Wrightsman, 2005, Vinson & Davis, 1993).

To the average juror, a police officer conveys an air of authority and respect. Officers should use this to their advantage, displaying a general attitude of confidence but not cockiness. They should maintain composure and dignity at all times and behave like professionals. This includes both voice and body language. Officers should sit up straight and avoid fidgeting or slouching. If there is a microphone, the officer should sit close enough so they do not need to lean over every time they speak. Notes, records, and presentation materials should be kept neatly organized in front of the officer, so he/she can find documents and exhibits when needed.

While testifying, the officer should look at the attorney while they are being questioned, then switch eye contact to the jury while answering the question, because jurors tend to find witnesses more credible when they feel directly and personally engaged. Officers should be neither overly aloof nor overly intense, but rather strive to appear open, friendly, and dignified. They should speak as clearly, slowly, and concisely as possible, keeping sentences short and to the point, and maintaining a steady and conversational tone of voice. The officer's overall attitude toward the jury should convey a sense of mutual respect: you are there to present the facts as you know them to a group of mature adults who, you are confident, will make the right decision.

The officer is well advised to listen carefully to each question before responding. If the question is not fully understood, the officer should ask the attorney to repeat it or rephrase it, and not be pressured into giving a quick answer, if they needs a couple of seconds to compose their thoughts. The officer should speak as clearly and concisely as possible and answer the question completely, but not over-elaborate or ramble. If the officer does not know the answer to a question, he/she should state plainly, "I don't know," and certainly not try to bluff his/her way out of a tricky question. The officer should avoid being baited into become defensive and should always answer questions honestly.

Attorneys will typically phrase questions in a way that constrains the witnesses' answers in the direction they want them to go. If the officer feels they cannot honestly answer the question by a simple yes-or-no answer, they should say so: "Sir/Ma'am, if I limit my answer to yes or no, I will not be able to give factual testimony. Is that what you wish me to do?" Sometimes, the attorney will voluntarily reword the question. If the attorney presses for a yes-or-no answer, at that point either the officer's attorney will pop up to voice an objection or the judge will intervene. The latter may instruct the cross-examining attorney to allow the officer more leeway in responding, or to rephrase the question, or the judge may simply order the officer to answer the question as it has been asked, in which case that's what they will do, to the best of their ability.

Another attorney tactic is to phrase questions in such a way as to force the officer to respond in an ambiguous manner, often prefacing the answer with such phrases as "I believe," "I estimate," "To the best of my knowledge/recollection," "As far as I know," "I'm pretty sure that," etc. If the facts warrant it, the officer should be as definite about his/her answers as possible; if they do not, the officer should honestly state that this particular piece of testimony may not be a clear perception or recollection, but the officer should be firm about what he or she *is* sure about.

In general, it is a good idea not to answer beyond the question. For example, if the attorney asks the officer to phrase his/her answers in precise measurements that are not relevant or that he/she cannot accurately recall, the officer should not hypothesize or speculate, unless that is what the attorney actually asks the officer to do.

Attorney: Officer Jackson, you say you saw the defendant take two drug vials out of his jacket pocket. How far away from the defendant were you when you made this observation?
Officer: About half a block away.
A: How many feet away would that be?
O: I don't know.

A: Surely, officer, you can estimate the distance. Was it a hundred feet? Two hundred? Fifty? Ten?

O: I really can't accurately estimate the number of feet. But on that block, between myself and the defendant, there was a liquor store, a dry cleaner, and the front steps of a post office. The defendant was standing right next to the first step, close enough to observe his hand movements clearly.

Again, if the officer does not know the answer to a question, he/she should just say "I don't know." Jurors and other factfinders will respect and appreciate honest ignorance of a few details far more than an apparent attempt to make everything "fit in" by appearing to fudge the testimony.

Law Enforcement Officer as Defendant

When the officer him/herself is the defendant in a criminal trial or civil lawsuit, the tension level understandably ratchets up because this time the personal stakes are higher and rules are a little different. Now the officer's role switches from dispassionate fact or expert witness to the person on trial. In this setting, the officer may not be afforded the same deference and respect as they might be in their official police officer witness role (Chambers, 1996; Griffith, 2005; Miller, 2009). Accordingly, the officer's demeanor, while still dignified and professional, should shade slightly more to the deferential and humble side. This does not mean that the officer should bow and grovel to the jury or judge, but the prevailing attitude should convey that this officer is confident in putting his or her fate in their hands and is trusting them to do the right thing. Otherwise, the principles of effective court testimony are the same as those discussed in the previous sections.

Psychologists on the Stand

A special issue relates more directly to the role of psychologists in the legal process. It is not uncommon for officers who are being internally investigated, criminally charged, or civilly sued to have undergone psychological counseling, stress debriefing, a psychological fitness-for-duty evaluation, or other mental health services (Miller, 1998a, 1998b, 2006a, 2006b). This raises issues of confidentiality and admissibility of psychological records. Generally, it is exceedingly rare for courts to order the release of confidential mental health records, except under the most extreme circumstances. Nevertheless, to reinforce confidence in the doctor–patient relationship, a practical piece of advice for any officer in treatment who is undergoing any kind of legal proceeding is this: If there is a piece of factual case evidence that you are not sure you should reveal, *ask your lawyer first*. And if the attorney advises the officer not to tell the clinician, then they should not. Therapist and patient can still do effective psychotherapy and counseling without the clinician having to know every technical detail and, that way, nobody is put in the position of having to worry about revealing a secret that has never been told.

In those rare cases where a treating psychologists is subpoenaed to testify, the line of questioning by the prosecutor or plaintiff's attorney can be skillfully used to make it look like the clinician is hiding something, or at least that he or she is an incompetent dupe:

Attorney:	Dr. Lopez, during the course of your psychological treatment of Officer Jackson, did he render to you a history of the events he is charged with and a description of what took place?
Psychologist:	He pretty much told me what's in the record regarding the circumstances of the charges against him.
A:	Did he tell you how many times he struck Mr. Williams after he had been handcuffed and restrained?
P:	No.
A:	Isn't that something you would want to know when taking a clinical history from Officer Jackson?
P:	The exact number of strikes isn't really an important detail at that point.
A:	Did he tell you how he felt during his struggle with Mr. Williams? Was he mad? Frightened? Enraged? Was he looking for revenge?

[At this point, the officer's attorney will probably object.]

P:	We really didn't discuss that in our first session. I was more concerned with his mental status at that time.
A:	And how was he feeling, doctor? Did he express remorse? Was he sorry for what he'd done? Or was he glad Mr. Williams got what he deserved?

[Probably another objection.]

P:	He was generally upset about the injuries Mr. Williams received, as that was not his intention. As it has already been well documented in the record, Officer Jackson maintains that the injuries were accidental, sustained while Mr. Williams was violently resisting arrest in a state of extreme intoxication.
A:	And that's it, doctor? That's all you got from Officer Jackson in that first session? You mean to say, you spent

> an hour with Officer Jackson, and all he told you was what was in his initial statement?
>
> *P:* I believe I just answered the questions you asked me.

The lesson here is that no party to the case is immune from manipulative cross-examination from aggressive opposing counsel. So the recommendation for both doctor and officer is to try to maintain as much composure and dignity as possible. Remember, an important part of trial testimony is the impression the witness makes on the jury by his demeanor, language, and grace under pressure, so witnesses should avoid being either cowed into submission or baited into an angry overreaction. That is one more reason to go over one's testimony before the trial: to anticipate challenges and become comfortable with the substance of the case.

Finally, remember that most citizens, including most jurors, want to believe that the people they place their trust in—doctors, police officers, public officials—have their best welfare in mind. This means that they will often mentally bend over backward to give police officers and doctors the benefit of the doubt if these professionals can give them a credible reason to do so. It also means that if the factfinders feel insulted or manipulated through witness dishonesty or disrespect, they may come down especially hard for betraying that trust. Officers, clinicians, and all witnesses should prepare carefully for their case, be clear and honest in their testimony, maintain dignity and decorum at all time, and given a meritorious case, in most instances the system will work for them, not against them.

Summary and Conclusions

An internal investigation, criminal charge, or civil suit can be among the most stressful experiences of a law enforcement career. Consequences of such actions may include suspension, demotion, criminal prosecution, civil litigation, or other actions. Psychological effects of such actions on the officer may include fear, guilt, hopelessness, anger, and a variety of clinical syndromes. Practical and psychological coping strategies for dealing with an internal investigation or legal action against the officer include forming a coherent strategy, obtaining proper legal counsel, constructively working the case, keeping a low profile, developing alternative long-term contingency plans, and seeking mental health counseling when necessary. Strategies for effective court testimony include adequate preparation, maintaining composure and dignity, using effective communication skills, and presenting an identifiable role model image of the law enforcement professional.

References

Anderson, W., Swenson, D. & Clay, D. (1995). *Stress Management for Law Enforcement Officers.* Englewood Cliffs: Prentice Hall.

Chambers, D. (1996). Police-defendants: Surviving a civil suit. *FBI Law Enforcement Bulletin*, March, 34–39.

Griffith, D. (2005). On the hook. *Police*, September, 42–51.

Miller, L. (1996). Making the best use of your neuropsychology expert: What every neurolawyer should know. *Neurolaw Letter*, 6, 93–99.

Miller, L. (1997). The neuropsychology expert witness: An attorney's guide to productive case collaboration. *Journal of Cognitive Rehabilitation*, 15(5), 12–17.

Miller, L. (2004). Good cop–bad cop: Problem officers, law enforcement culture, and strategies for success. *Journal of Police and Criminal Psychology*, 19, 30–48.

Miller, L. (2006a). On the spot: Testifying in court for law enforcement officers. *FBI Law Enforcement Bulletin*, October, 1–6.

Miller, L. (2006b). *Practical Police Psychology: Stress Management and Crisis Intervention for Law Enforcement.* Springfield, IL: Charles C. Thomas.

Miller, L. (2007). The psychological fitness-for-duty evaluation. *FBI Law Enforcement Bulletin*, August, 10–16.

Miller, L. (2008a). Stress and resilience in law enforcement training and practice. *International Journal of Emergency Mental Health*, 10, 109–124.

Miller, L. (2008b). *METTLE: Mental Toughness Training for Law Enforcement.* Flushing, NY: Looseleaf Law Publications.

Miller, L. (2009). You're it! How to psychologically survive an internal investigation, disciplinary proceeding, or legal action in the police, fire, medical, mental health, legal, or emergency service professions. *International Journal of Emergency Mental Health*, 11, 185–190.

Miller, L. (in press). *Posttraumatic Stress Disorder and Forensic Psychology: Applications to Civil and Criminal Law.* New York: Springer.

Mogil, M. (1989). Maximizing your courtroom testimony. *FBI Law Enforcement Bulletin*, May, 7–9.

Posey, A.J. & Wrightsman, L.S. (2005). *Trial Consulting.* New York: Oxford University Press.

Vinson, D.E. & Davis, D.S. (1993). *Jury Persuasion: Psychological Strategies and Trial Techniques.* Little Falls, NJ: Glasser Legalworks.

10

SPECIAL UNITS POLICING

Hostage Negotiation, Undercover, and Sex Crimes Investigation

Laurence Miller

From *Miami Vice* to *Law & Order: SVU* to *Criminal Minds*, the public continues to display a fascination with special unit policing, partly due to the often titillatingly lurid nature of the subject matter, and partly because such stories combine the features of vicarious danger and ultimate triumph (we hope) of good over evil. Of course, these portrayals typically overlook the plodding hard work that underlies most successful special unit operations, and obscures many of the psychological variables that can influence this kind of police work. As distinct from daily patrol, these special investigatory operations are typically carried out by trained detectives within a department or division of a law enforcement agency. This chapter will describe the role of psychological factors and services in three specialized area of policing: hostage negotiation, undercover operations, and criminal investigation.

Hostage Negotiation

Hostage negotiation has achieved iconic status in the world of popular drama. Probably in no other area of law enforcement response does the negotiating officer bring to bear the full range and depth of crisis intervention psychology as in his or her efforts to resolve hostage crises. Although only a small percentage of law enforcement critical incidents deal with actual hostage taking, in probably no other kind of law enforcement response are the stakes so high in terms of immediate threat to human life (Borum & Strentz, 1992; Greenstone, 2005; Hammer & Rogan, 1997;

Hare, 1997; McMains & Mullins, 1996; Miller, 2005, 2006a, 2006b, 2006c; Rogan, 1997; Slatkin, 2005).

There are three especially dangerous periods during a hostage crisis. The first is the initial 15–45 minutes when confusion and panic are likely to be at their peak. The second is during the surrender of the hostage-takers (HTs), when, hair-trigger emotions, ambivalence, and lack of coordination among negotiators, tactical team members, HTs, and hostages can cause an otherwise successful resolution to turn deadly. Finally, tactical assault by the SWAT team carries the highest casualty rate. Tactical assault results in a 78 percent injury or death rate to hostages and/or HTs. Sniper fire results in a 100 percent death rate to the target. However, containment and negotiation strategies yield a 95 percent success rate in terms of resolving a hostage crisis without loss of life.

Hostage Crisis Response Team Structure

Consistent with the evolving conceptualization of law enforcement *crisis teams* as mutidimensional response units, hostage negotiators need to see themselves as part of the larger context of crisis management that includes suicide, robbery, hostage, barricade, bomb threat, terrorist attack, and other emergencies (Fuselier & Noeser, 1990; Hare, 1997; Terestre, 2004). Different departments may have different team structures, depending on their individual needs, but some basic, universal components of team structure include the following (Blythe, 2002; Fusilier, 1986; Greenstone, 1995, 2005; Hammer, Van Zandt, & Rogan, 1994; McMains & Mullins, 1996; Miller, 2005, 2006c, 2007; Noeser, 1999; Regini, 2002, 2004; Rogan, Hammer, &Van Zandt, 1994).

The *team leader* is a senior officer who is instrumental in organizing the crisis response team, selecting its members, planning and overseeing training, and making deployment decisions in emergencies. His role may or may not overlap with that of the *on-scene commander*, who is the person in charge of the actual hostage crisis. This individual is responsible for everything that goes on at the crisis scene, from establishing perimeters and traffic control, to directing the activity of negotiators, to deploying the tactical team, to liaising with emergency medical and community services.

Of course, the essence of a hostage crisis response team is the *negotiator*. Depending on the size of the team and the nature of the emergency, there may be one or several negotiators. The preferred model is to have one *primary negotiator* and one or more *secondary* or *backup negotiators*.

The *intelligence officer*'s job is to gather information about the hostage-taker and hostages, including family members, past criminal and/or mental health treatment history, demographics, identity of the hostages and their relation to the HT, and any other intelligence that will be useful in planning and carrying out the negotiation.

The role of the *communications officer* is to keep in contact with all of the individuals and agencies that are important in successfully managing the crisis. These can include firefighting and emergency medical services, local electrical power and phone companies, public transportation agencies, local businesses, and the media. Many departments have a special *community affairs* or *public information officer* who is charged with the specific duty of dealing with the media and the general public, so that timely, accurate, and rumor-free information is appropriately disseminated, without compromising the operation.

The *tactical team* typically consists of a Special Weapons and Tactics (SWAT) unit, specialized marksmen, and other professionals whose sole job is to make a forced entry if and when it is determined by the on-scene commander that negotiations have failed and that hostages are in imminent danger.

Role of the Police Psychologist in Hostage Crisis Response Teams

Different law enforcement agencies emphasize different roles for the police psychologist in hostage crisis team training and operational assistance in negotiations (Baruth, 1988; Bohl, 1997; Fuselier, 1988; Hatcher, Mohandie, Turner, & Gelles, 1998; Greenstone, 1995, 2005; McMains, 1988a, 1988b; McMains & Mullins, 1996; Miller, 2005, 2006c, 2007; Slatkin, 2005; Van Hasselt & Romano, 2004), so this section will attempt to synthesize these views and present a practical consensus.

Team Selection, Development, and Training

One important role of the psychologist in team formation is in the selection of team personnel, including the negotiators. Selection procedures may be by way of clinical interview, record review, standardized psychological tests, or a combination of all three. But in many cases, the psychologist will come on board after the department's crisis team has already existed for some time, and may then become involved in continuing education and training, either within the department or through local police academies or criminal justice institutes. Psychologists may also assist in organizational development training and team-building, enhancing crisis team cooperation and morale, and advising supervisors and police administrators on the art and science of personnel management.

Psychological traits and characteristics of successful hostage negotiators include: (1) determination and success-orientation; (2) self-confidence and self-reliance; (3) assertiveness and decisiveness; (4) ambiguity tolerance and cognitive flexibility; (5) frustration tolerance, persistence, and

186

self-control; (6) general intelligence, practical intelligence, and emotional intelligence; (7) insightfulness and quick thinking; (8) logical and abstract thinking; (9) imaginative and creative problem-solving; (10) verbal communication skills; (11) interpersonal perceptiveness and intuitiveness; (12) ability to use "constructive manipulation"; (13) truthfulness and sincerity; and (14) total commitment to the negotiating approach (Allen, Fraser, & Inwald, 1991; Bolz, Dudonis, & Schultz, 1996; Flin, 1996; Fuselier, 1986; Getty & Elam, 1988; Klein, 1998; McMains & Mullins, 1996; Miller, 2005, 2006c, 2007; Misino, 2002; Russell & Beigel, 1990; Slatkin, 2005).

Operational Assistance

During an actual hostage crisis, the on-scene psychologist can monitor the progress of negotiations, usually through a *dead phone* (ear piece but no voice piece), and make recommendations based on the perceived mental status of the HTs and the negotiation strategies used. Part of the psychologist's job may involve HT profiling, based on a combination of on-scene monitoring and background information provided by the intelligence officer. Relevant information may range from broad diagnostic categories to moment-by-moment mental state; for example, intoxicated, exhausted, delusional. An important aspect of HT profiling and negotiation monitoring is the assessment of risk and danger level. All this may be relevant to the negotiation process and the strategies employed.

Hostage negotiation is among the most cognitively and emotionally demanding aspects of law enforcement work, in terms of both the responsibility for human life and the sheer grueling length of some episodes which can extend into hours or days. Accordingly, another important operational role for the psychologist is to monitor the stress levels of the team members themselves. Where the primary negotiator has become physically and mentally exhausted and needs to be replaced by a secondary negotiator, the psychologist can help the first negotiator deal with any disappointment, guilt, or resentment about not being allowed to "finish the job." Finally, after the crisis is over, the psychologist may participate in both operational and stress debriefings: the former to review and critique the incident in order to learn from it; the second to deal with the emotional repercussions of the incident on the part of the team members, especially in the minority of cases where the event has gone bad and people have been injured or killed.

Undercover Policing

An important part of gathering evidence to prosecute serious crimes involves the skillful infiltration of criminal groups by specially trained officers. While the targets of undercover operations carried out by law enforcement agencies may vary—narcotics, money laundering, illegal immigration, terrorism, and so on—the fundamental goal of all undercover operations is to develop prosecutable evidence by accessing subjects and their activities from the inside. In addition to types of targets, undercover assignments vary in terms of time frame, including everything from short-term buy-bust scenarios that may take minutes or hours, to longer-term "deep undercover" investigations lasting many months or (rarely) years (Barefoot, 1975; Hibler, 1995).

Even in this age of terrorism, narcotics continue to be the largest area of focus for undercover law enforcement. Undercover narcotics work is one of the most hazardous and stressful jobs in policing. Undercover officers (UCOs) must create and play a role that is not only dangerous but also puts them in daily intimate contact with the dregs of humanity and places them at risk of detection and violent retribution; UCOs are ten times more likely than uniformed officers to be shot or shoot someone else (Geller, 1993). In addition to the ever-present danger, the work is physically, intellectually, and emotionally demanding (MacLeod, 1995). Psychologically, then, the essence of all undercover operations is the same: undercover officers knowingly and purposefully develop relationships that they will ultimately betray (Band & Sheehan, 1999; Farkas, 1986; Girodo, 1985; Hibler, 1995; Miller, 2006b, 2006c; Smith, 1994).

Every major undercover operation is a team effort, and although most UCOs pay lip service to the idea that the UCOs cannot be held individually accountable for the final outcome, no officer can avoid feeling the disappointment and anger of a blown operation (Hibler, 1995); indeed, the pain of such a failure is matched only by the recriminations observed after a failed hostage negotiation (see above). The difference is, however, that while a hostage crisis typically evolves over hours or days, undercover operations may span weeks or months, heightening the sense of having "blown it big time" when something goes wrong.

Role of the Psychologist in Undercover Operations

As much as any operation in law enforcement, successful undercover work must be a model of planning, coordination, and timing. Probably in no other kind of operation are so many roles played by so many personnel over so long a period of time, under such sustained conditions of stress. Undercover police work is thus an area where police psychologists can make a vital contribution.

Phases of an Undercover Operation and the Psychologist's Role

Hibler (1995) has described a six-stage progression of an undercover operation that can be used as a framework for understanding the psychologist's role. The basic stages are: (1) *selection* of personnel for the undercover team; (2) *training* the team; (3) *planning* the operation; (4) *deployment* of the team and carrying out of the operation; (5) *termination*, or "closedown" of the operation, either upon successful completion or because of unforeseen complications; and (6) *reintegration* of the undercover officer into normal work and life roles (Miller, 2005, 2006c, 2007). Each of these phases has its own psychological implications, to be discussed below.

Screening and Selection of Undercover Officers

The screening and selection process includes the officer's knowledge of tactics, weapons, legal principles, undercover strategies, evidence collection and preservation, and other skills, as assessed by means of performance reviews, written tests, interviews, and role-play scenarios. The psychological component usually involves some combination of a structured clinical interview and psychological testing. These evaluations should be updated every 6 to 12 months and prior to every new major assignment (Band & Sheehan 1999; Hibler, 1995).

The following characteristics comprise a profile of the "ideal UCO" (Band & Sheehan, 1999; Hibler, 1995; MacLeod, 1995). Such UCOs should be experienced, seasoned investigators of reasonably mature age, with a secure police identity and prior experience in other areas of policing. They should have had some life experience outside the police force. They must be able and willing to accept training and supervision when necessary and to work hard at perfecting their craft. They should volunteer for undercover work because they believe in its goals and methodologies and have demonstrated appropriate moral and ethical values that correspond to their belief in the purposes of legitimate law enforcement activity in a free society. Their interest in undercover work should be motivated by a justifiable pride in their ability to excel in this type of endeavor. At the same time, this should not be pursued as a quest for glory or as an escape from less desirable work or an unpleasant personal life.

Undercover officers have to be able to show perseverance and resourcefulness in the face of complex, changing, ambiguous, and often dangerous circumstances, with very little external supervision or oversight. At the same time, they cannot become free agents or loose cannons, and must be comfortable taking direction and operating within their agency's policies, procedures, and guidelines. They must be highly proficient and flexible in their undercover role plays, be proficient actors, and at the same time be able to maintain their core identities and commitment to the mission. They must be able and willing to spend long intervals away from family and friends. Importantly, they must be able to purposefully and credibly establish, nurture, and maintain close, sometimes intimate, personal relationships with a variety of different types of people, knowing that these relationships will ultimately be betrayed as part of the larger mission and their overall dedication to law enforcement.

Training

As with any operation, the purpose of training is to develop and sharpen operational performance by acquiring knowledge and practicing skills necessary for functioning in the undercover arena. In fact, selection often overlaps with training as undercover candidates are further culled in the training process. Aside from any technical knowledge the undercover officer might need to fit into his or her role, the essential essence of undercover work involves interpersonal skills. These include the ability to deal convincingly with others, to be creative, flexible, and self-disciplined in carrying out the assignment, and to be able to exert good judgment and calm behavior under stress (Hibler, 1995; MacLeod, 1995).

Preparation and Planning

As noted above, a successful undercover operation is always a team effort, and no operation of any kind can succeed without proper planning and preparation (Anderson, Swenson, & Clay, 1995; Band & Sheehan, 1999; Hibler, 1995). This includes accurate intelligence-gathering; clear, mutually understood goals for the operation; and proper support of UCOs by the assignment of a *control officer,* who will meet with the UCO periodically to exchange information, to assess the officer's stress level and mental status, and to provide a reality-check when needed.

Target Profiling and UCO Profiling

For large-scale undercover operations, psychologists may assist in providing a psychological profile of the target of the investigation. In addition, internal profiling involves determining which particular officers might be the best match for a particular target (Hibler, 1995).

THE COVER IDENTITY

The central feature of all undercover operations is creating a *cover identity* for the UCO. Unlike Hollywood depictions of chameleonic "masters of disguise" who can seamlessly slip in and out of any persona, in real life the undercover role should never be a total masquerade; in fact, the closer it is to the officer's real identity and persona, the better the chances of successfully pulling it off. These planning efforts should also take into account the personality and working style of the individual UCO (Anderson et al., 1995; Buckwalter, 1983; Hibler, 1995).

Deployment

Now the operation is set to go. At this point, everybody involved in the mission—UCO, control officer, support personnel, command, and so on—should understand their respective roles and how to interact with one another.

STRESSES OF UNDERCOVER DEPLOYMENT

Perhaps due to rigorous selection, serious stress reactions to undercover deployment are rare, and most problems reported by UCOs consist of technical and strategic matters, rather than health or psychological concerns. Rarely does a UCO require pullout on mental health grounds alone and, in those few cases, this is usually out of concern for possible danger or due to sagging motivation on the part of the UCO, not for "going nuts," as often depicted in movies. Major sources of stress for UCOs under deep cover include the agent–supervisor relationship, maintaining the role requirements of the undercover operation, resisting overidentification with the targets, and strain on family and social relationships. Major psychological reactions include anxiety, paranoia, hypervigilance, feelings of isolation, relationship problems, and corruption of the agent's value system and commitment to the operation. A number of UCOs have noted that they would have liked the opportunity to speak with a psychologist during their deployment (Anderson et al., 1995; Band & Sheehan, 1999; MacLeod, 1995; Marx, 1988).

MANAGING DEPLOYMENT STRESS

Given that the UCO's personality and behavior are the crucial tools in a successful undercover operation, proper attention to the agent's ongoing mental status is as integral to the mission as maintaining the integrity of weapons or surveillance equipment. If the UCO's psyche breaks down, the mission breaks down. Conversely, effective, well-planned psychological monitoring and intervention services can assure that UCOs may function effectively for long periods of time (Band & Sheehan, 1999; Cheek & Lesce, 1988).

To begin with, the sheer weight placed on the UCO to carry out the mission successfully implies that, to a large degree, these officers must be responsible for monitoring their own stress levels and knowing when to take appropriate steps to maintain their bodies and minds in optimal performance mode. The next line of defense consists of regular meetings with the supervisor or control officer, who keeps the UCO informed of any strategic or logistical changes in the operation's goals or tactics and also functions as a "stress barometer" to assure that the UCO is dealing with the pressures of his role assignment in a reasonably healthy and adaptive way (Anderson et al., 1995; Band & Sheehan, 1999; Marx, 1988).

Finally, some departments build into the operation regular contact with a psychologist; in other departments, this is arranged on an as-needed basis; and in still other departments, there are simply no psychological services routinely available for undercover assignments (Anderson et al., 1995; Macleod, 1995). Obviously, psychologists in this role must have some understanding of undercover work and police psychology in general.

Termination and Reintegration

Variously labeled *closedown* or *decompression*, the termination phase of an undercover operation is the formal end of the undercover part of the mission. Less glamorous, but equally important, is the phase that follows termination, in which the undercover team organizes their evidence and prepares for trial (Hibler, 1995; MacLeod, 1995).

There are three basic reasons why an undercover operation is terminated (Marx, 1988). First, the mission has been successful, the evidence needed has been gathered, arrests have been made or sufficient intelligence has been obtained for the next phase of law enforcement action. Second, after sufficient expenditure of time and resources, it becomes clear that the goals and purposes of the operation cannot be accomplished within the scope of the undercover plan, and the operation is unceremoniously terminated. Finally, in the worst case, the operation may have to be terminated because cover is blown or the security of the UCO or others is jeopardized. Often, results are mixed: some useful evidence is gathered, some targets are apprehended, but all or most of the mission's objectives may not have materialized.

TERMINATION–REINTEGRATION STRESS

The undercover role allows the UCO a certain degree of freedom and autonomy of action and the return to routine police work can be quite a letdown, especially if the transition is abrupt. Former UCOs frequently complain of feeling micromanaged and babied by their subsequent routine police duties and of not receiving proper respect and appreciation for their special role and efforts. Others reported termination stresses and responses include impaired personal relationships, concerns about retaliation and safety, lingering sympathy and regret at betrayal of criminal "friends," inability or unwillingness to shed the cover identity, corrosion of the law enforcement value system, mild and transient post-traumatic stress reactions, and weight gain during the assignment (Anderson et al., 1995; Farkas, 1986; Girodo, 1991a, 1991b, 1991c; Hibler, 1995; Russell & Beigel, 1990).

DEALING WITH THE FAILED MISSION

As noted earlier, operations rarely go exactly according to plan, however, when an unproductive operation is terminated or unforeseen dangers crop up and fold the mission, there is a tendency to seek someone to blame for the failure, either others who have messed up or, just as commonly, one-self for overlooking some sign or clue that could have staved off disaster. A vicious cycle may ensue wherein the self-flagellating officer, unable to bear his crippling guilt, projects it onto others who then understandably resent being unfairly labeled as the screw-ups.

For such failed missions, Hibler (1995) recommends encouraging disappointed officers to see their jobs as akin to firefighters who are paid to be ready and able to give their best effort when called, but have no guarantee of how things will turn out. A floor may collapse, a cache of unknown chemicals may explode, someone may have negligently locked a fire escape door, and so on. Similarly, in MacLeod's (1995) program, all UCOs are considered successful at termination and officers are encouraged to reframe failure in terms of survival and sensible self-preservation by emphasizing that safety is priority one, and the success of the mission, while important, is secondary to the officers' well-being. While this may be enough to assuage the pain of some UCOs, others will still feel the sting of self-reproach if they suspect they have let others down, in which case, more targeted individual counseling may be necessary.

Homicide and Sex Crimes Investigators

Another major class of special unit policing consists of specialized homicide or sex crimes investigators who handle particularly brutal crimes, multiple murders, serial killings, or crimes against children (Anderson et al., 1995; Blau, 1994; Miller, 2006c, 2009; Rodgers, 2006).

Stresses of Criminal Investigation

A serial murder investigation or child homicide forces the detective or investigating officer to confront stressors directly related to his or her projected image of unwavering strength and determination, ability to respond competently and dispassionately to crises, and willingness to place the needs and demands of the public above his or her personal feelings. All this is amplified in high-profile cases with greater media attention. The sheer magnitude and shock effect of many mass murder scenes and the violence, mutilation, and sadistic brutality associated with many killings, especially those involving children, often exceed the defense mechanisms and coping abilities of even the most "hard-boiled" investigator. Revulsion may be tinged with rage when innocent victims or fellow officers have been killed or injured, and the murderer seems to be mocking law enforcement's attempts to capture and/or prosecute him (Henry, 2004; Miller & Schlesinger, 2000; Sewell, 1993, 1994).

As the investigation drags on, the inability to solve the crime and close the case further frustrates and demoralizes the assigned officers and seems to fly in the face of society's notions of fairness and justice. All the more disturbing are situations where the killer is known but the existing evidence is insufficient to support an arrest or conviction. Stress and self-recrimination are further magnified when the failure to apprehend the perpetrator is caused by human error; for example, when an officer's misguided actions or breach of protocol leads to loss or damage of evidence or suppression of testimony, allowing the perpetrator to walk (Sewell, 1993, 1994).

All of these reactions are intensified by a cumulatively spiraling vicious cycle of fatigue and cognitive deterioration, as the sustained and exhausting effort to solve the case may result in careless errors, eroding work quality, and fraying of home and workplace relationships (Rossmo, 2009). Fatigue also exacerbates the wearing down of the investigator's normal psychological defenses, rendering him or her even more vulnerable to stress and failure (Sewell, 1993, 1994).

Especially in no-arrest cases, and particularly those involving children, some homicide or sex crimes investigators may become emotionally involved with the victims' families and remain in contact with them for many years. Some detectives become obsessed with a particular case and continue to work on it at every available moment, sometimes to the point of compromising their work on other cases and leading to a deterioration of health and family life (Russell & Beigel, 1990; Spungen, 1998).

Adding to this stress is the sense of rivalry that exists in many law enforcement agencies, especially between homicide and sex crimes units, with homicide still regarded as the elite investigative unit in most departments. One way this prioritization manifests itself is in terms of allocation of departmental resources. For example, the case closure rate of homicides is almost always greater than that of sex crimes (about 70 percent to 50 percent, respectively), despite the fact that homicide victims are by definition deceased, while sexual assault victims are typically alive and able to recount their experiences to investigators (Lanning & Hazelwood, 1988). To outsiders and fellow officers alike, anyone who would actually choose to specialize in this type of repugnant crime may be imbued with a certain air of creepiness that serves to isolate and alienate them from the rest of their colleagues, thereby depriving them of a valuable source of collegial support in the battle against stress and burnout.

Selection and Training of Criminal Investigators

In many departments, the appointment of officers to homicide or sex crime units is more a matter of seniority and promotion, and less a matter of specific training and selection criteria, as is often the case with hostage negotiators, undercover officers, SWAT team members, or other special operations personnel (Henry, 2004; Lanning & Hazelwood, 1988; Miller, 2005, 2006a, 2006b, 2006c, 2009). Where more rigorous selection procedures are used, it should be noted that, aside from the technically savvy, investigators will spend a good deal of time speaking with victims, families, witnesses, suspects, and others who may be important to the case, so screening for good communications skills are essential (Henry, 2004).

Screening also involves weeding out unsuitable candidates. These include officers who have an overly lurid or voyeuristic motive for doing this kind of work; those who may be going into it mainly for personal reasons; officers who have particular religious or political agendas; and those who see investigation as an easy career move, without the requisite commitment to the hard and dedicated work involved (Lanning & Hazelwood, 1988).

Characteristics of Successful
Criminal Investigators

A number of traits and behaviors, as well as essential knowledge, skills, and abilities, appear to characterize the most successful criminal investigators. First, they possess a basic knowledge of the law and the legal system to guide their efforts. They have an extensive knowledge of investigative and forensic techniques and procedures and are able to take a broad and deep perspective on their cases, to perceive complex patterns and connections within standard typologies of criminals and crime scenes, but also to be able to creatively "think outside the box" when necessary. Successful investigators are able to marshal and sustain motivation and persistence to see the case through, from beginning to end. They have the patience to deal with frustration and disappointments, as well as the ability to be self-starters and resist boredom and burnout.

Certain cognitive and temperamental features characterize successful investigators. A curious and inquisitive mind is an asset, characterized by the desire to go deeper and know more about a phenomenon. This is aided by a highly developed attention to detail, enabling the investigator to perceive minutiae that are overlooked by other observers but that may well prove crucial to solving the case. Similar to hostage negotiators (see above), the best investigators are natural people-persons. They can read subtle interpersonal cues and can communicate effectively with suspects, witnesses, or civilians in ways that induce trust and the willingness to come forth with important information. They can also flexibly adapt their communication style to their audience, without appearing to be patronizing or faking it (Henry, 2004; Rossmo, 2009; Sewell, 2003).

Stress-Coping Strategies of Criminal Investigators

A variety of coping strategies are used by criminal investigators to help themselves and their colleagues carry out their assignments. Some of these are used spontaneously by the officers themselves, some can be encouraged by departmental supervisors, and some can be taught and trained by mental health professionals (Henry, 2004; Holmes & Holmes, 1996; Lanning & Hazelwood, 1988; Miller, 2000; 2006b, 2008; Miller & Schlesinger, 2000; Reese, 1987, 1988; Ressler, Burgess, & Douglas, 1988; Russell & Beigel, 1990; Schlesinger & Miller, 2003; Turvey, 1999).

Defense Mechanisms and Mental Toughening

A number of authorities have commented on the general mental hardening or toughening that takes place in the mental life of criminal investigators. This is the most familiar way of blocking out unpleasant material for personnel who are used to taking a tough, suck-it-up attitude toward unpleasant aspects of the job. However, most of this mental toughening or hardening response is intended to be utilized for time-limited stressful circumstances; when it persists, it can be less conducive to productive coping over the long term.

Compartmentalization or *isolation of affect* occurs when negative emotions are separated out and put in a "mental file cabinet," thereby allowing the remainder of the officer's cognitive faculties to keep functioning. Individuals differ in their ability to make this mental separation without undue emotional leakage into other areas of work and family life.

Intellectualization is the term used to describe the process of detoxifying an emotionally wrenching task or experience by adopting the stance of detached, objective, intellectual curiosity; for example, the emotional revulsion and horror of encountering the remains of a sexually mutilated corpse is diffused and diluted by immersion in the technical scientific minutiae of crime scene investigation and offender profiling.

Sublimation refers to the process of turning a "bad" impulse into a socially acceptable, or even admirable "good" activity or vocation. In the law enforcement arena, this often manifests itself in taking the morbid curiosity and anxiety we all have about sex and murder, and channeling it into a productive career in forensic analysis. In this regard, sublimation is aided by intellectualization, which gives the immersion in the world of gore a scientific rationale.

Humor involves being able to take an ironic perspective on things that make us uncomfortable. Humor enables officers to deal with the grotesque by removing it emotionally through several stages in the form of a joke. Healthy humor enables officers to defuse stress and anxiety, share an experience in a supportive atmosphere, and encourage a healthy bonding among members of an elite "club." By contrast, unhealthy humor mocks the officers or victims themselves, distresses surviving family members, and sullies the department's honor.

Peer support is one of the effects that healthy humor can have to cement supportive camaraderie among members of the investigative team and more widely among officers within the department. Typically, officers themselves report that recognition and support from their fellow officers constitute the most important stress-mitigating factor they can think of. Peer support can also be thought of more broadly in the form of collegial associations, such as memberships in professional societies, and accessing and contributing to relevant publications and online databases—that is, building a nationwide and worldwide *community of support,* in addition to that within the department.

Professionalism subsumes all of the adaptive coping strategies noted above, as well as being a constructive principle of law enforcement generally (Lanning & Hazelwood, 1988; Miller, 2006c). Professionalism is undergirded by a general service orientation and feeling of professional accomplishment and satisfaction that motivates the investigator to do his or her best job. Professionalism is reflected in the physical space the investigator works in and the dignified language and demeanor used to make victims, witnesses, other officers, and even suspects feel comfortable.

Mental Health Services

Even in the face of the most heinously traumatic investigations, the majority of homicide and sex crimes investigators will not require professional mental health intervention. However, where necessary, such services should be available in an easily accessible and nonstigmatized way. Mental health services may include several options, such as critical incident debriefing, individual stress-management counseling, or family therapy for emotional spill-over effects (Sewell, 1993, 1994; Miller, 2006c; Miller, 2008). These are covered further in separate chapters of this book. As always, the department's true commitment to its personnel is shown by the quality of support services it chooses to provide.

Summary and Conclusions

Special unit policing has certain stresses, challenges—and rewards—of its own. The three branches of special unit policing considered in this chapter, hostage negotiation, undercover policing, and sex crime investigation, all share in common an immersion in the worst elements of human nature, with the necessity to act with professionalism while enforcing the law. Some of the challenges are different; for example, in both hostage crises and undercover policing, there is ever-present danger of imminent injury or death, while for sex crimes investigators, it is the aftermath of horrific violence that must be dealt with. Coping mechanisms common to all three domains include intellectualization, expertise-enhancing activities, collegial support, professionalism, and opportunity for mental health services when required. Somebody has to do these dangerous and dirty jobs and these officers deserve our gratitude and respect.

References

Allen, S.W., Fraser, S.L., & Inwald, R. (1991). Assessment of personality characteristics related to successful hostage negotiators and their resistance to post traumatic stress. In J. Reese, J. Horn & C. Dunning (Eds.), *Critical Incidents in Policing*, pp. 1–15. Washington DC: US Government Printing Office.

Anderson, W., Swenson, D., & Clay, D. (1995). *Stress Management for Law Enforcement Officers*. Englewood Cliffs: Prentice Hall.

Band, S.R. & Sheehan, D.C. (1999). Managing undercover stress: The supervisor's role. *FBI Law Enforcement Bulletin*, February, 1–6.

Barefoot, J. (1975). *Undercover Investigation*. Springfield, IL: Charles C. Thomas.

Baruth, C.L. (1988). Routine mental health checkups and activities for law enforcement personnel involved in dealing with hostage and terrorist incidents by psychologist trainer/consultant. In J.T. Reese & J.M. Horn (Eds.), *Police Psychology: Operational Assistance*, pp. 9–20. Washington DC: Federal Bureau of Investigation.

Blau, T.H. (1994). *Psychological Services for Law Enforcement*. New York: Wiley.

Blythe, B.T. (2002). *Blindsided: A Manager's Guide to Catastrophic Incidents in the Workplace*. New York: Portfolio.

Bohl, N.K. (1997). Postincident crisis counseling for hostage negotiators. In R.G. Rogan, M.R. Hammer, & C.R. Van Zandt (Eds.), *Dynamic Processes of Crisis Negotiationi,* pp. 46–56. Westport: Praeger.

Bolz, F., Dudonis, K.J., & Schultz, D.P. (1996). *The Counter-Terrorism Handbook*. Boca Raton: CRC Press.

Borum, R. & Strentz, T. (1992). The borderline personality: Negotiation strategies. *FBI Law Enforcement Bulletin*, 61 (August), 6–10.

Buckwalter, A. (1983). *Surveillance and Undercover Investigation*. Boston: Butterworth.

Cheek, J.C. & Lesce, T. (1988). *Plainclothes and Off-Duty Officer Survival*. Springfield: Charles C. Thomas.

Farkas, G.M. (1986). Stress in undecover policing. In J.T. Reese & H. Goldstein (Eds.), *Psychological Services for Law Enforcement*, pp. 433–440. Washington DC: US Government Printing Office.

Flin, R. (1996). *Sitting on the Hot Seat: Leaders and Teams for Effective Critical Incident Management*. New York: Wiley.

Fuselier, G.D. (1986). What every negotiator would like his chief to know. *FBI Law Enforcement Bulletin*, 55, 1–11.

Fuselier, G.D. (1988). Hostage negotiation mental health consultant: Emerging role for the clinical psychologist. *Professional Psychology: Research and Practice*, 19, 175–179.

Fuselier, G.D. & Noeser, G.W. (1990). Confronting the terrorist hostage taker. *FBI Law Enforcement Bulletin,* July, 6–11.

Geller, W.A. (1993). Put friendly-fire shooting in perspective. *Law Enforcement News*, 18, 9.

Getty, V. & Elam, J. (1988). Identifying characteristics of hostage negotiators and using personality data to develop a selection model. In J.T. Reese & J.M. Horn (Eds.), *Police Psychology: Operational Assistance*, pp. 159–171. Washington DC: US Department of Justice.

Girodo, M. (1985). Health and legal issues in undercover narcotics investigations: Misrepresented evidence. *Behavioral Sciences and the Law*, 3, 299–308.

Girodo, M. (1991a). Symptomatic reactions to undercover work. *Journal of Nervous and Mental Disease*, 179, 626–630.

Girodo, M. (1991b). Personality, job stress, and mental health in undercover agents. *Journal of Social Behavior and Personality*, 6, 375–390.

Girodo, M. (1991c). Drug corruption in undercover agents: Measuring the risk. *Behavioral Sciences and the Law*, 9, 361–370.

Greenstone, J.L. (1995). Tactics and negotiating techniques (TNT): The way of the past and the way of the future. In M.I. Kurke & E.M. Scrivner (Eds.), *Police Psychology into the 21st Century*, pp. 357–371. Hillsdale: Erlbaum.

Greenstone, J.L. (2005). *The Elements of Police Hostage and Crisis Negotiations: Critical Incidents and How to Respond to Them*. New York: Haworth Press.

Hammer, M.R. & Rogan, R.G. (1997). Negotiation models in crisis situations: The value of a communication-based approach. In R.G. Rogan, M.R. Hammer, & C.R. Van Zandt (Eds.), *Dynamic Processes of Crisis Negotiation*, pp. 9–23. Westport: Praeger.

Hammer, M.R., Van Zandt, C.R., & Rogan, R.G. (1994). Crisis/hostage negotiation team profile of demographic and functional characteristics. *FBI Law Enforcement Bulletin*, 63, 8–11.

Hare, A. (1997). Training crisis negotiators: Updating negotiation techniques and training. In R.G. Rogan, M.R. Hammer, & C.R. Van Zandt (Eds.), *Dynamic Processes of Crisis Negotiation*, pp. 151–160. Westport: Praeger.

Hatcher, C., Mohandie, K., Turner, J., & Gelles, M.G. (1998). The role of the psychologist in crisis/hostage negotiations. *Behavioral Sciences and the Law*, 16, 455–472.

Henry, V.E. (2004). *Death Work: Police, Trauma, and the Psychology of Survival*. New York: Oxford University Press.

LAURENCE MILLER

Hibler, N.S. (1995). The care and feeding of undercover agents. In M.L. Kurke & E.M. Scrivner (Eds.), *Police Psychology into the 21st Century*, pp. 299–317. Hillsdale: Erlbaum.

Holmes, R.M. & Holmes, S.T. (1996). *Profiling Violent Crimes: An Investigative Tool*, 2nd ed. Thousand Oaks: Sage.

Klein, G. (1998). *Sources of Power: How People Make Decisions*. Cambridge: MIT Press.

Lanning, K.V. & Hazelwood, R.R. (1988). The maligned investigator of criminal sexuality. *FBI Law Enforcement Bulletin*, September, pp. 1–10.

MacLeod, A.D. (1995). Undercover policing: A psychiatrist's perspective. *International Journal of Law and Psychiatry*, 18, 239–247.

Marx, G.T. (1988). *Undercover: Police Surveillance in America*. Berkeley: University of California Press.

McMains, M.J. (1988a). Expanding the psychologist's role in hostage negotiations. *Journal of Police and Criminal Psychology*, 4, 1–8.

McMains, M.J. (1988b). Psychologists' roles in hostage negotiations. In J.T. Reese & J.M. Horn (Eds.), *Police Psychology: Operational Assistance*, pp. 281–318. Washington DC: US Government Printing Office.

McMains, M.J. & Mullins, W.C. (1996). *Crisis Negotiations: Managing Critical Incidents and Situations in Law Enforcement and Corrections*. Cincinnati: Anderson.

Miller, L. (2000). The predator's brain: Neuropsychodynamics of serial killers. In L.B. Schlesinger (Ed.), *Serial Offenders: Current Thought, Recent Findings, Unusual Syndromes*, pp. 135–166. Boca Raton: CRC Press.

Miller, L. (2005). Hostage negotiation: Psychological principles and practices. *International Journal of Emergency Mental Health*, 7, 277–298.

Miller, L. (2006a). Psychological traits and characteristics of successful hostage negotiators. *Inner perimeter: The official newsletter of the International Association of Hostage Negotiators*, 1, 3–4.

Miller, L. (2006b). Undercover policing: A psychological and operational guide. *Journal of Police and Criminal Psychology*, 21, 1–24.

Miller, L; (2006c). *Practical Police Psychology: Stress Management and Crisis Intervention for Law Enforcement*. Springfield, IL: Charles C. Thomas.

Miller, L. (2007). Negotiating with mentally disordered hostage takers: Guiding principles and practical strategies. *Journal of Police Crisis Negotiations*, 7, 63–83.

Miller, L. (2008). *METTLE: Mental Toughness Training for Law Enforcement*. Flushing, NY: Looseleaf Law Publications.

Miller, L. (2009). Criminal investigator stress: Symptoms, syndromes, and practical coping strategies. *International Journal of Emergency Mental Health*, 11, 87–92.

Miller, L. & Schlesinger, L.B. (2000). Survivors, families, and co-victims of serial offenders. In L.B. Schlesinger (Ed.), *Serial Offenders: Current Thought, Recent Findings, Unusual Syndromes*, pp. 309–334. Boca Raton: CRC Press.

Misino, D.J. (2002). Negotiating without a net. *Harvard Business Review*, October, 49–54.

Noesner, G.W. (1999). Negotiation concepts for commanders. *FBI Law Enforcement Bulletin*, January, 6–14.

Reese, J.T. (1987). Coping with stress: It's your job. In J.T. Reese (Ed.), *Behavioral Science in Law Enforcement*, pp. 75–79. Washington DC: FBI.

Reese, J.T. (1988). Psychological aspects of policing violence. In J.T. Reese & R.M. Horn (Eds.), *Police Psychology: Operational Assistance*, pp. 347–361. Washington DC: Federal Bureau of Investigation.

Regini, C. (2002). Crisis negotiation teams: Selection and training. *FBI Law Enforcement Bulletin*, November, 1–5.

Regini, C. (2004). Crisis intervention for law enforcement officers. *FBI Law Enforcement Bulletin*, October, 1–6.

Ressler, R.K., Burgess, A.W., & Douglas, J.E. (1988). *Sexual Homicide: Patterns and Motives*. New York: Free Press.

Rodgers, B.A. (2006). *Psychological Aspects of Police Work: An Officer's Guide to Street Psychology*. Springfield, IL: Charles C. Thomas.

Rogan, R.G. (1997). Emotion and emotional expression in crisis negotiation. In R.G. Rogan, M.R. Hammer, & C.R. Van Zandt (Eds.), *Dynamic Processes of Crisis Negotiation*, pp. 26–43. Westport: Praeger.

Rogan, R.G., Hammer, M.R., & Van Zandt (1994). Profiling crisis negotiation teams. *The Police Chief*, 61, 14–18.

Rossmo, D.K. (2009). *Criminal Investigative Failures*. Boca Raton, FL: CRC Press.

Russell, H.E. & Beigel, A. (1990). *Understanding Human Behavior for Effective Police Work*, 3rd ed. New York: Basic Books.

Schlesinger, L.B. & Miller, L. (2003). Learning to kill: serial, contract, and terrorist murderers. In R.S. Moser & C.E. Franz (Eds.), *Shocking Violence II: Violent Disaster, War, and Terrorism Affecting Our Youth*, pp. 145–164. New York: Charles C. Thomas.

Sewell, J.D. (1993). Traumatic stress of multiple murder investigations. *Journal of Traumatic Stress*, 6, 103–118.

Sewell, J.D. (1994). The stress of homicide investigations. *Death Studies*, 18, 565–582.

Sewell, J.D. (2003). Training strategies and techniques for criminal investigators. In M.J. Palmiotto (Ed.), *Policing and Training Issues*, pp. 235–258. Upper Saddle River: Prentice-Hall.

Slatkin, A.A. (2005). *Communication in Crisis and Hostage Negotiations*. Springfield: Charles C. Thomas.

Smith, B.L. (1994). *Terrorism in America: Pipe Bombs and Pipe Dreams*. Albany: State University of New York Press.

Spungen, D. (1998). *Homicide: The Hidden Victims. A Guide for Professionals*. Thousand Oaks: Sage.

Terestre, D.J. (2004). Talking him down. *Police*, March, 26–32.

Turvey, B. (1999). *Criminal Profiling: An Introduction to Behavioral Evidence ANALYSIS*. New York: Academic Press.

Van Hasselt, V.B. & Romano, S.J. (2004). Role-playing: A vital tool in crisis negotiation skills training. *FBI Law Enforcement Bulletin*, February, 12–17.

11

POLICE OFFICER STRESS

Syndromes and Strategies
for Intervention

Laurence Miller

> I've seen dead bodies—fresh ones and ripe ones. I've scraped
> an eyeball off a bedroom wall in a suicide shooting, I've
> investigated murder scenes you wouldn't believe. But this was
> different, this was a little kid, this could have been *my* kid. And
> there was no reason for it, just no reason.

This grim testimonial came from a veteran detective following the fatal
shooting of a young child by his mentally handicapped brother who had
been left unsupervised by the children's parents in the same house as an
unsecured handgun. It was not the worst death the emergency responders
had ever seen, it was not the grisliest, nor the most touch-and-go in terms
of lifesaving attempts—the child had apparently died instantly from a
.357 magnum round to the head. The main traumatizing effect of this
call was the sheer existential indigestibility of the death circumstances:
an innocent victim, even an essentially innocent perpetrator, both set up
by stupidly careless adults who should have known better—there was
just "no reason."

The men and women of law enforcement are exposed to special kinds
of routine and unusual traumatic events and daily pressures that require
a certain adaptively defensive toughness of attitude, temperament, and
training. Without this resolve, they could not do their jobs effectively.
Sometimes, however, the stress is just too much, and the very toughness
that facilitates smooth functioning in their daily duties now becomes an
impediment to these helpers seeking help for themselves.

This chapter first describes the types of critical incidents and other
stresses experienced by law enforcement officers. Many of these challenges
affect all personnel who work in emergency services, public safety, and

the helping professions, including police officers, firefighters, paramedics, dispatchers, trauma doctors, emergency room nurses, teachers, military personnel, and mental health clinicians (Miller, 1995, 1998b, 2006b; 2008b; 2010); however, the focus here will be on the stressors most relevant to law enforcement personnel, particularly patrol officers; stresses specific to different types of special unit policing are covered in separate chapters. Second, this chapter will outline the practical interventions and psychotherapeutic strategies that have been found most useful for helping cops in distress.

Stress and Coping in Law Enforcement

We know that police officers can be an insular group, and are often more reluctant to talk to outsiders or to show "weakness" in front of their own peers than other emergency service and public safety workers. Part of this may be because officers typically work alone or with a single partner, as opposed to firefighters or paramedics, who are trained to have more of a team mentality (Blau, 1994; Cummings, 1996; Kirschman, 1997, 2004; Reese, 1987; Solomon, 1995). This presents some special challenges for peers, supervisors, and clinicians attempting to identify and help officers in distress.

The essential nature of their jobs regularly requires police officers to deal with the most violent, impulsive, and predatory members of society, to handle citizens undergoing the most emotional events of their lives, and to confront cruelties and horrors that most civilians only read about or view on their TV or computer screens. At any moment, officers may be expected to put their lives on the line. In addition to the daily grind and unpredictable crises, officers are frequently the target of criticism and complaints by citizens, the media, the judicial system, adversarial attorneys, crusading politicians, "do-gooder" clinicians, social service personnel, and their own administrators and law enforcement agencies (Blau, 1994; Henry, 2004).

Police officers generally carry out their sworn duties and responsibilities with dedication and competence, but every officer has his/her breaking point. For some, it may come in the form of a particular traumatic experience, such as a gruesome accident or homicide, a vicious crime against a child, a close personal brush with death, the death or serious injury of a partner, the shooting of a perpetrator or innocent civilian, or an especially grisly or large-scale crime. For other officers, there may be no singular trauma, but the mental breakdown caps the cumulative weight of a number of more mundane stressors over the course of the officer's career.

In either case, the officer all too often feels that the department does not fully support him and that there is nowhere else to vent his distress. So he bottles up his feelings, acts snappish with coworkers, superiors, civilians, and family members, and becomes hypersensitive to small annoyances on and off the job. As his isolation and feelings of alienation grow, his health and home life begin to deteriorate, work becomes a burden, and he may ultimately feel he is losing his mind, or going "squirrelly."

Several authors (Carlier, 1999; Henry, 2004; McCafferty et al., 1990; McCafferty, McCafferty, & McCafferty, 1992; Sugimoto & Oltjenbruns, 2001; Violanti, 1999) have commented on the "death-saturated" culture that pervades many forms of police work, likening it to guerilla warfare or antiterrorist combat, right down to the military-style training and weaponry used and the us-against-them mentality that is often instilled in rookie officers. In some cases, the types of post-traumatic responses seen in police officers resembles that observed in military combat personnel (Corbett, 2004; Creamer & Forbes, 2004; Galovski & Lyons, 2004; Miller, 2008c, 2010; Nash & Baker, 2007; Nordland & Gegax, 2004; Rudofossi, 2007, 2009; Vasterling et al., 2010). Such an atmosphere may set the stage for traumatization when law enforcement critical incidents occur.

Most police officers deal with both the routine and the exceptional stresses of their work by a variety of situationally adaptive coping and defense mechanisms, such as repression, displacement, isolation of feelings, humor, and just generally toughing it out. Most officers prefer problem-focused and direct action methods of coping. Strategies include displacement onto colleagues or the public, delegating work, taking sick leave, using psychotropic medication, seeking spiritual help, engaging in physical exercise, relaxing, smoking, eating, using alcohol, or talking things out with colleagues (Alexander & Walker, 1994; Evans et al., 1993)

Officers frequently develop a closed society, an insular "cop culture," centering around what many refer to as *The Job*. Part of this closed-society credo is based on the shared belief that no civilian or outsider could possibly understand what they go through on a day-to-day basis. A smaller number of police officers spend most or all of their time with other cops, watch cop shows, read cop stories, log onto cop websites, and so on. For these few, *The Job* becomes their life, and crowds out other activities and relationships (Blau, 1994; Rodgers, 2006; Russell & Beigel, 1990).

Although earlier suppositions about rampant police stress and disability have been shown to be exaggerated (Curran, 2003), certain critical incidents, such as *officer-involved shootings* (OISs), can leave psychological scars in some officers, especially where the circumstances of the shooting are ambiguous or the legitimacy is contested (Miller, 2006a, 2006b; Sewell, Ellison, & Hurrell, 1988; Solomon, 1995; Solomon & Horn, 1986). However, by focusing too much on high-profile events like OISs, police supervisors often overlook the cumulative effect of more common critical incident and procedural stressors, such as long overtime shifts during disasters, dealing with child victims, attempting resuscitation on a person who eventually dies, or working a fatal accident where the officer personally knows the victim.

Emotional reactions of guilt, irrationally taking responsibility for events that were beyond one's control, and rage at being forced into a no-win situation—being "at the wrong place at the wrong time"—are common themes of law enforcement stress. This also includes escaping serious harm where others have been killed or wounded. Failure to resolve these issues often leads to a variety of maladaptive response patterns. Some officers begin to overreact to perceived or imagined threats, while others ignore clear danger signals. Some cops quit the force prematurely, while others become discipline problems or develop increased absenteeism, burnout, physical symptoms, substance abuse, or a host of other personal problems that can interfere with functioning at home and on the job (Barrett et al., 2011; Fischler, McElroy, Miller, Saxe-Clifford, Stewart, & Zelig, 2011; Miller, 2004, 2006b, 2007; 2011; Ostrov, 1991; Solomon, 1995; Solomon & Horn, 1986).

Perhaps the most tragic form of police casualty is suicide (Cummings, 1996; Hays, 1994; McCafferty et al., 1992; Miller, 2005; Seligman, Holt, Chinni, & Roberts, 1994). While the statistics are controversial, some estimates are that about twice as many officers take their own lives than are killed in the line of duty. In New York City, the suicide rate for police officers is more than double the rate for the general population. These totals may actually be higher, since such deaths are sometimes underreported by fellow cops and family members to avoid stigmatizing the deceased officer and to allow families to collect benefits. Most suicide victims are young patrol officers with no record of misconduct, and most shoot themselves off-duty. Often, problems involving alcohol or personal crises are the catalyst, and easy access to a lethal weapon provides the ready means.

Critical Incidents and Post-Traumatic Stress Disorder

Critical Incident Stress

A *critical incident* is defined as any event that has an unusually powerful, negative impact on law enforcement personnel. In the present context, it is any event that a police officer may experience that is above and beyond the range of the ordinary stresses and hassles that come with the job. (A full discussion of the state of the science of Critical Incident Stress Debriefing is given in Chapter 5 of this volume.) Major classes of critical incidents include: a line-of-duty death; serious injury to police personnel; a serious multiple-casualty incident such as a multiple school shooting or workplace violence incident; the suicide of a police officer; the traumatic death of children, especially where irresponsible or frankly malevolent adults were involved; an event with excessive media interest; or a victim who is a family member or otherwise well-known to one or more responding officers (Everly & Mitchell, 1997). Recent times have multiplied exponentially the range and scope of horrific law enforcement critical incidents to include acts of mass terror and destruction, involving multiple deaths of civilians, fellow officers, and other emergency personnel (Henry, 2004; Karlsson & Christianson, 2003; Miller, 1999, 2003, 2006c).

Susceptibility to stressful events varies among different persons, and many individuals are able to resolve acute critical incident stress through the use of informal social support and other adaptive activities (Bowman, 1997; Carlier & Gersons, 1995; Carlier, Lamberts, & Gersons, 1997; Gentz, 1991). However, critical incident stress that is not resolved adequately or treated appropriately in the first few days or weeks may evolve into a number of disabling psychological traumatic disability syndromes (Miller, 1998b).

Post-Traumatic Stress Disorder (PTSD)

The concept of critical incident stress grew out of the larger tradition of trauma psychology. Although persisting and debilitating stress reactions to wartime and civilian traumas have been recorded for centuries (Trimble, 1981; Wilson, 1994), *post-traumatic stress disorder* (PTSD) first achieved status as a codified psychiatric syndrome in 1980 (APA, 1980), and has been identified as a sequel of military combat and civilian trauma (Clary, 2005; Corbett, 2004; Galovski & Lyons, 2004; Nordland & Gegax, 2004; Paton & Smith, 1999; Tyre, 2004; Vasterling et al., 2010). Various other types of psychological syndromes, such as phobias, anxiety, panic attacks, somatization disorders, and depression may follow exposure to traumatic events (Miller, 1998b, 2008b), but the quintessential psychological syndrome following psychological traumatization is PTSD (APA, 2000; Meek, 1990; Merskey, 1992; Modlin, 1983, 1990; Weiner, 1992).

Diagnostically, PTSD is a syndrome of emotional and behavioral disturbance following exposure to a traumatic stressor that injures or threatens self or others, and that involves the experience of intense fear, helplessness, or horror. As a result, following a law enforcement critical incident, there may develop a characteristic set of symptoms, which include those listed below.

Anxiety. The officer experiences a continual state of free-floating anxiety and maintains an intense hypervigilance, scanning the environment for impending threats of danger. Panic attacks may be occasional or frequent.

Physiological arousal. The officer's nervous system is on continual alert, producing increased bodily tension in the form of muscle tightness, tremors, restlessness, heightened startle response, fatigue, heart palpitations, breathing difficulties, dizziness, headaches, or other physical symptoms.

Irritability. There is a pervasive edginess, impatience, loss of humor, and quick anger over seemingly trivial matters. Friends and coworkers may get annoyed and shun the officer, while family members may feel abused and alienated. Interactions with citizens on patrol may grow testy and lead to unwarranted confrontations.

Avoidance/denial. The officer tries to blot out the event from his mind. He avoids thinking or talking about the traumatic event, as well as news items, conversations, TV shows, or even coworkers that remind him of the incident. Part of this is a deliberate, conscious effort to avoid trauma-reminders, while part involves an involuntary psychic numbing that blunts incoming threatening stimuli. On the job, the officer may "lie low," minimizing his contact with the public and his fellow officers, and thereby underperform in his law enforcement duties.

Intrusion. Despite the officer's best efforts to keep the traumatic event out of his mind, the disturbing incident pushes its way into consciousness, typically in the form of intrusive images or flashbacks by day and/or frightening dreams at night.

Repetitive nightmares. Sometimes the officer's nightmares replay the actual traumatic event; more commonly, the dreams echo the general theme of the trauma, but miss the mark in terms of specific content. The emotional intensity of the original traumatic experience is retained, but the dream may partially disguise the actual event. For example, one officer who was jumped and beaten by a suspect in an unlighted room reported recurring dreams of "tripping over a rock and being bitten by a snake."

Impaired concentration and memory. Friends and family may notice that the officer has become a "space cadet," while supervisors report deteriorating work performance because the officer "can't concentrate on doing his job." Social and recreational functioning may be impaired as the officer has difficulty remembering names, loses the train of conversations, or cannot keep his mind focused on reading material or games.

Withdrawal/isolation. The officer shuns friends, schoolmates, and family members, having no tolerance for the petty, trivial concerns of everyday life. The hurt feelings this engenders in those rebuffed may spur resentment and counteravoidance, leading to a vicious cycle of mutual rejection and eventual social ostracism of the officer.

Acting-out. More rarely, the traumatized officer may walk off his patrol, wander out of his familiar jurisdiction, or take unaccustomed risks by driving too fast, associating with unsavory elements on his beat (or within his own department), gambling, using substances, being insubordinate, or acting recklessly with suspects and citizens, thereby putting himself or other officers in unnecessary danger.

Delayed, Displaced, or Prolonged Reactions

In some cases, especially if no treatment or other appropriate support has been provided, the after-effects of a traumatic incident may persist for many months or longer in the form of anger, hostility, irritability, fatigue, inability to concentrate, loss of self-confidence, neglect of health, increased indulgence in food or substances, or problems with authority and discipline. Many of these long-term effects obviously will interfere with work performance and threaten the stability of close personal relationships. Ultimately, they may be responsible for early retirement, burnout, or even suicide (Bohl, 1991, 1995).

In some cases, an officer may appear to emerge from a dangerous situation or series of emergencies emotionally unscathed, only to later break down and develop a full-blown PTSD reaction following a relatively minor incident like a traffic accident (Davis & Breslau, 1994). The fender-bender, certainly far less traumatic than the dramatic scenes encountered in emergency work, seems to have symbolized vividly the personal risk, sense of human fragility, and existential uncertainty that the officer's professional activities entail but that he is unable to face directly if he is to maintain his necessary defenses and get the job done. The stifled emotion may then be projected onto the minor incident because it is a "safer" target to break down or blow up at. Unfortunately, this may instigate a fear of losing control and going crazy, further propelling the vicious cycle of increased stress but greater reluctance to report it. Here, alert spouses, coworkers, or supervisors may be of help in urging the stricken officer to get the help he or she needs.

Risk and Resiliency Factors for PTSD and Traumatic Disability Syndromes

As noted previously, not everyone who experiences a traumatic critical incident develops the same degree of psychological disability, and there is significant variability among individual levels of susceptibility and resilience to stressful events. While many individuals are able to resolve acute critical incident stress through the use of informal social support and other adaptive activities (Bowman, 1997, 1999; Carlier & Gersons, 1995; Carlier et al., 1997; Gentz, 1991), in some cases, critical incident stress that is not resolved adequately or treated appropriately in the first few days or weeks may evolve into a number of disabling psychological traumatic disability syndromes (Miller, 1998b, 2008b).

Risk factors for PTSD or other traumatic disability syndromes in officers may be (1) *biological*, including genetic predisposition and inborn heightened physiological reactivity to stimuli; (2) *historical*, such as prior exposure to trauma or other coexisting adverse life circumstances; (3) *psychological*, including poor coping and problem-solving skills, learned helplessness, and a history of dysfunctional interpersonal relationships; and (4) *environmental/contextual*, such as inadequate departmental or societal support (Carlier, 1999; Paton, Smith, Violanti, & Eranen, 2000).

Equally important, but often overlooked, are *resiliency factors* that enable officers to withstand and even prevail in the face of seemingly overwhelming trauma. These include superior training and skill development; a learning attitude toward the profession; commitment to something meaningful; good verbal and interpersonal skills; higher intelligence; adequate emotional and behavioral self-control; optimism; an easy temperament; good problem-solving and adaptive coping skills; ability to frame problems as comprehensible and manageable; internal locus of control; seeing stresses as challenges to be mastered; ability to form meaningful relationships; and the ability and willingness to seek help and support where necessary (Hoge, Austin, & Pollack, 2007; Miller, 1998a, 1998b, 2008e; Paton et al., 2000). Proper intervention services for PTSD and other critical incident stress reactions should make good use of these inherent resiliency factors wherever possible (Antonovsky, 1979, 1987, 1990; Bifulco, Brown, & Harris, 1987; Brewin, Andrews, & Valentine, 2000; Garmezy, 1993; Garmezy, Masten, & Tellegen, 1984; Kobassa, 1979a, 1979b; Kobassa, Maddi, & Cahn, 1982; Luthar, 1991; Maddi & Khoshaba, 1994; Miller, 1990, 1998a, 1998b, 2008a, 2008e; Paton et al., 2000; Rubenstein, Heeren, Houseman, Rubin, & Stechler, 1989; Rutter, 1985, 1987; Rutter, Tizard, Yule, Graham, & Whitmore, 1976; Werner, 1989; Werner & Smith, 1982; Zimrin, 1986).

Mental Health Services for Law Enforcement Stress

For some traumatized or cumulatively stressed police officers, a Critical Incident Stress Debriefing (CISD) may not suffice and more extensive, intensive, and individualized approaches to fostering recovery may be required, invoking the services of mental health professionals. Unfortunately, sometimes for good reason (Max, 2000), police officers have traditionally shunned these services, often perceiving its practitioners as ferrets and shills who are out to dig up dirt that their departments can use against them. Other cops may fear having their "head shrunk," harboring a notion of the psychotherapy process as akin to brainwashing, a humiliating and emasculating experience in which they are forced to lie on a couch and sob about their most inner secrets. Less dramatically and more commonly, the idea of needing any kind of "mental help" implies weakness, cowardice, and lack of ability to do the job. In the environment of many departments, some officers realistically fear censure, stigmatization, ridicule, thwarted career advancement, and alienation from colleagues if they are perceived as the type who "folds under pressure." Still others in the department who may have something to hide may fear a colleague "spilling his guts" to the clinician and thereby blowing the malfeasor's cover (Miller, 1995, 1998b, 2006b).

But the goal of law enforcement psychological services following a critical incident should always be to make officers *stronger,* not weaker. Sometimes a broken bone that has begun to heal crookedly has to be re-broken and reset properly for the individual to be able to walk normally again and, while the re-breaking may hurt, the pain is temporary and the effect is to restore and re-strengthen the limb. In the same way, an officer who is responding to critical incident stress with an ossified, malformed defensive mindset that is impeding his or her job performance and personal life may need to have those defenses challenged in a supportive atmosphere, so he or she can benefit from a healthy resetting of his mental state to deal with life more adaptively and courageously. He or she needs to regain the psychological strength to learn to walk the path of life again (Miller, 2006b; Rudofossi, 2007, 2009; Toch, 2002).

Therapeutic Strategies for Recovery and Resilience

Psychotherapeutic strategies for law enforcement officers have been covered in detail elsewhere (Miller, 2006b). For the purposes of this chapter, the effectiveness of any therapeutic strategy in fostering resilient recovery will be determined by the timeliness, tone, style, and intent of the intervention. Effective psychological interventions with law enforcement officers and other service personnel share the following common elements (Blau, 1994; Fullerton, McCarroll, Ursano, & Wright, 1992; Wester & Lyubelsky, 2005).

Briefness. Clinicians should utilize only as much therapeutic contact as necessary to address the present problem. The officer does not want to become a "professional patient."

Limited focus. Related to the above, the goal is not to solve all the officer's problems, but to assist in restabilization from the critical incident or cumulative stressors, and provide stress-inoculation for future incidents.

Directness. Therapeutic efforts are directed to resolve the current conflict or problem to reach a satisfactory short-term conclusion, while planning for the future if necessary.

In light of Violanti's (1999) conceptualization of police work as "civilian combat," it is interesting to note that a very similar intervention model has recently been articulated by military psychologists for dealing with soldiers experiencing combat stress and trauma (Munsey, 2006). The program goes under the acronym, BICEPS, which stands for:

- *Brevity.* Treatment is short, addressing the problem at hand.
- *Immediacy.* Intervention takes place quickly, before symptoms worsen.
- *Centrality.* Psychological treatment is set apart from medical facilities, as a way to reduce the stigma soldiers might feel about seeking mental health services (although it could be argued that putting mental health treatment in a special category might make some soldiers feel alienated from their colleagues who have suffered "real" injuries; accordingly, clinicians should use their judgment).
- *Expectancy.* A soldier experiencing problems with combat stress is expected to return to duty.
- *Proximity.* Soldiers are treated as close to their units as possible and are not evacuated from the area of operations.
- *Simplicity.* Besides therapy, the basics of a good meal, hot shower, and a comfortable place to sleep ensure a soldier's basic physical needs are met.

These can easily be applied to clinical work with police offers, other public safety personnel, and all patients with a traditionally masculine orientation (Miller, 2008a; Wester & Lyubelsky, 2005).

Utilizing Cognitive Defenses for Resilience

In psychology, *defense mechanisms* are the mental strategems the mind uses to protect itself from unpleasant thoughts, feelings, impulses, and memories. While the normal use of such defenses enables the average person to avoid conflict and ambiguity and maintain some consistency to their personality and belief system, most psychologists would agree that an overuse of defenses to wall off too much unpleasant thought and feeling leads to a rigid and dysfunctional approach to coping with life. Accordingly, much of the ordinary psychotherapeutic process involves carefully helping the patient to relinquish pathological defenses so that he or she can learn to deal with internal conflicts more constructively.

However, in the face of immediately traumatizing critical incidents, the last thing the affected person needs is to have his or her defenses stripped away. If you sustain a broken leg on the battlefield, the medic binds and braces the limb as best as he can and helps you quickly hobble out of the danger zone, reserving more extensive medical treatment for a later, safer time and place. Similarly, for an acute psychological trauma, the proper utilization of psychological defenses can serve as an important psychological splint that enables the person to function in the immediate post-traumatic aftermath and eventually be able to productively resolve and integrate the traumatic experience when the luxury of therapeutic time and safety can be afforded (Janik, 1991).

211

Indeed, whether in their regular daily work or following critical incidents, law enforcement and public safety personnel usually need little help in applying defense mechanisms on their own. Examples (Durham, McCammon, & Allison, 1985; Henry, 2004; Taylor, Wood, J.V., & Lechtman, 1983) include:

- *Denial.* "Put it out of my mind; focus on other things; avoid situations or people who remind me of it."
- *Rationalization.* "I had no choice; things happens for a reason; it could have been worse; other people have it worse; most people would react the way I am."
- *Displacement/projection.* "It was Command's fault for issuing such a stupid order; I didn't have the right backup; they're all trying to blame me for everything."
- *Refocus on positive attributes.* "Hey, this was just a fluke—I'm usually a great marksman; I'm not gonna let this jam me up."
- *Refocus on positive behaviors.* "Okay, I'm gonna get more training, increase my knowledge and skill so I'll never be caught with my pants down like this again."

Janik (1991) proposes that, in the short term, clinicians actively support and bolster psychological defenses that temporarily enable the officer to continue functioning. Just as a physical crutch is an essential part of orthopedic rehabilitation when the leg-injured patient is learning to walk again, a psychological crutch is perfectly adaptive and productive if it enables the officer to get back on his emotional two feet as soon as possible after a traumatic critical incident. Only later, when he or she is making the bumpy transition back to normal life, are potentially maladaptive defenses revisited as possible impediments to progress.

And just as some orthopedic patients may always need one or another kind of assistive walking device, like a special shoe or a cane, some degree of psychological defensiveness may persist in officers so they can otherwise productively pursue their work and life tasks. Indeed, rare among us is the person who is completely defense-free. Only when defenses are used inappropriately and for too long—past the point where we should be walking on our own psychological two legs—do they constitute a "crutch" in the pejorative sense.

Survival Resource Training

As noted earlier, a recently evolving trend in trauma psychotherapy emphasizes the importance of accessing and bolstering the patient's natural powers of resilience, and the constructive marshalling of strength and resistance to stress and disability (Calhoun & Tedeschi, 1999; Dunning, 1999; Miller, 2008d; Stuhlmiller & Dunning, 2000; Tedeschi & Calhoun 1995; Tedeschi & Kilmer, 2005; Violanti, 2000). In this vein, Solomon (1988, 1991, 1995) has been ahead of the curve in capitalizing on the idea that constructive denial of vulnerability and mortality can be an adaptive response for law enforcement officers coping with past and ongoing critical incidents and their immediate aftermath.

Solomon (1988, 1991) points out that, following critical incidents characterized by fear, danger, injury, or death, officers often dwell on their mistakes and overlook what they *did right* in terms of coping with their emotions and getting the job done. Thus, being realistically reminded by the clinician of their own adaptive coping efforts may prove especially empowering because it draws upon strengths that came from the officer him- or herself. Termed *survival resource training*, this intervention allows officers to utilize the fear response to tap into a state of controlled strength, increased awareness, confidence, and clarity of mind.

In this technique, the clinician encourages the officer to view the critical incident from a detached, objective point of view, "like you were watching a movie of yourself," and to go through the incident "frame-by-frame." At the point where he imagines himself fully engaging in this activity (e.g., negotiating with a hostage-taker, arresting a dangerous felon, taking cover, firing his weapon), the officer is instructed to "focus on the part of you enabling you to respond."

In most cases, the survival resource training procedure leads to a mental reframe characterized by controlled strength, heightened awareness, confidence, and mental clarity, as the officer mentally zooms in on his capability to respond, instead of focusing on the immobilizing fear, perceptions of weakness, loss of control, or perceptual distortions. Often, this results in the officer's being reminded of how he put his fear on hold and rose to the occasion in order to get the job done. The reframing thus focuses on resiliency instead of vulnerability, strength instead of weakness.

In addition to processing past critical incidents, realistic feelings of efficacy and competence can also shade over into future incidents, as officers report increased confidence and ability to handle subsequent calls, such as arrests, shooting incidents, domestic disturbances, and traffic chases. In addition, officers have felt more confident in other nonemergency but stressful situations, such as court testimony and personal matters, such as resolving family conflicts (Solomon, 1988, 1991, 1995). It is especially gratifying to clinicians and officers alike when their mutual efforts can turn vicious cycles of demoralization and despair into positive cycles of confidence and optimism. Indeed, this is the essence of the resilience model of psychotherapy.

Organizational and Departmental Support

Not all interventions involve psychotherapy or debriefings. Following a department-wide critical incident, such as a line-of-duty death, serial homicide investigation, or mass casualty rescue and recovery operation, the departmental psychologist or consulting mental health professional can advise and guide law enforcement agencies in encouraging and implementing several *organizational response measures* (Alexander, 1993; Alexander & Walker, 1994; Alexander & Wells, 1991; DeAngelis, 1995; Fullerton et al., 1992; Palmer, 1983). Many of these strategies are proactively applicable as part of training before a critical incident occurs. Others apply even when there is no specific incident, but just involve cops in a jam seeking support and relief. Some specific organizational and leadership measures that can promote recovery and resilience include those listed below.

Encourage mutual support among peers and supervisors. The former typically occurs anyway; the latter may need some explicit reinforcement. Although not typically team workers like firefighters or paramedics, police officers frequently work as partners and understand that some degree of shared decision-making and mutual reassurance can enhance effective performance on the job, as well as helping to deal with tragedy.

Utilize humor as a coping mechanism to facilitate emotional insulation and group bonding. The first forestalls excessive identification with victims, the second encourages mutual group support via a shared language. Of course, as noted earlier, mental health clinicians and departmental supervisors need to carefully monitor the line between adaptive humor that encourages healing and gratuitous nastiness that only serves to entrench cynicism and despair.

Make use of appropriate rituals that give meaning and dignity to an otherwise existentially disorienting experience. This includes not only religious rites related to mourning, but such respectful protocols as a military-style honor guard to attend bodies before disposition, and the formal acknowledgment of actions above and beyond the call of duty.

Make productive use of grief leadership. This involves the commanding officer demonstrating by example that it is okay to express grief and mourn the death of fallen comrades or civilians, and that the dignified expression of one's feelings about the tragedy will be supported, not denigrated. Indeed, this healthy combination of masterful task-orientation and validated expression of legitimate grief has largely characterized the response of rescue and recovery personnel at the New York World Trade Center and other mass-casualty disaster sites (Henry, 2004; Regehr & Bober, 2004).

Show respect for psychological issues and psychological services. If the departmental brass do not believe that encouraging the appropriate utilization of psychological services is a valid way of expressing their concern and support for their troops' welfare, then the rank and file will not buy it either. Psychological referrals should be destigmatized and supported as a health and safety measure, the same as with medical referrals and general fitness maintenance.

Summary and Conclusions

In their daily work, law enforcement officers are exposed to the possibility of both traumatizing critical incidents and cumulative stressors. Some of these are severe enough to produce critical incident stress, post-traumatic stress disorder, or other traumatic disability syndromes. Certain traits and behaviors characterize individuals who are either unusually susceptible or unusually resistant to the effect of potentially traumatic events. Such vulnerability and resilience factors are important to take into consideration when working clinically with law enforcement officers. Therapeutic options include critical incident stress debriefing and specialized psychotherapy modalities that emphasize the creation of a meaningful narrative of traumatic events and the bolstering of adaptive resilience to cope with future stressors.

References

Alexander, D.A. (1993). Stress among body handlers: A long-term follow-up. *British Journal of Psychiatry*, 163, 806–808.

Alexander, D.A. & Walker, L.G. (1994). A study of methods used by Scottish police officers to cope with work-related stress. *Stress Medicine*, 10, 131–138.

Alexander, D.A. & Wells, A. (1991). Reactions of police officers to body-handling after a major disaster: A before-and-after comparison. *British Journal of Psychiatry*, 159, 547–555.

American Psychiatric Association (APA). (1980). *Diagnostic and Statistical Manual of Mental Disorders*, 3rd ed. Washington DC: American Psychiatric Association.

American Psychiatric Association (APA). (2000). *Diagnostic and Statistical Manual of Mental Disorders*, 4th ed., text rev. Washington DC: American Psychiatric

Antonovsky, A. (1979). *Health, Stress, and Coping*. San Francisco: Jossey-Bass.

Antonovsky, A. (1987). *Unraveling the Mystery of Health: How People Manage Stress and Stay Well*. San Francisco: Jossey-Bass.

Antonovsky, A. (1990). Personality and health: Testing the sense of coherence model. In H.S. Friedman (Ed.), *Personality and Disease*, pp. 155–177. New York: Wiley.

Barrett, J.E., Johnson, W.B., Johnson, S.J., Sullivan, G.R., Bongar, B., Miller, L., & Sammons, M.T. (2011). Psychology in extremis: Preventing problems of professional competence in dangerous practice settings. *Professional Psychology: Research and Practice*, 42, 94–104.

Bifulco, A.T., Brown, G.W., & Harris, T.O. (1987). Childhood loss of parent, lack of adequate parental care and adult depression: A replication. *Journal of Affective Disorders*, 12, 115–128.

Blau, T.H. (1994). *Psychological Services for Law Enforcement*. New York: Wiley.

Bohl, N.K. (1991). The effectiveness of brief psychological interventions in police officers after critical incidents. In J.T. Reese, J.M. Horn, & C. Dunning (Eds.), *Critical Incidents in Policing*, pp. 31–38. Washington DC: US Department of Justice.

Bohl, N. (1995). Professionally administered critical incident debriefing for police officers. In M.I. Kunke & E.M. Scrivner (Eds.), *Police Psychology into the 21st Century*, pp. 169–188. Hillsdale: Erlbaum.

Bowman, M. (1997). *Individual Differences in Posttraumatic Response: Problems with the Adversity-Distress Connection*. Mahwah, NJ: Erlbaum.

Bowman, M.L. (1999). Individual differences in posttraumatic distress: Problems with the DSM-IV model. *Canadian Journal of Psychiatry*, 44, 21–33.

Brewin, C.R., Andrews, B., & Valentine, J.D. (2000). Meta-analysis of risk factors for posttraumatic stress disorder in trauma-exposed adults. *Journal of Consulting and Clinical Psychology*, 68, 748–766.

Calhoun, L.G. & Tedeschi, R.G. (1999). *Facilitating Posttraumatic Growth*. Mahwah, NJ: Erlbaum.

Carlier, I.V.E. (1999). Finding meaning in police traumas. In J.M. Violanti & D. Paton (Eds.), *Police Trauma: Psychological Aftermath of Civilian Combat*, pp. 227–240. Springfield: Charles C. Thomas.

Carlier, I.V.E. & Gersons, B.P.R. (1995). Partial PTSD: The issue of psychological scars and the occurrence of PTSD symptoms. *Journal of Nervous and Mental Disease*, 183, 107–109.

Carlier, I.V.E., Lamberts, R.D., & Gersons, B.P.R. (1997). Risk factors for posttraumatic stress symptomatology in police officers: A prospective analysis. *Journal of Nervous and Mental Disease*, 185, 498–506.

Clary, M. (2005). War vets besieged by stress. *South Florida Sun-Sentinel*, March 28, 1–2.

Corbett, S. (2004). The permanent scars of Iraq. *New York Times Magazine*, February 15, 34–41, 56–61.

Creamer, M. & Forbes, D. (2004). Treatment of posttraumatic stress disorder in military and veteran populations. *Psychotherapy: Theory, Research, Practice*, 41, 388–398.

Cummings, J.P. (1996). Police stress and the suicide link. *The Police Chief*, October, 85–96.

Curran, S.F. (2003). Separating fact from fiction about police stress. *Behavioral Health Management*, January/February, 38–40.

Davis, G.C. & Breslau, N. (1994). Posttraumatic stress disorder in victims of civilian and criminal violence. *Psychiatric Clinics of North America*, 17, 289–299.

DeAngelis, T. (1995). Firefighters's PTSD at dangerous levels. *APA Monitor*, February, 36–37.

Dunning, C. (1999). Postintervention strategies to reduce police trauma: A paradigm shift. In J.M. Violanti & D. Paton (Eds.), *Police Trauma: Psychological Aftermath of Civilian Combat*, pp. 269–289. Springfield: Charles C. Thomas.

Durham, T.W., McCammon, S.L., & Allison, E.J. (1985). The psychological impact of disaster on rescue personnel. *Annals of Emergency Medicine*, 14, 664–668.

Evans, B.J., Coman, G.J., Stanley, R.O., & Burrows, G.D. (1993). Police officers' coping strategies: An Australian police survey. *Stress Medicine*, 9, 237–246.

Everly, G.S. & Mitchell, J.T. (1997). *Critical Incident Stress Management (CISM): A New Era and Standard of Care in Crisis Intervention*. Ellicott City: Chevron.

Fischler, G.L., McElroy, H.K., Miller, L., Saxe-Clifford, S., Stewart, C.O., & Zelig, M. (2011). The role of psychological fitness-for-duty evaluations in law enforcement. *The Police Chief*, August, 72–78.

Fullerton, C.S., McCarroll, J.E., Ursano, R.J., & Wright, K.M. (1992). Psychological responses of rescue workers: Firefighters and trauma. *American Journal of Orthopsychiatry*, 62, 371–378.

Galovski, T. & Lyons, J.A. (2004). Psychological sequelae of combat violence: A review of the impact of PTSD on the veteran's family, and possible interventions. *Aggression and Violent Behavior*, 9, 477–501.

Garmezy, N. (1993). Children in poverty: Resilience despite risk. *Psychiatry*, 56, 127–136.

Garmezy, N., Masten, A.S., & Tellegen, A. (1984). The study of stress and competence in children: A building block for developmental psychopathology. *Child Development*, 55, 97–111.

Gentz, D. (1991). The psychological impact of critical incidents on police officers. In J. Reese, J. Horn, & C. Dunning (Eds.), *Critical Incidents in Policing*, pp. 119–121. Washington DC: US Government Printing Office.

Hays, T. (1994). Daily horrors take heavy toll on New York City police officers. *Boca Raton News*, September 28, 2A–3A.

Henry, V.E. (2004). *Death Work: Police, Trauma, and the Psychology of Survival*. New York: Oxford University Press.

Hoge, E.A., Austin, E.D., & Pollack, M.H. (2007). Resilience: Research evidence and conceptual considerations for posttraumatic stress disorder. *Depression and Anxiety*, 24, 139–152.

Janik, J. (1991). What value are cognitive defenses in critical incident stress? In J. Reese, J. Horn, & C. Dunning (Eds.), *Critical Incidents in Policing*, pp. 149–158. Washington DC: US Government Printing Office.

Karlsson, I. & Christianson, S.A. (2003). The phenomenology of traumatic experiences in police work. *Policing: An International Journal of Police Strategies and Management*, 26, 419–438.

Kirschman, E.F. (1997). *I Love A Cop: What Police Families Need to Know*. New York: Guilford.

Kirschman, E.F. (2004). *I Love A Firefighter: What the Family Needs to Know*. New York: Guilford.

Kobasa, S.C. (1979a). Personality and resistance to illness. *American Journal of Community Psychology*, 7, 413–423.

Kobasa, S.C. (1979b). Stressful life events, personality, and health: An inquiry into hardiness. *Journal of Personality and Social Psychology*, 37, 1–11.

Kobassa, S.C., Maddi, S., & Cahn, S. (1982). Hardiness and health: A prospective study. *Journal of Personality and Social Psychology*, 42, 168–177.

Luthar, S.S. (1991). Vulnerability and resilience: A study of high-risk adolescents. *Child Development*, 62, 600–616.

Maddi, S.R. & Khoshaba, D.M. (1994). Hardiness and mental health. *Journal of Personality Assessment*, 63, 265–274.

Max, D.J. (2000). The cop and the therapist. *New York Times Magazine*, December 3, 94–98.

McCafferty, F.L., Domingo, G., & McCafferty, E. (1990). PTSD in the police officer: Paradigm of occupational stress. *Southern Medical Journal*, 83, 543–547.

McCafferty, F.L., McCafferty, E., & McCafferty, M.A. (1992). Stress and suicide in police officers: Paradigms of occupational stress. *Southern Medical Journal*, 85, 233–243.

Meek, C.L. (1990). Evaluation and assessment of post-traumatic and other stress-related disorders. In C.L. Meek (Ed.), *Post-Traumatic Stress Disorder: Assessment, Differential Diagnosis, and Forensic Evaluation*, pp. 9–61. Sarasota: Professional Resource Exchange.

Merskey, H. (1992). Psychiatric aspects of the neurology of trauma. *Neurologic Clinics*, 10, 895–905.

Miller, L. (1990). *Inner Natures: Brain, Self, and Personality*. New York: St. Martin's Press.

Miller, L. (1995). Tough guys: Psychotherapeutic strategies with law enforcement and emergency services personnel. *Psychotherapy*, 32, 592–600.

Miller, L. (1998a). Ego autonomy and the healthy personality: Psychodynamics, cognitive style, and clinicial applications. *Psychoanalytic Review*, 85, 423–448.

Miller, L. (1998b). *Shocks to the System: Psychotherapy of Traumatic Disability Syndromes*. New York: Norton.

Miller, L. (1999). Critical incident stress debriefing: Clinical applications and new directions. *International Journal of Emergency Mental Health*, 1, 253–265.

Miller, L. (2003). Psychological interventions for terroristic trauma: Symptoms, syndromes, and treatment strategies. *Psychotherapy*, 39, 283–296.

Miller, L. (2004). Good cop–bad cop: Problem officers, law enforcement culture, and strategies for success. *Journal of Police and Criminal Psychology*, 19, 30–48.

Miller, L. (2005). Police officer suicide: Causes, prevention, and practical intervention strategies. *International Journal of Emergency Mental Health*, 7, 101–114.

Miller, L. (2006a). Officer-involved shooting: Reaction patterns, response protocols, and psychological intervention strategies. *International Journal of Emergency Mental Health*, 8, 239–254.

Miller, L. (2006b). *Practical Police Psychology: Stress Management and Crisis Intervention for Law Enforcement*. Springfield, IL: Charles C. Thomas.

Miller, L. (2006c). Critical incident stress debriefing for law enforcement: Practical models and special applications. *International Journal of Emergency Mental Health*, 8, 189–201.

Miller, L. (2007). The psychological fitness-for-duty evaluation. *FBI Law Enforcement Bulletin*, August, 10–16.

Miller, L. (2008a). *METTLE: Mental Toughness Training for Law Enforcement*. Flushing, NY: Looseleaf Law Publications.

Miller, L. (2008b). *Counseling Crime Victims: Practical Strategies for Mental Health Professionals.* New York: Springer.

Miller, L. (2008c). Military psychology and police psychology: Mutual contributions to crisis intervention and stress management. *International Journal of Emergency Mental Health*, 10, 9–26.

Miller, L. (2008d). Stress and resilience in law enforcement training and practice. *International Journal of Emergency Mental Health*, 10, 109–124.

Miller, L. (2010). Psychotherapy with military personnel: Lessons learned, challenges ahead. *International Journal of Emergency Mental Health*, 12, 179–192.

Miller, L. (2011). Policing the police psychologist: Ensuring health and competence. *Professional Psychology: Research and Practice*, 42, 100–102.

Modlin, H.C. (1983). Traumatic neurosis and other injuries. *Psychiatric Clinics of North America*, 6, 661–682.

Modlin, H.C. (1990). Post-traumatic stress disorder: Differential diagnosis. In C.L. Meek (Ed.), *Post-Traumatic Stress Disorder: Assessment, Differential Diagnosis, and Forensic Evaluation*, pp. 63–89. Sarasota: Professional Resource Exchange.

Munsey, C. (2006). Soldier support. *Monitor on Psychology*, April, 36–38.

Nash, W.P. & Baker, D.G. (2007). Competing and complementary models of combat stress injury. In C.R. Figley & W.P. Nash (Eds.), *Combat Stress Injury: Theory, Research, and Management*, pp. 65–94. New York: Routledge.

Nordland, R. & Gegax, T.T. (2004). Stress at the front. *Newsweek*, January 12, 34–37.

Ostrov, E. (1991). Critical incident psychological casualties among police officers: A clinical review. In J. Reese, J. Horn, & C. Dunning (Eds.), *Critical Incidents in Policing*, pp. 251–256. Washington DC: US Government Printing Office.

Palmer, C.E. (1983). A note about paramedics' strategies for dealing with death and dying. *Journal of Occupational Psychology*, 56, 83–86.

Paton, D. & Smith, L. (1999). Assessment, conceptual and methodological issues in researching traumatic stress in police officers. In J.M. Violanti & D. Paton (Eds.), *Police Trauma: Psychological Aftermath of Civilian Combat*, pp. 13–24. Springfield: Charles C. Thomas.

Paton, D., Smith, L., Violanti, J.M., & Eranen, L. (2000). Work-related traumatic stress: Risk, vulnerability, and resilience. In J. Violanti, D. Paton, & C. Dunning (Eds.), *Posttraumatic Stress Intervention: Challenges, Issues, and Perspectives*, pp. 187–203. Springfield: Charles C. Thomas.

Reese, J.T. (1987). Coping with stress: It's your job. In J.T. Reese (Ed.), *Behavioral Science in Law Enforcement*, pp. 75–79. Washington DC: FBI.

Regehr, C. & Bober, T. (2004). *In the Line of Fire: Trauma in the Emergency Services.* New York: Oxford University Press.

Rodgers, B.A. (2006). *Psychological Aspects of Police Work: An Officer's Guide to Street Psychology.* Springfield, IL: Charles C. Thomas.

Rubenstein, J.L., Heeren, T., Houseman, D., Rubin, C., & Stechler, G. (1989). Suicidal behavior in "normal" adolescents: Risk and protective factors. *American Journal of Orthopsychiatry*, 59, 59–71.

Rudofossi, D. (2007). *Working with Traumatized Police Officer-Patients: A Clinician's Guide to Complex PTSD Syndromes in Public Safety Professionals.* Amityville, NY: Baywood.

Rudofossi, D. (2009). *A Cop Doc's Guide to Public Safety Complex Trauma Syndrome: Using Five Police Personality Styles.* Amityville, NY: Baywood.

Russell, H.E. & Beigel, A. (1990). *Understanding Human Behavior for Effective Police Work*, 3rd ed. New York: Basic Books.

Rutter, M. (1985). Resilience in the face of adversity: Protective factors and resistance to psychiatric disorder. *British Journal of Psychiatry*, 147, 598–611.

Rutter, M. (1987). Psychosocial resilience and protective mechanisms. *American Journal of Orthopsychiatry*, 57, 316–331.

Rutter, M., Tizard, J., Yule, W., Graham, P., & Whitmore, K. (1976). Research report: Isle of Wight studies, 1964–1974. *Psychological Medicine*, 6, 313–332.

Seligmann, J., Holt, D., Chinni, D., & Roberts, E. (1994). Cops who kill—themselves. *Newsweek*, September 26, 58.

Sewell, J.D., Ellison, K.W., & Hurrell, J.J. (1988). Stress management in law enforcement: Where do we go from here? *The Police Chief*, October, 94–98.

Solomon, R.M. (1988). Mental conditioning: The utilization of fear. In J.T. Reese & J.M. Horn (Eds.), *Police Psychology: Operational Assistance*, pp. 391–407. Washington DC: US Government Printing Office.

Solomon, R.M. (1991). The dynamics of fear in critical incidents: Implications for training and treatment. In J.T. Reese, J.M. Horn, & C. Dunning (Eds.), *Critical Incidents in Policing*, pp. 347–358. Washington DC: Federal Bureau of Investigation.

Solomon, R.M. (1995). Critical incident stress management in law enforcement. In G.S. Everly (Ed.), *Innovations in Disaster and Trauma Psychology: Applications in Emergency Services and Disaster Response*, pp. 123–157. Ellicott City: Chevron.

Solomon, R.M. & Horn, (1986). Post-shooting traumatic reactions: A pilot study. In J.T. Reese & H. Goldstein (Eds.), *Psychological Services for Law Enforcement*, pp. 383–393. Washington DC: US Government Printing Office.

Stuhlmiller, C. & Dunning, C. (2000). Challenging the mainstream: From pathogenic to salutogenic models of posttrauma intervention. In J. Violanti, D. Paton, & C. Dunning (Eds.), *Posttraumatic Stress Intervention: Challenges, Issues, and Perspectives*, pp. 10–42. Springfield: Charles C. Thomas.

Sugimoto, J.D. & Oltjenbruns, K.A. (2001). The environment of death and its influence on police officers in the United States. *Omega*, 43, 145–155.

Taylor, S.E., Wood, J.V., & Lechtman, R.R. (1983). It could be worse: Selective evaluation as a response to victimization. *Journal of Social Issues*, 39, 19–40.

Tedeschi, R.G. & Calhoun, L.G. (1995). *Trauma and Transformation: Growing in the Aftermath of Suffering*. Thousand Oaks, CA: Sage.

Tedeschi, R.G. & Kilmer, R.P. (2005). Assessing strengths, resilience, and growth to guide clinical interventions. *Professional Psychology: Research and Practice*, 36, 230–237.

Toch, H. (2002). *Stress in Policing*. Washington DC: American Psychological Association.

Trimble, M.R. (1981). *Post-traumatic Neurosis: From Railway Spine to Whiplash*. New York: Wiley.

Tyre, P. (2004). Battling the effects of war. *Newsweek*, December 6, 68–70.

Vasterling, J.J., MacDonald, H.Z., Ulloa, E.W., & Rodier, N. (2010). Neuropsychological correlates of PTSD: A military perspective. In C.H. Kennedy

& J.L. Moore (Eds.), *Military Neuropsychology*, pp. 321–360. New York: Springer.

Violanti, J.M. (1999). Death on duty: Police survivor trauma. In J.M. Violanti & D. Paton (Eds.), *Police Trauma: Psychological Aftermath of Civilian Combat*, pp. 139–158. Springfield: Charles C. Thomas.

Violanti, J.M. (2000). Scripting trauma: The impact of pathogenic intervention. In J. Violanti, D. Paton, & C. Dunning (Eds.), *Posttraumatic Stress Intervention: Challenges, Issues, and Perspectives*, pp. 153–165. Springfield: Charles C. Thomas.

Weiner, H. (1992). *Perturbing the Organism: The Biology of Stressful Experience*. Chicago: University of Chicago Press.

Werner, E.E. (1989). High-risk children in young adulthood: A longitudinal study from birth to 32 years. *American Journal of Orthopsychiatry*, 59, 72–81.

Werner, E.E. & Smith, R.S. (1992). *Overcoming the Odds: High Risk Children from Birth to Adulthood*. Ithaca, NY: Cornell University Press.

Wester, S.R. & Lyubelsky, J. (2005). Supporting the thin blue line: Gender-sensitive therapy with male police officers. *Professional Psychology: Research and Practice*, 36, 51–58.

Wilson, J.P. (1994). The historical evolution of PTSD diagnostic criteria: From Freud to DSM-IV. *Journal of Traumatic Stress*, 7, 681–698.

Zimrin, H. (1986). A profile of survival. *Child Abuse and Neglect*, 10, 339–349.

12

MANAGING MENTALLY ILL INDIVIDUALS

Recommendations for Police Officers

Laurence Miller

Dealing with mentally ill or neurologically impaired individuals is a necessary part of police patrol work. Many officers actually feel less comfortable handling mentally ill citizens than they do criminal suspects because the latter, ironically, are often more predictable and appear more responsible for their behavior than the former. There also remains the social stigma attached to the mentally ill which colors the opinions of most people, including most police officers.

Nevertheless, most officers perceive a need for special training in dealing with the mentally ill (Borum, Deane, Steadman, & Morrissey, 1998; Hill, Quill, & Ellis, 2004; Vermette, Pinals, & Appelbaum, 2005). Accordingly, this chapter provides some insight into the variety of mentally ill citizens that officers are most likely to encounter in their patrol work. It also offers some practical strategies for dealing with mentally ill citizens in a way that preserves the balance between respect for individual rights and dignity, and enforcing the law and maintaining social order within the community.

Approximately 5 percent of the American population has some form of serious mental illness. In jail or prison populations, this proportion rises to 16 percent. Almost three-quarters of these mentally ill inmates have a coexisting substance abuse problem. Most mentally ill persons are not violent, but there seems to be a somewhat higher incidence of violence among the seriously mentally ill than in the general population. The factors most often associated with violence are *paranoid schizophrenia* with *command hallucinations*, that is, auditory hallucinations telling the subject to do something, as well as coexisting psychosis, substance abuse, and antisocial personality disorder. However, the mentally ill are far more often the victims of crime than the perpetrators, and are three times more likely than ordinary citizens to be crime victims. When mentally ill persons do commit a violent crime, the victim is familiar to them in more than half the cases; indeed, most perpetrators of violence have some personal connection with their victims (Borum et al., 1998; Carter, 1993; Cordner, 2000; Dupont & Cochran, 2000; Finn & Stalans, 2002; Miller, 2006, 2008b; Reuland & Margolis, 2003).

Across the United States, mental health calls account for 5–10 percent of calls for police service, ranking on a par with robbery calls. A significant number of these mental health calls relate to aggressive behavior, making them at least as dangerous as robbery calls. A large number of mental health calls overlap with domestic disturbance calls, which are themselves potentially dangerous situations for responding officers. Officers tend to view mentally ill subjects as more dangerous and less in control of their actions than other citizens. Officers are more likely to try to use *civil commitment* as an alternative to arrest and jail detention if they believe that the mental health system will accept potentially violent cases, but placement space is typically limited (Borum et al., 1998; Bonta, Law, & Hanson, 1998; Eccleston, Brown, & Ward, 2005; Hill et al., 2004; Monahan, 1996; Vermette et al., 2005; Wiley, 2005).

Responding to Mentally Disturbed Citizens: Basic Strategies for Patrol Officers

Underlying and framing the individual approaches for specific mental disorders to be described below are some general considerations that apply to dealing with mentally ill citizens of all types (Borum, Swanson, Swartz, & Hiday, 1997; Borum et al., 1998; Fyfe, 2000; Janik, 1992; Miller, 2006, in press; Rodgers, 2006; Russell & Beigel, 1990).

Proper response to the mentally ill begins with the call. Sometimes, officers will just happen upon a situation involving a mentally disordered subject, but in many cases, such calls come over the radio, usually in the form of someone "acting crazy" on the street, or in a store or home. Such calls should be answered by more than one officer, preferably in uniform, so there is no doubt in the subject's mind as to the identity of the law enforcement responders. One officer should try to engage the subject in conversation, while others control any crowds that might contribute to a spectator circus.

The first priority for officers is to ascertain the physical health and safety of the subject and others who may be at the scene. When first approaching the subject, keep your distance and move slowly. One officer should be the talker and the rest keep silent, to avoid simultaneous conversation, which will be confusing and irritating to an already disturbed subject. Employ the technique of a *calm show of force*: by a combination of strength of numbers and fair-but-firm demeanor, make it clear to the subject that you would prefer him to comply willingly and will respect his decision to do so, but you are prepared to use physical restraint if he leaves you no other choice.

In line with this, provide reasonable assurance that you are there to make things better, not worse. With angry and agitated subjects, avoid unnecessary threats and try to meet hostility with deflection and de-escalation, but be cautious about letting down your guard; remember that mentally disordered persons can be unpredictable. Even though the subject appears disturbed, try to keep your conversation geared to that of a normal, reasonable person. As much as possible, do not lie, deceive, manipulate, or treat the subject like a baby.

If the subject expresses delusional thinking, neither dispute nor agree with the content. Arguing against someone's subjective perception is likely to be irritating and alienating, while too quickly agreeing with the *delusion* (false belief) or *hallucination* (false perception) may be taken for the phony camaraderie that it is, further convincing the subject that he can trust no one. A better strategy is to present yourself as an honest broker who frankly cannot pretend to see or believe everything the subject does, but is prepared to keep an open mind in the service of helping the subject: "Sir, I really don't know if they're after you or not, but if you think they are, let's figure out how to keep you safe for now, okay?"

It is a good idea to record the gist of the subject's delusional content because this may prove valuable to both criminal justice and mental health follow-ups, especially if this involves overtly paranoid, aggressive, or suicidal ideation. Note any threats made, especially if directed against specific persons or agencies. If no arrestable offense has been committed and the subject is basically cooperating, exercise due caution, but utilize the same tact and respect as you would with any citizen. Even if things seem to have calmed down, stay with the subject until help arrives. Sometimes it may be your role to transport the subject to the appropriate facility, so know which facilities exist in your community. Usually, any such transport will be made by the paramedics you have contacted, and if the subject declines to be treated or transported, they may be the ones to make the call as to whether or not to involuntarily commit the person. In the simplest cases, you may have no option other than to let the subject go peaceably on his way.

Dealing with Different Mental Disorders:
Abnormal Psychology 101 for Police Officers

To supplement the basic general recommendations above, the following sections offer more specific advice for handling subjects with particular kinds of mental disorder, and this material can be used by mental health and behavioral science professionals as the foundation for training curricula in police psychology. While not intended as a formal course in psychopathology and psychotherapy, this information is more focused toward the kind of street-level crisis intervention that virtually all officers inevitably have to deal with in their patrol activities. In addition, officers may be charged with the responsibility of locating appropriate services for these individuals (APA, 2000; Garner, 1995; Miller, 2006, in press; Mohandie & Duffy, 1999; Rodgers, 2006; Russell & Beigel, 1990).

Schizophrenia

Psychotic disorders comprise a group of syndromes, the main common feature of which is a significant break with reality, characterized by severe disturbances of mood, thought, interpersonal relatedness, and goal-directed action. The most common form of psychotic disorder is *schizophrenia*, which is a progressive syndrome, usually first presenting in adolescence or early adulthood (although childhood forms occur), and characterized by delusional thinking and the presence of hallucinations, which are typically auditory (hearing voices), and more rarely, visual (seeing things). Untreated schizophrenics may suffer episodic bouts of delusional and hallucinatory psychosis, between which they may appear simply odd or weird, unable to maintain any consistent work or other goal-directed activity.

Many of these individuals are seen among the ranks of the "street people" comprising a proportion of an officer's patrol district in any major metropolitan area, and represent the largest group of calls for service for a mentally ill citizen. Although diagnostic overlap is common, schizophrenia may be primarily of the *paranoid* type, characterized by delusions of persecution and accusatory hallucinations; the *disorganized* type, characterized by general aimlessness and lack of contact with reality; the *catatonic* type, which is more commonly seen in institutional settings because of their near-immobility; or the *undifferentiated* type, which may comprise features of the other three classifications or show additional symptoms (Miller, 2006, in press).

Schizophrenia: Risk Factors for Violence

Although not intended to needlessly stigmatize the mentally ill, the clinical evidence to date does suggest that subjects with schizophrenic disorders do have a somewhat higher risk of violence than the population at large. The rate of schizophrenia is three times higher in prisons than in the general population, although this may reflect differential rates of arrest or access to competent legal representation, as untreated mental illness is typically associated with poverty and lower social status. When asked to describe their own behavior, the prevalence of self-reported violence is five times higher among schizophrenic subjects than among the general population.

Paranoid schizophrenic subjects may be an especially dangerous group (Shore et al., 1985, 1988). Certain factors serve to increase the risk of violence among psychotic subjects. Some of these are associated with generic violence risk factors, such as access to weapons and coexisting substance abuse and antisocial personality disorder. More syndrome-specific risk factors include the presence of *persecutory delusions* which may impel psychotic subjects to lash out as a way of protecting themselves, that is, a "preemptive strike." Another important risk factor is *command hallucinations* that order the subject to use offensive or defensive aggression.

Schizophrenia: Police Response

Officers who encounter a psychotic individual should observe a few basic rules of engagement (Mohandie & Duffy, 1999). First, if possible, assess the nature of the subject's psychotic state and overall behavior before approaching. This is to prevent either a lapse of precaution on the one hand, or an unnecessarily aggressive response on the other. Approach the subject as slowly and as nonthreateningly as possible. If more than one officer is present, keep the sensory overload to a minimum by having only one officer speak at a time. Try to determine if the subject can be verbally engaged. Always speak and act slowly, firmly, and deliberately.

If the subject is willing to talk, encourage venting, but not ranting. If the subject expresses delusional ideas and beliefs, neither argue nor agree with the delusions. Through their painful life experiences, most schizophrenics have learned that other people do not believe their delusional ideas, so pretending to do so may only serve to further alienate or enrage an already-disturbed psychotic subject. Conversely, it is highly unlikely that trying to "talk sense" into a delusional subject is going to make him suddenly see things more rationally. Instead, acknowledge the content of the delusion and try to ally yourself with the subject's perspective and perception of the situation, while keeping the focus on present reality: "Let me try to understand this. The terrorists have been sending you messages through your radio and cell phone, telling you of their plots to kill people, and you're trying to fight them off. Do I have that right? That must be pretty frightening." Utilize active listening skills with the goal of calming the situation as much as possible (Miller, 2006).

One thing to be especially alert for in the content of a psychotic subject's verbalization is the risk of suicide or violence, particularly if expressed toward specific targets ("They can't keep trying to ruin my work and get away with it—I'm gonna teach that supervisor a lesson!"). Again, it is probably futile to try to correct the subject's misinterpretations of reality, so keep your statements simple, concrete, and focused on the subject's safety and well-being.

Because many psychotic subjects are especially sensitive to physical boundary issues, try to make productive use of personal space and body language, as well as verbal and nonverbal calming techniques. Unless and until physical restraint becomes necessary, keep a reasonable distance and inform the subject of what you are about to do: "Sir, I'm going to reach into my pocket to take out a pen and a pad so I can write down some notes, okay? It's just a pen and pad." Then move slowly. Always use caution, however, because the subject may become panicked and turn violent in a flash.

If physical restraint or arrest is required, utilize appropriate backup and safe takedown procedures. Once the decision to restrain the subject has been made, do so quickly and purposefully, while, if at all possible, allowing for some degree of the subject's self-respect to be preserved. Remember that psychotic subjects can be very unpredictable—sitting and mumbling distractedly one moment, thrashing and kicking violently the next. If an arrest is not made, transport the subject to an appropriate medical or psychiatric receiving facility. Unfortunately, many mentally ill subjects who would best be served by a medical–psychiatric unit are nevertheless turned away from such facilities due to lack of funding or the facility's refusal to accept intoxicated or potentially violent patients. In such cases, officers often have no choice but to let the subject go or arrest him on a misdemeanor charge in order to transport him to jail for his own and others' safety.

Alcohol and Drug Intoxication

Aside from schizophrenic subjects, alcohol- and drug-intoxication disturbances comprise the second most common type of mental disorder-related police patrol interaction (Garner, 1995; Miller, 2006; Rodgers, 2006; Russell & Beigel, 1990). In fact, the two diagnoses frequently overlap, as many mentally disturbed individuals are also abusing substances at any given time.

Intoxication and Withdrawal: Signs, Symptoms, and Syndromes

Signs of *alcohol intoxication* are familiar to any officer who has ever pulled over a drunk driver or attended a New Year's Eve party: slurred speech, unbalanced posture, impaired coordination, and so on, although it is possible for many drinkers who are legally intoxicated to act relatively normally, especially when trying to impress the officer with their intactness. Alcohol has varying effects, depending on the particular user, with some inebriated drinkers becoming more mellow and tractable, others becoming more angry and agitated. In general, alcohol and most other drugs lower inhibitions and self-control, so any intoxicated person has to be approached with caution.

Less common, but potentially more serious, are signs and symptoms of *alcohol withdrawal* in subjects who are physiologically addicted to alcohol. This usually presents as an agitated state with tremors ("the shakes"). In severe cases, this can be accompanied by hallucinations and/or seizures. An acute state of agitated delirium, characterized by intense fear and tactile and visual hallucinations of vermin crawling on the skin, is called *delirium tremens* ("the DTs"). Typically, such individuals will be so clearly impaired that the need for transport to a medical facility is obvious.

A rare, but more dangerous syndrome is *pathological intoxication*, where even small amounts of alcohol trigger violent rages in susceptible individuals, which is thought to be due to an electrophysiological disturbance in sensitive limbic areas of the brain. Witnesses will describe an explosion of rage in which the subject appears to be "on automatic" or "like a runaway train," fueled by adrenalin and capable of inflicting severe damage to anyone who gets in their way. During these brief episodes, it is useless to try to talk the subject out of their aggressive action. The only effective strategy is to use appropriate physical restraint to keep them from harming others.

Other substances of abuse have different effects on behavior, depending on their biochemical action within the nervous system. *Stimulants* ("uppers"), such as cocaine and amphetamine, produce a "racing" kind of high, with rapid thought and speech, erratic and impulsive behavior, and a ramped-up energy level. Such individuals may occasionally become violent, but more commonly, they will present as simply annoying and raucous, quite similar to the manic phase of bipolar disorder, described below; in fact, many manic subjects deliberately use stimulants to enhance and extend their natural high. Danger may arise when their overconfidence and impulsivity leads to temper flare-ups provoked by confrontations with police.

Central nervous system *depressants* ("downers"), such as barbiturates (e.g., Quaaludes) or benzodiazepines (e.g., Valium), have effects similar to alcohol, which include a calming effect, but accompanied by a loosening of inhibitions, which may lead to impulsive and illegal actions. Most calls for service for these users tend to be due to their passing out unconscious in a public place, but they may become combative if they are still confused and disoriented when police or paramedics arrive.

The effects of *hallucinogens,* such as marijuana, LSD, or angel dust, may range from mellow loopiness to violent delirium. *Organic hydrocarbons*, such as the glue and paint thinner used by sniffers or "huffers," tend to produce a toxic delirious state; these latter substances are also extremely injurious to brain tissue and can produce long-term cognitive impairment.

Police Handling of Intoxicated Subjects

Because a behaviorally deteriorated state can be caused by a variety of factors, it is first important to distinguish drug or alcohol intoxication from other medical or psychiatric conditions. Remember, several syndromes may go together; for example, the delusions of a paranoid schizophrenic may be exacerbated by using cocaine, so he smokes some pot to calm down and begins hallucinating, so then he drinks some beer to quiet the voices, and this interacts with the postconcussive effects of a recent head injury he sustained in a fight. Now you are faced with a fearful, angry, and confused person whose behavior is erratic and unpredictable.

In most cases of alcohol use, the subject's breath will give him away. Otherwise, you may have to rely on your knowledge and experience (observational and personal) of intoxicated states. Always approach an intoxicated person with caution. Try to gather as much information as possible about how that person has gotten to where he or she is and whether there is a need for medical attention. Check for weapons and generally assess for danger to self or others. Use tact, patience, and verbal intervention skills—but only to a point. Remember, you are dealing with a person whose powers of perception, comprehension, reasoning, and self-control have all been impaired by the substance they have ingested.

If necessary, call for backup and be prepared to use defensive and/or control techniques, such as spray, impact, taser, or restraint, if necessary. If the subject has not yet committed an arrestable offense, but yet cannot be safely left on his own, arrange for transport to a receiving facility: better to call the paramedics and let them handle the medical aspects if the subject is refusing treatment or transport.

Mood Disorders

Mood disorders are generally classified into unipolar and bipolar types, depending on whether the extreme changes in mood are in one direction (down-depressed) or both directions (down-depressed and up-elated or up-angry). *Major depressive disorder* is characterized by episodes of depressed mood that may last for weeks or months at a time. In severe cases, the individual may be virtually immobilized. More characteristically, subjects feel dejected, demoralized, helpless, and hopeless. Sleep and appetite may be impaired; alternatively, some individuals become hypersomnic (sleep virtually all the time) or may binge-eat. Concentration and memory may be affected to the point where individuals feel they are becoming demented. Gone is any motivation or enthusiasm for work, play, or family activities. Accompanying emotions may include anxiety, panic, irritability, or anger. The disorder usually occurs in cycles over the lifespan, and, in most cases, is very responsive to treatment.

Bipolar disorder, also known as *manic-depressive illness*, is characterized by extreme shifts in mood, from elation to depression, spanning over the course of hours or days, often with an absence of normal mood in between: for such individuals, there are only highs and lows. The *manic phase* typically begins with the individual feeling energized, overconfident, and "pumped." He becomes hyperactive and grandiose, spinning all kinds of half-baked unrealistic plans, but acting increasingly impulsive and distractible. Thinking and speech become rapid and forced. Need for sleep decreases and the individual may be hypersexual; all appetites are on sensory overdrive. The overall impression is of someone on stimulant drugs and, indeed, such individuals may abuse amphetamines, cocaine, or alcohol to enhance the natural high and try to keep it going.

At the beginning of the manic phase, the individual may appear quite engaging and entertaining, but as the manic phase progresses, he becomes increasingly short-tempered, irritable, anxious, and paranoid. Inevitably, the individual cycles into the *depressed phase*. At this point, he may increase his use of stimulants to try to prolong the high, but eventually even this is not enough to stave off the depressive crash. Suicide is a distinct risk at this stage. In other bipolar patients, the manic episodes do not involve much elation at all, but are characterized mainly by irritability, anger and paranoia, and may be misdiagnosed as schizophrenia.

Mood Disorders: Law Enforcement Response

The most frequent law enforcement crisis intervention context for a depressed subject is potential suicide; depressed subjects are frequently seen in correctional and other institutional settings, as well as on daily street patrol. The first priority is safety. In these cases, assess for suicidality and emphasize the subject's well-being, especially since the police response is often associated with a confrontation: "I'm Officer Smith and this is Officer Jones. We're here to make sure you're okay and to get you any help you need right now."

Violence against others is rare in unipolar depression, although it may occur as part of a "suicide pact" with another person, usually an elderly couple with a serious illness or disability. Violence is a more likely risk for bipolar manic individuals who may be angry and delusional. Move slowly and take your time, avoiding any unnecessary intimidation. Use verbal and nonverbal calming techniques, and employ cautious physical restraint where necessary. Subjects in a manic state may not initially intend to attack you, but may be subject to explosions of anger upon hair-trigger provocation. And if they do get physical, you will be dealing with a huge adrenalin factor and it is going to take a lot of force to keep this person under control, so injuries on all sides are a distinct risk. Especially in these cases, then, your judicious use of verbal and nonverbal de-escalation techniques can make the difference between a subject who gets talked down and treated at a psychiatric facility and one who gets arrested and taken to jail for assaulting an officer. Assuming no arrest is called for but the subject requires further disposition, transport him or her to an appropriate medical or psychiatric receiving facility.

Dementia

The term *dementia* refers collectively to a range of organic brain syndromes that impair perception, thinking, language, memory, and behavior. As the American population continues to age, police officers can expect to deal with an increasing number of such individuals in their daily patrols. The main causes of dementia in the elderly are Alzheimer's disease, Parkinson's disease, and strokes. In younger subjects, dementia may occur as the result of AIDS, toxic-metabolic, and medical syndromes such as kidney or liver disease, or from heavy drug use or overdose.

Symptoms of dementia include *disorientation* to *time* ("What day is this? What year are we in?"), *place* ("What street are we on? Do you know what city we're in? Where do you live?"), and *person* ("What's your name?" "How old are you?"). *Aphasia* is a disturbance of language and can involve the comprehension of speech, the production of speech, or both. The difficulty an officer will have in dealing with a subject with organic dementia is largely determined by how severe the disorder is. Mildly impaired subjects may seem only a bit befuddled and absentminded, while more severely demented citizens will be unable to communicate or understand you, and will be virtually oblivious to their surroundings, aimlessly wandering, and becoming fearful and combative if restrained or feeling threatened.

Police Handling of Citizens with Dementia

Most cases of law enforcement contact with brain-impaired individuals will involve trespassing, where the subject simply wanders onto private property; theft or shoplifting, where they pick up a store item because they think it is theirs or just because it is there; assault related to defensively lashing out when they feel threatened, such as when confronted by an irate shopkeeper; or, more rarely, sexual offenses based on inappropriate comments or physical contact with others.

When encountering such a person, do not overlook the obvious—check for ID. Most nursing home residents have wristbands. Assess if there is any medical need. Even if not ill or injured, many such subjects may be malnourished or dehydrated because they literally forget to eat or drink. In your interactions with the subject, assess for specific signs or symptoms such as perceptual disturbances, difficulty completing sequences of actions, or language difficulties. If the subject is confused, frightened and agitated, use very basic calming techniques, such as slow even pace of voice, easy body language, and short, simple, reassuring phrases ("It's okay, we're going to take you home"). Most of these subjects will be reassured more by the demeanor and tone of what you say than by the content.

Be gently directive—tell and show the subject what you want him to do; most cognitively impaired subjects will display an easy, childlike compliance as they do not feel threatened. If you can identify where the subject resides, call the home or institutional facility and offer to transport the subject back there. If it is unclear where the subject lives, or if there appears to be any injury or other medical problem, call for paramedic backup or transport the subject to a hospital. Relatives looking for missing elderly family members will usually call hospitals first.

Mentally Retarded Subjects

The formal definition of *mental retardation* is a measured IQ of below 70 which results in impairment of any major life activity, such as education, employment, or socialization. Although mental retardation is not a mental illness per se, it may be associated with other kinds of mental disorder, so it is possible to see mood disorders, anxiety disorders, or psychotic disorders coexisting with intellectual deficiency.

Mentally retarded subjects may become involved in the criminal justice system in a number of ways. Their often childlike impulsivity may make them prone to misdemeanor crimes, such as shoplifting or public nuisance. When confused or frightened, they may become silent and withdraw or they may lash out defensively. They are also hardly immune to alcohol and drug abuse, and this may make their behavior even more unpredictable. Ordinarily, they tend to be quite compliant and trusting, and thereby make perfect patsies for other criminals to use as drug couriers or stashers of stolen goods. Mentally retarded offenders comprise about 5–10 percent of the convicted prison population (Bowker, 1994).

Police Handling of Mentally Retarded Subjects

Most of the mentally retarded citizens that officers encounter on their street patrols will not be found in the course of committing a crime, but are more likely to be lost and confused. In most cases, a brief interaction will be sufficient to determine that something is not right about this person. Pay attention to missing, excessive, or disheveled clothing or other unusual styles of dress. There may be peculiarities in the subject's

gait and movement, as many mentally retarded individuals also have disturbances in motor coordination. The subject's speech may have a simplistic, childlike quality, it may be characterized by various speech disorders, such as lisps, stutters or variations of volume and pitch, or it may sound relatively normal. When confronted by authorities, such as the police, these subjects are likely to become afraid or confused, or to be overcompliant and dependent.

If it is unclear as to whether the subject is mentally retarded or suffering from some other form of disorder, Bowker (1994) recommends a few curbside tests of cognitive and intellectual functioning. Can the subject identify their name and residence? Can they give coherent directions to where they live or where they are going? Can they repeat a question in their own words? Can they write their names clearly? Can they recognize coins and make change? Tell time? Use a telephone?

If you come across the scene of a crime or other disturbance involving a mentally retarded subject and other people, it may not be immediately clear who is the suspect, victim, witnesses, or bystanders. The mentally retarded subject may be intimidated and remain silent while the others do the talking and make their own cases. Be careful to question everyone present very carefully, and document these interviews. If you must arrest the mentally retarded subject, ensure that Miranda rights are understood; for example, ask the suspect to rephrase them in his own words. This might not always be possible. If a mentally retarded suspect has to be criminally detained, all care should be taken not to house him with the general population, where he may be abused. Of course, this will depend on the realities of the situation and available facilities.

Other Syndromes

More rarely, a variety of neurological and psychiatric syndromes may be seen by police officers on patrol.

Epilepsy

Epilepsy is a neurological syndrome characterized by repeated seizures. Most convulsive *grand mal* seizures are fairly unmistakable while they are occurring. However, there are a number of seizure types that produce disturbances primarily in thought, consciousness, and complex behavior; these may not be readily identifiable as manifestations of a neurological disorder. For example, in *temporal lobe epilepsy,* or TLE, the subject's awareness of his surroundings may be severely disturbed, and his behavior may not appear to be under his control. The seizure has an abrupt onset and gradual recovery, and can last for several seconds to minutes (Miller, 1994a).

The TLE symptoms most likely to get the subject into trouble are collectively known as *automatisms*, which are stereotyped, repetitive actions that, in themselves, are normal in the proper contexts, but occur during the seizure in an inappropriate form or circumstance. These behaviors include wandering; dressing and undressing; sexual and bathroom behavior; picking up and carrying off objects; and approaching others with short, repeated vocalizations. One of my patients had several arrests for indecent exposure for taking off his clothes and walking around a supermarket and up and down the street. Another patient was arrested for gathering up objects in a barbershop while waiting for a haircut. Defensive violence may occur if the confused subject feels threatened or restrained during a seizure.

If you suspect a citizen is having a TLE seizure, check for a medical ID bracelet or other identification. Also check for medication containers that may yield clues to what illness is being treated. If this is a true TLE seizure, it will pass in a few minutes. In the meantime, use the minimum amount of restraint necessary to control the situation. Do not waste time trying to talk the subject down because it is unlikely he will comprehend complex verbal interventions—if he hears you at all. Instead, try the "herding" technique: simply stand a few feet in front of, or off to the side of, the subject and gently guide him in the direction you want to go, using slow, easy body language and gestures. Simple, direct instructions may work with some subjects: "This way, it's okay." Try not to rush or crowd the subject; remember cases of violence during TLE episodes almost always occur when the subject feels confused, confined, or threatened. When the seizure passes, determine if medical treatment is necessary. When in doubt, call for paramedic backup.

Narcolepsy

Narcolepsy is unrelated to epilepsy and is a medical sleep disorder characterized by poor quality of night-time sleep and excessive daytime sleepiness. The subject typically experiences vivid, dreamlike hallucinations that occur just when he is falling asleep (*hypnogogic hallucinations*) or waking up (*hypnopompic hallucinations*), and these may be associated with *sleep paralysis*, the transient inability to move while experiencing these "waking dreams." During the day, the subject may experience *sleep attacks*, causing him to abruptly fall asleep in the middle of whatever he is currently doing. These attacks may be associated with *cataplexy*, which is a sudden loss of muscle tone that causes the subject to abruptly collapse and fall. These episodes can be triggered either by boredom or, conversely, by sudden strong emotion.

A likely scenario for patrol policing involves a driver who becomes excessively drowsy at the wheel and acts like he is intoxicated, weaving all over the road. When apprehended by police, he becomes frightened and promptly passes out. Of course, true intoxication and many kinds of medical condition can cause a person to lose consciousness, but in narcolepsy the person will usually awaken after a few moments with little or no residual symptoms. The most important thing an officer can do in such circumstances is to assure the subject's safety and call for medical attention.

Tourette Syndrome

Beginning in childhood, *Tourette syndrome* (TS) is characterized by the progressive development of multiple *tics*, which are rapid, involuntary, coordinated spasms of small muscle groups. Most TS tics are of the motor variety, in which case the subject may appear characteristically "twitchy." A smaller number of TS patients have vocal tics, which usually consist of throat-clearing, grunts, single syllables, or other simple vocalizations. A minority of TS patients suffer from *coprolalia*, in which they utter various kinds of foul language, typically involving sexual or racial epithets, probably because most of these words contain hard consonants and are emitted with explosive breath—the vocal equivalent of a motor tic. Not surprisingly, these subjects may get into big trouble if they are heard to be uttering offensive curse words in a public place. Merchants may call police because the subject is driving away customers, or fights may break out due to the words being uttered.

Of course, people curse at each other for any number of reasons, and most do not have a brain syndrome. Although an officer need not make a formal diagnosis, note if the subject seems to be in control of his utterances, and whether the verbal curses occur in the context of overall twitchy, agitated behavior. Usually, in addition to coprolalia, TS subjects will manifest a number of other vocal and motor tics. If this seems to be the case, and no real harm has been done, escort the subject to a location where his involuntarily obnoxious verbiage is less likely to get him into trouble.

Traumatic Brain Injury

Individuals who have received a blow to the head may suffer temporary or permanent brain damage producing a *postconcussion syndrome* (Miller, 1993, 1998; Parker, 2001). Physical symptoms include headache, dizziness, disturbance of equilibrium, and hypersensitivity to light and sound. Cognitive symptoms include attention and concentration, poor short-term memory and, in severe cases, general disorientation and confusion. Emotional–behavioral symptoms include increased irritability and anger, poor frustration tolerance, lack of good judgment, and impulsivity.

The most likely setting for a police officer's interaction with a brain-injured subject is at the scene of an assault or accident, immediately following the injury. The subject may have difficulty answering the officer's questions and giving a coherent account of what happened. If the subject was unconscious for any length of time, he will have trouble remembering events following his regaining of consciousness (*anterograde amnesia*), as well as for several seconds, minutes, or hours prior to the actual impact, as those memories had not had sufficient time to be consolidated to long-term storage prior to the injurious blow (*retrograde amnesia*). Some subjects show a *lucid interval*, where they will appear relatively normal immediately following the accident or assault, and may even give the responding officer a reasonably coherent account of events, before then slipping into unconsciousness, from which they emerge with no recollection of the preceding interaction with the officer.

Occasionally, officers may encounter subjects with past head injuries who are still showing residual postconcussion effects months or years later. These individuals may seem confused and disoriented and may be mistaken for being intoxicated. Or they may well *be* intoxicated in addition to having a brain injury, which can have an additional impairing effect on thinking and behavior. Especially when the damage occurs to the brain's *frontal lobes*, the subject may develop an impulsive behavioral dyscontrol syndrome and engage in antisocial behavior. In fact, one often sees a vicious cycle, in which individuals with an already impulsive, sensation-seeking lifestyle, often involving the use of drugs and alcohol, are more likely to drive unsafely, get into fights, and otherwise expose themselves to risk for brain injury which, in turn, only worsens the behavioral syndrome (Miller, 1993, 1994b, 1998, 2006, in press). In practical terms, treat these subjects as you would any cognitively impaired citizen: utilize safety precautions, assess for medical need, apply verbal de-escalation strategies, and take appropriate action if necessary.

Summary and Conclusions

I often emphasize in my training classes that officers are the real "street psychologists," because they have to think and act fast with mentally disordered subjects, while most mental health professionals get to do their work from the comfort of a soft chair and air-conditioned office. Training in mental health issues is becoming more and more common in law enforcement curricula; hopefully, at some point in the near future, it will be a standard component of police training.

References

American Psychiatric Association (APA). (2000). *Diagnostic and Statistical Manual of Mental Disorders-TR*, 4th ed., text rev. Washington DC: American Psychiatric Association.

Bonta, J., Law, M., & Hanson, R.K. (1998). The prediction of criminal and violent recidivism among mentally disordered offenders: A meta-analysis. *Psychological Bulletin*, 123, 123–142.

Borum, R., Deane, M.W., Steadman, H.J., & Morrissey, J. (1998). Police perspectives on responding to mentally ill people in crisis: Perspectives of program effectiveness. *Behavioral Sciences and the Law*, 16, 393–405.

Borum, R., Swanson, J., Swartz, M., & Hiday, V. (1997). Substance abuse, violent behavior, and police encounters among persons with severe mental disorder. *Journal of Contemporary Criminal Justice*, 13, 236–250.

Bowker, A.L. (1994). Handle with care: Dealing with offenders who are mentally retarded. *FBI Law Enforcement Bulletin*, July, 12–16.

Carter, D.L. (1993). Police response to street people: A survey of perspectives and practices. *FBI Law Enforcement Bulletin*, March, 5–10.

Cordner, G.W. (2000). A community policing approach to persons with mental illness. *Journal of the American Academy of Psychiatry and the Law*, 28, 326–331.

Dupont, R. & Cochran, S. (2000). Police response to mental health emergencies: Barriers to change. *Journal of the American Academy of Psychiatry and the Law*, 28, 338–344.

Eccleston, L., Brown, M., & Ward, T. (2005). The assessment of dangerous behavior. In P. Fitzkirk & S.P. Shohov (Eds.), *Focus on Behavioral Psychology*, pp. 85–125. Melbourne: Nova Science Publishers.

Finn, M.A. & Stalans, L.J. (2002). Police handling of the mentally ill in domestic violence situations. *Criminal Justice and Behavior*, 29, 278–307.

Fyfe, J.J. (2000). Policing the emotionally disturbed. *Journal of the American Academy of Psychiatry and the Law*, 28, 345–347.

Garner, G.W. (1995). Street smarts: Safely handling intoxicated persons. *FBI Law Enforcement Bulletin*, December, 10–13.

Hill, R., Quill, G., & Ellis, K. (2004). The Montgomery County CIT model: Interacting with people with mental illness. *FBI Law Enforcement Bulletin*, July, 18–25.

Janik, J. (1992). Dealing with mentally ill offenders. *FBI Law Enforcement Bulletin*, July, 22–28.

Miller, L. (1993). *Psychotherapy of the Brain-Injured Patient: Reclaiming the Shattered Self*. New York: Norton.

Miller, L. (1994a). The epilepsy patient: Personality, psychodynamics, and psychotherapy. *Psychotherapy*, 31, 735–743.

Miller, L. (1994b). Traumatic brain injury and aggression. In M. Hillbrand & N.J. Pallone, (Eds.), *The Psychobiology of Aggression: Engines, Measurement, Control*, pp. 91–103. New York: Haworth.

Miller, L. (1998). Brain injury and violent crime: Clinical, neuropsychological, and forensic considerations. *Journal of Cognitive Rehabilitation*, 16(6), 2–17.

Miller, L. (2006). *Practical Police Psychology: Stress Management and Crisis Intervention for Law Enforcement.* Springfield, IL: Charles C. Thomas.

Miller, L. (in press). *Criminal Psychology: Nature, Nurture, Culture.* Springfield, IL: Charles C. Thomas.

Mohandie, K. & Duffy, J.E. (1999). Understanding subjects with paranoid schizophrenia. *FBI Law Enforcement Bulletin*, December, 8–16.

Monahan, J. (1996). Violence prediction: The last 20 years and the next 20 years. *Criminal Justice and Behavior*, 23, 107–120.

Parker, R.S. (2001). *Concussive Brain Trauma: Neurobehavioral Impairment and Maladaptation.* Boca Raton: CRC Press.

Reuland, M. & Margolis, G.J. (2003). Police approaches that improve the response to people with mental illness: A focus on victims. *The Police Chief*, November, 35–39.

Rodgers, B.A. (2006). *Psychological Aspects of Police Work: An Officer's Guide to Street Psychology.* Springfield, IL: Charles C. Thomas.

Russell, H.E. & Beigel, A. (1990). *Understanding Human Behavior for Effective Police Work*, 3rd ed. New York: Basic Books.

Shore, D., Filson, C.R., Davis, T.S., Olivos, G., DeLisi, L., & Wyatt, R.J. (1985). White House cases: Psychiatric patients and the Secret Service. *American Journal of Psychiatry*, 142, 308–312.

Shore, D., Filson, C.R., & Johnson, W.E. (1988). Violent crime arrests and paranoid schizophrenia: The White House case studies. *Schizophrenia Bulletin*, 14, 279–281.

Vermette, H.S., Pinals, D.A., & Appelbaum, P.S. (2005). Mental health training for law enforcement professionals. *Journal of the American Academy of Psychiatry and the Law*, 33, 42–46.

Wiley, K. (2005). Crisis intervention team: It's more than just training. *Training Wheel: The Training Journal of the Las Vegas Metropolitan Police Department*, April–June, 10–15.

13

FATAL CRASH INVESTIGATION

First Responder Issues

R. Trent Codd, III

Introduction

Law enforcement officers (LEOs) have unique duties relative to other first responders when working the scene of a fatal crash. Additionally, they are often the first ones to arrive on the scenes of such incidents. Extensive literature pertaining to the sources of stress and post-traumatic stress disorder for LEOs exists. For example, a particularly potent factor identified in this literature is dealing with death, including the death of a child or colleague (Horn, 1990; Spielberger, Westberry, Grier, & Greenfield, 1981; Violanti & Aron, 1995). However, while this factor is experienced by LEOs during fatal crash investigations and is of demonstrated importance empirically, very little empirical attention has been paid to other psychological factors as they pertain specifically to fatal crash investigations. Most of the literature pertaining to fatal crash investigation examines the prevention of, as well as the risk for onset of, a post-traumatic stress reaction.

This literature is important and addresses an important aspect of LEO psychological functioning in this area. However, additional psychological factors likely exist in these contexts. For example, the officer who works a fatal crash scene may experience a high negative emotional valence, which they perceive to be distressing, while engaging in numerous tasks simultaneously (which itself is likely stressful). After completion of his or her work at the scene, there is an expectation that they will return to a calm emotional baseline and carry on with other duties remaining during their shift. Still further, at the completion of his or her shift and on returning to their family and off-duty life, there is an expectation that their emotional calm will endure and not impact their functioning in these other domains. These expectations are at odds with the normal human response and seem worthy of empirical examination and intervention.

An extensive literature search by the author failed to identify published studies which had empirically examined many of these issues as they specifically pertain to an officer's fatal crash investigation duties. Some related literature was identified, however. In this chapter some of this related literature is reviewed briefly, but the primary focus is on factors that have not been directly examined in the existing empirical literature.

This chapter was written for the mental health professional working with LEOs in either a psychotherapeutic capacity or as an organizational behavior management consultant. The goals of this chapter are to (1) humanize the emotional distress experienced by officers in these specific contexts by fully explicating the tasks and experiences typical of such work duties, (2) discuss literature related to the psychological needs of LEOs who conduct fatal crash scene investigations, and (3) discuss ways of addressing the LEO's mental health needs, in this specific context, and how one might do so at both the individual and the organizational level. The last two goals will be addressed by introducing a psychological model that is both parsimonious and well-supported empirically across a range of individual and organizational contexts. The potential usefulness of this model for context that is the subject matter of this chapter is discussed. Finally, recommendations for future research and resources for further study are provided.

Research in the Civilian Sector

Stress

The literature pertaining to stress in the civilian sector is voluminous and too extensive to fully review here. In brief, Lazarus and Folkman (1984) defined stress as a relationship between the person and the environment that is appraised by the person to exceed his or her resources and endangering their well-being. Interventions examined to date have focused on impacting the stressors themselves and/or an individual's perceptions of stressors.

A growing body of research emphasizes the latter intervention point, but in a slightly different way than what is present in the literature historically. Specifically, an individual's response to stressors (i.e., their psychological flexibility/inflexibility in the presence of stress) rather than their evaluation of them is being increasingly targeted with promising results. This approach is discussed below.

Acceptance and Commitment Therapy (ACT) has been evaluated for its impact on stress within the civilian population. For example, Bond and Bunce (2001) evaluated an ACT for worksite stress program. Their results indicated that the ACT intervention improved employees' general mental health, depression and their propensity to initiate innovations at work, relative to a control group of employees. Other research has produced similar findings with respect to the impact of ACT interventions on worksite stress (Bond & Bunce, 2000, 2003; Flaxman & Bond, 2006) and, additionally, a randomized controlled trial showed ACT to be effective in reducing burnout in drug and alcohol counselors (Hayes et al., 2004). Thus, there is basic support for this model of intervention with civilian employee stress.

PTSD

Findings from epidemiological studies are clear that most persons exposed to a traumatic event are resilient and only a small percentage of these persons go on to develop PTSD (Varra & Follette, 2004). Researchers have examined and identified a number of variables that separate those who develop PTSD from those who do not. However, one set of identified factors, those related to individual coping styles, are among the most important because those are the primary factors amenable to intervention. Thus, these will be briefly reviewed here. One of the most robust coping styles implicated in the development and maintenance of PTSD is avoidance. This has been described in a number of ways by various research teams, but the concept of experiential avoidance is probably the most useful because it is the most comprehensive (i.e., many forms of avoidance discussed in the literature are essentially collapsed under this variable). It is also useful because this concept is known to be amenable to intervention as evidenced by the success of the empirically supported treatment originally designed to target experiential avoidance specifically: Acceptance and Commitment Therapy (Hayes, Strosahl, & Wilson, 2011).

Experiential avoidance is the tendency to attempt to alter the form, frequency, or situational sensitivity of private events (e.g., traumatic thoughts, distressing emotions) even when doing so interferes with behaving in ways that are important and effective. A vast literature (see Hayes, Wilson, Gifford, Follette, & Strosahl, 1996) demonstrates experiential avoidance to be one of the most pathological known psychological processes. Several studies have demonstrated a relationship between experiential avoidance and PTSD (Boeschen, Koss, Figueredo, & Coan, 2001; Cameron, Palm, & Follette, 2010; Plumb, Orsillo, & Luterek, 2004; Polusny, Rosenthal, Aban, & Follette, 2004; Roember, Litz, Orsillo, & Wagner, 2001; Shipherd & Beck, 1999; see Walser & Hayes, 2006, for a review of experiential avoidance as it pertains to trauma). Relatedly, Thompson and Waltz (2010) found a negative relationship between mindfulness, a core psychological process targeted by ACT that is typically disruptive of experiential avoidance, and PTSD symptom severity.

Research in LEO Populations

An extensive literature review failed to identify studies that examined the psychological needs of LEOs in the specific context of fatal crash investigations. Related literature was identified, however. This literature examined the impact of stress on quality of life, factors related to the development of post-traumatic stress disorder following experiences with traumatic events, and the utility of critical incident stress debriefing. This literature is briefly reviewed here to provide the reader with appropriate context. More extensive reviews of this literature can be found in other chapters of this same volume (see Miller; Violante; Bisson; Olson & Wasilewski; this volume).

Research on Police Stress

Law enforcement officer stress has been a topic of interest in the empirical literature for many years. There remains some controversy about the extent of stress in policing relative to other professions (Terry, 1983; Swanson & Territo, 1982; Gaines, Southerland, & Angel, 1991), but the research is pretty consistent in demonstrating a relationship between clinically significant stress and policing (Burke, 1993; Copes, 2005; Hart & Cotton, 2003; Kerley, 2005; Violanti & Aron, 1994; Violanti, Marshall, & Howe, 1985). More specific to LEOs and fatal crash scenes, one research team found traffic officers to be more susceptible to stress than their colleagues because their duties involved less predictability and a greater likelihood of involving traffic fatalities (Brown, Fielding, & Grover, 1999).

While one would intuitively assume stress to largely be a function of experiences with traumatic events, researchers have identified many sources of police stress not involving traumatic events (e.g., Brough, 2005; Brown & Campbell, 1990; Evans & Coman, 1993; Hart, Wearing, & Headey, 1995; Huddleston, Stephens, & Paton, 2007; Reiser, 1974; Sigler & Wilson 1988; Spielberger et al., 1981; Violanti & Aron, 1993). Researchers have divided these stressors into the two broad categories of job content and job context (Evans & Coman, 1993). Many studies have found that organizational stressors (job context) have a greater impact on police officer stress than job content (Huddleston et al., 2007; Violanti & Aron, 1995). Stephens and Pugmire (2008) examined the role of minor daily events (which they termed "hassles" and "uplifts") in eliciting psychological distress in a sample of New Zealand Police officers. Hassles were defined as minor but frequent negative events, whereas uplifts were characterized as small but frequent positive events. They found that hassles worsen health outcomes whereas uplifts improve them. They recommended that police organizations should target both types of environmental events. This was an important finding given that much existing literature tends to emphasize intervention with hassles to the exclusion of uplifts.

Traumatic events, as would be experienced on the scene of a fatal crash, are a major source of stress for LEOs. For example, research has demonstrated stressful effects for an officer attending the scene of a sudden death (Anshel, Robertson and Caputi, 1997; Brown et al., 1999; Duckworth, 1986). In particular attending the scene of the death of another officer has been reported as among the most distressing (Horn, 1990; Spielberger at al., 1981; Violanti & Aron, 1995).

A police organization's impact on officers' orientation to death is significant. In particular, organizations where contingencies support emotional detachment and maintenance of emotional control (Pogrebin & Poole, 1991; Reisser & Geiger, 1984), including the importance of physical and mental strength (Waddington, 1999), have been found to negatively impact officer stress. Several studies have confirmed this notion that the police culture influences the felt distress in response to acute stressors (Brown et al., 1999; Reisser & Geiger, 1984). Dick (2000) examined the police culture's impact on the meaning that individual officers give to acute stressors. She found that some acute stressors impacted officers in the way a chronic stressor might (e.g., by eliciting the belief that "the world is beyond help and that it is pointless to intervene"). She found that the meaning stressors have for an individual are crucial for determining the experience of felt stress and that these meanings are influenced by the police culture. These findings highlight the importance of the mental health professional who works with LEO organizations working to alter the organizational variables that influence how officers respond to adverse events. Indeed some researchers have suggested the use of organizational psychologists in addition to clinical psychologists (Goolkasian, Geddes, & DeJong, 1985; Hart et al., 1995).

Specific coping strategies are highly related to officer psychological well-being. Specifically, emotion-focused strategies were found to be maladaptive relative to problem-focused strategies (Hart et al., 1995). This is concerning because several research teams identified and noted the extensive use of emotional avoidance among police officers (Carlier, Lamberta, Gersons, 1997; Mann & Neece, 1990; Pogrebin and Poole, 1991). Indeed, Williams, Ciarrochi, and Patrick Deane (2010) found avoidance and emotion identification deficits to be predictive of poorer mental health in a sample of police officers they followed longitudinally.

Development of Post-Traumatic Stress
Disorder in LEO Populations

Post-traumatic stress disorder is an important area of concern for the clinician working with LEOs. Fortunately, findings are generally consistent in reporting that a minority of officers are experiencing traumatic stress levels and in need of clinical intervention (Brown et al., 1999). For officers who do experience clinically significant symptoms, events experienced on fatal crash scenes are likely to be responsible.

The role of traumatic incidents in producing stress has been examined (Alexander & Wells, 1991; Stratton, Parker, & Snibbe, 1984). Factors related to the degree of symptom development include the severity of trauma exposure (Hodgins, Creamer, & Bell, 2001), number of successive traumatic events exposed to (Stephens, Long, & Miller, 1997), and previous trauma exposure (Regehr, LeBlanc, Jelley, Barath, & Daciuk, 2007). In a sample of police recruits, Regehr et al., (2007) found three variables increased vulnerability to psychological stress responses: lower levels of social support, previous traumatic exposures, and pre-existing symptoms of traumatic stress. Importantly, though, they did not find that prior trauma exposure increased vulnerability to psychological distress in an acute situation suggesting this may not be a risk factor for disrupted performance during fatal crash investigations.

Coping style appears to also be important in the development of PTSD for LEOs. For example, Stephens et al. (1997) found that denial of emotional expression was a significant risk factor for the development of PTSD following the experience of a traumatic event in a sample of New Zealand police officers. They went so far as to suggest that the police culture may model and reinforce these strategies and thus encourage the development of PTSD.

Critical Incident Stress Debriefing

Critical Incident Stress Debriefing (CISD), in brief, is an intervention designed to be preventative of the onset of PTSD and is used quite widely with first responders (Gist & Taylor, 2008). A comprehensive review of this intervention is beyond the scope of this chapter and the reader is again referred to the chapter in this volume which reviews the state of the science with CISD. It is important, however, to briefly note that the empirical research suggests this intervention may at best be inert and has shown that for some recipients of the intervention it impedes the natural recovery process (see McNally, Bryant, & Ehlers, 2003 for a review). This finding has spawned a number of guidelines cautioning against the routine use of this procedure (see Forbes et al., 2007; Gray & Litz, 2005; National Institute for Clinical Excellence, 2005; Rose, Bisson, Churchill, & Wessely, 2009). For these reasons the author cautions against the use of this procedure and suggests that the therapist who works with a police officer after experiencing a traumatic event as part of a fatal crash scene develop fluency with the principles of psychological first aid (see Ruzek et al., 2007). Gist and Taylor (2008) also provide some guidelines for use with EMS workers that are likely to be applicable to the care of police officers in this context. The reader is referred to their manuscript where these guidelines are discussed. Finally, it is worth highlighting this as another area of the LEO organization the clinician should work to impact as it too influences an officer's development of PTSD.

Psychological Intervention with Law Enforcement Officers

Examination of the above research review leads one to conclude that a clinician working with LEOs who work fatal crash scenes would benefit from a model that is flexible enough to be used with individual officers as well as the organizations within which they operate and which supports factors that encourage the development of clinically significant levels of distress. Further, it seems that a model that also possesses flexibility around delivery format, such as brief and lengthy formats, would be most useful. One such model is Acceptance and Commitment Therapy (Hayes et al., 2011). This model points to a small set of variables that are thought to be relevant to a wide range of individual and organizational difficulties. Further, this model has been delivered in brief (e.g., Robinson, Gould, & Strosahl, 2011) and long-term formats. Although ultimately an empirical question, it seems reasonable to speculate that ACT may be delivered effectively in these various ways with LEOs and LEO organizations.

Overview of Model

The ACT model of stress and emotional disorders proposes that attempts at regulating emotional distress are at the core of these disorders rather than the presence of particular levels of distressing emotion. Alteration of the functional effects of inner experiences are targeted with much less concern for the form, frequency, or likelihood of any particular category of inner experience such as anxiety, irritability, or intrusive thoughts. Decreasing avoidance of these inner distressing experiences as the dominant response is a primary goal so that the repertoire of responses in the presence of them is broadened. Repertoire broadening of this kind results in psychological flexibility, which is defined as the ability to openly experience distressing emotions while moving in personally chosen directions. This is accomplished through targeting the six psychological processes thought to be responsible for the onset and maintenance of emotional disorders from an ACT perspective: being present, acceptance, defusion, self-as-context, values, and committed action (Hayes, Luoma,

Bond, Masuda, & Lillis, 2006; see Hayes et al., 2011, for a full handling of the theory and clinical interventions). Thus far, support for ACT processes is decent (as reviewed in Hayes et al., 2006), but only work involving Stress, PTSD and Organizations will be reviewed below.

ACT with Stress and PTSD

Case studies support the effectiveness of ACT with PTSD (Orsillo & Batten, 2005; Twohig, 2009). The target process of ACT (psychological inflexibility) has consistently been shown to be highly and significantly correlated with anxiety disorders in general (Hayes et al., 2004), PTSD (e.g., Marx & Sloan, 2005), and experiencing distressing emotions including anxiety and depression (Campbell-Sills, Barlow, Brown, & Hoffman, 2006). Also, Codd, Twohig, Crosby and Enno (2011) found ACT to be effective in the treatment of four anxiety disorders including PTSD in the civilian sector. The significance of their study was that ACT was shown to be effective as a unified protocol for several anxiety disorders. This is a desirable feature for the LEO clinician as multiple problems can be addressed utilizing the same procedures.

ACT in Organizations

The Acceptance and Commitment Therapy model has been utilized in organizational contexts and the effects examined empirically. Two randomized controlled trials showed that an ACT intervention reduced worksite stress (Bond & Bunce, 2001; Hayes et al., 2004). Other studies showed that interventions designed to impact acceptance and psychological flexibility (two central processes targeted in the ACT model) lead to increased job performance, fewer work errors, increased ability to learn new work skills, and greater mental health (Bond & Bunce, 2003; Bond & Flaxman, 2006). Thus, there is broad support for the use of this model at an organizational level.

Case Vignette

A case vignette is presented below. The purpose of this vignette is to describe for the clinician what a typical experience on the scene of a fatal crash may be like and to suggest a typical presenting complaint.

Description

Chris, a ten-year highway patrol veteran, arrives on the scene of an accident. He is the first responder on the scene. At first glance it appears to him that this accident involves a fatality. His initial assessment gives him the sense of urgency that accompanies the need for life-saving efforts. As the first officer on the scene, it is his responsibility to collect information (on individual identities and vehicles) and to notify dispatch of the support units he needs. He feels as though he is experiencing controlled chaos. He needs, for example, to request the Reconstruction Team to process the scene of the fatality and take measurements to insure the entire scene can be re-constructed later in the event of a criminal or civil action. He has to identify the deceased and make a next-of-kin notification. He does this himself as he can answer questions that a chaplain cannot. Once the Reconstruction Team has control of the scene, the deceased has been transported to the Medical Examiner's office and death notification has been made, he makes himself available for the next call.

Throughout this process he must handle radio traffic, cell phone traffic, and collect information on everyone and every vehicle involved. He has to identify any witnesses and, if any are identified, he must document their information as well as separate them from each other. Simultaneously he must also close the road and re-direct traffic by posting marked units at key places. This helps insure that there is not a secondary accident while this one is being worked. He must also evaluate all the information available to him so that he may determine the exact nature of the circumstance. He must maintain a level of readiness throughout this process as accidents are not always what they appear to be. Sometimes there is foul play involved.

He provides very little in terms of medical help as he, like most officers, has limited medical training and does not carry equipment to provide more than very basic first aid. Someone who needs "basic" first aid can wait on the ambulance, which is seconds to minutes away. Someone who needs more than basic first aid is usually beyond a law enforcement officer's ability to help. He may provide CPR.

He is scared of getting a stranger's blood on him and believes his role does not involve providing medical treatment. He believes his role is to control the scene (i.e., protect the injured person lying in the road from being run over by another motorist) and comforting injured victims until the medical personnel arrive. He also recalls that many times in the past he has discovered that the victim was a violent criminal who wrecked because he was fleeing a crime scene. Also salient for him are the number of times he has had to arrest victims at these scenes. These arrests were for driving under the influence which caused his/her passenger's or someone else's death or for outstanding warrants which he discovered after he "run" them.

He attempts to suppress his feelings throughout the incident. He remembers well that when he was in the academy the first 48 hours were dedicated to making the weak-minded quit. He also remembers that his Field Training Officer (FTO) taught him to practice distracting himself and suppressing his feelings. He firmly believes that not only do his fellow officers and department require him to be Spartan, but also the public.

After he arrives home at the end of his shift, he wakes his children up and tells them he loves them. This incident was particularly difficult for him because it involved the loss of life of a truly innocent party—a child (it did not involve someone fleeing the crime scene or who was driving drunk).

Following this event he experiences intrusive images of the dead child, disrupted sleep, and increased irritability. These symptoms persist for several months after this event and have a negative impact on his functioning at both home and work. For example, he finds himself "snapping" at his wife and children with some frequency. He increasingly avoids his children because seeing them prompts additional occurrences of the aversive images of the deceased child victim. In combination, his irritability and avoidance has led to significantly decreased contact with his family and less meaningful, and more aversive, interactions with them when he does spend time with them. At work, he also finds himself "snapping" at his peers as well as members of the public. This bothers him because he values his tight relationships with his fellow officers and because it has always been important to him to maintain a good relationship with the citizens in his community.

He does not self-determine that he could benefit from some counseling. One of his peers suggests he talk to the department counselor just to "check in." He is fearful of following through on this recommendation because he fears that interfacing with the counselor could place his job in jeopardy. Although he is reassured by his peer that any conversations he has with the counselor are confidential (and by the counselor's literature), he is not confident that information he discloses would not subsequently be shared or otherwise utilized to his detriment. After persistent and worsening symptoms, as well as continued prompting from his concerned peer, he reluctantly commits to scheduling an appointment in order to simply "check in."

Discussion of Vignette

This officer is experiencing persistent symptoms that are beginning to impair his functioning and quality of life, and he only interfaces with a mental health professional reluctantly. It is notable that what prompted him to seek help was a peer. Ideally, the law enforcement clinician works to arrange the environment in such a way that peers are willing to reach out to their fellow officers to prompt help-seeking when appropriate. It is likely that they will be more willing to suggest to a peer that they pursue help rather than self-identifying themselves as personally in need of help. The LEO clinician would also do well to train officers in effective methods of prompting peers to seek help. Effective prompting contains a number of components. One crucial element is limiting suggestions to mere "treatment sampling" (e.g., "Why don't you just check it out to see whether you think it will be useful—there's nothing that says you have to go more than once") rather than to immediately commit to a lengthy course of treatment. It is typically much easier to solicit agreement to this smaller initial commitment. It can also be useful to provide instruction around when to approach a peer to suggest help. This includes learning the signs that would warrant such a discussion as well as learning to factor timing (i.e., when a peer may be more or less receptive) into the conveying of one's concerns. Since prompting help-seeking involves behavior (i.e., the behavior of prompting), it is best learned through behavioral rehearsal rather than didactic presentation alone. It may be useful to have officers role play this behavior so that their behavior can be shaped. This also allows strengthening of this behavior through a lot of reinforced practice. Importantly, experiential avoidance should be targeted during role-play practice. Such targeting may remove or reduce emotional barriers to the emitting of this behavior such that the likelihood of generalization from role-play practice to real contexts is increased.

Because of his reluctance to seek help, unless he is mandated by his department, it is unlikely a lengthy course of therapy will ensue. Many circumstances will likely be addressed effectively on the basis of brief intervention in which some of the core ACT processes, which were described earlier, are addressed. It is also likely to make the behavior of coming to such an intervention less aversive and may occasion future visits.

This officer's reluctance to seek help, which is not atypical, also speaks to the value of targeting these core processes at an organizational level. Interventions at this level may result in less experiential avoidance at baseline, reducing the risk of clinically significant stress reactions following such events. Furthermore, this level of intervention helps circumvent the difficulty with officers who remain steadfast in their refusal to seek help.

Future Research

Stress research with law enforcement populations is mature. Sources of stress, their relative impacts and moderators of stress have been identified. Additionally, researchers have identified factors which increase the risk of development of PTSD in law enforcement populations.

This literature can progress with attention to other important areas. Suggestions for future research include:

1   Examination of the core ACT processes in the LEO fatal crash scene context. One strength of the ACT model is its parsimony. The aforementioned psychological processes are thought to play a role in

many forms of disrupted emotional functioning and psychopathology. Theoretically, then, these same processes should be present with the LEO in fatal crash scene contexts. Nevertheless, this should be verified empirically.

2 Investigation of the utility of the ACT model at law enforcement organizational level. Completed work investigating ACT in organizational contexts is growing and to date the results are promising. Although this literature is not yet fully mature, there is sufficient reason to believe it may be useful to the law enforcement organizations.

3 The impact of the psychological sequelae of participating in fatal crash scene investigations on subsequent law enforcement duties and tasks should be examined more fully.

4 The impact of ACT interventions on LEO stress and post-traumatic stress should be evaluated. Much of the existing research on LEO stress and post-traumatic stress is descriptive and does not provide the clinician with manipulable variables to target in the service of helping LEOs. For example, severity of traumatic event and history of trauma have been identified as variables related to clinically meaningful symptoms. While instructive, these variables are not amenable to intervention and thus not optimally useful for the practitioner (i.e., they allow prediction, but not influence). The ACT model provides a number of variables that can be impacted by the practitioner. Thus, future research with this model in this context is strongly encouraged.

5 The consequence of targeting ACT processes on LEO decision-making in fatal crash scenes should be evaluated. For example, if there is a relationship between psychological flexibility and decision-making in these contexts (which need to be empirically evaluated), then decision-making may potentially be optimized through ACT interventions.

Reader Resources

Readers interested in learning more about this model, especially as it pertains to the LEO population involved in fatal crash scene investigations, should pursue some of the resources listed below.

Web Resources

Association for Contextual Behavior Science (ACBS) www.contextualscience.org
    Visit this location to learn of clinical trainings, conferences and peer-reviewed research pertaining to the ACT model.
http://buildingsafetycommitment.com, or www.mindfulemployee.com
    Visit these locations to learn more about an application of ACT to organizations.

Books

PTSD and ACT

Walser, R.D. & Westrup, D. (2007). *Acceptance and Commitment Therapy for the Treatment of Post-traumatic Stress Disorder and Trauma-related Problems: A Practitioner's Guide to Using Mindfulness and Acceptance Strategies.* Oakland, CA: New Harbinger Publications.

ACT in Organizations

Bond, F.W., Flaxman, P.E., & Livheim, F. (2013). *The Mindful and Effective Employee: An Acceptance and Commitment Therapy Training Manual for Improving Well-Being and Performance.* Oakland, CA: New Harbinger Publications.

Hayes, S.C., Bond, F.W., Barnes-Holmes, D., & Austin, J. (2006). Acceptance and mindfulness at work: Applying Acceptance and Commitment Therapy and Relational Frame Theory to Organizational Behavior Management. Binghamton, NY: Haworth Press.

Moran, D.J. (2013). *Building Safety Commitment.* IL: Vital Living Books.

References

Alexander, D.A., & Wells, A. (1991). Reactions of police officers to body-handling after a major disaster. A before-and-after comparison. *The British Journal of Psychiatry*, 159(4), 547–555.

Anshel, M.H., Robertson, M., & Caputi, P. (1997). Sources of acute stress and their appraisals and reappraisals among Australian police as a function of previous experience. *Journal of Occupational and Organizational Psychology*, 70(4), 337–356.

Boeschen, L.E., Koss, M.P., Figueredo, A.J., & Coan, J.A. (2001). Experiential avoidance and post-traumatic stress disorder: A cognitive mediational model of rape recovery. *Journal of Aggression, Maltreatment & Trauma*, 4(2), 211–245.

Bond, F.W. & Bunce, D. (2000). Mediators of change in emotion-focused and problem-focused worksite stress management interventions. *Journal of Occupational Health Psychology*, 5(1), 156.

Bond, F.W. & Bunce, D. (2001). Job control mediates change in a work reorganization intervention for stress reduction. *Journal of Occupational Health Psychology*, 6(4), 290.

Bond, F.W. & Bunce, D. (2003). The role of acceptance and job control in mental health, job satisfaction, and work performance. *Journal of Applied Psychology*, 88(6), 1057.

Bond, F.W. & Flaxman, P.E. (2006). The ability of psychological flexibility and job control to predict learning, job performance, and mental health. *Journal of Organizational Behavior Management*, 26(1–2), 113–130.

Brough, P. (2005). A comparative investigation of the predictors of work-related psychological well-being within police, fire and ambulance workers. *New Zealand Journal of Psychology*, 34(2), 127–134.

Brown, J.M. & Campbell, E.A. (1990). Sources of occupational stress in the police. *Work & Stress*, 4(4), 305–318.

Brown, J., Fielding, J., & Grover, J. (1999). Distinguishing traumatic, vicarious and routine operational stressor exposure and attendant adverse consequences in a sample of police officers. *Work & Stress*, 13(4), 312–325.

Burke, R.J. (1993). Work⊠family stress, conflict, coping, and burnout in police officers. *Stress Medicine*, 9(3), 171–180.

Cameron, A., Palm, K., & Follette, V. (2010). Reaction to stressful life events: What predicts symptom severity? *Journal of Anxiety Disorders*, 24(6), 645–649.

Campbell-Sills, L., Barlow, D.H., Brown, T.A., & Hofmann, S.G. (2006). Effects of suppression and acceptance on emotional responses of individuals with anxiety and mood disorders. *Behaviour Research and Therapy*, 44(9), 1251–1263.

Carlier, I.V., Lamberts, R.D., & Gersons, B.P. (1997). Risk factors for posttraumatic stress symptomatology in police officers: a prospective analysis. *The Journal of Nervous and Mental Disease*, 185(8), 498–506.

Codd, R.T., Twohig, M.P., Crosby, J.M., & Enno, A. (2011). Treatment of three anxiety disorder cases with acceptance and commitment therapy in a private practice. *Journal of Cognitive Psychotherapy*, 25(3), 203–217.

Copes, H. (2005). *Policing and Stress*. Pearson College Division. Upper Saddle River, NJ: Pearson Prentice Hall.

Dick, P. (2000). The social construction of the meaning of acute stressors: A qualitative study of the personal accounts of police officers using a stress counselling service. *Work & Stress*, 14(3), 226–244.

Duckworth, D.H. (1986). Psychological problems arising from disaster work. *Stress Medicine*, 2(4), 315–323.

Evans, B.J., & Coman, G.J. (1993). General versus specific measures of occupational stress: An Australian police survey. *Stress Medicine*, 9(1), 11–20.

Flaxman, P.E. & Bond, F.W. (2006). Acceptance and commitment therapy (ACT) in the workplace. *Mindfulness-based Treatment Approaches: Clinician's Guide to Evidence Base and Applications*, 377–402.

Forbes, D., Creamer, M., Phelps, A., Bryant, R., McFarlane, A., Devilly, G. J., et al. (2007). Australian guidelines for the treatment of adults with acute stress disorder and post-traumatic stress disorder. *Australasian Psychiatry*, 41(8), 637–648.

Gaines, L., Southerland, M.D., & Angel, J.E. (1991). *Police Administration*. New York: McGraw-Hill.

Gist, R. & Taylor, V. H. (2008). Occupational and organizational issues in emergency medical services behavioral health. *Journal of Workplace Behavioral Health*, 23(3), 309–330.

Goolkasian, G.A., Geddes, R.W., & DeJong, W. (1985). *Coping with Police Stress*. U.S. Department of Justice, National Institute of Justice, Office of Development, Testing, and Dissemination.

Gray, M.J. & Litz, B.T. (2005). Behavioral interventions for recent trauma empirically informed practice guidelines. *Behavior Modification*, 29(1), 189–215.

Hart, P.M. & Cotton, P. (2003). Conventional wisdom is often misleading: Police stress within an organisational health framework. *Occupational Stress in the Service Professions*, 103–141.

Hart, P.M., Wearing, A.J., & Headey, B. (1995). Police stress and well-being: Integrating personality, coping and daily work experiences. *Journal of Occupational and Organizational Psychology*, 68(2), 133–156.

Hayes, S.C., Strosahl, K.D., & Wilson, K.G. (2011). *Acceptance and Commitment Therapy: The Process and Practice of Mindful Change.* New York: Guilford Press.

Hayes, S.C., Luoma, J.B., Bond, F.W., Masuda, A., & Lillis, J. (2006). Acceptance and commitment therapy: Model, processes and outcomes. *Behaviour Research and Therapy*, 44(1), 1–25.

Hayes, S.C., Bissett, R., Roget, N., Padilla, M., Kohlenberg, B.S., Fisher, G., et al. (2004). The impact of acceptance and commitment training and multicultural training on the stigmatizing attitudes and professional burnout of substance abuse counselors. *Behavior Therapy*, 35(4), 821–835.

Hayes, S.C., Wilson, K.G., Gifford, E.V., Follette, V.M., & Strosahl, K. (1996). Experiential avoidance and behavioral disorders: A functional dimensional approach to diagnosis and treatment. *Journal of Consulting and Clinical Psychology*, 64(6), 1152.

Hodgins, G.A., Creamer, M., & Bell, R. (2001). Risk factors for posttrauma reactions in police officers: A longitudinal study. *The Journal of Nervous and Mental Disease*, 189(8), 541–547.

Horn, J. (1990). Critical incidents for law enforcement officers. In J. Reese, J. Horn, & C. Dunning (Eds.), *Critical Incidents in Policing*. Washington, DC: U.S. Government Printing Office.

Huddleston, L., Stephens, C., & Paton, D. (2007). An evaluation of traumatic and organizational experiences on the psychological health of New Zealand police recruits. *Work: A Journal of Prevention, Assessment and Rehabilitation*, 28(3), 199–207.

Kerley, K.R. (2005). The costs of protecting and serving: Exploring the consequences of police officer stress. *Policing and Stress*, 73–86.

Lazarus, R.S., & Folkman, S. (1984). Coping and adaptation. In W.D.Gentry (Ed.), *Handbook of Behavioral Medicine*, pp. 11–21. New York: Guilford Press.

Mann, J.P. & Neece, J. (1990). Workers' compensation for law enforcement related post traumatic stress disorder. *Behavioral Sciences & the Law*, 8(4), 447–456.

Marx, B.P. & Sloan, D.M. (2005). Peritraumatic dissociation and experiential avoidance as predictors of posttraumatic stress symptomatology. *Behaviour Research and Therapy*, 43(5), 569–583.

McNally, R.J., Bryant, R.A., & Ehlers, A. (2003). Does early psychological intervention promote recovery from posttraumatic stress? *Psychological Science in the Public Interest*, 4(2), 45–79.

National Institute for Clinical Excellence. (2005). *Post-traumatic Stress Disorder (PTSD): The Management of PTSD in Adults and Children in Primary and Secondary Care.* London: National Institute for Clinical Excellence.

Orsillo, S.M. & Batten, S.V. (2005). Acceptance and commitment therapy in the treatment of posttraumatic stress disorder. *Behavior Modification*, 29(1), 95–129.

Plumb, J.C., Orsillo, S.M., & Luterek, J.A. (2004). A preliminary test of the role of experiential avoidance in post-event functioning. *Journal of Behavior Therapy and Experimental Psychiatry*, 35(3), 245–257.

Pogrebin, M.R. & Poole, E.D. (1991). Police and tragic events: The management of emotions. *Journal of Criminal Justice*, 19(4), 395–403.

Polusny, M.A., Rosenthal, M.Z., Aban, I., & Follette, V.M. (2004). Experiential avoidance as a mediator of the effects of adolescent sexual victimization on negative adult outcomes. *Violence and Victims*, 19, 109–120.

Regehr, C., LeBlanc, V., Jelley, R.B., Barath, I., & Daciuk, J. (2007). Previous trauma exposure and PTSD symptoms as predictors of subjective and biological response to stress. *Canadian Journal of Psychiatry. Revue Canadienne de Psychiatrie*, 52(10), 675–683.

Reiser, M. (1974). Some organizational stresses on policemen. *Journal of Police Science and Administration*, 2(2), 156–159.

Reiser, M., & Geiger, S.P. (1984). Police officer as victim. *Professional Psychology: Research and Practice*, 15(3), 315.

Robinson, P., Gould, D., & Strosahl, K. (2011). *Real Behavior Change in Primary Care: Improving Patient Outcomes and Increasing Job Satisfaction*. Oakland, CA: New Harbinger Publications.

Roemer, L., Litz, B.T., Orsillo, S.M., & Wagner, A.W. (2001). A preliminary investigation of the role of strategic withholding of emotions in PTSD. *Journal of Traumatic Stress*, 14(1), 149–156.

Rose, S.C., Bisson, J., Churchill, R., & Wessely, S. (2009). Psychological debriefing for preventing post-traumatic stress disorder (PTSD). Cochrane Database of Systematic Reviews.

Ruzek, J.I., Brymer, M.J., Jacobs, A.K., Layne, C.M., Vernberg, E.M., & Watson, P.J. (2007). Psychological first aid. *Journal of Mental Health Counseling*, 29(1), 17–49.

Shipherd, J.C. & Beck, J.G. (1999). The effects of suppressing trauma-related thoughts on women with rape-related posttraumatic stress disorder. *Behaviour Research and Therapy*, 37(2), 99–112.

Sigler, R.T. & Wilson, C.N. (1988). Stress in the work place: Comparing police stress with teacher stress. *Journal of Police Science & Administration*, 16(3): 151–162.

Spielberger, C.D., Westberry, L.G., Grier, K.S., & Greenfield, G. (1981). *The Police Stress Survey: Sources of Stress in Law Enforcement*. Tampa, FL: National Institute of Justice.

Stephens, C. & Pugmire, L.A. (2008). Daily organisational hassles and uplifts as determinants of psychological and physical health in a sample of New Zealand police. *International Journal of Police Science and Management*, 10(2), 179–191.

Stephens, C., Long, N., & Miller, I. (1997). The impact of trauma and social support on posttraumatic stress disorder: A study of New Zealand police officers. *Journal of Criminal Justice*, 25(4), 303–314.

Stratton, J.G., Parker, D.A., & Snibbe, J.R. (1984). Post-traumatic stress: Study of police officers involved in shootings. *Psychological Reports*, 55(1), 127–131.

Swanson, C. & Territo, L. (1982). *Police Administration, Structures, Processes, and Behaviors*. New York: MacMillan.

Terry III, W.C. (1983). Police stress as an individual and administrative problem: Some conceptual and theoretical difficulties. *Journal of Police Science and Administration*, 11(2), 156–165.

Thompson, B.L., & Waltz, J. (2010). Mindfulness and experiential avoidance as predictors of posttraumatic stress disorder avoidance symptom severity. *Journal of Anxiety Disorders*, 24(4), 409–415.

Twohig, M.P. (2009). Acceptance and commitment therapy for treatment-resistant posttraumatic stress disorder: A case study. *Cognitive and Behavioral Practice*, 16(3), 243–252.

Varra, A.A. & Follette, V.M. (2004). ACT with posttraumatic stress disorder. In S.C. Hayes & K.D. Strosahl (Eds.), *A Practical Guide to Acceptance and Commitment Therapy*, pp. 133–152. New York: Springer.

Violanti, J.M. & Aron, F. (1993). Sources of police stressors, job attitudes, and psychological distress. *Psychological Reports*, 72(3), 899–904.

Violanti, J.M. & Aron, F. (1994). Ranking police stressors. *Psychological Reports*, 75(2), 824–826.

Violanti, J.M. & Aron, F. (1995). Police stressors: Variations in perception among police personnel. *Journal of Criminal Justice*, 23(3), 287–294.

Violanti, J.M. Marshall, J.R., & Howe, B. (1985). Stress, coping, and alcohol use: The police connection. *Journal of Police Science & Administration*, 13(2), 106–109.

Waddington, P.A. (1999). Police (canteen) sub-culture. An appreciation. *British Journal of Criminology*, 39(2), 287–309.

Walser, R.D. & Hayes, S.C. (2006). Acceptance and commitment therapy in the treatment of posttraumatic stress disorder. In V.M.R. Follette & I. Josef (Eds.), *Cognitive-Behavioral Therapies for Trauma*, 2nd ed., pp. 146–172. New York: Guilford Press.

Williams, V., Ciarrochi, J., & Patrick Deane, F. (2010). On being mindful, emotionally aware, and more resilient: Longitudinal pilot study of police recruits. *Australian Psychologist*, 45(4), 274–282.

14

POST-TRAUMATIC GROWTH IN POLICE OFFICERS

Guidelines for Facilitating Post-Traumatic Growth

Stephen Joseph, David Murphy, and Stephen Regel

Introduction

Traumatic stress and its effect has been the focus of much research effort since 1980 when the diagnostic category of post-traumatic stress disorder (PTSD) was first introduced. Research has shown that emergency service personnel often experience work-related stressors that can result in PTSD and other problems that impair social and occupational functioning. For example, an early study by Spielberger, Westberry, Grier, & Greenfield (1981) into what events police officers experienced as traumatic found that homicide, domestic abuse, shootings, fatal road traffic incidents, and responding to child abuse were the most stressful events that police officers face. Policing requires daily direct exposure to potentially life-threatening situations as well as indirect exposure to the suffering of others.

Exposure to the pain, suffering, and traumatic experiences of others can lead to PTSD and related reactions. These reactions have been described as vicarious traumatization. They often manifest in changes in systems of meaning, a lack of trust in others, a disruption of the individual's self-protective beliefs about safety, control, and predictability. In particular, studies of police officers investigating serious, violent offences, particularly those involving children (e.g., child abuse, neglect, child sexual abuse) have also suggested that these groups are at risk of developing traumatic stress symptoms as highlighted above. Usually individuals working in such situations often develop coping strategies in order to function effectively while engaged in such challenging tasks. Often many

256

attempt to disengage emotionally in order to remain objective. However, there is constant exposure to viewing images of abuse and violence such as video clips of torture and beheadings, which have often been found on the computers of those involved in terrorism or attempting to radicalize others.

As a consequence, much effort has been made to introduce mental health interventions within police work and to make psychological debriefing procedures routinely available for staff. Yet while such efforts to recognize the negative effects of work-related stressors are to be welcomed, there is a danger that this has created a culture of expectation in which PTSD is an expected outcome. Research shows that in general people are relatively resilient to the effects of trauma. Resilience is the term used to refer to people who seem to show a capacity for coping in the face of adversity. We might think of resilient people as like trees that stand unbending in the wind. Alexander (1993) studied officers following the Piper Alpha oil rig disaster, showing that most did not exhibit signs of distress at three months. The ability to be able to maintain "business as usual" in the face of adversity is of course desirable in police officers.

Yet while it is important to recognize resilience, there are times when police officers do succumb to the traumas they face. Much has been written about the devastating psychological impact of trauma, but over the past decade it has become increasingly recognized that there can also be positive changes in the aftermath of adversity. The aim of this chapter is to provide an overview of post-traumatic growth and, drawing on our developing clinical experience in this area, some guidelines on how it can be promoted.

Post-Traumatic Growth

Most people are familiar with the adage, "what doesn't kill me, makes me stronger." It a quote from the philosopher Nietzsche (1997/1889) which, on the one hand, oversimplifies complex human experiences, but, on the other, we think captures something very true that police officers will instantly recognize. Psychologists have also begun to recognize that traumatic events do not necessarily lead to damaged and dysfunctional lives, but that for some can also be a springboard to a higher level of psychological well-being. Various terms, such as "benefit-finding," "flourishing," and "positive changes" have been used to describe this process of how trauma can lead to higher levels of psychological well-being, but the term that is most widely used is *post-traumatic growth* (Tedeschi & Calhoun, 1996).

We propose that interventions for traumatized staff should not only seek to address the psychological problems of PTSD but also to promote post-traumatic growth. Post-traumatic growth is a relatively new topic for research and clinical intervention that promises to be of considerable interest to those involved in working with police officers who have experienced traumatic events and to police officers themselves and those managing police officers.

It takes us to begin to listen differently to our clients to begin to notice their growth. A case from one of us (David) shows how in the midst of distress and despair there may be pockets of positive change that in turn point to the person's recovery. Working as a police officer had been Tom's ambition for as long as he could remember. His father had been a police officer and so were two of his uncles. Tom was definitely part of the police family and on joining the service he saw them very much as his family. After about nine years of service Tom felt as though he had seen quite a bit. He had attended a modest number of fatal road traffic incidents and sudden deaths, and been involved in apprehending a number of violent individuals often made more hazardous due to their intoxication through substance misuse or alcohol. He had come across instances of child abuse and neglect and had processed hundreds of people for thefts, burglaries, and other volume crimes. So when he got the call over the radio to attend "just another" road traffic incident nothing quite prepared him for his reaction.

Eleven years on Tom was sat in the chair opposite me having been referred for psychological assessment. This was in response to a period of sickness absence that had flagged him to the HR department. Looking at Tom's sickness record, it was possible to see how a pattern started to emerge in his sickness absence at around the period he had served nine years. This was the time of the unsuspecting incident in which Tom had been adversely affected by what he witnessed. A mother and her daughter had been tragically killed in a car crash and Tom had been called to attend the scene. Tom started to tell me how he was not the first to arrive and the paramedics were already doing what they could. Tom said he had worked through the incident as he would any other and managed the scene effectively and efficiently, trying his best to make sure that everything that could be done was and that other road users and passersby not involved were minimally affected.

So why this event and why the sickness absences and poor attendance ever since? It seems that it was by pure chance that we stumbled on the opportunity to help Tom. A routine referral through HR had created an opportunity for Tom to discuss his plans for the remaining ten years of service he had ahead of him. At first glance Tom appeared in pretty good shape, a well-built guy with a big smile that it would be easy to take at face value and not offer a second thought to the possibility that something might be going wrong behind the veneer of this outwardly projecting image of "I'm doing okay.' However, even just a marginally closer look into Tom's eyes and it was clear there was much more going on. The almost glassy opaqueness of his skin around his eye sockets, the fact that sitting still in the chair for more than a few seconds without fidgeting was a near impossible task were additional tell-tale signs. Further inquiry revealed a number of GP prescriptions of antidepressant medication and two, albeit brief, previous visits to welfare suggested that something was not quite right.

Simply asking Tom about his poor sleep was like opening the floodgates. He described his experience of being kept awake at night for hours upon hours lying there thinking about the incident involving the mother, and specifically her daughter, that he attended over a decade prior. Asking about the rest of his life seemed to suggest that most areas were satisfactory. However, the persistent lack of sleep over the last ten years had put a significant degree of pressure on his marriage, he had been forced to call in sick on occasions when he was more truthfully exhausted through lack of sleep. He had avoided front line duties for many years, taking on roles that meant he was in the back office providing support to the first responders, a role he had previously loved to do himself. In addition to avoidance, intrusive thoughts and the obvious heightened agitation had led to Tom becoming depressed, holding little hope for the future, and being unable to see any other option than medical retirement on the grounds of post-traumatic stress.

However, an obvious omission from Tom's record was that he had pretty much avoided any contact with psychological help. When I asked about what troubled him most while he could not sleep, he gave a fairly detailed description of an image from the scene of the fatal road traffic incident he had been asked to attend. He recalled himself having returned to get something from the car and of looking back out of his rear view mirror. The reflection in the mirror was of the little girl being stretchered into the car and that pretty much all he could see was a pair of green patent leather shoes shining brightly in the winter sun that shone down. He said the image was "etched" into his mind and that he just couldn't get it out of his head at night-time.

Inviting Tom for a series of therapy sessions, it seemed that the best I could hope for was for him to start to get a good night's sleep and be free from the intrusive thoughts that prevented this from happening. Tom came to sessions and we worked with pretty much whatever it was that Tom felt was most important. Almost invariably, after a few minutes of talk he would get on to the topic of the green shoes. Each time he spoke about this incident the image was described with greater clarity and he would often weep at the sadness he experienced. Tom said he was totally shocked how he felt about this event given the passage of time. He had truly believed that the longer he avoided thinking about what had happened then eventually it would go away. He said that until now he had thought there was no point in discussing it as he believed this would simply have the effect of making it worse. As we talked, Tom began to make connections with other things that had been happening in his life at the time of incident. He had a daughter of his own who was at the time about the same age as the girl killed in the accident. He also recalled having been asked to go to the hospital after the incident where he had met the father of the little girl and how he now remembered identifying with the father's grief and getting caught in a cycle of panic for his own daughter's well-being.

Our sessions were few in number but were incredibly intense experiences. Tom would weep for the many traumatic losses he had experienced that all seemed to be symbolized in this little pair of green shoes being put into the ambulance. However, the freedom, the unconditional acceptance of him and our joint venture at gaining a deep understanding of what the whole incident meant to him seemed to have a profound effect on Tom. The opaqueness under his eyes gradually became replaced with more color and Tom's smile seemed to more accurately reflect how he felt. He reported that since starting to get a little more sleep and feeling as though he had more energy, he had been able to invest more time in his relationship with his family. This was proving a great success and he said he felt less depressed and was back in discussions with HR about returning to work, possibly to see out his remaining ten years of service. Tom had a wealth of experience that was highly valued within the job and he finally made a return to work in an area he could contribute to with pride. He went on to take up a role of training new police drivers and preparing them for being on the scene of fatal road traffic incidents. More than this, he was instrumental in instituting a shift in policy within his organization, seeing a system of peer support for all officers after attending a fatal, thus opening the way for others to get help sooner rather than later should it be required.

Tom's experiences are common. There are three major ways in which people talk about how they change following trauma. Post-traumatic growth refers to the constellation of positive changes that people may experience following exposure to psychological trauma, and has been described as consisting of three broad dimensions. First, people may report that their relationships are enhanced in some way; for example, that they now value their friends and family more, and feel an increased compassion and altruism toward others. Second, survivors may develop improved views of themselves in some way. For example, they may report having a greater sense of personal resiliency and strength, which may be coupled with a greater acceptance of their vulnerabilities and limitations. Third, survivors may report positive changes in life philosophy, such as finding a fresh appreciation for each new day, or renegotiating what really matters to them.

Various self-report psychometric tests are available with which to assess post-traumatic growth (see Joseph & Linley, 2008 for a review on measurement). The Psychological Well-Being Post-Trauma Changes Questionnaire (PWB-PTCQ: Regel & Joseph, 2010) is an 18-item measure (e.g., "my *life has meaning*," "*I have strong and close relationships in my life*"). Respondents are asked to rate how much they have changed on each item as a result of their experience on a 5-point scale ranging from '*much less so now*' (1) to '*much more so now*' (5), so that scores have a possible range of 18 to 90, with higher scores indicating greater growth. Scores of over 54 indicate the presence of positive change. Such measures as the PWB-PTCQ are useful in documenting change and for research purposes, and also help to validate anecdotal evidence that growth is often experienced by police officers following some of the most horrific work.

We asked a small team of specialist forensic investigators to complete the PWB-PTCQ. The team consists of police officers (N = 7) and civilians (N = 2), who would frequently have to view images of torture, beheadings, and other forms of violence on computers seized in the course of complex terrorist investigations. The viewing would often have to be repeated in the course of cataloguing and rank ordering evidence. The police officers were all experienced forensic investigators with an average of 28 years experience in policing and forensic investigation. The civilians had no police experience but had three years of forensic investigation. In addition all had postgraduate qualifications in forensic investigation. The team is close knit with firm evidence of good peer and supervisory support, with minimal episodes of sickness throughout the life of the unit at the time of writing.

We found that scores of the police officers ranged from 54–62 with a mean of 57. Scores of the civilians ranged from 65–66. The civilian investigators scores are somewhat higher, reflecting a higher level of positive change and qualitatively; they also described their work as rewarding and fulfilling. It has also to be acknowledged that all these individuals have an exceptionally high level of technical skill with information technology and approach their roles and tasks with great meticulousness and professionalism. There is strong sense of camaraderie together with good peer support together with efficient and supportive supervisory input.

In the longer term, post-traumatic growth seems to be adaptive. Helgeson et al. (2006) conducted a meta-analytic review of 87 studies, concluding that benefit finding was related to lower depression and more positive well-being. Linley, Joseph, and Goodfellow (2008) found that people who report growth are less likely to experience problems of post-traumatic stress at six months. Affleck, Tennen, Croog, and Levine (1987) reported that heart-attack patients who found benefits immediately after their first attack had reduced re-occurrence and morbidity statistics eight years after the attack (for a recent review of the literature, see Joseph & Butler, 2010).

In many instances of post-traumatic growth, the changes might be small and even not noticed by many, it is essential for professionals in the field to be able to be tuned to the signs for growth and to facilitate their flourishing, which in our experience is promoted through warm, supportive therapeutic relationships as much as anything we might actually do. Calhoun and Tedeschi (2008), two of the pioneers of this field, advise practitioners to learn about the phenomenon of post-traumatic growth themselves, and then 'become the expert companion' on the patient's potential journey to growth, a view which we would agree with through our own experience of person-centered practice (see Worsley & Joseph, 2007). Below, we unpack this in some more detail and offer ten principles to promote growth.

Promoting Post-Traumatic Growth: Ten Principles

As Calhoun and Tedeschi emphasize, it important that the practitioner must not push the idea of post-traumatic growth as this might lead to pressure and anxiety for the client as well as disappointment if they do not experience post-traumatic growth. Based on some of our previous writings (see Murphy, Durkin, & Joseph, 2010) we suggest ten principles that can be useful toward facilitating growth after trauma (see Table 14.1). Below we will discuss each of these in more detail.

1. To Let the Idea of Growth and Its Directions Emerge from the Client

Some people very quickly begin to see positive benefits arising from their experiences, but for others it takes longer. Either way this is something that

Table 14.1 Ten principles to promote growth

1	To let the idea of growth and its directions emerge from the client.
2	To recognize that growth emerges from the struggle to make sense of the experience, not from the experience itself.
3	To respect the person's right to self-determination
4	To show the client unconditional respect as a person of worth.
5	To aim toward an understanding of the client's experience as it is for them.
6	To be open and communicate understanding and acceptance of the client's experience.
7	To be always prepared to work with the traumatic material.
8	To acknowledge, respect, and respond to the whole of the client's experience.
9	Not to place an expectation for growth on the client.
10	To acknowledge and work toward a therapeutic relationship based on mutuality.

Taken from Murphy, Durkin, & Joseph (2010).

has to come from the person themselves when they are ready. Suggesting to someone who has come through trauma that they ought to see positive benefits in their experiences is likely to be self-defeating and push the person to a defensive position where they are hostile to the idea of positive change.

We now routinely include self-report psychometric tests alongside the traditional measures of post-traumatic stress within our assessment batteries to ask about post-traumatic growth. This can be useful in opening up the conversation with the client about positive changes, but only in directions that come from what they have told us.

2. To Recognize that Growth Emerges from the Struggle to make Sense of the Experience, not from the Experience Itself

It is misleading we think to talk of post-traumatic growth arising from the traumatic events themselves. We are careful not to suggest to clients that the traumatic event itself is to be welcomed as a good thing in their lives, but that it is an inevitable fact now of their lives and it is in their struggle to deal with it that something positive can emerge.

Exposure to the inimitable shock of some aspects of police work has the potential to threaten existing beliefs and change the person's whole world view, thus shattering the sense of what is considered to be normality. However, if a police officer is to carry on with the work and remain psychologically healthy, as most officers do, somehow they must find a way to piece back together the shattered assumptions that were once in place with a new worldview that has integrated the newly encountered trauma and the learning that takes place as a result.

There is no doubt that policing or working in a police organization changes the way one sees the world. A study by Marshall (2006) of American State of Delaware police officers showed that a number of significant changes in worldview occurred as a result of cumulative traumatic stressful events at work—officers showed a reduction in trust in others, and felt that the world was not a safe place. What these officers described is something that many in the field of policing will be able to relate to—that some people cannot be trusted and that the world is not necessarily a safe place—this learning arises through police work and represents the officers developing new worldviews that are in line with their experiences. As such, the task of professionals working in the field of policing is to help officers in their struggle to make sense of their experiences.

From my own (David's) experience of clinical work in the field of trauma and abuse, I noticed the distress, fear, shock, loss of sleep, being kept awake at night by intrusive thoughts, and feeling sorrowful at the extent of the problem of abuse in our society. The fact that abuse was much more prevalent than had previously been believed had changed my worldview. This was a new fact in life for me that had to be integrated. As difficult as I still find this fact, through the help provided by supervision and peer support I am able to take this new information on board and use it constructively in my life. How?

3. To Respect the Person's Right to Self-determination

How a person makes sense of their experiences, whether they use it constructively or destructively, is ultimately their choice we believe. But the more we are able to stand back and respectively trust people to make their own decisions, the more likely they are to be constructive.

It is important to avoid the tyranny of positive thinking (Held, 2002, 2004). Therapists should be aware of the potential for positive change in their clients following stress and trauma. But it must also be recognized that adversity does not lead to positive change for everyone. Therefore therapists need to be careful not to inadvertently imply that the person has in some way failed by not making more of their experience, or that there is anything inherently positive in the person's experience. Personal growth after trauma should be viewed as originating not from the event, but from within the person themselves through the process of their cognitive–emotional struggle with the event and its aftermath.

We cannot make someone find growth in their experiences. Research tells us that the affected person's reported approach to coping is one of the most important determinants of growth. Problem-focused acceptance and positive reinterpretation coping are the important ways of coping that promote growth. For this reason, it is important to provide coping-skills training that people can turn to if they struggle to use these ways of coping.

4. To Show the Client Unconditional Respect as a Person of Worth

When we talk about standing back from the person, we mean standing back in the sense of realizing that respecting people means not trying to make decisions for them but to trust them as adults. But we do not mean standing back in the sense of not caring—rather the opposite. We mean caring in the sense of valuing the person not for what they have, or what they have accomplished, or what decisions they are making, but in the sense that they are a unique human being like ourselves doing their best in life.

5. To Aim Toward an Understanding of the Client's Experience as it is for Them

This is about doing all we can to see things through their eyes. Our task is to understand what it was like for them, not what it would have been like for us, or what we think it should be like for them.

6. To be Open and Communicate Understanding and Acceptance of the Client's Experience

In trauma therapy, people tell us things that many people would find shocking, or embarrassing, shameful, or disgusting. What is important if we want our clients to be able to feel safe to move in growthful directions is that they feel accepted, no matter what they tell us. Our task is to provide clients with a level of acceptance that they do not feel the need to be defensive with us, or more importantly with themselves.

7. To be Always Prepared to Work with the Traumatic Material

Often people get stuck in their traumatic memories, or in thoughts of what they did or failed to do, and until they are able to make sense of their memories, rid themselves of feelings of shame or guilt, they will struggle to move in growthful directions. For this reason, we must be prepared to always work with whatever the traumatic material is. This involves making sure people have the time to talk through whatever is troubling them. It is important not to rush this.

8. To Acknowledge, Respect, and Respond to the Whole of the Client's Experience

There will often be so many things goings on in the session that it is easy to overlook some part of what the client is telling us. Trauma inevitably has both negative and positive aspects, and each needs to be acknowledged.

9. Not to Place an Expectation for Growth on the Client

It is not appropriate to put pressure on the client to report growth. This might seem obvious, but the pressures can be subtle and hard to avoid, and it requires extra vigilance to ensure that it is ok with us if the client has nothing positive to say.

10. To Acknowledge and Work Toward a Therapeutic Relationship Based on Mutuality

We may be experts on psychological therapy and post-traumatic stress, but we are not experts on what our client should be feeling, or how they should think. They are their own best experts and we need to respect that and see ourselves as mutual companions alongside them on their journey. We are there to learn from them as much as they are there to learn from us.

265

Changes in worldview can be used in either destructive or constructive ways and it is in the struggle officers have with their shifting worldviews that we can offer them the most support. Ideally, we wish to create a mutually supportive environment in which officers can be open with each other and provide a level of peer support that encourages constructive rather than destructive use of the new worldviews.

Within the field of trauma we have learnt that many factors mediate the effects of exposure to a traumatic event on the development of later psychological difficulties, but because the most important factor in predicting how people adjust is their social support. Marmar et al. (2006) in a study of police officers found that those who had the poorest social support from their work colleagues were most likely to develop PTSD. More recently, Burns, Morley, Bradshaw, and Domene (2008) looked at police teams investigating internet child exploitation. They highlighted several factors associated with effective coping, notably the quality of supervision (managers' understanding attitude being seen as vitally important), humour (for bonding the team together and releasing the tensions at difficult moments), a sense of control (i.e., having control over one's work), candidate selection (a key factor here was to select people based on their ability to cope and to give meaning and purpose to their work in the field), organizational support (included aspects such as access to training, equipment and access to psychological support), social support (involved access to other positive relationships beyond the immediate team), and finally psychological support (which included annual psychological assessments, psycho-education and training in coping skills).

Some of these principles might also be helpful in shaping the way we develop support among peers or for team leaders to adopt and model for their team to be influenced by. It might be worth considering how you could bring change within your own team or your organization that might begin to create the kind of social environment within which growth is able to occur.

Conclusion

One of the most remarkable advances in our knowledge of trauma in recent years is that in the aftermath of the struggle with adversity it is common to find benefits. The above are guidelines for promoting post-traumatic growth in working with traumatized people. Research into the clinical facilitation of post-traumatic growth among survivors of a variety of events is beginning to flourish, with reports of interventions with war veterans, cancer patients, survivors of sexual abuse, and terrorism, for example, reporting positive results (Joseph & Linley, 2008). The perception of benefits, in turn, may lead to higher levels of psychological functioning and improved health. Research indicates that reports of growth are related to longer-term adaptation such as lower levels of depression, post-traumatic stress as well as higher levels of well-being. As yet there is little research with police officers, but from our own experiences of working with the police we have seen post-traumatic growth for ourselves and know that for many this is one of the trajectories of adjustment to traumatic events that can arise.

References

Affleck, G., Tennen, H., Croog, S., & Levine, S. (1987). Causal attributions, perceived benefits, and morbidity after a heart attack: An 8-year study. *Journal of Consulting and Clinical Psychology*, 55, 29–35.

Alexander, D.A. (1993). Stress among police body handlers: A long-term follow up. *British Journal of Psychiatry*, 163, 806–808.

Burns, C.M., Morley, J., Bradshaw, R., & Domene, J. (2008). The emotional impact on and coping strategies employed by the police teams investigating internet child exploitation. *Traumatology*, 14, 20–31.

Calhoun, L.G. & Tedeschi, R.G. (2008). The paradox of struggling with trauma: Guidelines for practice and directions for research. In S. Joseph & A. Linley (Eds.), *Trauma, Recovery, and Growth: Positive Psychological Perspectives on Posttraumatic Stress*, pp. 325–337. Hoboken, NJ: Wiley.

Held, B.S. (2002). The tyranny of the positive attitude in America: Observation and speculation. *Journal of Clinical Psychology*, 58(9), 965–991.

Held, B.S. (2004). The negative side of positive psychology. *Journal of Humanistic Psychology*, 44(1), 9–46.

Helgeson, V.S., Reynolds., K.A., & Tomich, P.L. (2006). A meta-analytic review of benefit finding and growth. *Journal of Consulting and Clinical Psychology*, 74, 797–816.

Joseph, S. & Butler, L. D. (2010). Positive changes Following Adversity. *PTSD Research Quarterly*, 23(3), 1–8. Available at: www.ptsd.va.gov.

Joseph, S. & Linley, P.A. (2008). Psychological assessment of growth following adversity: A review. In S. Joseph, & P.A. Linley, (Eds.). *Trauma, Recovery, and Growth: Positive Psychological Perspectives on Posttraumatic stress*, pp. 21–38. Hoboken, NJ: Wiley.

Linley, P.A., Joseph, S., & Goodfellow, B. (2008). Positive changes in outlook following trauma and their relationship to subsequent posttraumatic stress, depression, and anxiety. *Journal of Social and Clinical Psychology*, 27, 877–891.

Marmar, C.R., McCaslin, S.E., Metzler, T.J., Best, S., Weiss, D.S., Fagan, J., Liberman, A., Pole, N., Otte, C., Yehuda, R., Mohr, D., & Neylan, T. (2006). Predictors of posttraumatic stress in police and other first responders. *Annals of New York Academy of Sciences*, 1071, 1–18.

Marshall, E. (2006). Cumulative career traumatic stress: A pilot study of traumatic stress in law enforcement. *Journal of Police and Criminal Psychology*, 21, 62–71.

Murphy, D., Durkin, J., & Joseph, S. (2010). Growth in relationship: A post-medicalised vision for positive transformation. In N. Tehrani (Ed.), *Managing Trauma in the Workplace*. London: Routledge.

Nietzsche, F. (1997/1889). *Twilight of the Idols*, trans. R. Polt. Indianapolis, IN: Hackett.

Regel, S. & Joseph, S. (2010). *Post-traumatic Stress: The Facts*. Oxford: Oxford University Press.

Spielberger, C.D., Westberry, L.G., Grier, K.S., & Greenfield, G. (1981). *The Police Stress Survey: Sources of Stress in Law Enforcement*. Tampa, FL: Human Resources Institute.

Tedeschi, R.G. & Calhoun, L.G. (1996). The posttraumatic growth inventory: Measuring the positive legacy of trauma. *Journal of Traumatic Stress*, 9, 455–471.

Worsley, R. & Joseph, S. (Eds.), *Person-centred Practice: Case Studies in Positive Psychology*. Ross-on-Wye: PCCS Books.

15

THE LAW ENFORCEMENT CHAPLAIN

Grief, Loss, Honor, and Compassion

Robert E. Douglas, Christine M. Heiny,
and Sharon M. Freeman Clevenger

Overview

Chaplain is defined as a "Christian Clergyman attached to a private chapel of a prominent person or institution or ministering to a military body, professional group, etc." (World English Dictionary). A police chaplain is a minister in a law enforcement setting. Each police department is free to set the requirements and conditions upon which police chaplains serve. Two such organizations that offer guidelines, and training, for police chaplains are the International Conference of Police Chaplains and American Police Chaplains Association based out of Michigan. The American Association of Police Chaplains is a distinctly Christian nonprofit organization. The statement of purpose for the American Police Chaplains Association is: "When we are able to rescue others, we should do so at all costs. Ask God for direction—then act! He may have placed you here 'for such a time as this!'" (Esther 4:14, New King James version, in American Police Chaplains Association, n.d.).

The International Conference of Police Chaplains has a written Canon of Ethics for Law Enforcement Chaplains and a set of qualifications and qualities devised to maintain professionalism in law enforcement chaplaincy (International Conference of Police Chaplains ICPC).

The qualifications are:

1   A law enforcement chaplain (LEC) should be an ecclesiastically certified person in good standing and endorsed for law enforcement

chaplaincy by a recognized religious body, with (5) years' experience in ministry.

2 An LEC should have a specialized interest in law enforcement chaplaincy by training, working experience and appointment.

3 An LEC should be able and willing to be carefully screened by a local LEC committee and/or appointed authorities.

4 An LEC should be available to serve on a 24-hour call basis, determined, and governed by the head LEC and/or chief of police.

5 An LEC should manifest a broad base of experience and professional ministry, emotional stability and personal flexibility.

6 An LEC should be tactful and considerate in approaching all people regardless of race, sex, creed, or religion.

7 An LEC should be willing to become involved in training programs that enhance one's efficiency in meeting and dealing with people in crisis and should be familiar with community medical, psychiatricn and other helping resources in the local area.

Chaplains consist of clergy, sworn law enforcement officers (LEOs) who are also clergy, and lay ministers. The LEC strives to "protect and serve" those who "protect and serve" by nourishing the spirit of those who deal constantly in the onslaught of man's inhumanity to man. Behind the badge is a human being and dire is the situation when that is forgotten.

What does the LEC actually do? The chaplain works with issues of grief, loss, honor, remembrances, spirituality, and the impact of police work on LEOs and their families:

> The chaplain may be called upon to give death notifications, provide confidential counseling to police department personnel, provide a moral and ethical foundation to police personnel, provide referral and resource assistance when requested, provide pastoral functions at special events (i.e., graduations, award ceremonies, etc.), preside at weddings, funerals or other religious events as requested, assist with Critical Incident Stress Debriefings (CISD), serve as a liaison with other local clergy, and liaison with police families in the event of a line of duty injury or death.
> (www.south-haven.com/pages/police chaplain)

In addition chaplains may be called upon to counsel families of LEOs, visit sick or injured officers, provide assistance to victims, assist at suicide incidents, provide for the spiritual needs of prisoners, deal with transients and homeless, serve on review boards, teach stress management, ethics, family life, and pre-retirement classes, and furnish expert responses to spiritual questions (ICPD, 2014). The purpose of this chapter will be to focus on the role of police chaplains to help LEOs access spirituality to deal with the effects of grief, loss, politics, alcohol and drug abuse, suicide, on duty deaths of fellow officers, rampant crime, street violence, physical trauma, judicial system inequities, relationship problems, and personal and family crisis. The best approach for the LEC is a holistic approach, including spirituality, and must be implemented by leaders of law enforcement agencies nationwide if we are going to meet the needs of our officers successfully. This is a very critical period in law enforcement professions. The United States has experienced increased demand on over 18,000 law enforcement agencies because of terrorist-related issues, along with serious financial challenges facing our city, county, and state governments. When added to the already routine stress-related issues that LEOs face on a daily basis, it is no wonder that the officer is struggling physically and emotionally, not only on the job, but also within their families as well.

The first author of this chapter has served as police chaplain for over 32 years and has personally experienced an alarming number of LEO-related suicides. In recent years an increase in the number of homicides/suicides has escalated. Dr. James T. Reese (FBI Retired) made this observation on self-destructive actions of LEOs:

> We must accept the task of moving into the 21st century with the renewed hope this act of self-destruction will cease. Fortunately, as the 20th century closed, many law enforcement trainers focused on holistic wellness. The entire field of police stress seemed to realize "the enemy without" did not cause the greatest amount of job dissatisfaction and self-destructive behaviors. The "enemy within" posed the biggest threat.
>
> (Rupert, n.d.)

The above statement begs the question: If the greatest concern for officer safety lies within, how can the Police Chaplain or Spiritual Advisor help meet the needs of the LEO and their family in order to reduce the threat of suicide?

Defining the Role

Cyndee Thomas, Senior Chaplain and current President, International Conference of Police Chaplains (ICPC), made the following observations to co-author Robert Douglas:

> The Chaplain needs to be able to 'leave their pulpit' when providing spiritual support to Law Enforcement. When the Chaplain first meets the emotional needs, officers and family

members will be more inclined to ask for Spiritual guidance as well as direction on moral and ethical issues. The Chaplain will do more harm than good if personal theology and proselytizing are part of his or her agenda.

Ms. Thomas further stated that: "the chaplain who is more interested in being an officer 'wannabe,' or is only interested in the thrill of deference received as a result of their position, will cause not only skepticism on the part of the officer, but a sense that the chaplain has the wrong motive and therefore cannot be trusted." In other words, the LEC should understand the ministry of a chaplain is a support role to law enforcement personnel, not an LEO themselves. As the LEO experiences that the chaplain is not there to judge, but rather to offer spiritual counsel when asked, provide emotional support develop relationships in order to walk through the good and bad times, then the chaplain will be accepted and welcomed into the law enforcement family. The hope is that by developing those relationships ahead of time when the times of crisis come, the chaplain will be called by the officer, spouse, or child for the guidance and support needed to get through the crisis.

There are numerous definitions as to the role and responsibilities of a chaplain. The definition from the Omaha Police Chaplain Corps in the Omaha Police Department states that "the Police Chaplain will seek to lighten the burden of the officers by performing tasks that have a greater spiritual or social nature rather than law enforcement nature." The Chaplain Corps strive to strike a balance between serving the needs of LEOs in their personal and professional lives and serving the Omaha Metro Area at large.

The key to successfully supporting the LEO then is to maintain a "balance of service" by establishing a balance between the LEOs, the community in which they serve, and the LEO family. It is all too easy for the LEC, because of their day-to-day exposure to LEOs, the LEO environment and in some cases their designated "rank" and uniform, to begin to think and act more like an LEO than a chaplain. It cannot be understated that this kind of attitude and action becomes a great liability for the chaplain's program because their ability to serve as a chaplain begins to blur, and even cease to exist. They are now looked at as almost fellow officers rather than as a police chaplain.

Stay on Point

As an example, when an officer is killed, it is common for other officers in the agency to respond to the hospital to be with their fellow officers and the family of the officer who was killed. This is a time of great emotions and stress. In this example, the chaplain arrived and immediately started to hold defusing sessions with the LEOs involved with the incident. The LEC role should have been to provide spiritual support for the families and the officers who were there. As a result of this blurring of roles, the Peer Support Team Supervisors had to remove the chaplain in the above example from the defusing session because the chaplain took on a departmental task that was only to be done by Critical Incident Stress Management (CISM) team members. This one incident placed this particular chaplain in jeopardy of losing their role in that agency. What this chaplain failed to understand was the importance of retaining their ability to balance effectiveness and credibility.

Maintaining Spiritual Neutrality

Typically, a pastor of a church, or parish, generally ministers to a group with similar beliefs. This is not true of an LEC. As a chaplain you must also be able to provide services to diversified groups of individuals. Everyone, regardless of their spiritual beliefs, needs to benefit from the services of the chaplain. Every chaplain comes with his or her beliefs and religious background that could impact how services are provided to their agency and community. Police officers often have different "life styles" from the chaplain. The chaplain is there to listen and see what steps need to be taken to meet the LEO's immediate concerns.

A case example would be one in which an LEO had recently left his wife and children because of perceived failings or mistakes and was seeking counsel from the chaplain via telephone. The officer admitted that he was contemplating suicide as a solution to his problems. The chaplain became concerned that he would also harm his wife and children because of his despondency. The chaplain had no indication where the officer was calling from, and became anxious about calming the officer down and preventing a tragedy, using only words. The chaplain chose to listen carefully to what the officer was saying, relaying to him that his past mistakes could not be altered, but that his decisions at this point would either bring about greater hurt and lasting pain for those who loved him and those he loved, or it could be the beginning of a "renewed life" that with time and effort could restore the respect of his wife and children. The conversation lasted what felt like hours to the LEC, but were probably only minutes while the LEC sent a distress text to a supervisor. This situation ended well with the officer getting help by professional mental health counselors, but left the chaplain reviewing the conversation in his head for days. Later, the chaplain said: "I don't know if I had anything to do with the outcome, I hope so, but in my heart as a chaplain I knew that I didn't make things worse and hopefully expressed a deep concern for the hurts he felt responsible for in his life." In this situation, the chaplain remembered that it is important to not take responsibility for things you cannot control when dealing with officers in crisis. The chaplain is not a clinical mental health professional.

Handling Invisible Wounds

The previous example reminds us that most LECs are not licensed psychologists or therapists, and as a result there are some professional limitations. However, not being licensed may provide them with some flexibility when helping the LEO deal with some problems caused by emotional pains, guilt, and frustrations that are common in post-traumatic stress disorder (PTSD), cumulative career trauma stress (ccts), and compassion fatigue.

PTSD is defined by the *Diagnostic and Statistical Manual*, fifth edition (DSM-5) (APA, 2013) as the development of characteristic symptoms following exposure to an extreme traumatic stressor involving direct personal experience, or vicarious exposure, to an event that involves actual or threatened death or serious injury, or other threat to one's physical integrity; or witnessing an event that involves death, injury, or a threat to the physical integrity of another person; or learning about unexpected or violent death, serious harm, or threat of death or injury experienced by a family member or other close associate. The person's response to the event usually involves intense fear, helplessness, or horror. In addition, the person may experience persistent re-experiencing of the traumatic event, persistent avoidance of stimuli associated with the trauma and numbing of general responsiveness, and persistent symptoms of increased arousal.

The development and treatment of PTSD in LEOs is discussed in greater detail in other chapters in this volume. However, for the purposes of this chapter, the reader is reminded that depending on jurisdiction and locale, most LEOs are exposed to traumatic events on a regular basis. They will function as their occupation designates, but what they deal with affects them and it accumulates in a very harmful way. One traumatic event can "shut down" a civilian for a lifetime, while LEOs continue to function, often in repeated traumatic situations, over and over, which often leads to a phenomenon referred to as "Cumulative Career Traumatic Stress" (CCTS) (Marshall, 2006)

Researchers out of Delaware have studied the effects of traumatic stress on LEOs. It was observed that officers may experience trauma symptoms sporadically throughout a career as a result of being routinely exposed to many traumatic events over a period of time (Marshall, 2006). Marshall referred to this experience as "Cumulative Career Traumatic Stress." She goes on to state:

> The symptoms of CCTS are similar to Posttraumatic Stress Disorder (PTSD) but rather than presenting suddenly as a result

of a single traumatic event directly experienced by the officer, such as a shooting, the officer may experience one of a combination of symptoms sporadically throughout a career as he or she is exposed to a myriad of traumatic events over a period of years. The trauma symptoms that are experienced fail to fit the duration criteria for PTSD, but are none-the-less frequently experienced and left unacknowledged. This in turn creates a slow and subtle deterioration of the officer's psychological and emotional stability.

(Marshall, 2006)

The LEO is a specialized client group. They are split from general society by their uniform presence and their position of authority and control. They are expected to die on their job if need be. They are different because they respond often to horrific trauma. The police world is never stable or comfortable. In a fraction of a second they can go from boredom to terror. Police are not called when things are going well. "Imagine the most horrific things that happen in this city that no one really hears about or sees. Homicides, rapes, car accidents, violent assaults, this is the kind of stuff we deal with on a daily basis. Some of these cases involve teenagers and children" (Muller, 2013).

Many of the officers you deal with may be suffering from undiagnosed PTSD in some degree. LEOs may claim to be desensitized to what they deal with but they never forget the tragedies they see. Consequently, they may share details with you of incidents that civilians, including some professionals, do not want to hear. Do not judge them, recoil, or criticize. You are there to help and not hurt the situation by adding the stress of judgment or second-guessing. They may have no one to listen to them except you. Other officer's might listen to a point but showing weakness is taboo. And, asking for help shows weakness. "Police officers generally think of themselves as problem-solvers, not people who have problems" (Violanti, 2013).

Police officers are also highly susceptible to compassion fatigue, which is often defined by Violanti as "the cost of caring without reward or result" (Violanti & Gehrke, 2004). It is hypothesized that individuals exposed to frequent, and repeated trauma eventually develop a state of compassion fatigue through a secondary process of emotional compassion fatigue (Violanti, 2004). Burnout, which is a separate and distinct process, is systemic desensitization and demoralization occurs when there is chronic emotional depletion, especially in a work environment. First responders and crisis personnel like LEOs are not only exposed to frequent and repeated exposure to traumatic incidents, they also absorb the traumatic emotional stress of those they help. No police officer is truly prepared for the high cost of caring about the people and the events they will experience. In fact the compassion and desire to help others in crisis that lead many to a career in police work are the very traits that set an officer up for compassion fatigue. Over time the constant emotional distress wears them down.

Given that individuals who choose a career in law enforcement often have very personal reasons for becoming an LEO, they experience the powerlessness of the victim of a crime as a personal failure. In actuality, police work does not often allow for protection and correction of a wrong done to someone, the personal sense of mass injustice accumulates. The officer begins to believe that they will "never make a difference" because there are too many victims, too many "bad guys," and too little justice. "Unrecognized and untreated compassion fatigue causes cops to leave their professions, fall into the throws of addictions, or in extreme cases become self-destructive or suicidal" (Panos, 2007).

It is in these cases, when someone is suffering from an overwhelming feeling of futility, that the LEC can offer compassion, support, and recognition for making a difference to the LEO. "Isolation is a symptom of compassion fatigue and is ultimately dangerous. To be resilient you need to have good support and connections with others" (Panos, 2007).

The role of an LEO is service, which means to serve, and to give of themselves whenever possible. It is not unusual for a police officer to buy someone a meal, pay for their taxi fare, purchase milk or diapers if needed, and provide other compassionate assistance out of their own finances. As a result, it is foreign, unusual, and often uncomfortable for an LEO to have another human being offer service, and hope, to them. Robert Douglas (co-author) believes there are at least 20 options of hope they could choose instead of suicide for each reason. These are not absolute solutions to their deep concerns, but each one offers them a different choice. Police officers do not expect you as a chaplain to have all the answers to their personal and professional issues, but they do expect you to be there for them and their family during crisis. By the time an officer is in crisis for whatever reason, he or she has tunnel vision. You can share realistic options that might bring new insight to their thought process (Douglas, 2014, personal communication).

Several years ago when the National Police Suicide Foundation was holding a Police Suicide Awareness (PSA) Train the Trainer program outside of Baltimore, Maryland each of the trainers was asked to give a presentation on what they would say when they became trainers of the class they would be teaching back at their agency. When it was time for one of the trainers to give his presentation, he stood in front of our class and made this statement: "I would not be here today if not for my chaplain." He went on to tell the class how he had been struck by a vehicle on a car stop that resulted in serious back and neck injuries which caused serious emotional and physical trauma to him and his family. He stated that for more than two years this chaplain provided assistance to his family and spiritual encouragement for him (Douglas, personal communication). What Chaplain Douglas did not realize at the time was that his chaplain had come to this training, and she was in the room when he was making his presentation. He walked over to her table and stated to her, "I have never told you this, but I deeply appreciate all that you have done for me and my family. I do not know if you realize this or not, but you have been our 'lifeline' for the past two years." The officer then broke down emotionally and there was not a dry eye in the training room. Always be giving and respectful to reach these men and women where they need you the most. Never forget that despite their demeanor or appearance, LEOs are very vulnerable human beings.

Often the chaplain will find that the life styles of LEOs are not always in line with the chaplain's spiritual beliefs and personal conduct. Chaplains that have no tolerance will alienate everyone. For example, when this author (Robert Douglas) was serving as chaplain for Baltimore City FOP Lodge 3, the Baltimore City Police Department had just started their Police Chaplain's Corp. They assigned a police chaplain for each of their nine police districts. On one particular evening we had an officer who shot and killed a suspect. After spending several hours at our Homicide Unit downtown, the officer returned to his district to continue filling out his paper work on the incident. The chaplain for that district was contacted about the shooting and responded to the district to check on the officer who did the shooting. When the chaplain attempted to speak with the officer, the officer replied that he was very busy at the present time and he would speak with him later. Instead of honoring the officer's request, the chaplain insisted that the officer speak with him and stated he needed to talk about how he felt. The officer turned to the chaplain and told him to leave him the "****" alone and returned to his paperwork.

The chaplain was offended by the profanity of the officer and contacted his district commander and made an official complaint against the officer. That one act by that chaplain shut down any communication between the officers in that district and the Chaplains Corp and wiped out months of working to develop a relationship of trust between the officers and the chaplains. The conduct of the officer was unprofessional, but under the circumstances was not unexpected or abnormal. If the chaplain had given the officer a little time and space, the results would have been entirely different. It is all about the feelings of those we serve and not our own feelings.

Understanding the Characteristics of Grief and Loss

The LEO deals with grief and loss on a regular basis. An unnamed officer said once "we are with people during the worst twenty minutes of their lives." The lines blur for officers because of the constant silent irrational expectation that nothing bad should happen as long as they are doing their job. Society, police administration, training, all drill into them over and over that they are all that stands between a criminal and an innocent citizen. Not every crisis you are called into will be duty related. Some of the hardest are the death of a close family member, the death of a fellow officer, the loss of a child through death or parental separation, and the loss of a relationship. Grief and loss often are not totally acknowledged by officers because they learn to compartmentalize their emotions in order to "stay on point." Civilians who do not understand the necessity of putting your feelings aside in order to maintain safety and control believe that LEOs are cold-hearted with no feelings. Traits that make for a good police officer are not necessarily conducive to being a good family man or woman. Paranoid traits are healthy on the job for an LEO, even crucial, are considered cold and unfeeling in the civilian world (Anderson, 2002). This automatic ability to compartmentalize feelings contributes to distance between the LEO and their family members.

The LEC maintains an understanding of these characteristics in the LEO in order to help the law enforcement family understand their LEO's feelings, and to therefore move through loss, and even the grief, from regular effects of a law enforcement career. An example of loss of an officer's nephew will be used to illustrate the process of grieving from an LEO perspective. Sgt. Jones (fictitious LEO) arrived on the scene of a fist fight at a school football field. Sgt. Jones was the first officer on the scene and saw what appeared to be 12–13 youths wielding baseball bats and other weapons at a smaller group of adolescents. As Sgt. Jones approached the group, he was struck from behind by one of the participants causing him to crumble to the ground in the midst of the melee. He grabbed one of the combatants but saw that he was now the target of other assailants, one of which was reaching for his duty weapon, which he had unclipped, ready to use with his hand on the handle of the gun. He could hear sirens from other responding officers in the distance, but knew there was no way they could get to the scene in time to help him, and to prevent further danger. As the assailant grabbed the handle of his gun, another was sitting on his legs, another on his chest while a third was striking him in the legs with a club. He grabbed the hand on the gun and pulled the gun away from the assailant. As he did so, the weapon discharged because the youth had his finger on the trigger of the weapon. The noise of the gun firing caused the assailants to scatter. Sgt. Jones was rising to get up and realized he had a broken right leg from the beating he had taken. Other officers were arriving on the scene and asked if he was alright, seeing his injuries, they called for an ambulance and began to secure the scene. What Sgt. Jones was not aware of at that moment was that his nephew, who had seen Sgt. Jones arrive, was running toward the brawl to warn his uncle. When the gun discharged, the bullet struck his nephew in the leg, severing his femoral artery causing him to rapidly bleed out. He was unable to be saved and died shortly thereafter. Sgt. Jones was horror-struck, felt responsible and second-guessed every action he had undertaken, blaming himself for the death. An investigation concluded that he had followed all procedure, had prevented additional death or injury through his actions and was placed on sick leave to "recover" at home.

Sgt. Jones experienced severe guilt, anger, grief, and depression in the months that followed. He refused to participate in his own rehabilitation because "what was the point." Elizabeth Kubler-Ross's groundbreaking work in 1969 outlining the "Five Stages of Grief" (Kübler-Ross, 1969) described coping with death and dying as having five distinct components: (1) Denial, (2) Anger, (3) Bargaining, (4) Depression and finally, (5) Acceptance. These stages are not meant to describe all emotions that someone goes through when coping with major loss, however, they are meant to be a starting point. In fact, it has been observed by clinicians that people may move up and down through the stages as progress is not a linear experience. The original stages of grief have been expanded upon many times. Kennel, Slyter, and Claus (1970) recommended Lindemann's ten stages of grief hypothesis (1944) to describe the death of a neonate (infant). The ten stages of grief will be used to illustrate the case of an officer's loss of his nephew:

Stage of grief	Example
Shock	Shock that is felt by the person experiencing the loss acts as a temporary anesthetic and numbs them to the whole overwhelming experience. This process may be helpful because the LEO does not have to comprehend the magnitude of the loss of the child.
Reality of the loss	The family, and the LEO, will have a tendency to be angry at God along with showing irritability and anger toward each other, friends, and relatives. They may question how God could allow this to happen and expect a direct answer to this question. This reaction is normal and has nothing to do with their religious faith. It is a recognition of their own loss of control, and realization that "no one has control!"
Depression	At some point, his colleagues and even his family, has stopped coming around and its back to life as usual for most of his acquaintances. The officer may also be feeling that as a "protector" he or she failed, and feel hopeless, helpless and question their choice of career.

(continued)

(continued)

Stage of grief	Example
Physical symptoms of distress	Some of the symptoms can be a feeling of tightness in the throat, choking with shortness of breath, fatigue, loss of appetite, insomnia, and anxiety attacks. Many LEOs are able to experience these physical symptoms because it is accepted to be physically ill, but not emotionally ill. Parents who have lost a child have stated they experience severe aching in their arms because of the need to hold their child one more time.
Failure and fear	Feeling that he has failed his nephew, and his brother (the nephew's father), the LEO's feelings of helplessness and guilt expand causing increased self-examination focused on the incident. An LEO may not want to be alone and they may have unreasonable fears of danger. If they have other children, or young family members, they may fear for their safety as well.
Guilt	During this period there is deep self-evaluation with the focus on guilt regarding the outcome of death. An LEO is at a greater risk of taking their life during this phase. Police officers are used to being in control. Since an officer feels he had no control over the situation resulting in the death, he now has no control over what is happening at the current time. The officer may distance themself from their family and focus almost exclusively on their job believing that the job is an emotionally "safe" place for them.
Anger	This phase is characterized by overt hostility toward anyone they think may have contributed to the loss of the child. In other words, they are looking for someone to blame. They may focus on the medical profession (for not saving him), the person responsible for the accident (themselves or other officers for not responding quickly enough), or toward their spouse or family ("why didn't you tell him he should never approach a dangerous situation!") Over-focusing on the job can result in aggravation of their anger and therefore cause great pressures on their own marriage and could lead to separation or divorce.
Inability to tolerate "normal" situations	Often friends and family set a time limit on when they feel everything should return to normal. This is not always possible and can be very difficult for an individual to return to their daily routines with any degree of enthusiasm. This is even more difficult for a police officer whose daily routine may include the accidental death of other children that will continually remind them of their loss, and guilt. At work, other officers may avoid the grieving LEO out of concern that they might somehow be "infected" by the "abnormal" behavior.

| Beginning of recovery | The intensity of the symptoms gradually decline, although for many years occasional remembrances will occur. A resurgence of anger, guilt and/or grief may occur on important anniversaries, such the loved one's birthday, date of their death, holidays, and significant other "firsts." If there was an injury involved in the event, such as Sgt. Jones's broken leg, every time they experience pain, it reminds them of the incident. |
| Reaching out | The last stage includes the desire, and the ability, to reach out to others who are grieving. This can be the part of the grieving process that is the most "healing." For by helping others, we help ourselves. Many support groups began with individuals reaching this stage and using it to help others. In this case, Sgt. Jones my reach out to other LEOs who experience a tragedy of their own. |

Adapted from Lindemann (1944).

Remember a person who is grieving may walk away from you. If this occurs, let them go and watch for an opportunity when they are more approachable. Be aware, police officers may be very resistant to being touched unless there is great trust between you. They are constantly on guard of their space for safety purposes, both emotionally and physically. Do not take that personally.

Support Systems

Be aware of LEO support systems in your community and what they each have to offer. Check to make sure any support service is familiar enough with LEOs to actually help them. If possible, keep a list available to give them along with phone numbers and a contact person they may call. Some families may need a very specific support group that deals with their particular kind of loss or other issue. For example, if they lost a loved one to suicide or homicide, they may not feel comfortable in a grief support group where everyone died from a prolonged illness. Many police departments have their own psychologist and police counselors on staff. However, in some cases there is a deep reluctance to trust anyone associated in any way with the administration for fear of exposure or retaliation, no matter how good the counselors or psychologists are. A primary goal for the LEC is to help the LEO express any spiritual or emotional feelings in a neutral, accepting manner.

Recent research indicates that spirituality is a very effective tool to use with the challenges of police work. According to an article by Neil (2012) in the periodical *Law Enforcement Today*:

Spirituality enables stress management, accelerates performance, enhances practice, governs intuitive policing, governs emotional intelligence, nurtures ethics, and fosters longevity.

Absent intentional spirituality, the coping mechanisms people adopt to manage stress often increases it. Then, they become a stressor to others. Thus, it seems reasonable to conclude that law enforcement training academies should consider stress management and spirituality as complementary disciplines.

Summary

The law enforcement chaplain has a primary goal to strive to see the big picture and never lose sight of the value of service to others. They work with issues of grief, loss, honor, remembrances, spirituality, and the impact of police work on LEOs and their families. Being an LEC is one of the richest experiences someone can experience. The LEC has an opportunity to learn and give more than anyone can possibly imagine, and yet is at risk for their own emotional exhaustion and disappointment. In order to be of service, the police chaplain must understand the culture of the law enforcement community, have basic understanding of a variety of religious practices and fully understand the stages of grieving.

Spirituality and religion can offer an enormous foundation of strength, resiliency, perspective, and hope to people in crisis and pain. No two individuals will define, and experience, this concept in the same manner. Hopefully, the police chaplain can help the LEO, or their family member, personally access what this foundation means in their own lives, and help them establish a routine of supportive consistent awareness that they can carry forward into anything they might face.

References

American Police Chaplains Association (n.d.) Our *History, Our Statement of Purpose*. Retrieved from htpp://americanpolicechaplain.org/ (August 10, 2013).

American Psychiatric Association. (2013). Post-traumatic stress disorder: Diagnosis and criteria. In *The Diagnostic and Statistical Manual of Mental Disorders*, 5th ed. Arlington, VA: American Psychiatric Publishing.

Anderson, B.J. (2002). Echoes of violence in the police family. *A Gift From Within*. Retrieved from http://giftfromwithin.org/html/Police-Stress-Management.html (January 24, 2014).

International Conference of Police Chaplains (2014). *Qualifications and Qualities of the Police Chaplain*. Retrieved from www.icpc4cops.org/chaplaincy-intro/chaplain-qualifications.html (January 21, 2014).

Kennel, J.H., Slyter, H., & Claus, M., (1970). The mourning response of parents to the death of a newborn infant. *The New England Journal of Medicine*, August 13, 344–349.

Kübler-Ross, E. (1969). *On Death and Dying*. New York: Routledge.

Lindemann, E. (1944). "Symptomatology and Management of Acute Grief," and "Ten Stages of Grief Resolution," read at the Centenary Meeting of the American Psychiatric Association, Philadelphia, Pa. May 14–18.

Marshall, E. (2006) Cumulative Career Traumatic Stress (CCTS): A pilot study of traumatic stress in law enforcement. *Journal of Police and Criminal Psychology*, 21(1), 62–71.

Muller, R. (2013). www.psychologytoday.com/blog/talking-about-trauma/ 201302/toughing-it-out-posttraumatic-stress-in-police-officers (Accessed 08 December, 2013).

Neil, R. (2012). *Weapon for Wounded Warriors*. February 15. Retrieved from htpp://lawenforcementtoday.com/tag/police-chaplain-2/ (July 17, 2013).

Panos, A. (2007). *Understanding and Preventing Compassion Fatigue—A Handout for Professionals*. Retrieved from www.giftfromwithin.org/html/prvntcf.html (January 28, 2014).

Rupert (n.d.) *Suicide and Law Enforcement*. Behavioral Science Unit, FBI Academy, Quantico, VA, Forward VIII: 2001.

Violante, J.M. (2013). *The Badge of Life*. Retrieved from www.badgeoflife.com/data.php (January 29, 2014).

Violanti, J.M. & Gehrke, A. (2004). Police trauma encounters: Precursors of compassion fatigue. *International Journal of Emergency Mental Health*, 6(2), 75–80.

INDEX

assaults: against correctional officers 146, 147; against LEOs 13, 17; *see also* violence
assessment 23–43; civilians 26; errors 28–31; Fitness-for-Duty Evaluation 4, 25, 33, 34–39, 40; future directions 39–40; military law enforcement officers 139, 140, 141; pre-employment evaluation 24–25, 27–31, 32, 40; recent developments 24–26; self-assessment 33–34; special police populations 31–33; undercover officers 189
assessment centers 25
automatisms 234
autopsies, psychological 26
availability heuristic 105
avoidance 118, 207, 241–242, 243, 248, 249, 259, 274

Baker, D.N. 155
Baker, Monty 5, 70–98, 145–167
Balch, Robert W. 9
Baltimore City Police Department 277
Bannister, C. 81
Battlemind Training 80
Batts, A.W. 29
beliefs 60
Ben-Porath, Y.S. 27
BICEPS program 210–211
bipolar disorder 230–231
Bisson, J.L. 81, 82, 83
Black, R. 151
Blascovich, J. 160–161
Bliese, P.D. 136
blood pressure (BP) 46, 47–48, 71, 152
body language 227
Boggild, H. 52
Bohl, N. 79
Bond, F.W. 240–241
Bono, J.M. 89
Boston Marathon bombing (2013) 6, 8
Bowker, A.L. 233
BP *see* blood pressure
Bradshaw, R. 266
brain processes 55–57
Brockman, Andrea M. 5, 145–167
Bunce, D. 240–241
Burke, K. 58

burnout 34, 205, 275; correctional officers 148, 149, 151, 152, 153, 154–155, 162; post-traumatic stress disorder 208; stress impact on 145
Burns, C.M. 266
Burque, Brandi 5, 70–98, 131–144, 145–167

Caces, B. 52
Calhoun, L.G. 262
California Psychological Inventory (CPI) 27
calm show of force 223–224
Caplan, G. 72
cardiovascular disease (CVD) 49–55, 60–61; allostatic load 45; cortisol levels 46; exposure to trauma 47–48, 50–52; shift work 52–55
Castellano, C. 90, 159
Castro, C.A. 32
cataplexy 234
CBSM *see* cognitive behavioral stress management
CCTS *see* Cumulative Career Traumatic Stress
challenge appraisals 160–161
chaplains 7, 269–283; correctional officers 157–158; dealing with grief and loss 277–281; handling invisible wounds 274–277; military members 116; qualifications 269–270; role of 271–273; spiritual neutrality 273–274; support systems 281–282
Cheek, F. 146
child abuse 81, 102, 106, 256, 257, 263–264, 266
child exploitation investigators 31, 34, 266
child homicide 193, 194
child victims 202, 205, 206, 256, 275
Churchill, Winston 8
Ciarrochi, J. 243
CISD *see* Critical Incident Stress Debriefing
CISM *see* Critical Incident Stress Management
civil commitment 223
civil lawsuits 172, 180
civilian police (CP) 135
Claus, M. 279

disorder 47, 103–104, 121–123;
psychological assessment 31–33,
36; public perception of violence
105–106; responding to need
117–119; returning home 100–101;
return-to-duty programs 139–141,
143; risk factors 104, 106–107,
108, 110, 117, 121; stigma
116–117; suicide 110–116, 118;
trauma 101–102
military veteran law enforcement
officers (MVLEOs) 131,
136–139, 143
Miller, Laurence 6, 142, 171–183,
184–201, 202–221, 222–238
Miller, M. 146
mindfulness 241–242
misconduct 27, 171, 176
Mitchell, J.T. 71, 74, 83, 87–88, 91
Mitchell, R. 159
MLEOs see military law enforcement
officers
MMPI 27, 33, 40
mood disorders 229–231, 232
Morey, R.A. 56
Morley, J. 266
motivation: correctional officers
152–153; criminal investigators 195
Muller, R. 275
Murphy, David 7, 256–268
MVLEOs see military veteran law
enforcement officers

narcolepsy 234–235
narcotics work 188
National Center for Women and
Policing 10
National Guard (NG) 113–114, 137,
138, 139, 140–141, 143
National Institute of Mental Health
(NIMH) 80
National Law Enforcement Memorial
Fund 13
National Organization for Victim's
Assistance (NOVA) 84
Navy 80, 112, 113, 115, 132
Neil, R. 281–282
neurological processes 55–57
New Jersey Port Authority Police
Department 90
NG see National Guard
Nietzsche, F. 257
nightmares 207

NIMH see National Institute of
Mental Health
norms 60, 148
NOVA see National Organization for
Victim's Assistance

obesity 52, 54–55, 60–61, 71
offensive language 235
officer-involved shootings (OISs)
204–205
Omaha Police Department 272
organizational climate 58–59
organizational commitment
152–153, 154
Ostrov, Eric 38–39

Page, Wade Michael 99, 108–109
Panetta, Leon 114
panic attacks 206
Panos, A. 276
Paoline, E.A. 147, 150
paranoid schizophrenia 222,
225, 226, 229
Parker, G.F. 161
pathological intoxication 228
Paton, D. 48, 58
Patrick Deane, F. 243
peer support 87–88, 90, 140–141,
157–158, 197, 214, 260, 266; see
also social support; support
Pembroke Pines Police Department
(PPPD) 89–90
PEPSA see Psychological Evaluations
for Police Special Assignments
personal information 38–39
personal space 227
personality characteristics 9–10, 25;
assessment of 27, 33; criminal
investigators 195–196; hostage
negotiators 186–187
Petty, C.M. 56
physical restraint 227, 229
physiological arousal 48, 207
Plionis, E. 90
police chaplains 7, 269–283; dealing
with grief and loss 277–281;
handling invisible wounds
274–277; qualifications 269–270;
role of 271–273; spiritual neutrality
273–274; support systems 281–282
police chiefs 35
police officers see law enforcement
officers

mischaracterization of PTSD 107–
108; post-traumatic growth 266;
post-traumatic stress disorder 47,
103–104, 121–123; psychological
assessment 31–33, 36; public
perception of violence 105–106;
responding to need 117–119;
returning home 100–101; return-to-
duty programs 139–141, 143; risk
factors 104, 106–107, 108, 110, 117,
121; stigma 116–117; suicide 110–116,
118; trauma 101–102; *see also*
military law enforcement officers
vicarious traumatization 256
victims of crime 78–79, 276; child
victims 202, 205, 206, 256, 275;
mentally ill people 223
Vietnam War 77
Violanti, John M. 4–5, 44–69, 71,
210, 275
violence: bipolar disorder 230–231;
daily dealings with 275; domestic
6, 36, 107, 110, 159; epileptic
patients 234; images of 257, 261;
media coverage 105–106, 123n5;
mental illness 222, 223, 225–226;
military members 100, 106–107,
121; mischaracterization of PTSD
107–108; number of violent crimes
4; prisons 145, 146, 150, 161; risk
factors 5, 104, 106–107, 109, 110,
121; against women 10; workplace
violence assessments 25; *see also*
shootings
vulnerability factors 9, 19–20, 21

Walklate, S. 99
Waltz, J. 241–242
Warrior Resilience programs 5
Weiss, P.A. 24
Welch, L. 60
Wessely, S. 82
Westberry, L.G. 256
Whitehead, J. 151
Williams, C. 50
Williams, V. 243
Wilson, Deloria 5, 131–144
Wirth, B. 88
Wisconsin shootings (2012) 99, 105,
108–109
withdrawal 207
witnesses 176–177, 182
Wittenberg, P. 161
Wolk R. 52
women 10–11; cardiovascular disease
46; correctional officers 150, 154;
military members 102
Work Stress Scale for Correctional
Officers (WSSCO) 155
WorkAbility Evaluation 39–40
World War I 26, 76
World War II 72, 76–77
worldview, changes in
263–264, 266
Worlock, P. 81
Wozniak, J. 147
WSSCO *see* Work Stress Scale for
Correctional Officers

Yalom, I.D. 85
Yehuda, R. 47